ALSO BY PATRICK SYMMES

Chasing Che:
A Motorcycle Journey in Search of the Guevara Legend

THE BOYS FROM DOLORES

THE BOYS
FROM DOLORES

FIDEL CASTRO'S SCHOOLMATES FROM
REVOLUTION TO EXILE

Patrick Symmes

PANTHEON BOOKS, NEW YORK

Library of Congress Cataloging-in-Publication Data

Symmes, Patrick, [date]
The boys from Dolores: Fidel Castro's Schoolmates from Revolution to Exile /
Patrick Symmes.
p.   cm.
Includes index.
ISBN-13: 978-0-375-42283-6
1. Castro, Fidel, 1926—Contemporaries.   2. Colegio de Dolores
(Cuba)   3. Cuba—Description and travel.   4. Symmes, Patrick,
1964—Travel—Cuba.   I. Title.
F1788.S96 2007   2006030323

www.pantheonbooks.com

Printed in the United States of America

First Edition

2   4   6   8   9   7   5   3   1

FOR MY MOTHER,
WHO ENCOURAGED ALL MY VENTURES, GREAT OR SMALL

I want to leave today for the island of Cuba, which I believe to be Japan . . . The Indians . . . say it is very large and has people there with one eye in the forehead, as well as others they call cannibals . . . I also understand that, a long distance from here, there are men with one eye and others with dog's snouts who eat men.

—FROM THE LOGBOOK OF CHRISTOPHER COLUMBUS

Contents

THE BOYS FROM DOLORES

MIAMI SPRINGS

"This has been a difficult year for the Sad Ones," Pedro Haber said, but before he could continue, there was a metallic purr, which grew quickly into a feedback loop. The sound squawked over the ballroom, a room full of wrinkled men in brown suits and ageless women in immovable bouffants. Pedro tried to continue. He said, "Four who regularly attend these reunions have fallen, God has them in all his glor—"

But he was cut off now, fatally. The screech made even a busboy put down his bread rolls and cover his ears. A devilish *skeeeeeeeeTWAAAAAAAAAA-weeeeeeSKEEEEE* refracted off the rented glassware and the golf club plates, a piercing white noise like a fax machine in your head. Old, trembling hands rose reaching for hearing aids.

Pedro, class of '59, stood calmly and stared at the microphone. One more betrayal in a lifetime of disappointments.

SKWEEEEEEEEEE-BWAAAAAAAAAA-SOOOOOOOOOO.

Pedro ran the reunions because he was the most stalwart, reliable, and capable of the men from the old days. But this was exactly why he disliked being called on to manage things, yet again. He was a friend to everyone. He did nothing to deserve this. Stress was bad for a man his age. But duty was duty: at sixty-two years of age, he was one of the younger men in the room.

Unplug. Fiddle with knobs. Move cables. Start over. Forget to replug. Replug. Readjust knobs. Tap tap. "Can everyone hear me?" He was back in business. But nobody, all night, could handle the microphone. Not even the singer.

Pedro Haber didn't actually start by saying that it was "a difficult year for the Sad Ones." He had said that it was a difficult year for the *Dolorinos*. The word is rooted in *dolor,* meaning "pain, ache; sadness, grief." When Pedro said *Los Dolorinos* it sounded like all of those things, a world of aching and grieving, the ones who suffer. But it had another meaning, for these were the men who, as boys, came from a happy place. Dolores was their old school, the Catholic academy, run by Jesuits. The Colegio de Dolores where they had all met had been a boarding school in eastern Cuba, once upon a time. The sadness had come later.

Everyone in the room, from the busboys on up, spoke the twin languages of this nation-within-a-nation. But not everyone is equally ambidextrous, and thought and speech leapt between Cuba and the United States. At the far right of the room, near the entrance, was a special table reserved for VIPs and the guests of honor. Pedro Haber and I were sitting there, and the accents and vocabulary at this table were a mixture of proper upper-crust Castilian Spanish and plain American English. Two spots over to my right was Pedro Roig, a Dolores alumnus and Bay of Pigs veteran, who was now head of TV Martí in Washington. Immediately on my left was Lundy Aguilar, retired from his professorship at Georgetown University. And directly across the table was the Reverend Father Juan Manuel Dorta-Duque, one of the last surviving teachers from the old school in Cuba. He was a Jesuit, or more properly, a member of the Society of Jesus, perhaps the most influential of all Catholic orders. Dorta-Duque was eighty-four years old now, but that wasn't old enough to have known Fidel Castro. Dorta-Duque told me that he didn't arrive at Dolores until 1951. But he had known all the Jesuits who had taught Fidel, as well as some of the younger boys from those days, or the younger brothers of the boys who had studied with Fidel. Dorta-Duque lived in a Jesuit home now, retired from all work but that of joining his fellow Jesuits in their duties of worship and contemplation.

"Yes, I remember them," Dorta-Duque said, leaning forward. He meant that he remembered the students and teachers from long before the Revolution, when the future of the country was in the hallways of Dolores. "But they are all dead," he added.

One of them was sitting at the same table, actually. A survivor, just a few feet away. But Lundy Aguilar didn't hear the remark, and Dorta-Duque's mistake did no harm.

Two languages, two minds, a Cuban inside every American. Even here, at their own high school reunion, among their very own, they were unmoored, their homes, lives, even their manner of speech, somehow without footing.

Cuban exiles are on a journey that cannot be finished in one lifetime, a two-hundred-mile transmigration of the soul that is at once irreversible, and incompletable. The survivor suffers from temporal confusion, at once in eastern Cuba in 1941 and in Miami Springs in 2005. Equally at home in that lost Atlantis, the mythical Cuba from "before," and in the Dade County real estate market. What a difference between the old Santiago de Cuba, in the long-ago republic, in a time of youth, privilege, and revolution, and this age of old faces at a golf club near Miami International? Weren't these the same people? Like a snail, the exile carried his world along with him.

The phrase *Los Dolorinos* harked back to a starting point, before any expulsion from any garden. The Colegio de Dolores was the capital school of Cuba's second city, the best education available in eastern Cuba. The richest gathering of the richest part of Cuba, a school of the chosen few. All Pedro Haber had meant, what he truly said, was that they, the *Dolorinos,* had lost yet more friends. Four had fallen from the ranks this year. For this room of Cuban exiles, locked in an actuarial competition with Fidel Castro himself, attrition was a difficult subject.

The reunion was held in late September, the middle of a very bad hurricane season. There had been eleven inches of rain in a month. The water table was up to the grass. It had rained again this morning, hard. Low clouds, lit up by the ground beacons of Miami International, by the strip malls along Le Jeune, and by the floodlights of an industrial park across the road, scudded over the golf course. Turbulent and wet, the clouds passed without releasing drops, for now. Black patches of night sky winked in and out.

The old *Dolorinos* and their wives had started arriving en masse at 7:00 P.M., most of them not just on time for the cocktail hour, but early. Over the next hour heavy American cars kept rolling into the lot, and then the same progression of aged legs crossed the street. The grass lawn of the country club would hiss as someone explored the possibility of taking a shortcut. A dress shoe came back out of the grass with a sucking sound, and a high heel stabbed an indentation in the lawn that began to fill with runnels of silt. The click of heels on brick soon followed. These men and women, averaging somewhere in their early sixties, cut no cor-

ners. Moving slowly, often supporting each other, they made right-angle
turns on the brick walkways, which were uneven and slicked with algae.
The men, in a mixture of brown and black suits, or sometimes the long-
sleeved guayaberas, were jovial, even the one who arrived using a walker.
The women had formality and reserve. (It wasn't their reunion; Dolores was a boys school.) Or maybe the women had, in their upright car-
riage, just the composure required by cream gowns and structured black
cocktail dresses, by shoulder wraps of the very gauziest pastels. Their hair
was stiff. Usually short, a tropical reality, but fixed in uplifted construc-
tions. Their lips and eyelashes were lacquered with precision. Even on the
men, every hair was in place—brushed back, Brylcreemed, ordered and
clipped. You had to draw the line somewhere and this was it: neatness of
tonsure was a way of fighting back, of defending civilization against its
enemies.

The banquet hall of the Miami Springs Country Club is called the
Legends Room, but it isn't very big. There were 105 people in there by
8:00 P.M., and most of them were talking, a raucous atmosphere of jokes,
bragging, disbelief, laughter, shouts, argument, and monologue, all of it
bouncing off long tables of rented glass and dull knives. The crowd was
prone to thick glasses and hearing aids, but functional, still able to dance
and to argue. The men touched one another constantly, putting a hand
on another's arm, pressing a shoulder in their grip, even clutching one
another's lapels in a kind of menacing embrace. They wore pins in those
lapels, showing off their allegience to political movements, their qualifi-
cations as survivors of various disasters, their enlistment in Masonic
Lodges, the Elks, Lions, Odd Fellows, and Rotary, or ethnic allegiances,
sporting clubs, religious leagues, cultural groups, charitable drives, and
other bulwarks against the loss of everything. Ariel Dorfman, a Chilean,
said that an exile had only two possessions, the language of his birthplace
and the keys to a house that no longer exists. Cubans are joiners, filling
their empty pockets with new things.

On the way into the Legends Room, the door charge was $5, collected
as a donation to the welfare fund for impoverished alumni of the school.
For that money, you received a printed program for the reunion event. It
listed the speakers, and featured page after page of pictures, old shots of
the Colegio de Dolores in Santiago. There were many of the students of

past days, and shots of the signature buildings of Santiago and the surrounding region.

In America, someone is always standing by to sell you your history, so
more of the same photography was available for sale at the back of the
room. Two women in icy competition were selling similar arrays of souvenirs and memorabilia related to Cuba. Photographs and paintings.
Antebellum cigar box labels. Stamps of the old Republic of Cuba. Tickets
from the Spanish lottery. Coins. Most of it was fake.

They both had maps for sale. One, a reproduction of early Spanish car-
tography, showed Cuba in outline only, with the interior a blank unknown,
a paradise of the imagination. Even in such an old map, you could see
what Cubans always claimed to see, the island shaped like a sleeping alli-
gator, snout to the west and the long thin body stretching out to the east,
with the tail tucked back under the body to make the stubby shape of
Oriente province. It mapped out well enough. Medallions around the
borders of the old map showed the four winds, and the native peoples in
their imagined costumes. There were modern maps for sale, but not too
modern. The most recent maps were still fanciful in their way, also decorated around the edges with symbols of never-was Cuba. Thatched bungalows. The old capitol building in Havana, now abandoned because
it looks exactly like the U.S. Capitol. An American navy ship steaming
past eastern Cuba. Up north some seventeenth-century natives paddled
canoes. Hokey peasants on carts with huge wheels rolled up the middle of
the island, passing schematic palm trees.

In the south, somewhere near Grand Cayman, was a legend that said:
THIS MAP HAS BEEN CREATED TO PRESERVE THE MEMORY, KNOWL-
EDGE, AND PATRIOTISM OF THE YOUNG CUBAN IN EXILE. And next to
that was a list of "facts" about Cuba, including the statement that "Three
fourths of all Cubans are white, of Spanish descent," which wasn't true in
whatever past was being mapped here, and certainly isn't true today.

These were charts to a Cuba that didn't, hadn't, couldn't, and wouldn't
exist. They were accurate in their way, though, as charts of the peculiar
mental geography of Cuba in exile. Whether printed in great detail, framed
and placed on a wall in a home, or distributed on disposable place mats in
Cuban diners, these maps for exiles show a Cuba of six provinces, the
original Spanish imperial demarcations dating back to the days of the Con-

quest. From west to east these six were Pinar del Río, Havana, Matanzas, Las Villas, Camagüey, and Oriente. Almost everyone here at the reunion tonight identified themselves as being *oriental,* an easterner, from around the region that surrounded Santiago de Cuba. There were a few Havana people here, because there were always Havana people. But no matter who you were, wherever you came from, when they asked you your place of origin you answered with one of those old names, the provinces.

That was Cuba, but that isn't Cuba. Oriente doesn't exist anymore. Fidel Castro had literally redrawn the map, turning the traditional six into a new fourteen. The old provinces and identifications were blown up and replaced with rational borders and, sometimes, names commemorating Castro's own life. Part of old Oriente was broken off and renamed Granma province, because Castro had run his boat *Granma* aground there. How could an exile say he was from such a place? The old Isle of Pines, where a young Castro had served jail time, had been split off to make a province called the Isle of Youth, contractually dedicated to education. Who could acknowledge such things?

They didn't sell accurate road maps, either. Never mind if Castro had built a new highway down the middle of Cuba, or that a better map would reveal all the satellite housing cities and rural polytechnic universities that had sprung up across Cuba. Nobody was going to that Cuba. The less accurate the map the better.

I browsed through some copies of old photographs of Santiago, with men in straw hats, and views of the bay, or the old Bacardi rum factory. Next down the table was a Havana telephone guide from 1959. This old phone book, full of period illustrations and corporate optimism, is the single best selling item at the Cuba Nostalgia Fair, a memorabilia mart that draws thirty thousand people to a convention center in Miami once a year.

The same brisk commerce was available the rest of the time from dozens of shops around the city: an endless supply of Cuban flag paintings, regional histories, and posters of Elián, the sacred child of the rafters, who was often shown being carried across the waves on a dolphin's back. Just the day before, driving along Calle Ocho in Little Havana, I'd counted four stores in seventeen blocks that specialized in memories of Cuba. The latest, Havana To-Go, featured "Made in Manzanillo" T-shirts. The owner wasn't even Cuban.

I'd already bought myself a copy of the 1959 Yellow Pages there, on Calle Ocho. But after ten years of visits, I didn't need a guide to Havana; it was Miami that mystified me. I knew the street grid of Vedado in the dark; the highways of Dade County left me confused and frightened. I'd been to Miami half as often as Havana, often for just a few hours. The Cubans I knew were in Cuba.

Flipping through the pages of the phone book was seeing Cuba through the wrong end of a telescope. Distanced, rendered small, the Cuba of this vision was perfectly useless as a guide to anything but memory. The photographs in the ads showed a Havana where the avenues were crowded with commercial signs, bustling with banks, airlines, department stores, liquor promotions, society institutions, and cheap entertainments. For a Cuban phone book the amount of English was startling: Westing-house, General Electric Cuba, Eagle Electrical Specialties, Mercury Air Cargo, Orkin, Nelson, Singer. The commercial dominance ran on and on. But the Cubans had their pride, too, like the Tropicana, listed under "cabarets" as the *"Night-club más bello del mundo!"* There was a full-page ad for an efficient-looking bus company, with seven departures a day for Santiago, all on the latest equipment. Waiting now for the cocktail hour to end, I flipped through the restaurant listings for 1959, which made me sad.

The first call to sit for dinner was ignored. The phone book had a White Pages listing as well, and idly killing time, I looked under C and found this:

Castro, Raúl—14 no. 109 Mnao—29-4770

That's to say, Raúl Castro, Dolores class of 1945. There was no listing in the phone book for his older brother, Fidel. The 1959 phone book would have been put together during 1958, a year that Fidel and Raúl spent fighting in the mountains. Apparently they had kept their phone on.

The Cuban-American poet Orlando Ricardo Menes warned against all this. He met a man who painted sunsets of Havana, the kind of sunsets where the clouds are underlit, the sea is blue and calm, palm trees obscure the foreground, and at rear, a Cuban flag ripples from the battlements of the old castle, El Morro. Such pictures were for sale everywhere in Miami. Ricardo Menes cautioned the man:

> Mi Cuba collapsed from corruption, greed, and violence.
> Idyllic memories are a jeweled noose.

At the second call for dinner, a few people actually sat down, mostly us outsiders. There were a few Cubans here who weren't from the old school. After Dolores had been closed by the Revolution, it had been re-created in Miami, but not as Dolores. The students-in-exile had been merged with the pupils from two other Cuban Jesuit schools at a new campus in Florida. But the new school took the name of the largest of the old ones, the Colegio Jesuítico de Belén. Belén had always been a sister school to Dolores, and the student bodies were intimately tied together— many Dolores students, including Fidel Castro and Lundy Aguilar, had actually graduated from Belén—but were also rivals. Belén was Havana, Dolores was Santiago. So the Legends Room was full of a confusing mix of Dolores alumni, some old, some young, some graduates from Santiago, but others from Belén in Havana, with younger ones from Belén in Miami. It had always rankled. Half a century ago the Dolores boys had felt like hicks when they showed up at Belén, transfer students lost on the sixty-acre campus in the bustling, alien capital. Now at their own high school reunion half the people were from Belén.

A third call to sit for dinner, this time with the lights flicking off and on, but people just kept talking. Ten minutes went by, the waiters squawking haplessly at clots of Cubans engaged in furious rounds of handshaking, exchanging addresses and bits of old news, wrapping up old stories and starting new ones. After fifteen minutes the head of cater-ing came out, clapped his hands furiously, and marched around the rooms shouting *DAMAS Y CABALLEROS POR FAVOR*. Slowly, people began to pry apart, to exchange business cards, to release lapels and sit. Pedro Haber reached for the fatal microphone and began to flick switches on the sound system.

Disorder bubbled along pleasantly for the rest of the evening. Through dinner, and the scheduled remarks, and the events, and even the prayerful invocation, a few people kept talking loudly in the back, or wandering around shamelessly shaking hands. There was a great crash during one speech when someone posing for a disposable camera backed over a chair, flipped, and brought down a tablecloth, shattering a dozen plates. Craggy faces kept popping up from the long tables, waving to each other, signal-ing or passing notes, no different than the Dolores lunchroom.

One of every ten Cubans have fled the island since Castro's revolution. There are Cubans in Burundi and Bilbao, Mexico City and Manhattan. Several thousand live in Australia. But the capital of exile is Greater Miami. In a diaspora of more than a million Cubans, 833,000 are in Florida. That ratio was reflected in the Legends room. A few determined alumni had made the long slog to this dinner from Houston or Los Angeles or Puerto Rico. They were the exiled exiles. But there were a few who, even though they lived in Miami, were strangers here. One short, wrinkled man in glasses, standing alone, told me he had attended the Colegio Dolores for only one year, in the 1950s. He didn't know anyone here. The idea of Dolores, the most prestigious school in eastern Cuba, still drew him, even as many of the alumni who knew the school best, who had been there through entire childhoods, skipped this night entirely.

The attendees from outside Miami were self-selected by enthusiasm, the most delighted, the loudest, the most prone to interrupting anything for photographs, the first to pass business cards, the last to sit down. While dinner was finally being served, a thoracic surgeon from Texas jumped the gun, stepping to the empty microphone and turning it on before anyone had quite realized what he was doing. He introduced himself to the crowd at a blasting volume, announced that he was about to tell a funny joke, and then took a piece of paper from his jacket and unfolded it.

"I'm sorry for speaking in English," he said.

"Habla español!" a woman at the VIP table shouted.

The surgeon opened his mouth, closed it, and stared at the abruptly silent room. "I apologize for speaking English," he said again. And, weaker: "The joke has to be told in English."

He'd done more than break form. He'd betrayed something, turning his back on the old language, preferring the new. He might as well have said the unspeakable into that microphone: *We aren't really Cubans.*

Nobody here was Cuban, anymore. Exile remade them, separated and changed them. Nobody had planned to spend the rest of their lives abroad, but they had. Cuba had gone on living the decades without them. The exiles might have been been born in Cuba. They might be Catholic, and speak Spanish, and have Cuba engraved in their hearts. But they weren't the Cubans anymore. Nine out of every ten had stayed. That was Cuba, over there. The island of memory and old phone books was something different. The exiles had gone through defeats and abandonments, and were now stranded in other places, the tide receding. They were never going home.

Were they Americans? Some were citizens, certainly. But exile is defined by leaving, not arriving. You drifted a line whose course went only away, leaving you between worlds and languages, neither here nor there. Neither one nor the other. How could you be a Cuban if you didn't live in Cuba? How could you be an American if you still lived, in your head, in Cuba?

For years I had sat under the scissors of a Cuban barber in New York, who had lost his natural confidence in Spanish without ever gaining an equivalent comfort in English. He had become a stranger in his own mouth, suffocated. For these older exiles, too long in Cuba to fully leave it and never entirely at home in America, language was a perilous landscape, freighted with subtle signifiers. They heard their own children flitting from Spanish to English between syllables, and saw their grandchildren stare back dumbly when asked a simple question in Castilian. Even those older people at ease in English could feel their abilities fading with the years, their minds gravitating back toward Spanish and Cuba.

The surgeon was a rare exception. Maybe he'd been isolated among English speakers in Houston, because he'd gone so far into English he couldn't come back. The woman who shouted *habla español* was declaring that he had abandoned them.

The doctor from Houston told his unauthorized joke, in English. It flopped. He sat down to polite applause.

The business of the evening flowed quickly. With roast beef on our plates, Pedro Haber kept it all moving, and after a quick prayer of invocation from Father Dorta-Duque, Haber went straight in to the business of handing out honors.

Pedro Roig leapt up from the VIP table to receive the first. Roig ran, among other things, TV Martí, a television station funded by the U.S. government and staffed by Cuban exiles. Broadcast from an aircraft over U.S. water, TV Martí offered "free" television to captive Cubans. But it was a signal to nowhere. The 90-mile distance from Key West to Havana was simply too far for television transmission. I had never met anyone in Cuba who had seen the channel. It was a bit of heated rhetoric hurled into the ether. Year after year, an alliance of anti-Castro congressmen and exile influence workers kept federal funding for TV Martí. Even if no one could see it, they argued, the mere fact of its existence was vital.

Cutting the funding would be nothing less than giving in to Castro. An illusion of that size was impressive.

Then Lundy Aguilar got up, with a bashful smile for an old man. At the podium he was not exactly steady. Lundy, class of '43. Nearing eighty, he was small, bent, skinny as ever, now as always a model of self-control. As Haber described it, the plaque was presented in honor of Lundy's achievements as an illustrious professor, a newspaper columnist since the 1950s, a philosopher of liberty, a member of distinguished academic bodies, and a campaigner for democracy both before and after the Revolution. He'd done the things other people talked about. He'd known and rejected Castro. He'd protested for democracy and then fought the new tyrant. His early predictions—that the Revolution would produce a tyrant, that the tyrant would drive them out, and that pragmatism was the only response—had fallen on deaf ears. But they had come true. He was still at it, publishing occasional articles in the *Miami Herald,* or the *Diario Las Américas,* and knocking out weekly Internet postings on liberty, or history, or the god of Marxism, or Stalin, or Castro as a salesman auctioning off Cuba. This habit of pouring out commentaries and publishing revelations was common enough among Cubans—ubiquitous, even—but Lundy was different. His friends actually did call him the Prophet. Sustaining a realism like that, among Cubans, was award-worthy.

Sitting down with his plaque, Lundy looked tiny, and boyish, fondling the award while smiling easily and talking with the Reverend. Dorta-Duque leaned foward, tilting over the table in his high white collar, and asked Lundy where the rest of his Dolores classmates were. Lundy said they weren't here. There had been only thirteen boys in his final year, 1943.

"Four or six should still be alive," Dorta-Duque suggested.

"No, Father," Lundy said.

"Three?"

"No, Father."

"Two?"

"No, Father. Only one. I am the only one left alive."

Tragedy is stale news to Cubans, and the evening slid right into celebration. The music was bad, loud, and popular. A baritone dressed entirely in black, even to the dye in his mustache, pressed some buttons on a karaoke console. Instrumentals erupted, and he began to belt along to *son* standards. He was effective. The combination of the music and his striving, melodramatic voice was deafening, but many of the people in the room were already partly deaf, and these were Cubans, so the small dance floor filled up before the midpoint of the first song. Couples in their fifties and sixties danced with the easy flow of people who have spent decades together on the floor. Many of them had been dancing together for half a century; the divorce rate was minuscule. There was a mambo, danced cheek to cheek. And a *son,* a classic Benny Moré number. And then a cha-cha, with everyone chanting along, as happy as children to be shouting it out, throwing their hands into the air: *"Cha cha CHA!"* More dancers piled in, taking the last spots on the parquet dance floor, and then filling up the carpet around the edge. Then a conga line, which was invented by a Dolores man.

It was real dancing, blessedly unselfconscious, everyone bumping elbows, turning, their butts colliding, men calling out to one another, cutting in, reclaiming partners, and starting over with the next song. It wasn't 9:30. Between tunes the crooner would briefly ruin the mood by pressing buttons, so that the tape screeched backward and forward as he looked for different tracks. Or he might accidentally knock his microphone into one of the speakers, producing a clap of thunder and a yelp of feedback. But then there would be another tune, his melodramatic voice, and the dancers picked right up again.

The route to the bathroom was lined with black and white pictures of golfers: Arnold Palmer, Sam Snead, Jack Nicklaus, Jackie Gleason, and 1950s faces I didn't know. A sign taped on the wall said, in quick handwriting, DOLORES REUNION—LEGENDS ROOM. At the urinal, two Cubans took the spaces on either side of me and began to quiz me while relieving themselves. Was I Cuban? No, Irish from Virginia. What was I doing here? Looking for people from the old days, I said. To tell their stories.

They volunteered theirs: although they had never met until standing at these urinals, they'd both attended Dolores in the 1950s. And, they said, the old days were nothing compared to what they'd been through since. One guy was "in agriculture," he said. The other interrupted to say that he was also in agriculture. The first had a farm near Tampa. Oh, really? The second had a farm in Nigeria. Well, the first man came to Miami with nothing, he said, and built up a whole agricultural business, from farming and packaging to transport and added value, all from scratch. Amazing, the second man said quickly, because he himself had come to America with nothing, not one cent, and had supported his entire family and their extended clan by simultaneously opening a medical practice and starting a ranch in Venezuela. The first man cut in: he was growing five kinds of root vegetables in commercial quantities, including a very profitable manioc crop. *Muy rentable,* he shouted at one of my ears. The second man shouted at the other ear: over in Nigeria he'd crossed Holsteins with the African cattle, and they were getting ten thousand gallons of milk a day.

"Well," the first man said, zipping up. "I didn't know anything about farming, but with this exile, we have to do what we can."

We all washed up, but they pursued me toward the Legends Room, insisting that I write about them. Under cross-examination, the second man admitted that he had a *plan* to produce ten thousand gallons of milk a day in Nigeria. As I walked away, he yelled out, "But we really taught that bastard a lesson!"

I knew not to ask who he meant. *That bastard.* The name missing from the mailing list of this high school reunion. He was here, of course, if only because he was rolled up and hiding in my pocket. Only when the party began to wind down, around 10:15, did I clear away some strawberry shortcake and unroll the print, a particularly large copy of the picture that had brought me here. Twenty people were soon gathered around.

They remembered the building. Not just the men, who had been students there, but their wives, too, some of whom had seen Dolores for themselves, as visitors back in the girlhood of their 1940s or 1950s, and others who had merely encountered a thousand stories and snapshots in the decades since. The photograph I had unrolled was a straight shot of the entire student body at the Colegio de Dolores, taken in the fall of 1941. Two hundred and thirty-eight boys in uniform, lined in eight ranks, the youngest at the bottom, the oldest at the top. Around the edges of the frame were glimpses of railings, Mudejar archways, tall doors, and whitewashed walls. I pointed out where Lundy Aguilar, then fifteen years old, was standing, next to the Cuban flag.

There was another face in this picture, a ghost missing from this room. I saw a few people bend in, to look for it.

Discussion died out. People fell into an intense scrutiny of the long page, whispering "Do you see him?" Fear of success matched fear of failure. But they had to know how close they had stood.

It always gave people a shock when they finally recognized him. The uniforms made all the students look indistinguishable, but once I put the nail of my pinkie across his open, round face, his raked-back visage, that cocky gleam in his eye, there was a collective gasp. It was him. Third row down from the top, fifth from right. A tall boy, with his head tilted back. Instead of a necktie, like the boys on either side of him, his collar was open.

Him. A willful, wild little man, fourteen years old.

"It's him," a woman said. A man in a gray suit took out his glasses, cleaned them with a purple cloth, put them on, and studied the picture.

"Look at that son of a bitch," he said.

But I couldn't. I couldn't look at the man whom Guillermo Cabrera Infante called Cyclops, the terrible giant who ruled over his own island. You go blind from staring at the sun. Better to turn away. Let the eyes adjust to the shadows. There was more than one man in Cuba, and more than one boy in Dolores. His history was not the sum total of Cuban history.

Some called him messiah, others worse than Stalin, but I myself was not even sure he existed. Was he a real creature, or a myth that walked? Once in Havana, I had stood as close to him as the VIP table was to the microphone, close enough to see his hands trembling, but was he real? It wasn't possible for one man to have done everything in Cuba, no matter what the television in Havana and the radio in Miami said. There were other forces at work, a river of decisions and actors, accidents and intentions, that shaped the bends of generations. One life—even one very long, century-spanning life—was not enough. One alloy in the Cuban tragedy was this willingness to believe that it was all him, for good or ill. Cubans were gullible, Lundy Aguilar had once warned, for they "don't believe in anybody and they believe everybody." They grasped for bitter heroes.

He, the only he, whose name tasted like ashes in their mouths, liked it that way, too. A personalized history, full of his actions, his glories, his insight. The enemies of Cuba were *his* enemies, who despised and demonized *him*. He talked constantly of assassination plots, which equated the killing of the Revolution with the killing of him, personally. His enemies sometimes did him the courtesy of getting caught with .50 caliber sniper rifles, proving the equation.

But there were other men. You could draw a frame around any collection of Cubans, really. So why not these ones?

Old people go to bed early. By 10:30, the crowd was done. Done fingering my photograph, and done pressing stories, e-mails, business cards, accusations, phone numbers, advice, and obsolete addresses in Hialeah and Camagüey upon one another. There were only a few stragglers still on the dance floor. One of them, a woman of about sixty, danced toward me, took my hand, pulled me onto the floor, and then wrapped me in an inebriated hug. As we danced in this embrace, sashaying slowly around the floor, my nose was buried into the airy confection of her hair. The stiff hit of hair spray woke me up.

"Remember," she shouted up at me as we circled. "We are 99 percent Republicans. Put that in your book!"

The only thing Cubans agree on is that they are completely reasonable, and that everyone agrees with them.

But the real figure is 80 percent.

Lundy's house lay offshore, hove-to like a wise sailor on the security of Key Biscayne. The next afternoon, with the wet storm weather blown out by fierce winds, I paid a dollar for the toll and drove out the long causeway, leaving behind Miami. The road rose up, becoming a long white bridge, the blue of Biscayne Bay to my right, dotted with wind surfers, and the skyline of downtown Miami behind, on the left. It was Sunday, and cruise ships were outbound, nosing through the crowded waters like white buses. The road swooped down onto the brief Virginia Key, and then onto the long, flat island itself:

> *You said you'd bring to me*
> *Biscayne Bay*
> *Where the Cuban gentlemen sleep all day*

The road ran new through parkland, where crabgrass grew from sand, and past the old Winter White House of Richard Nixon. Key Biscayne runs five miles, sticking out from the side of Miami, a low barrier island that shields the city itself from hurricane swells. The highest point on the key is a pile of landfill beside the sewage plant. The island looks so flat and featureless that a stiff roller from the Gulf Stream might surge through the mangroves and submerge the whole thing briefly.

The beaches out here were poor, by Miami standards, and smelled of sulfur. That, plus the dollar toll on the causeway, kept most people out. Seldom visited, with only a few hotels, it was a prosperous residential neighborhood. As I drove into what passed for the center of town, I saw that the parking lot of the Key Biscayne Yacht Club was filled to overcapacity.

Lundy Aguilar's house was on a side street, off a side street. It was a modest one-story ranch, with slatted louvers on the windows, and royal palms growing in front and back. It was nestled in a tight row of similar houses. Lizards, mostly alive, dotted the road and driveway. Vera, Lundy's wife, sent me into the living room to wait for him.

Lundy had taught Latin American history at Georgetown University, but his was no dry and academic affection. He wallowed in history like a boy in a mud bog. He collected and painted toy soldiers for a hobby, and these were laid out on three bookcases beside the white armchair where I waited. On the left, the shelves supported twenty-five lancers and hussars of the Napoleonic infantry, the men in huge bearskin hats, with each little pom-pom painted red. These were facing an equal number of English Life Guards, their swords and breastplates gleaming in hand-daubed silver. Their French and British standards were accurate, and all the figures were mounted on small black stands. Below that were fifty-four more soldiers—a platoon of the Black Watch, with some skirmishers out front, and an assortment of Wellington's officers on horseback. The bottom shelf had more of the same.

Down the middle row there were soldiers from Cuba, from the war of two names. To the Americans this war was called the Spanish-American War, best remembered for the neat charge up San Juan Hill in 1898. But that was not Lundy's war: the figures here were mostly Cuban fighters from what he and other Cubans called the War of Independence. This was a struggle, fought with interruptions over thirty years, that was all but over by the time the Rough Riders arrived. In this conflict, the enemy soldiers—the Spanish troops—still looked, in miniature, much like the Napoleonic soldiers that had preceded them. They wore an imperial uniform of white breeches, epaulets, and flashy belts. But Lundy's shelves were mostly taken up with something new on the battlefield. His Cuban fighters were a ragtag bunch under a new red, white, and blue flag. These toy rebels wore wide straw hats and rough peasant clothing. Some were barefoot. Their cavalry were the mambises, the irregular squadrons of Afro-Cuban men who fought with only the sharp edge of their machetes. This was an insurgency, a people's war. A liberation struggle. No Americans on this shelf, or the lower ones.

Over on the right, the last three shelves were divided among an odd-ball assortment of Vikings, French knights, samurai, brass cannons, and finally some Americans: a squad of Confederates and a few disordered Yankees. Below that were the Romans, in hand-to-hand melee with some Ottoman janissaries. A few Cossacks were rushing in. Saxons occupied the bottom shelf, along with a dozen crumbling leather books.

Lundy came in, stooped, but spry and lean. He smoothed his hair and sat down in a red armchair, close by his battalions. Above and behind him on the wall there was an antique sword crossed against a kind of small blunderbuss. He told me right away that he had known Fidel Castro for five years at Dolores, and then four more years at the University of Havana. Lundy was older, and had been a calendar year ahead of Fidel.

"I didn't like Fidel," Lundy said. "We were friends, but we never became close." But at a small school with 238 boys spread across eight grades, those of similar ages were thrust together, inevitably intimate in some way. The school was also too small to tolerate division: there were, Lundy said, no cliques or separation by social class, the way he saw later at Belén, the bigger and more socially stratified sister school. At Dolores, everyone was pulled together by proximity, and pushed together toward something larger. The school had a mission.

"The Jesuits were the vanguard of the Catholic Church," Lundy explained. "They were born in Spain, and the order grew because the founders believed in studying science, that the kids in the Jesuit schools should know what the scientific movement was doing. In Cuba, when you reached a school of the Jesuits, you felt that you were in the avant-garde."

Fidel Castro had made much the same point. In one of the only interviews in which he ever mentioned Dolores, Castro told the theologian Frei Betto, a sympathetic leftist from Brazil, that he'd been impressed on arrival there. The school was run by "people who were much more rigorous, much more prepared, with much more vocation for teaching, in reality, [people] of much higher capacity, discipline, incomparably superior" to the teachers he had known before. "In my judgment," he said, it was "a school I wanted to join."

Lundy took me into the back of the house. There was a small nook, between the bathroom and the TV room, which had been curated into a kind of memory chamber. There were trophies and bits of antique armor, but mostly there were photographs from the old days, whether that meant Cuba in the 1940s and 1950s, or America in the 1960s and 1970s. The biggest of the photographs was the same one I had shown around at the reunion, a broad black and white panorama of the student body at Dolores in the fall of 1942. The 238 boys lined up, the whole student body of boarding and day students. It was Lundy who had first given the shot to me.

Even this, which was my original, was a copy of a copy of a large-format negative. Multiple generations had smudged the faces, softening the lines of the eyes, smoothing out the clothing, draining the shadows of detail. Scratches, a tear, and several spots of mold on an earlier print were all faithfully reproduced here.

The picture showed the boys in the patio, as they called the school's inner courtyard. It was split into upper and lower sections by a wall, which was topped with a black iron railing. Most of the boys, six full rows, were arrayed below that divide.

Up, behind the iron railing, were two rows of class leaders, honorees, members of the band, and assorted flag bearers. Lundy pointed himself out in this group. "There I am, holding the flag," he said. "Taking notes on everything with my eyes."

He had dressed that day in the full uniform that they rarely wore: black shoes, white trousers, a dark blue blazer over a white shirt, with a white Sam Browne belt running up and over the left shoulder.

Lundy wore a solid dark necktie; the other 237 boys wore a variety of ties, striped or solid, and a small number, like Fidel, were tieless. Fidel was one row below Lundy, on the other side of the railing. Fifth in from stage right, his shoulders brushed with the folds of a white school flag. You could have projected arrogance onto the way his hat was cocked, if you wanted, but this was simply a fourteen-year-old boy.

Cuba never had an upper class in the European sense, and there were only a few boys at Dolores who could claim an important Spanish name or old money. What Cuba had was a few super-rich people, often of new fortune and dubious background, and a relatively large middle class. Most of the boys at Dolores, Lundy said, were sons of professionals, or of businessmen, or came from poorer families that strove to produce professionals and businessmen. The boys at Dolores were less concerned with intellectual attainment than with sports and getting into a university. The parents were mostly interested in seeing their boys established in a good career. "Most of them," Lundy said, pointing again at the picture, "didn't go on to study history or law. They went on to be physicians or engineers. They were not analytical types. I was in the other category, a kid reading history all the time."

Lundy's son and namesake now crowded in behind us. Named Louis Aguilar, he was known as Lou, and had the same rangy, lean face as his father. In his mid-forties, wearing a white T-shirt, Lou was a screenwriter in L.A. But he was fed up with Hollywood, and was spending more and more time in Miami, living with his parents. Born in Cuba, he'd left that island before he could form any memory of it, and had grown up in Florida and Washington, D.C. But Cuba, even at the remove of imagination, had impressed itself in his form. It was Lou's generation, the first Cuban-Americans, who had a kind of baby boomer affinity for "Made in Manzanillo" T-shirts and declarative nostalgia. In polling data, the younger Cuban-Americans generally held more liberal views than their parents, but they were also less realistic about Cuba. Untempered by any actual experience, their views lacked proportion. Lou, hearing his father mention the young Fidel, interrupted.

"He's worse than Hitler," he said.

"Well," Lundy said. "Not really. He's not a Hitler."

"Dad, he—"

"He didn't make a Holocaust," Dad said.

Lou didn't even believe it himself, but making the comparison was common enough. On the seething AM bands of South Florida you could hear Castro compared to Hitler, or Stalin, or Pol Pot, or Ceaușescu, or Mao, every week.

But they didn't talk that way in the house of a historian, a man of Jesuitical balance. Lundy frowned at his son and went off to sit in his office. A few minutes later, I found him there, laughing. "Me!" he said. "Defending Castro!" But it was true, he repeated. The Cuban dictator was no Hitler.

He sighed. "That doesn't mean I wouldn't like to kill him," he added, mildly. "But as a historian, I have to be as objective as possible. I define myself as a skeptic, a humanist, a man from the Renaissance. A person who asks questions, who looks for everything."

That was, as clearly as I ever heard it put, the Jesuit education in a nutshell. Lundy had started with Jesuit teachers at Dolores, and had spent a thirty-year career teaching at Georgetown University, another Jesuit institution. He was one of the best educated people I had ever met. I had to ask him: had so much love of history, so much study of nuance, so much reading, prepared him for what happened? For the Revolution? For this?

He was still, a long time. Finally he swung his face side to side, as if exhausted. He had been naive, he said. Despite his own doubts, some of them voiced in the newspapers, he hadn't fully understood what was going to happen until it was too late to stop it. The moment he first saw the future, he said, was "on the third or fourth day of the Revolution," meaning the third or fourth day of January 1959. Castro was triumphant, but hadn't even reached Havana yet.

"I went into the center of Santiago," Lundy said. The city had never been taken by the rebels, but when the old regime collapsed they moved in immediately. Santiago was home base to many of the guerrillas, and full of supporters. It was the scene of the greatest rebellion, and the widest repression, under the old government. And by the third or fourth day of that new year, and era, Santiago was in an ecstatic uproar, delirious, the streets full of people, and every hour bringing some new celebration. Castro was driving toward Havana, slowly, and the criminals, the torturers, and the corrupt were being caught and punished. Swept up in the mood, Lundy went that morning to see "some people."

The first was a man, described by Lundy as "a mulatto who had worked with Raúl Castro." The fellow had been an underground courier for the guerrillas, and would certainly know the latest news. Lundy arrived at his house, excited by walking through the city, a huge smile on his face.

"Professor," the courier said. "Nice to see you. Are you celebrating all this?"

Lundy stood there, grinning.

"I thought you intellectuals were more intelligent than that," the man said. "Don't celebrate, Professor. These kids only know the whip. It's going to be a government of the whip. The only thing they know is the machine gun and the whip."

A government of the whip? Nonsense. Castro's platform was there for anyone to see: constitutional law, free elections, more schools, and independence from foreign meddling. What machine guns? The mulatto was crazy. But that phrase stuck in Lundy's head. *Un gobierno del fuete. A government of the whip.*

That night it happened again. He was heading to a party at a friend's house. A wealthy friend. As he walked along, seeing the city lit up, full of banners and music, reconciliations and reunions, Lundy's mood soared, and he whistled the official hymn of the rebels. Even today, the sound of that anthem is "very moving," Lundy confessed, and in 1959 he was enthusiastically tweeting it through the streets as he reached the house. A gardener was watching the door. Lundy knew him.

"You are whistling the hymn of hunger," the gardener said.

Castro was caravanning toward Santa Clara, uncontested at this point, but the gardener said he already knew what would happen when the rebels reached Havana. "If those guys win power," he said, "hunger will come to Cuba."

Those were "the people who told me first," Lundy said now. The first to have the gift of foresight. "Not that I didn't have my doubts," he added. History had few examples of good revolutions. And just from knowing Fidel Castro, Lundy had some doubts about his character.

Lundy had doubts about the character of *all* Cubans. In an article called "El Profeta" he had warned a visitor that Cubans lived in a permanent state of contradiction:

Don't try to get to know them, because in their souls they live in the impenetrable world of dualism. Cubans drink happiness and bitterness from the same cup. The make music from their weeping and laughter from music. They take jokes seriously and make everything serious a joke.

Never underestimate Cubans. The right arm of Saint Peter is a Cuban and the Devil's best advisor is also Cuban. Cuba has never produced a saint nor a heretic. But Cubans pontificate among heretics and blaspheme among the saints. Their spirit is universal and irreverent. Cubans believe in Catholicism, Changó, in charades and horoscopes all at the same time. They will appeal to your gods and make fun of your religious rights. They don't believe in anybody and they believe everybody. They will never give up their illusions and they never learn from their delusions.

Don't argue with them, ever. Cubans are born inherently wise. They don't need to read, they know everything. They don't need to travel, they have seen everything. The Cubans are the chosen people . . . chosen by themselves. They pass among lesser peoples like a ghost passing over water.

Cubans are characterized individually by their sympathy and intelligence and as a group by their shouting and passion. Every one of them carries the spark of genius and no geniuses are tolerated. That's why it is easy to reunite Cubans, and impossible to unite them.

"El Profeta" was written in 1986, and the article swiftly became Lundy's most successful: widely reprinted, translated, taped up in Cuban diners, put under glass in waiting rooms, or pinned to bulletin boards. His self-mockery tapped some frustration among a people gradually getting used to failure, to the idea that they were not going to defeat their enemy, that they were not going home, that they were in exile to stay.

I asked Lundy what had happened to the boys in the photo, as a whole. He shook his head. "That is a melancholy question. The casualties are already very high. That was fifty years ago." He repeated his conversation with Dorta-Duque of the night before. I'd been sitting between them, listening as they talked, but some stories need retelling, and Lundy carefully repeated his dialogue about the number of survivors in his class. Six? Four? Two? *I am the only one left alive.* But now Lundy broke into a smile and added, with relish, "and I am still a-smiling."

Most of the boys from Dolores had scattered after the Revolution. "Of twelve or thirteen in my class in Dolores," he said, "only one stayed in Cuba." They'd gone everywhere, Lundy said. Florida, of course, but also the rest of the Caribbean basin, from Venezuela to the Dominican Republic, Puerto Rico to Mexico. They were in Toronto and Bilbao and Houston. One boy in the photograph was living in a Dade County trailer park. Another was in Havana, at the desk of the president of the republic.

"Try to find José Antonio Roca, in Spain," he said. He picked out a figure, a long face, next to his own. Roca was carrying a flag, the huge standard of Dolores itself, emblazoned with a Madonna and heraldic knights and castles. Lundy explained that Roca had nearly been killed while working for Castro during the Revolution. He was a dentist now.

"And this is Pepín Bou," Lundy added, looking at another face. "He lives right here on Key Biscayne. A few blocks from here. But this fellow, I think is dead. And Juan Grou, there, he was a Bacardi guy who lives in Mexico now. He went hiking in the mountains with Fidel a lot. Enrique Hechevarría is here somewhere, but he is in Puerto Rico. Maybe Arturo de Jongh is here somewhere, I can't see. He lives in Miami."

He spoke as if Miami was some distant place. Maybe, from retirement, with the causeway and the toll, it was. Cubans joke that the nice thing about Miami is how similar it is to the United States. If Miami was already that way, more Cuban than American, then that was doubly true for Key Biscayne, offshore, detached. You could close your eyes out here and smell your Caribbean youth. Spanish was the idiom of the island. There was a familiar brine on the wind. At night, in bed, you heard the clatter of dry palm leaves that haunted your dreams.

As Lundy, already tired from two hours of talk, ushered me out of the house, I asked about a line buried in his résumé. Slipped in among the entries on education, publication, and career was a reference to "some not very successful attempts to ship arms to the anti-Castro resistance." What did that mean?

Lundy waved me silent. He dug into the alluvial deposits on the desk, emerging with a sheet of white paper and a black ballpoint pen. He drew a small crocodile in one corner, with its tail tucked under its back feet; Cuba, in overview. Then he made a larger, hasty sketch of eastern Cuba, marking Santiago de Cuba, Manzanillo, the Sierra Maestra, Guantánamo, and so on, all in a few seconds. Concentrating, he filled in more details of Oriente: some swamps in the south, and then a big bay on the north side. He couldn't remember the name of the bay, he said. Nipe, I told him. It had to be Nipe Bay.

But Lundy was lost in memory. His hand now came down from the top, drawing a slow, unsteady line that wiggled down and hit Nipe Bay. The line smudged out there, the pen rubbing back and forth. Then he sketched in three other lines, quick arrows that darted in from the east, touching different points along the coastline.

"We only went four times," he said, handing me the map. "The spring of '61."

He wouldn't say anything else, at all. He simply packed me off, pushing me out of the office and, for a little old man, doing it with dispatch. I was out the door before I'd even looked over the map.

As I stood on the lizard-bedecked driveway, looking at his four lines on white paper, Lou came over. He was the screenwriter of some commercially released B- and C-grade films: *Dark Queen: The Movie, Sisters of Sin,* etc. We'd known each other, very slightly, for years.

"You know he has Alzheimer's," Lou said. "Right?" I didn't know.

"Yeah, he's losing it," he said of his father.

"He's shot," he added, with a chop of the hand. "He's done."

Most of the houses on Key Biscayne look the same—one-story ranches and bungalows in earth tones, with long roof overhangs to keep the rainy season at bay. It was only a few blocks to the house of Pepín Bou, one of the men Lundy had mentioned. Lundy had given me the address, but he had specified that I should pay no attention to the house number. Instead I was to watch for three big palm trees with crossing trunks. Indeed the trees, unusually tall and thick for palms, were visible from a block away.

Pepín wasn't surprised to see me, although I hadn't called. The old Cuban way remained in him: people made social visits, stopped by, dropped in, did the rounds, and called on each other, rather than called each other. I mentioned Lundy, and Pepín invited me in. We sat in a dining room that ran across the back of the house, looking through glass doors at a small pool.

He was tall and very pale for a Cuban, the pinkest of men, with fine hair that was white-blond in his youth and now entirely white. His real name was José, but Josés were so common that they had to be separated by nicknames. For no reason at all, Josés are usually called Pepe. But at Dolores there were already so many Josés that the usual nicknames— Pepe and even Pepito—were already taken. On arrival at Dolores he was thus given the nth derivation, Pepín, to differentiate him.

I asked him why I hadn't met him at the reunion of Dolores alumni in Miami Springs. "I went to a few of those," he said. "You go to those reunions and you don't know who anyone is, and the ones who were there last year are dead. Personally, I find it depressing."

Pepín was *oriental,* the son of a Santiago engineer. He described his childhood as privileged, especially in comparison with the squalid life of the black sugarcane cutters who were the main workforce in the province. Like a lot of boys from Dolores, he'd gone on to the University of Havana with Fidel, and this personal connection had gotten him mixed up, against his will, in the early days of the revolutionary government. While quietly plotting his escape, he'd double-crossed Raúl Castro, and one of his last acts in Cuba had been to lie calmly to Che Guevara.

He'd left in 1961 "with nothing," Pepín said, and then corrected himself. "All I had was a dime." They'd had to abandon their house and leave behind all their possessions and money. Even their luggage had been trimmed down at the last minute, by regulations that governed the number of pairs of underpants they could carry out of Cuba. At the airport the revolutionary militia had confiscated the gold band of his watch. But in midair, halfway between Cuba and Miami, an Englishman on the plane had taken pity on Pepín. He'd given him an American dime, just enough money to make a phone call.

We went into the kitchen and he rooted around in a drawer, and then another drawer. He checked between the blender and the refrigerator, but it wasn't there. He looked under a pile of bills and found it. It was hard to lose: the dime, blackened with age, was encased in a block of clear Lucite, four inches wide by six inches tall, and two inches thick. He set it out on the coffee table, upright, a tombstone for everything that had been lost. Or perhaps it was the reverse. Maybe the dime was a memorial for all that had been regained. The house. The family. The job. The friends. The pool in back.

I mentioned the photograph of all of them together in 1942. "This one?" he asked, and went into the next room and brought out a framed copy of the same shot. He'd gotten it from Lundy years ago.

He flipped the frame, carefully, and there on the back were two dense columns of ballpoint writing. Names.

Pepín's sister was married to another one of the Dolores boys in the photograph, a fellow called Alberto Casas. "He made this list when he was here in the house one night," Pepín said. "He has a phenomenal memory, a really incredible memory. He knows all the faces. He had it all up here," he said, touching his temple. "You should talk to him."

Alberto Casas was a wild man, Pepín said, grinning. He lived down in Puerto Rico now. "His family had the biggest cattle farm in Cuba," Pepín said, "and now they have the biggest cattle farm in Puerto Rico."

I stared at the list. Everything that had happened to Cuba since 1942 had happened to, through, or among them.

Of course, you couldn't find them *all*. Out of 238 boys in the picture, Alberto Casas had identified just 65, and some of those were only partially named, or were followed by question marks. There were a lot of nicknames (Fatso Rabelo, Little Rocket Festari, or just Basquito). Even I recognized some of the names. The Bacardi boys were here, scions from the rum dynasty, a family that also ran Santiago politics. And of course, a couple of Castro brothers.

The boys were listed by row, left to right and back to front. The names were a file of diminutives and oddities, from Socrates to John. There were many brothers. The boys who had died were marked with a demure "E.P.D.," meaning *en paz descansa,* or rest in peace. The Castro brothers were both followed with the notation that they were "(H.P.)," or sons of bitches. A couple of names—just a couple—were already marked "Miami" or "P.R." But the fate of the rest was speculation.

Pepín snorted when I asked where they were. *"Se fueron,"* he said, waving a hand at the glass doors, the pool, Biscayne, the world. They'd gone. Most were in Florida, elsewhere in the Caribbean, maybe Europe. For sure, other parts of the United States. Even Australia.

Any still in Cuba? "No," he said.

But he didn't know that. That was Cuban thinking. To believe that everyone had decided the same as you. To believe there was only one right answer. If you had left Cuba, then everyone should have left.

Cuban thinking makes Cuban reality tolerable. The Revolution had taken a dull knife to Cuban society, cleaving it. People had been left on one side or the other, divided by timing, flights of persuasion, accidents, the seductions of power, or the terrors of it. The only rule was that every family, every city, every group, and every institution in Cuba had been divided against itself. There was no reason the Colegio de Dolores should be any different.

As he let me out, even Pepín began to remember this. He had insisted that none remained in Cuba, but now he recalled that there was one. One single *Dolorino was* there, apparently. Some Miami friends had visited Cuba recently, and had shown him a video they filmed. They'd recorded all over Santiago, capturing the old places that Pepín remembered. The Parque Céspedes at the center of town. The Cathedral. The harbor. The old Bacardi distillery. At one point they'd visited the old church in Vista Alegre, the swank neighborhood where most of them had grown up. Pepín remembered seeing an old-timer in the film there, a Dolores alumnus. He couldn't remember the fellow's name. "Maybe Llanez, or Llanova," he said, and shook his head. "Llibino. Or Yoruba or something."

He tried on a few more names, and then said abruptly, "No. I don't know. But even if I did know someone who was still there, I wouldn't know him, you know what I mean?"

Alberto Casas was married to Pepín's sister, Hortensia. Pepín had told me that the couple were living in Puerto Rico, but even though he had given me their phone number, it was hard to get Alberto on the telephone, and even harder to keep him on it. He lived in San Juan, the biggest city, but on most days he kept to the habit of a lifetime, rising before dawn to travel out into the countryside, where he had his pastures.

Over the course of the next year I did reach Casas, sometimes. I caught him on his cell phone as he stood in a field under the summer sun. But the conversation would be intermittent, interrupted by the yelling of cowboys as they moved a hundred head through a gate, or by Alberto himself shouting at some recalcitrant beast, bovine or human. He hung up once in an obvious emergency. I reached him at home at 7:30 in the evening once, and he pleaded that he had just walked in the door, "covered in mud," and needed a shower. He was seventy-five.

When we did talk, it was as Pepín had said: Alberto did all the talking. Standing in a pasture once, he spent the whole call denouncing Puerto Ricans and all things Puerto Rican, the "collective cowardice" and "corruption" of their politics, the ruined society they had made. He poured indignation into the cell phone until his battery died. After twelve months of these exchanges I flew down to Puerto Rico.

The island was an alternate vision of Cuba, a could-have-been brought to life. ("Two wings of the same bird," José Martí said.) Seized by the

Americans at the same moment, it was openly annexed. Now Puerto Rico was a Caribbean island where English and Spanish were intertwined, where the people held American passports and took domestic flights to New York but were grown from the same rootstock as the Cubans, the same African and Spanish elements. Casas held them in contempt for this very thing: they were like the Cubans, but had never had the strength that Cubans did. Not the strength to resist the Spanish, nor to resist the Americans. Even the Cuban exiles had come in here and taken the place over, he said.

But Puerto Rico, with all its faults, had to make do, for it was as close as a Cuban exile could get. The heart of the city, Old San Juan, was puny compared to Old Havana, but it did have the same star-shaped fortresses along the harbor, the same step-through doorways and pastel houses. Out in the countryside the conditions for cattle were the same as in Cuba. The language and social arrangements all echoed what I had seen in Cuba, but with American highways and brands everywhere.

I had picked a cheap oceanfront hotel out of a guidebook, and after checking in I walked the few steps to the beach, which was wide and lovely, with a few men in tiny bathing suits lounging around. I was planning on spending the entire weekend with Alberto, touring his farm and meeting over meals with various Dolores alumni he knew in Puerto Rico. But when I called him from my room, Casas barked that there was an emergency. A relative in the Dominican Republic was sick, and he was leaving that very night. Before I could say anything he announced that it was now or never: he would be at my hotel in thirty minutes.

He strode into the lobby half an hour later looking every bit the *guajiro* in a short-sleeved shirt and straw hat, his face bronzed by the sun, his rough hands like slabs. He was enormous, a barrel-chested man with a sagging belly below, and big shoulders spread wide. His head was the only delicate part of the man, set with intense, darting eyes and washed with lively expressions of all kinds. He'd rounded up one friend on short notice, Juan Sotus, Dolores '48, a quieter, less animated character who arrived in a blue blazer.

Long before, Casas had described himself on the telephone by telling me, "I'm trouble, and I always have been. I'm a bad mix of Yon Wayne and Clint Eastwood."

Now, as we sat down at a plastic table under an awning, he started right in, talking right over the efforts of his friend, Sotus, to add comments, and ignoring the slow parade of guests, mostly skinny men, mostly from New York, mostly in the very tiniest bathing suits. Alberto didn't look left or right as he launched into stories about Dolores, cackling gleefully as he recalled working out a way to muffle the alarm on the emergency exit at the rear of the school bus. When the bus pulled up to school each morning, he would stifle the alarm, open the back door, and lead a stealthy jailbreak, four or five boys dropping from the back of the bus unseen and scattering to avoid mass. "There was a lot of that," he said, pleased. "I wasn't the only one."

I went to the bar and bought three *daiquiris naturales.* Carrying the white plastic cups back, I noticed that the hotel had a lot of rainbow flags. The flyers on the table next to us were for gay nightclubs. But Casas didn't notice, then or later. He made his own weather.

Almost as soon as I sat down again, Alberto jumped up so hard he slammed the table, splattering the drinks. "Squeeze this," he said. He made a muscle. "SQUEEZE IT!"

I did. He was almost twice my age, and his biceps was double my own. A cannonball. He'd spent his whole life in labor. At eighteen, he'd been put in charge of operations at the family dairy. It hadn't been, as other alumni claimed, the very largest cattle ranch in Oriente; no, it was merely the second largest dairy operation in the province. And his current ranch, here in Puerto Rico, wasn't the very largest on the island, as Pepín in Miami had told me. It was the second largest feedlot operation.

When I asked if he'd gone on, like so many Dolores kids, to the University of Havana, he scoffed. "I went to *la universidad de acosta,*" he said. "THE SCHOOL OF HOW-YOU-SAY HARD KNOCKS HA HA HA!"

Happily deprived of further education, Alberto had savvy in place of philosophy. He reduced the last half century to two sentences ("Cuba was the *querida,* the woman, of the U.S. And when Castro kicked out American corporations, the war was on") that were impossible to dispute.

A big man knows something of appetite. For decades, the conflict over Cuba had flowed from that possessive desire, that need to dominate, to have a *querida.* Alberto was Cuban, and emphasized his credentials as a nationalist and a patriot. He was quick to condemn Batista and the disgraceful American meddling of the 1930s and 1950s. But he had never believed that Castro was really on the side of Cuba. All he remembered of

Fidel was enough: the older brother of the pesky Raúl, Fidel was a domineering presence in the patio, always with a high opinion of his own
judgment. As Fidel and Raúl led the guerrilla war in '57 and '58, Alberto
sat out the conflict, minding his cattle. But Casas was wealthy, and when
the Revolution came he needed no prophets to tell him what the future
held. He bolted in February 1959, earlier than Lundy the Prophet, earlier
indeed than anyone I had met. He was allergic to authority.

Alberto had barely touched his daiquiri. He claimed he didn't waste
his time thinking about Dolores or the old days. He thought about Puerto
Rican life, Puerto Rican business, and Puerto Rican politics. He'd become
a leader of the cattlemen's association here and a lobbyist for all the agricultural exporters, and had redirected his ire from various idiots in Cuba
to various idiots in Puerto Rico. He had a weekly radio show that he used
to denounce the current government, whoever it was. He mocked the
Cuban exiles who talked about the past too much. There was a special
beach in Puerto Rico, Alberto said, which was known as Used to Have
Beach, because it was full of Cuban exiles who sat on their butts all day,
talking about what they used to have in Cuba.

At Dolores, Alberto's many discipline troubles were all the fault of the
Jesuits, he explained. He praised the Jesuits enthusiastically, for about ten
seconds, and then talked for ten minutes about how awful some of them
were. Dolores was full of "unbearable priests," Alberto said. They were
narrow-minded, unfair, disagreeable, smelly, authoritarian, unreasonable,
and were, he finally concluded, nothing but "a little Gestapo." He mocked
their lisping Spanish accents, the way they called him "Alberto Cathath."

A Gestapo, I asked? Wasn't that a little strong?

"A GESTAPO!" he shouted. He smiled as he talked, a provocateur taking psychic revenge. The worst of all the Jesuits was Father López, the head
vigilante, who was responsible for discipline, but Alberto also denounced
the rector, Father Pedro, at length, and the Jamaican teacher of English,
Mr. Tremble, and would have gone on scourging priests if Sotus had not
interrupted him, successfully for once.

"Most of the Jesuits are buried now in the Dominican Republic," Sotus
said soothingly, trying to tamp down his friend's ardor. Sotus noted that
the Jesuit teachers had been forced to leave Cuba, and many had settled in
Jesuit schools elsewhere in the Caribbean, particularly the Dominican

Republic. They had continued their work there, Sotus explained, living "without possessions," sacrificing for the betterment of the world.

Like many lifelong friends, Sotus and Casas shared a cozy contempt. Sotus revered the memory of Dolores, the priests, and the close-knit school feeling. His own background was "from the docks," he said, but he wasn't a wharf rat or sailor. His family had *owned* three of the main docks in Santiago, as well as farms. He mentioned the sleepiness of Santiago, and said the momentous event of their childhood had been the opening of the concrete Central Highway in 1932, which sped a flood of commerce into the city and created easy contact with Havana for the first time in four hundred years.

Alberto rolled his eyes when he saw me taking notes. "Don't write about him," he said, waving a dismissive hand at Juan. "His brother Jorge is the one you should write about." Jorge was "the James Dean of the family," Alberto explained. Indeed, Jorge Sotus, who graduated before his brother, had participated in many of the key events of the Cuban Revolution. He'd joined the urban underground, rising to the rank of captain. He'd led sabotage missions and fought in a failed uprising in Santiago in 1956. Sotus was later trusted with large amounts of cash and sent on gun-buying sprees in the United States and Central America. An early dissident, he had formed a militant cell in Mexico, and later died in Miami.

Juan, by contrast, had stayed out of the war, living quietly, keeping his head down. The antiromantic survivor.

When I showed Alberto and Juan the 1941 school photo, and the list of names attached to the back of it, written in Alberto's own handwriting, they both studied it intensely. Pepín had said that Alberto recognized more of the faces than anyone else alive. "It's true," Alberto announced, "I have a phenomenal memory. And every time I look at the photo I remember someone new I didn't remember before. My memory is superb." To prove it he leaned forward and, flipping back and forth between the front and back of the photo, began adding names to the list.

"Rolando Cisneros," he wrote in his neat Dolores cursive, followed by the notation "Miami?" And then Evaristo Tercilla, Ceferino Catá, René Fernández. It had been several years since he had made the list for Pepín and he updated the old names, writing "passed away," in English, beside Juan Ascanio. For some reason he switched to Spanish, writing *en paz des-*

cansa, next to Eduardo Marmul, and Adolfito Dangillecourt Bacardi, and Felipito Fernándes de Castro. Jacky Fioc was "NY" and Jongo Ramírez Cisneros was "BALT. PHYSICIAN." John Grist was "ARGENTINA?" Rocky Festari, known in a bilingual pun as *cohetito,* Little Rocket, had passed away in Santiago recently. Fatso Rabelo was in "CUBA," along with Kiki de Jongh and Charles Magrans, who was a doctor, a nephrologist. I'd find José Antonio Cubeñas in New York, and José Antonio Roca in what Alberto inscribed as "VA./SPAIN."

Despite his low opinion of the Jesuits, and his insistence that he rarely concerned himself with the past, Alberto still met, frequently, with his old friends from the school. There were a half-dozen *antiguos alumnos* in Puerto Rico, and they got together *a menudo,* informally. They ate a big meal and just hung out, Alberto said. But he disliked the reunions in Miami, which weren't really Dolores reunions at all, he explained. "When we talk about the old alumni of the Jesuits, and we get together here, we are 100 percent *Dolorino,*" he explained. "But when they have the reunion in Miami, there are all these people from Belén. That doesn't interest me. I'm 100 percent *Dolorino* and will always be 100 percent *Dolorino.*"

Before leaving to catch his flight for the Dominican Republic, he asked me who else I would interview. I mentioned some names from the old days, many of them taken from his own list. Others I would find as I could. He grew uncharacteristically quiet. "Any you speak to," he said, "tell them of me."

Alberto flew away that night. I had allowed time to tour his dominions, so I spent the rest of the weekend roaming around San Juan, idly, killing time, just as I did in Havana. Crime is much higher in San Juan than in Havana, guns are more common, unemployment and drugs are both chronic, and police corruption is an ongoing scandal. The hoteliers urged me not to go exploring, especially at night, but I prowled the old city center, very like Old Havana, but smaller. Cruise ship customers flooded into the bars and restaurants for a few hours around dinnertime. In the afternoons, and late at night, it was almost empty.

In the rest of the city, in the folds between the beachfront hotels and the *casería* housing projects, there was good food, but the waiters warned me not to come back alone. Though Puerto Ricans are American citizens, many spoke to me as if New York City was an impossible remove, never to be achieved.

The flight home was easy, cheap, direct, and simple, just the opposite of a return from Cuba. The exit from Havana was slow and bureaucratic, hours of paperwork and searches in the airport, with the increasingly hostile question ("Why do you come to Cuba so often?" they said, and I erased their doubts by saying, like everyone else, "I have a woman"). The trip home from Cuba was expensive, passing through more airports, and third countries, usually overnighting somewhere, often flying ridiculous routes, heading north to Canada and then doubling south again, or going west to Mexico to turn around and head east, via Charleston, before going north.

And then, on reentry to the United States, more lines and paperwork, and either evasion (the careful management of deceptions, the juggling of passports, the hiding of rum and cigars) or admission (an automatic red circle around the word CUBA, called out of line, inspection of credentials, quizzing, confession, confusion, supervision, the production of rum and cigars) at the desk. Either way, I would be waved through, exhausted, two days after setting out.

But in San Juan, all I needed was my driver's license, a cheap ticket on American Airlines, and three hours later I was standing in the domestic lounge in a New York airport. That was life without the drama of Cuban politics.

A few weeks after getting home, I called Alberto. We laid plans to continue the interviews, to eat *a menudo,* to visit the ranch. But just a couple of months later, when he was working in the fields, early, the habit of a lifetime, he felt faint. By nightfall he was in a hospital, diagnosed with a fast-moving bronchial infection, and it killed him within a week.

THE COMPANY

Dawn is the childhood of time. Even on a crocodile-shaped island, prone beneath heat spells and doldrum humidity, time had its small moments, chill intimations before consciousness. Day arrived in the soft separation of blackness from the not-black, of silence from the not-quite. Beauty is decay; time is always gone. Every day in the tropics starts with this disillusionment, the cool and transient moment before. Before light. Before day. Before the riot and rot of all days. Cubans are expelled from Eden 365 times a year.

This exile began softly enough. No hard lines, at first, sometime in the fifth hour. Just the unity of darkness within sleep and without. Neither light nor darkness, movement or stillness. The *internos,* the sleeping boarders, first crossed back and forth between those two realms, slowly, easily, repeatedly. Blackness was blackness, an inky continuum inside and out, from sleep to wakefulness, from eyes closed to eyes open. Closed. Open. And then closed again.

The next time you opened your eyes, something had passed out of the room, leaving a deep indigo. Night had peeled off a layer, dividing black from not-black. A single lonely bird cried persistently, shockingly loud in the absence of all else. *Where are you,* it called in its persistent language of longing. *Where are you Where are you Where are you?*

While you dozed again, just for a second, the colors of Cuba began: dark blue, then blue-gray, then gray. Light created shapes from nothing. Window frames. A dark door against a less dark wall. Silhouettes of columns against the courtyard. Another bird, distant, suddenly shouted back in birdsong: *I'm over here I'm over here I'm over here.*

Where are you, and then, as if no time had passed, not even an instant, there were a dozen birds, a thousand, a whole city's worth. Santiago rose.

There is a chill to the Caribbean dawn that is always unexpected, even to born-and-never-left islanders. The ocean chill, even far from the ocean. This brief flight of all warmth is both feared and loved by those raised under the blanket of wet Caribbean heat. Cubans think that shivering is a sign of imminent death. The mothers claimed that even a brief exposure to cold like that could kill you. You feared it right up until it was gone, and then you thought about it all day.

Now a new pace to the changes, an urgency. The gray coolness—yes, the chill was gone already—gave rise to colors, which quickly became as plain as day: purple, red, orange, yellow, and then, abruptly, the real light itself, not just its shadow.

In the arrival of real day, between their waking at six with that first light and their rousting by the 7:45 bell for mass, the world came to Dolores in the form of noise and light. For the sleeping students the first sounds seemed loud only because they stood alone. The quiet shifting of a blanket. The slide of a drawer. Then these domestic sounds seemed even quieter as new sounds insisted on attention. In the distance now came the broken-throated cry of a rooster, and then the consequences of motion, of city life: footsteps, bells, doors, voices echoing up, first from within the school's own courtyard, and then from the street. The first car passing through the rectangular plaza outside, the long, tree-shaded block that slouched downhill toward the harbor. Then the sound of shutters rolling up on the stores around the plaza, and a ship horn in the harbor, long and soft, and then the hard-throated cries of the first foot vendors, carrying their baskets or pushing small carts up Heredia Street out back. Each vendor had a particular chant that was the first music of the day, a little song of commerce. Called *pregones,* these were simple rhymes and catalogues of goods, salted with double entendres. *Ice ice ice,* someone shouted in a husky, all-day voice, *keep cool at a good price.* Or, *fruits pineapples mango and yes gentlemen papaya too you know you like it.*

Inescapable, endless, burning, the sun arrived too soon and stayed too long, melting the dreams off every Icarus in the building. In the tropics there is no lingering half-light or golden hour. Nothing about sunrise here is subtle or slow. There is a revolution from night, to light, in half an hour, an unsentimental amount of time. This flip from one state to the next is unknown in the sun's more glancing latitudes. But in Cuba it could be dark out when you started brushing your teeth, and when you stepped out of the bathroom a moment later, it was day. Like autumn in New England, or spring in Virginia, a dawn in Cuba is a memory even as it happens, a kind of anticipated nostalgia.

The difference, of course, is that those other examples occur once a year. The everyday dispersions of a Cuban dawn, the losses right there, before anything else had even happened, were the reason Cubans are nostalgic. The cool time from before, before the sun or any other problem, was the only time worth having.

Cuba is sprawled out across the sea, lazy, long, and ripe, a continent more than an island, almost half the land and people of the whole Caribbean, its vast planes of thick topsoil divided up by small, sharp ranges of mountain. A shape-shifting island, a little of everything, with something everywhere. Out in the farthest east, on the black sand beaches of Baracoa, you stared down a raging Atlantic; in the west, beyond Pinar del Río, orchid-fringed mountains reached for Central America. Cuba is big, and by tradition, wealthy and powerful. It alone was free of the crippling smallness of scale that V. S. Naipaul blamed for stifling the economies, and crimping the minds, elsewhere in the Caribbean. With the biggest cities and busiest harbors in that round sea, Cuba felt itself at the crossroads of the world; there was none of the isolation that Derek Walcott lamented as the defining tragedy of island life.

At 746 miles long, Cuba was unmeasurable. The landmass, a long and recumbent crocodile of 47,000 square miles, was less a nation and more an approximation. Twisted, multi-limbed, bumpy, and wrapped in sub-islands and slithering archipelagoes, "Cuba" was actually composed of either 1,600 or 4,000 islands and islets, depending on how you counted. The northern and southern coasts were fringed with strings of islands, called "gardens," which included everything from big islands covered with forests, farmland, towns, and swamps, down to tide-shaped *cayos,* spits of sand barely higher than a storm wave. The *cayos* were always in motion, whether eroding slowly over decades, or disappearing, relocating, and rebuilding in a single hurricane. Cuba crawled, too slow to track, the idea of one known country supplanted by the suggestion of a reigning consensus.

Columbus set the course for all these misapprehensions. After passing smaller islands, he touched down in Cuba, in Oriente, perhaps at Baracoa, on October 27, 1492. Arawak Indians told him that the island was inhabited by a race of one-eyed giants, who ate human flesh and had the snouts of dogs. It was this report—one-eyed giants!—that Guillermo Cabrera Infante would take literally almost half a millennium later, when he insisted that Castro himself was the Cyclops, the terrifying monster who stalked the island. But Columbus, no novelist, disdained their words, and thought he knew better: this big landmass in front of him was, at last, the mainland of the Orient, a land of fabled riches and grandiose palaces, not of monsters. He wrote a letter to the "Great Khan," a title and address that had been obsolete for more than a century, and dispatched it into the interior with two men. These were not diplomats or princes, but belowdecks sailors, chosen because they spoke Hebrew and Greek. They returned after two days, having found neither the Khan nor China nor India. Columbus was some ten thousand miles short of his goal; if his theory about a sea route to Asia had been correct, he would have starved to death. But chance favored him, and he was made Admiral of the Ocean Sea for discovering what he continued to insist was "the Indies," even when he began to suspect otherwise. He spent the rest of his life extolling the beauty of Cuba, and exaggerating the richness of what he had found on the greatest of islands.

In the history that followed, few who touched Cuba did any better. The island exerted a magical grip, a dream of fortune glittering under blue skies and palm trees. By 1941, when the boys at Dolores were waking up to their world, that old Cuba of the Conquest, of one-eyed giants and gentle Arawak people, had been sublimated into a folk memory, the original story of a time before, of paradise won and lost. The pearl of the Antilles they saw around them now was nothing so rustic or mystical, but a bustling nation, coursing with the profits available during a time of war in Europe and Asia.

This Cuba was a society in flux, reaching for its democratic high point, but also unbalanced and divided. In Havana, in 1941, the Communist Party of Cuba was a legal organization, feeble but full of bureaucratic Marxists and academic revolutionaries. They divided Cuban society into three rigid social classes, each with its diligently differentiated subgroups and categorical imperatives. At the top was a ruling class, itself composed of two separate subclasses. The first, and most obvious, was the tiny, plutocratic elite in Havana, whose fortunes, and therefore power, often came from big businesses or inheritances or Europe. Out in the rest of the country, the ruling class was a broader and more uniform group of Creoles, the white, Spanish-descended planters. Their power and wealth usually came from gigantic landholdings, often preserved generation after generation, even across centuries. This provincial elite depended on the land, which is to say on the rain and the sun, but also on the size of the American sugar quota, and on the availability of cheap, tractable labor. Although politics could do nothing about the weather, it could arrange the rest neatly.

Below them was a middle class, small, but still bigger than was found in most of the rest of Latin America. The number of telephones and automobiles per capita lagged behind only Argentina and Venezuela, the traditional powerhouse economies. Cuban cities were filled with professionals. This native class of intelligentsia was enhanced by a large flow of immigrants from Europe and the United States during the 1920s and 1930s, who brought talent and resources to fuel the economy.

And then, *los humildes*. The poor were millions, a majority distributed everywhere from the wide plains of Santa Clara to the nooks and crannies of the harbor towns. They were day laborers in the stockyards of Matanzas, and the sons of slaves who farmed tiny plots in the Guamuhaya Mountains. Above all, the poor were beholden to the system of big agriculture. At the very bottom of Cuban society was the thing that held Cuba up: the *macheteros,* the cane cutters, an army of starvation-wage victims who moved in great waves through the countryside, hopping from plantation to plantation, doing dirty, dangerous, exhausting labor in the hot sun. In any given place the *zafra,* the cane harvest, lasted for only about 120 days. Most *macheteros* could string together employment for barely six months of the year. Hunger was common, malnutrition chronic. The per capita intake of calories (2,800 a day) looked sufficient on paper, but there is no average between rich and poor, and by 1941, amid a stable and expanding market for sugar, the average consumption of meat was actually falling in Cuba. The poor simply could not afford it: they lived on rice, beans, and especially the empty calories that come from gnawing on a stalk of sugarcane. As Che Guevara later pointed out, leaving children to starve for several months each year, with nothing but *guarapo,* the

weak juice from crushed cane, to survive on, was all the justification anyone needed for a revolution.

The extremes of wealth and poverty were striking, and therefore deliberately evaded in the consciousness of Cuba's elite. The state schools and
hospitals were pathetic, with little budget and few facilities, but still, they
could say, the University of Havana was one of the greatest schools in the
Americas. Peasants in the countryside had to travel to a city to have any
hope of treatment in one of the very few public hospitals, but still, it had
to be mentioned that Cuba had some of the best doctors in the world.
Havana might be ringed with shantytowns, but it was the most advanced
city in the Caribbean, the envy of a hundred islands. In the countryside
people were rotting from the inside out on a diet of cane juice, but epic
fortunes had been made through slavery, sugar, alcohol, gambling, corruption, hotels, and even through hard work, and Cuba gleamed in the sun.

The classes could be divided up almost indefinitely—lumpen and proletariat, petit and grand bourgeois, vanguard and exploiter—but one thing
was always the same. In memory, no matter how it had been, the sun was
always shining, the sky blue, the palm trees swaying in a breeze. It didn't
matter what lies were told by the statistics, or even memory, because everything was always perfect in the old days, by definition. Even the weather.

Everything good and bad in Cuba comes from the east, from Oriente.
Santería, the syncretic Afro-Cuban religion that marries Roman Catholicism to the demigods of West Africa. *Son,* the infectious Cuban rhythm
blending the Spanish guitar and the drum with the liberation of jazz.
Slavery and sugarcane, which were planted together in the fertile plains of
Oriente. The New World itself, born when Columbus found, instead of
his one-eyed monsters, a land of "exceeding riches," with a population so
gentle they could be enslaved "by fifty men with swords."

Something about Oriente invites exaggeration. It is the hottest part of
Cuba, the most mountainous, the first settled, and the earliest to achieve
glory and shame. Santiago (named "de Cuba" to differentiate it from the
one in Spain) was founded in 1515, by Diego Velázquez. That was only
one generation after the Muslims were driven out of Spain; just one generation after the Jews were expelled. There were men present at the

founding of the city who had known Columbus himself, and the 1515 date was so early that it rooted Santiago more in the European Middle Ages than in the new world to come. Santiago was the first capital of Cuba, reigning for forty years before eventually losing out to Havana, an insult never forgotten. The city served as a kind of Jerusalem to the Americas, spreading the new faith of conquest, and the new tongue of Castilian. Cortés had sailed from the harbor of Santiago to conquer the Aztecs. The gold and silver of the Incas had all passed back through the ports of Cuba. Sugarcane, one of the world's great cash crops, was introduced first in Oriente; the first slaves were landed at Santiago in 1554.

Enslavement produced sugar, sugar produced fortunes, and fortunes led to a flowering of culture. Cuba's great champions of liberty were from Oriente, and the real, original Cuban revolution was seeded here, when the generals Máximo Gómez and José Martí landed to begin their war of independence from Spain. A few years later, Teddy Roosevelt and his Rough Riders came ashore in Oriente, conquering San Juan Hill, just outside Santiago. The great names of Cuba—Bacardi, Castro, Desi Arnaz—are Oriente names.

In 1942, Santiago de Cuba was a city of just 200,000 people, intimate, folded inside its ring of hills, far from the rest of Cuba, and joined by sea to other influences. It was more Caribbean than the capital. The people of Santiago described themselves as more passionate than the materialistic *Habaneros*. Santiago people spoke quickly, dropped their *R*s, and larded their speech with Bahamian English from the harbors; Yoruba and Hausa terms imported with the slaves; and French and Haitian Creole from Tivoli, a quarter settled by refugees from the 1791 slave revolts in Haiti. In the early twentieth century black Jamaicans took jobs in the harbor, bringing words and a dance—the limbo—that became part of city tradition. By 1940, with a war in Europe driving Cuban agriculture, a new generation of Haitians was arriving to cut cane.

Havana had little of the formal racial segregation found in America, and Santiago was less rigid than Havana. In the big capital, Cubans were influenced by the racial codes imported by North Americans. But in Santiago there was an informal détente. Race mattered in Santiago, deeply. It was the blackest city in the blackest region, the Afro-Cuban metropolis par excellence, but Santiago was still ruled by whites, who preferred to think of Santiago as a city with "easy" or "warm" relations between races.

That was only because blacks knew their separate place, and kept to it. After an obscure political conspiracy in 1912, white mobs had lynched blacks in Santiago, a demonstration of arbitrary power not lost on Afro-Cubans. Black Cubans had to channel their energy into achievement and survival within their own community.

Still, in the Cuba of 1942, racial mixing occurred routinely in a variety of ways that would have been unacceptable, or even illegal, in the United States. In a country and city with people of every possible shade, a routine color bar was impractical. Interracial marriages were disapproved of, but not unknown, and "good" blacks were admitted to some elite schools and institutions, even as they were systematically excluded from the best social clubs. In politics, alliances reached across color lines, so that in Santiago during the 1940s, the mayor was Justo Salas, a black who was elected chiefly with the support of the white middle class, and who defeated a white candidate supported chiefly by blacks.

Sugar was grown all over the island, but the two greatest belts of cane ran across Oriente province. One was on the interior, or western, face of the Sierra Maestra, and the other, the greatest in Cuba, flowed across the rich soil of the north, wrapping itself around the Bay of Nipe, and enveloping Birán, the town where the Castro family lived. These cane lands were among the most profitable possessions in Cuba, and the wealth they generated flowed through Santiago. Oriente also had the richest mineral deposits in Cuba—iron ore in the Sierra Maestra, just to the west of Santiago, along with manganese and copper. Rich strikes of chromium, cobalt, and nickel had been found in the northeast.

As the largest of the old Spanish provinces, Oriente was still never large enough to contain the egos of people who lived there. To live in Santiago was to walk tall, if slowly. Residents absorbed, by osmosis, the enormous pride of the city, the geocentric presumption that age confers superiority. All Cubans were in agreement that their island was the jewel in the crown of Spanish Empire; that it was the center of the modern Caribbean, the most progressive and enlightened of all island nations. This lunatic self-regard reached even greater heights in the east, and was distilled to an essence in Santiago, where it occupied the thoughts of everyone, from Santiago's oldest families, with their triple-barreled surnames, to those who had no surname at all. White or black, poor or rich, the *Santiaguero* insisted with a straight face that fruit is riper, the sun stronger, the women more passionate, the politics more sincere, the talk more profound, the cemeteries more grand, even the night darker, than elsewhere in Cuba. The *oriental* insisted that not only was Cuban music the best music in the world, which everyone already knew, but Oriente was the only source of the Cuban music.

Even when they were excited, Oriente people could be smug and complacent. In the middle of raging parties they would shout at the musicians, *todo está inventado ya,* or, *no hay nada que inventar!* That's it. There is nothing left to invent. Everything has already been invented. They meant this as encouragement: progress stopped right here.

The Colegio de Dolores, prepatory academy and boarding school, emerged from sleep a self-contained community, enclosed behind high walls, and sealed against the outside world by a pair of tall, flat-topped doors that were locked with a heavy iron key at night. The doors seemed huge, looming over the tallest boys, high enough even to accommodate the Virgin of Fatima, a statue on a bier that was carried through the doorway on the shoulders of a dozen boys every January 18. Despite a few such public events, it was only the boys and the families of Dolores who came inside, not the rest of the world. There was a division. Inside the walls were an elect. Outside was the world that would be led.

The physical plan of Dolores was simple and typically Spanish: a regular rectangle constructed around a courtyard, whitewashed, with high ceilings and arched galleries. But the true shape of Dolores was hard to fathom, since the grid of exterior streets pressed the building into the side of one of Santiago's many hills. Looking at the school from outside, on the nearest tree-shaded plaza—named the Plaza Dolores, of course—it seemed to be a two-story building with unusually tall windows, but there were actually three stories on this, the downhill, side, and an irregular fourth story added onto the back, to compensate for what was swallowed below by the encroaching hillside, with a second small patio dug into the rear.

While blue-gray still ruled below, that fourth floor was the first to feel the touch of direct sunlight, which came peering over a slanted roof of curved red tiles. Boarding students lived one level down on the third floor, in shared rooms. There were only twenty-two of these *internos* living in the school, full-time enrollees who ate all their meals at Dolores, slept and woke within the walls, and were entirely captive of the school's educational climate. These boys were all from other parts of the province, sent in by their parents to make sure that rural life or small-town limitations did not keep their children from rising within Cuban society, whether that rise was achieved through merit, or a superb Jesuit education, or connection to the most prominent families of eastern Cuba, or all of the above.

The *internos* slept two to four to a room, with brothers normally housed together. Sleeping in the communal and monastically quiet atmosphere of a religious institution, they went to bed early and often woke up long before required, stirred from the blackness of slumber by the first hint of sound, the first, most subtle changes in the darkness. The late risers would certainly be provoked by the growing noises, the daylight peering into the upper stories.

Before the 7:00 A.M. breakfast, every *interno* was expected to make his bed, order his room, wash up, gather books and shine shoes. The bathrooms were communal, a crowd gathering at the end of the corridor to clean faces and hands, brush teeth, wet and tame hair from ardor to order. Then the remaining minutes before seven were for preparing their homework and schoolbooks. On normal days, they dressed in any white trousers and a light-colored shirt with the sleeves rolled down. Dark neckties were expected, but not required. With this, the common outfit of day-to-day education, they didn't have to wear their dark blazers, or don the hated officer's caps, which were big white things with stiff black visors, heavy and hot. Nor the awkward Sam Browne belt, of white leather, that was difficult to clean, hard to adjust, and annoying to put on or remove. That outfit—the formal uniform—was reserved for feast days, days with important visitors, days with academic ceremonies, or the special public days with theatrical performances, oratory competitions, and school pageants. There are constant feast days in Catholicism, and a few of the Jesuit fathers loved to see their boys dressed up in military perfection, so the formal outfit was liable to be evoked at the slightest opportunity.

There were many sets of brothers within the walls, triples and doubles, genetic repeats that kept the school intimate and familiar in the most literal sense. The three Castellvi brothers, the three Tercias, and the three Ravelos. Then there were David, Arturo, and Enrique (or "Kiki") de Jongh, with their unusual last name for old-fashioned Oriente. Their grandfather, a Dutch physician, had immigrated to Curaçao in the service of the Netherlands army, then followed a Cuban woman to the island in the early 1900s. The three sons, though born and raised in Cuba, full of Oriente pride, were creatures of many worlds. Catholic, but of Jewish heritage. Cuban, but of Dutch origins. Spanish speakers, but with an English-speaking, American-educated father, and their own private language at the school, the encrypted chatter of Papiamiento, a lingua franca of the Netherlands Caribbean that mixed Dutch, Spanish, English, and Arawak words. The three de Jonghs were day students, who lived in a big house with many servants, and had cars. They looked as similar as three pennies.

And there were the Castros: Ramón, the gangly eldest, dark-haired, one of the tallest boys in the school but destined never to shine with brilliance. Ramón made little impression on people: he was a conformist, firstborn, certain to inherit the land and fortune his father had cultivated. He was interested mainly in agricultural equipment and sports. Then Fidel, almost as tall as Ramón, with a round face and pale gray-blue eyes that, combined with his rapidly increasing height, made him a natural standout on a dark-eyed island. A second son, he would inherit only his father's determination. He was in constant conflict with the old man, which both of them seemed to enjoy.

And then Raúl, the odd man out. Raúl was short, and darker-skinned than Ramón or Fidel. His face little resembled that of his older brothers. His eyes were almost Chinese, and only a fool would ever mention aloud at Dolores the rumor that he was really fathered not by Angel, but by a Chinaman in Birán, or a local military officer. In the small world of the Oriente elite, such a thing would preclude an advantageous marriage.

Bad reputations were hard to shake. The Casas brothers, for example, were known troublemakers. There was Americo, who died at fifteen of appendicitis while away from Dolores, and Ignacio, and then Alberto. Their grandfather had built up the largest dairy farm in eastern Cuba, and they had five hundred milk cows. Every boy in the school knew that the milk on the breakfast table was Casas milk, in Casas bottles. Friends of the brothers would make trips to the family plant, a state-of-the-art dairy on the outskirts of Santiago, filled with roaring machinery and hay, vacuum tubing and rubber hoses, refrigeration and steaming manure, huge animals and foul-mouthed men who somehow, in an orchestra of chaos, produced truckloads of clinking glass bottles delivered to the entire network of city streets. A playground beyond all playgrounds.

A boy raised this way, as a prince in a rustic empire, could say no. Alberto Casas said no. He had already compiled the worst disciplinary record at Dolores. There were infractions for speaking out of turn, for stubbornness, for mocking the Jesuits openly, for fighting with other students. But Alberto had recently broken with his regular offenses, for the worse. His older brother had asked him to pick up something at the hardware store during the day: four boxes of .22 caliber bullets. These are the kind of tiny bullets used for target shooting. There was nothing unusual about this; Cubans have an almost American affinity for guns, and for the idle occupations of target shooting, wandering around in fields looking for birds to shoot, and blasting tin cans. Alberto bought the bullets during his lunch break, but when he returned to Dolores he was stopped at the front door by a hissing voice.

"Alberto Cathath, what are you carrying?" It was Padre López, the chief disciplinarian. Alberto told him what he had: four boxes of bullets.

López looked in the bag. "For carrying bullets in school," he said, "you are sentenced to detention until 6:00 P.M."

Alberto erupted. "You teach us to tell the truth and that's what I told you!" He shouted up at the padre's face. "I didn't lie and say it was candy in the bag!" He announced he would take the issue right to the Padre Prefect.

For arguing, López extended the punishment to a full week. Six P.M. detention every evening.

Alberto went into the detention hall—a dreaded second-floor room all the way back on the right—for that first afternoon. There was nothing to do for more than two hours except read stupid books, do homework, and make faces whenever Padre López looked his way. Alberto was used to spending his afternoons roaming the dairy, looking in on "his" cows and pursuing his whims. Now he stewed. He already knew the detention hall well and hated the hours here. His friends had already gone home. Even the *internos* were more free than he was, a day student trapped in the building. He was supposed to sit here, studying and suffering right through the afternoon heat, until 6:00 P.M.

López was old, weak, and slow-moving. He spent all his time sitting down scowling at Alberto. López was a toothless tiger, and when he turned away that afternoon, just for a moment, Alberto jumped up, climbed from his chair to a desk, and yanked open the tall window shutters. Before the padre could even stand up, Alberto leapt onto the sill and threw himself out the window. It was a second-floor window.

It was a long way down to Heredia Street, but the rise of the hill cut the distance somewhat, and though he hit very hard, Alberto had the elasticity of youth. He rolled, got up, and with the cry *Alberto Cathath* trailing after him, vanished at a run into the city.

Before mass the next morning, Father López was waiting on the front steps. "You are expelled," he said when he saw Casas. But another Jesuit was there, and quietly overrode the verdict, sending Alberto into the school.

For Alberto, this little victory was almost worse than defeat. He was infuriated by the unfairness of López, by his punishments, and by the absolute power of the administration, even when it overruled those punishments. So furious that Alberto plotted quietly to expose this injustice. Working with friends and the school mimeograph machine, he printed up a little newspaper, a revival of a student paper called the *Dolores Critic* that had died of indifference some years before. Alberto wrote the articles dealing with the unfairness of discipline and the hypocrisy of the school. He even managed to run off some copies before the Padre Rector saw one. After reading the *Critic,* he confiscated the issue and ordered the mimeograph locked away.

Alberto noted this down. There was no justice in his small world.

Up high, where the morning sunlight first struck Dolores, the school looked like a perfectly regular construction. On the third floor, the short sides of the rectangular layout were lined with four arches, directly echoing the four doors of the four bedrooms there, each used as a dormitory by three or four boarding students. The longer sides of the floor held a dozen arches, and a dozen more small rooms, typically shared by groups of brothers.

But the pleasing symmetry of life on the third floor began to dissolve as sunlight slipped down below. The second floor was less regular, with the arches misaligned against the entrances to classrooms, and a few doors that were taller and wider. The classrooms were airy, with the high ceilings and tall windows necessary to purge the Santiago heat. The classrooms were lined with appropriate exhibits of educational value. There were rooms decorated with math tables, or diagrams of plant circulation, but aside from the science lab the greatest fun in the building was the Museum of Cuban Birds. The second classroom on the right, it was lined with dark cabinets that went almost to the ceiling. Behind the glass were dozens of stuffed and mounted birds from the shores and peaks of the island, as well as a few mounted fish and a small stuffed shark to round out the picture. Atop the cabinets were paintings of the rest of the animal kingdom. The natural history classroom was likewise lined with cabinets of rock samples, plants, insects, and a few more birds, all under the stern gaze of a portrait of Ignatius Loyola, the founder of the Jesuit order, high overhead. The science classroom was even more transporting than stuffed birds: here were an assortment of antique but effective telescopes, Bunsen burners, and a large cabinet dedicated to the wonders of electricity, complete with a tiny generator for delivering experimental jolts.

Down at the bottom, the whole idea of order gave out. Entering from the Plaza Dolores, the first floor began with a lofty ceiling near the entryway, which opened out quickly to the courtyard. Here the arches made Moorish *pasillos,* the shaded walkways. But the *pasillos* seemed to erode: as they ran away, they buried themselves into the hillside that backstopped Dolores, remaining dark all day but also airless.

To accommodate the rise of this steep city, the large courtyard itself had to be stepped, divided by a six-foot wall into lower and upper patios. That wall, topped with an iron railing, was an obstacle to every sport, but there was still enough room on the lower patio for stickball, and the wall itself served as a mount for one basketball hoop, with the boys playing a short-court game back and forth between the wall and a hoop mounted near the chapel.

An obstacle to sports, the wall was a gift to ritual. The students would stand and face it for assemblies, to receive instruction, and to hear proclamations. A proscenium arch would be erected for plays and pageants. The oratory contests would be presented here, with boys practicing the bombastic tone and clenched-fist style of declamation. They would put on plays here, choral works, and, where the railing provided a jumping-off point, it was an irresistible place for show-off contests.

This, of course, was where the boys lined up for the school photo, which was made annually, by the same photography studio, during a special assembly in mid-morning, while the courtyard was still in shadow. The boys dressed in their "gala" uniforms, the blue blazers and white officer's caps. On the lower half of the courtyard, rows of chairs and then a bleacher were set up. Two men arrived from Foto Mexicana, the high-society studio of Santiago. The photographer was an anonymous technician; it was the brand name that mattered. Cubans, who conceded little glory to other countries, associated Mexico with artistic genius; in the 1930s that country was a beacon of artistic progress, a "revolutionary state" crowded with painters, sculptors, muralists, and photographers. There were other photography studios in Santiago, but Foto Mexicana was the choice of the elite, and the studio's trademark—a rosette stamp on the lower right corner of a photo—appeared in official church portraits and in the shots taken at country clubs, all the leading schools, and at wedding celebrations.

The Foto Mexicana studio was located at the heart of the business district on Enramada. Right across the street was the Woolworth's, an icon of consumerism that Cubans called, thanks to its low prices, El Ten Cent. There were commercial landmarks all around it: El Encanto, the gleaming, air-conditioned department store, and La Muñeca, where the boys from Dolores (and all the other parochial schools in Santiago) bought their uniforms. Foto Mexicana was the chronicler of this world, of the best of Santiago, and when they came to Dolores it was not merely to shoot the entire student body, but to continue with the students broken down into separate classes, with individual portraits of the graduating seniors, the student brigadier who supervised each division, and of the various *dignidades*.

After arriving in the courtyard, the Foto Mexicana technician would prepare for work by first draping a black cloth around his neck, a kind of velvet cowl that was a badge of office for photographers. He would stand with his back to the basketball hoop, directing an assistant—a young bull—to carry the equipment as he fetched first the heavy wood tripod, then the big box camera itself, usually a large-format Dearborn from Chicago. Then he brought in the film: a special suitcase packed with individual 8 x 10 negatives, each sheet of film pre-loaded into a slider, a metal frame. Even a negative this big would have to be printed at double size to produce a clear shot of such a big group.

And then—only then, once the camera was prepared—would the students themselves appear, led by the *reguladores* into their rows, with the Jesuits, standing behind the camera, directing and demanding. It was essential to work quickly. In the front, the smallest and youngest boys, just seven years old, were arrayed on folding chairs, thirty-three across. Some of them are too small to touch the floor with their toes. Each row was older and bigger, until, in the last row of bleachers, standing with their backs to the wall, the tallest. Then, behind them, looking down from the railing of the upper patio, two more rows of boys.

It was the morning of a bright day, but the sunlight striking the top of the walls had not reached down to the patio yet. The white stucco rising on all sides, however, served as an ideal reflector, softening and bouncing back the sunlight, brightening faces and filling in dark areas around the eyes. The photographer could estimate from experience that the lens aperture should be wide, and the exposure fast. Just one-sixtieth of a second, so fast that not one face out of 238 would blur with movement. But he would calculate the exposure anyway, with a light meter, to verify his instinct. The shutter speed and aperture would both be set on the lens itself, by moving tiny sliders.

He then stepped behind the camera, facing the ground glass, the image. The camera had a long accordion bellows, which stretched between two standards, or frames. Bending down to focus, he flipped the black monk's cowl over his head with a practiced gesture, dropping it over the camera top, concealing himself in darkness. Now it was possible to study the image on the ground glass clearly, looking at it from a couple of inches away. He would fiddle with the bellows, drawing the image into sharp relief, then check that the frame was filled, moving it in or out, slightly, and refocusing. After these swings and tilts, there were only a few seconds for the difficult art of *scheinflug,* or matching the focus plane to the natural tilt of the composition. The boys at the bottom of the frame were much closer to the camera than those at the top, eight rows back, so the front standard had to be tilted to match, using a small gear. And then the overall focus had to be reset, so that every face was equally crisp. Foto Mexicana made its money by selling copies of the pictures to every family represented; even one boy out of focus was a lost sale.

After popping the cloth up and back behind his neck, he stood up and raised his hands like a conductor, to draw their focus. *Everyone hold still.* Now the clock was ticking.

He stuck out a hand and was given, by the assistant, a slider, the metal film holder. Maybe he would throw the cowl over himself and the camera one last time, to check the focus, compulsively, because the slowest thing was to rush the job. But he had to stand, in the end, because you couldn't take a picture with this kind of camera while looking through the lens. With a slam, he would rack the film holder in, depositing the negative in front of the ground glass, and then reach forward and throw a toggle to close the shutter on the lens. Probably standing beside the camera, still focused more on the boys than his machine, he pulled the slider out, leaving the film naked. *Look here,* he would say, loudly, pointing to the lens. *Not at me.* And then click. Just a simple, light pressure on the shutter switch. It was over in a sixtieth of a second.

When shooting small groups, the photographers had a rule of thumb: one exposure per subject, but that wasn't possible with a group of this size. Even the most disciplined children will quickly lose their patience and begin to move. With large groups there is about a minute, or ninety seconds at most, to finish such a job. Three or four exposures would be enough, but a professional would do six in that time, perhaps. It wasn't necessary to bracket the exposures or change anything; exposure could be fixed easily in the printing process. But multiple shots gave some proof against blurred and blocked heads. So, in roughly ninety seconds, a steady rhythm: bang, reload, bang, reload, bang, reload. At some point the photographer would notice that the boys were wavering, losing their focus, so he might make a commanding reminder, halfway through: *If you can't see me, I can't see you.*

About two minutes after it started, all the negatives were tucked away, sealed in the Foto Mexicana suitcase, and the Jesuits would clap with satisfaction and release the boys.

Before he touched the bell, Lundy Aguilar had it easy. He was rail-thin, knock-kneed in his white trousers, already wearing a long face by age thirteen. Aguilar had a preoccupied mind and a love of books. A day student, he tried to read as he walked to school each morning, even though he sometimes strode into lampposts or mailboxes. Pleasing to his parents and to the Jesuits, he was bathed in extraordinary freedom for an adolescent boy. Every day, he would wake up in his own home, on his own time, make his own bed, and dress himself without consulting his parents. They even let him prepare his own breakfast, as he wished. His father, by day a grave supervising judge in the criminal courts, was at home tolerant and even indulgent, for little Lundy excelled at many things, and could not be found guilty of much. Lundy's mother trusted him. The boy was diligent, punctual, thorough, and could seemingly do no wrong. Even the Jesuits, who were always generous with praise, gave special credence to this oddly serious boy.

Having eaten or not, as he wished, Lundy hit the streets of Santiago around 7:15 and began his daily ramble through the noble city. Although the Lundy family had *oriental* roots going way back, Lundy had lived his early years off in central Cuba. Until the age of seven, his whole world had been a small cow town outside the larger cow town of Santa Clara. The land there was all flat plain, cowboy country, with some sugarcane, lines of royal palms, and little else. The village had close horizons—familiar faces throughout, a few dirt streets churned only by horse hooves, and a special welcome everywhere for the son of the town judge. But the lack of spectacle, of variety and new things, was what had driven Lundy into books. He devoured stories of history, of adventure and travel, of the conquistadors and buccaneers, of early Cuban heroes and of desperate battles between cavalrymen and Indians. When his father was promoted to Santiago, Lundy began to walk to his new school every day in a kind of rapture, convinced he had stepped into the pages of his true life at last. The voluptuous hills of the city were gifted with sudden vistas, and surprises lay around every corner. Tram cars! Woolworth's! Air-conditioned buildings! (And so many of them!) Ship horns blasting in the harbor. Immigrants. Foreigners. Two hundred thousand Cubans in every walk of life. The stores were packed with American toys and European fashions. This was the genuine city where the conquistadors in Lundy's books had once strode about in armor, plotting their departures for new lands. Santiago was big and energetic, just like the *Nueva York* shown in movies. Lundy knew that he was walking through his kingdom, and that Santiago stood at the center of the world.

No matter how many times he walked to the Colegio de Dolores, year after year, there was always something to see. It was only six blocks, up the never flat streets, through the Plaza Dolores, and then, just past the chapel, up the stairs and inside the two tall, thin doors. You could vary the route, watch the cars, poke into shops, pass the houses of friends, sit on benches, talk to children and adults, watch strangers, see projects and works in progress. You could see something, always. You could take it all in.   .

The Jesuits had made Lundy a *regulador,* one of the class officers charged with keeping order among his own age group, making sure that everything happened on time. As the most punctual and well regarded of all the *reguladores,* he was given the special duty of sounding the assembly bell for mass, literally ringing in the school day.

His badge of office was the wristwatch, given to him as a prize by the Jesuits for his good grades. Trust came with the watch: with diligence came power, and with power responsibility. The model student was a clock spring turning steadily toward a larger goal. For the Jesuits time was of the essence. Dolores was located on Calle Reloj, Clock Street. In colonial times, the presence of a church here had meant the ringing of hourly bells, to keep the faithful on *hora inglesa.* The school displayed time everywhere, in the classrooms and on the walls, in the dormitories and the dining room. There were clocks, and bells, boys with ordinary wristwatches, and then special boys with special wristwatches, given to them expressly for keeping everyone else on time. The Jesuits tried to think about the very long term, as if centuries were minutes, but they also insisted that minutes be treated like seconds, caught and used before they flew away. *Hora inglesa* means "English time," which is to say, on time. Punctuality was a double good: symbol of diligence, and maker of it.

But these were boys, after all. They all shared the dangerous habit of drifting off, as if time didn't matter and childhood was forever. Their natural state was the reverse of the Jesuit ideal: children drew out the minutes, and made time itself into another servant. That was what the bell and the *regulador* were for: to keep everyone on *hora inglesa,* following the orderly life within these walls, and then without them.

At half past seven on most mornings, Lundy would turn the corner on the Plaza Dolores, sweep up the short staircase, and enter the school. The *internos* had finished their breakfast and scattered. He might stop to read the notices, but soon he would be on the second floor, checking his watch against the office clock and taking possession of the hand bell. It was brass, with a thick clapper and a wood handle. At 7:44 he went to the railing overlooking the courtyard and watched his watch. When the second hand swept past the top, he threw his hand down, and up, down and up, harder and harder:

Bam bam bam bam bam bam bam.

Seven times, or seventeen times, as many and as loud as he could get away with. It made every kid jump. They had 180 seconds to get to their places.

Those three minutes, starting every day at 7:45, were the prelude to holy mass, and then classes, and they were the most frenzied minutes of the day. The bell set a machine of 238 gears in motion. Boys came out of every doorway in the school: the bathrooms, the classrooms, the dining room, the chapel, the dormitories, the science lab, and the offices. Scores of late or skylarking boys came crowding in through the front door all at once, a wave of children that met with a smaller number of boarding students tumbling down from the third floor. The courtyard began to fill up, and dawdlers jumped the steps two at a time. Single-digit boys, the seven- and eight-year-olds, were pushed around and mixed in among those twice their age, everyone trying to sort into lines by age, prodded by *reguladores*. With seconds to go, amid muffled collisions and play shoves, two hundred and thirty-eight boys formed up, the military drill crescendoing to a sudden and practiced perfection. Nine lines filing across the patio. The youngest and oldest students were always fewest in number, while the middle grades often had twenty or even twenty-five boys each.

When the three minutes were up, and everything ready, the sudden stillness was undercut by tiny murmurs, encrypted busts of insult, arrangement, and gossip:

"Tonight, Fatso."

"Move it, Leadbutt."

"Did you?"

"Shut up, moron."

"Moron!"

Then the black-robed Jesuits themselves, sweeping in among the snaking lines, straightening postures, squaring shoulders. The last slackers would be chased into file by a few syllables of over-articulated Castilian:

Quick. Hurry up. Keep quiet.

And for the blabbers and fidgety, just the sharp, attention-getting interrogative: *And you?*

The routine was the same: everyone was called to attention, gave a military salute—sometimes accompanied with a goofy face—and then the long lines would begin to snake through the courtyard, beneath the gallery, and through a side entrance, into the chapel attached to Dolores. The youngest boys marched in front and took seats in front; then the next class, and the next, in order, pushed from behind, a *regulador* policing each group, keeping them moving, until the pews were full. In the space of a few minutes the 238 students had remade themselves into one.

Dolores was a military academy without weapons. The Jesuit order is explicitly based on military structure. Their founder, Ignatius Loyola, was a hardened Spanish soldier who lost a leg to a cannonball in 1521. After making an unexpected recovery, Loyola dedicated himself to religion, conceiving a new order, his Society of Jesus, that would mirror the administrative efficiency, scientific modernism, and dedication to mission of a trained European army. The head of the Jesuits, residing in Rome, is called the General. The worldwide structure is divided into provinces, each run by a "Provincial." All the way down to the student *reguladores,* the Jesuit way was structure, order, attentiveness. Everything in its right place, on time, clean, neat. Focused. Disciplined. Modern.

Capable, educated, connected through their schools to the powerful and the wealthy of Europe, the Jesuits often stood too close to power for their own good. In theory, the order had no politics, only an agenda of service to the Pope. But at different times the Society has been accused of being too radical (for opposing slavery in South America in the 1700s), too conservative (for backing the doctrine of papal infallibility in 1870), too rightist (it was banned in Switzerland until 1972) and too leftist (for criticizing Central American generals in the 1980s). As a result, the Society has an epic history of expulsions and censure. The Jesuits were banned in Japan in 1587; thrown out of Portuguese dominions in 1759; banned from France, Sicily, and the Spanish Empire by 1767; and entirely suppressed by the Pope in 1773. The order always reconstituted itself after these setbacks, and was restored globally in 1814, returning to Cuba in 1854.

By eight o'clock *hora inglesa,* the boys stood in the pews, watched by some three dozen Jesuit instructors and Cuban staff. Teachers and students alike faced front and clasped their hands together, and waited. At 8:01, when the priest rose, the assembled body fell still and silent. The future had begun.

Morning upon morning, week upon week, fall, winter, and spring, year after year, the same. The bell at 7:45, crying out *bam bam bam bam bam bam bam.* Then assembly. Lines. The march. The pews. And mass: from eight onward, a crowded fifteen minutes of joint prayer, homily, and ritual. On some saint's days, mass was extended an hour for extra readings and studies on the particular man or woman being celebrated. But on most days it was fifteen minutes, the briefest episode in the school day.

It was repetition, not length, that counted. The Church needed to remind people. Despite its status as the official faith of Cuba, Catholicism had a weak grip on the island. More than 90 percent of Cubans described themselves as Catholic, but 75 percent did not practice and only 2 percent were regular churchgoing Catholics who took the sacraments.

It was fine to feed the poor, as the actions of Cuban priests often showed, but it was wrong to ask why they were hungry. The Church did not challenge the authorities of Cuban life or the precepts of capitalism. The traditional tripartite alliance in Latin America—landowner, military officer, and priest—held sway here, too. There was no Vatican II yet, no Liberation Theology, no "preferential option for the poor." The Church was attached to Cuba's ruling class. Catholic schools, charities, and outreach projects were disproportionately located in Cuban cities, often concentrated in well-to-do neighborhoods. The Cuban church was tied to the elite, and hardly Cuban at all: out of 681 priests on the island, only 125 were actually born there. The vast majority were Spaniards, often sympathetic to rulers like Francisco Franco in Spain and Mussolini in Italy. Franco was a champion of the Catholic Church, who vowed to smite the radical anarchists and communists who had persecuted and even executed priests during the Spanish Civil War.

Fascism was on the rise, outside the school walls. The Nazi war machine had already flattened Poland, Holland, Belgium, and France.

Airwar raged over London; U-boats were on the offensive in the Atlantic and were sinking British and Dutch oil tankers right off the coast of Cuba. The Japanese, already in control of much of China, had signed a new tripartite alliance with Hitler and Mussolini. Yet at Dolores, the subject of this global fighting rarely came up; in history class, the war they were studying was the Trojan War. Yet there was little doubt which side most of the instructors identified with. Sometimes a Jesuit at the blackboard would let slip a comment about "the wonderful job that Mussolini is doing, putting all the people to work."

It was another war that occupied the time and thought of students and instructors. Relentlessly, in class and after it, in instruction and conversation, they discussed this other war, the real war, a conflict more profound, more subtle, and more widespread. This war was the struggle between the legions of Christ and the armies of hell. A perpetual conflict fought today and tomorrow, here and everywhere, for the free will of every human being. The Jesuits were governed by one of Loyola's central maxims, the urge to "find God in all things," meaning that even the humblest activities could be done to the glory of God. As they sat at their desks, walked to school, even as they played sports or ate their meals, the children were troops in this larger war.

Nomenclature at Dolores reflected this military framework. The children were divided into age cohorts, called divisions. The largest division was Lundy's own, the *mayores,* who ran from seventh grade through the end of high school. The *segundos* followed, with the boys from the main years of elementary school. The last division, the smallest in both number and height, was *los primeros,* the very youngest boys. The three divisions lined up in the courtyard separately, stood separately, studied different courses in different classrooms, and met only for meals, mass, the celebration of patriotic days, and plays and religious parades.

Discipline was rarely needed during morning lineups, or any other time. It was a matter of applying layers of chiding, gentle wisdom, confinement in the *sala de disciplina* after hours, and the occasional bout of physical persuasion. Tugging on ears, slapping boys on the head, and threatening them with a ruler were not unheard of. The Jesuits were inventive. Two boys who antagonized each other, routinely and endlessly, were ordered to climb up to the top floor sunroom, that made a kind of fourth floor, and fight it out. They were left alone, and did fight, but it was one of the hottest days of the school year and the sunroom was like an oven. It took only twenty minutes for the boys to return, reconciled.

In a culture of conformity and middle-class aspirations, most of the boys could be brought into line with nothing more than a glare, or a lisped *Qué patha?* from one of the Spaniards.

In religion, Cubans spoke in their particular dialect of doubled meaning, an internal language of punning and inversion. The central fact of life at Dolores was an orthodox Catholicism of the most traditional kind. The day began with mass and ended with prayers before bedtime. They learned them all. The Hail Mary. The Apostles' Creed. The Litany of the Blessed Virgin Mary. The Act of Contrition. Sanctifying Grace. The Ten Commandments. The Seven Virtues. The Seven Sacraments. The Seven Deadly Sins.

First Communion was the apogee of a calendar stuffed with Catholic scheduling. With more than four thousand saints in the Catholic panoply, every day in the year was associated with several. There were too many to memorize, but the boys were expected to be familiar with all of the important ones. Francis of Assisi was especially beloved, the patron of animals and small children. The boys liked the exciting Teresa of Lisieux, too—the patroness of pilots and foreign missions. San Cristobal protected travelers, Santa Gertrudio the teachers. Saint John the Apostle was invoked to watch over printers, editors, book binders, and all others in the line of scribes. Saint Martín Porres, a black martyr of Peruvian origins, was noted in Santiago because he was the patron of anyone of mixed race, and there were endless more saints to learn, those protecting conquistadors and fiddlers, altar boys and carnival workers, bald men and the youth of Mexico, the royalty of France and girls living in the countryside, those who needed rain and those who needed protection from rain, those who overslept and those who bottled champagne. It was more than anyone could absorb, and daily mass at Dolores was too brief to do more than mention a saint a day.

Occasionally, in the quick moment after the recitation of one such hero or martyr, the boys would hear a darker note slip into the daily. They would hear the priest denounce superstition. Foolishness. Fortune-telling. Strange and particular warnings, Cuban warnings, in a tone that stood apart. The priest might use terms like *brujeria,* witchcraft. Or adult words they had never heard before: *Obscurantism. Satanic cult. Black mass. Criminal anthropophagy.*

When mass ended, such notions floated away on the sunlight of the patio, in the chaos of 238 voices. The bell for classes rang, and good Catholic boys were not troubled.

By witchcraft they meant Santería. What you oppose defines you, and in Cuba, Catholicism attacked Santería because they were too close, as close as black beans and white rice. Santería is the "Way of the Saints," an Afro-Cuban cult built around venerating the same Catholic saints held up to the boys of Dolores at morning mass, but done in a very different way, often at night, amid drumming and cigar smoke, alcohol and even chicken blood. The saints were called different names, summoned for different purposes, attended by different officiates (though often as not, the followers of one cult would be seen at rites of the other). The Catholic Church attacked this low faith, the religion of the common people, as witchcraft, the work of Satan, a dangerous nocturnal creed of criminals and the ignorant. But Santería was more popular, more influential in Cuba, than daylight Catholicism itself.

Santería is a veneer of Christianity over African faiths. Principally Yoruba and known formally as "The Rule of Ocha," it was widely practiced in Cuba, especially in Oriente, where there was a strong black majority. To *santeros,* the pictures of Santa Barbara and Martín de Porres had other meanings. The saints were portals into the complex reality of a universe crowded with gods and demigods, malevolent spirits and shape-shifting divines.

Christ became the face of Obatalá, guardian of the unfinished creation. Ogún, the patron of hunters and blacksmiths, was a drunkard who appeared in the guise of Saint John the Baptist. Yemayá, the blue goddess of the seas, was also Our Lady of Regla, the Catholic patroness of Havana harbor. Oshún, the yellow-clad beauty who represented erotic love, was twinned with the Virgin of El Cobre, Cuba's most important Catholic shrine, just outside Santiago.

For white, middle-class kids, Santería was the faith of the housemaid, of the gardener or chauffeur. But even good Catholics peered into its shadowy realm from time to time. If the priest denounced the old African rites during mass, then how many mothers of boys at Dolores blushed, having sought out fortune-tellers and arrangers of love affairs? How many fathers had laughed at the Rule of Ocha, or one of the other, parallel Africanized cults, but then covered their bets by leaving a lottery ticket at the Catholic shrine of El Cobre, with a muttered appreciation of the good fortune that Changó or his rival Ogún might allow them? How many professed the doctrine of the Universal Church, and then refused to cut down a kapok tree because it was foolish to offend Iroko, the resident spirit?

This was hypocrisy, but centuries of slavery and repressive politics had taught Cubans to be expert at *doble cara,* "two faces," the practice of saying one thing and doing another, of keeping two separate and even contradictory truths in place at the same time. *Doble cara* allowed opposition and loyalty at once, dissent and conformity side by side. You could aspire to democratic rule and then work for the latest tyrant; you could practice Holy Roman rituals on Sunday and, the next night, have a fortune told, a love affair arranged, or a trial influenced, amid cigar smoke and turtle bones.

Nothing about the boys of Dolores was typical or average. Dolores was a Jesuit school, one of three on the island, and by design the Jesuits and their students stood apart. Santiago had several good private schools, run by the Christian Brothers and other orders, as well as academies for girls, like Sagrado Corazón, which was run by nuns but applied the same educational principles as the Jesuits. But there was only one top school, and it was Dolores. To be a *Dolorino* was to walk through the Plaza Dolores as if you owned it, and to step right past students in the uniforms of other *colegios* without comment. Dolores acknowledged no equals.

The *colegio* was imbued with Loyola's original impulse to forge a new Catholic vanguard. The wealthy and powerful families of Santiago were themselves determined to accomplish the same goal of training their children to rise up in life. For the Jesuits, wealth was fine, an old name was good, but the larger cause needed talent. A boy who showed skill in academics, and who demonstrated potential, was too fine a prize to turn away, even if his father was humble, his name unknown. The school gave places to families that could not afford them, so that a department store employee's son like José Antonio Roca sat beside a landowner's scion like Fidel Castro.

The exception was race. Dolores was a segregated school. Black students, no matter how intelligent, were excluded by a social dictum enforced by white families to protect their own privileges. At the country clubs, restaurants, and schools that served the elite, white was the only color that counted. In the 1940s, Dolores was no different.

But Cuba had always known an amorphous racial climate, not of blacks and whites, but gray areas—or brown ones. For centuries, Cubans have lived in the reality of a mulatto society, acknowledging a wide spectrum of skin tones with frank language unknown to the north. This vast middle ground was comprised of mulattoes, but mulattoes themselves were unselfconsciously described as octoroons, or white mulattoes, or dark whites, or clear octoroons, or Creole. Blacks were labeled by shade: "Congo" (pure black) or "blue black" or "red black" or "black like a raisin" or "black-haired" (meaning nappy), all of which denoted subtle differences along the spectrum of Africanness. Even whites were also rated on a scale of whiteness, ranging from the dark-haired *gallegos* ("Galician," meaning of Spanish descent) like Fidel Castro, on up to *claros,* the palest Cubans, like white-haired Pepín Bou, or the Dutch-Cuban de Jongh brothers, with their translucent skin. And of course anyone with even a touch of indigenous blood (rare in Cuba) or any type of Asian background (much more common) was bluntly labeled *chino.* (A joke held that Cubans were half white, half black, and half Chinese.) With so many gradations, Cubans could use the subtlest signals to convey color, like dragging two fingers over the back of their hand, to indicate that someone was "marked," or colored.

The Jesuits opened the doors of their schools to admit, if not a cross section of Cuban society, at least a wide sample of the middle and upper classes. That made the students at Dolores typical not of Cuba, but of the people who ran it: the powerful, the rich, the talented, and the useful. And they were typical of the future, too, for it was their generation of young, frustrated, middle- and upper-class boys that would shape, through its internal feuds and frustrations, the Cuban Revolution. Fidel Castro would use, and eventually consume, his own family, his own cousins and neighbors, his relations by marriage, and those whom he knew through schooling, first from Santiago, and later from Havana. He would use Dolores when he needed it—to protect him physically or politically, and in turn those who helped him would join the ranks of the regretful.

Whether bred, recruited, or raised, these boys were from an elite, and part of a world that rested on an overhang, unstable. Locked behind their high walls, the *Dolorinos* were invisible to the larger world, meant to be separated out of it, in order to shape it. Dolores fulfilled this mission, albeit disastrously for itself. It did make rulers, of two; it made the rest, across decades, into survivors.

Not everyone endured: some withered, here or in exile. But the most common sight, a lifetime later, would be a man, surrounded by his family, who had survived hardship and loss, and reestablished himself with an astonishing degree of consistency, true to his education, profession, and religion, and the memory of a place that will never come again.

Some of them would even become the elite they were meant to be, wealthy in business or industry or agriculture, leaders in medicine and academia. Just not here, in what they had been told was their city, and their Cuba.

The day students lived in an expansive world the boarding students could hardly credit. Every single day, often for hours at a time, they got to wander in the wider life of city streets. At night they had the deep comforts of a kitchen table, a mother, many generations, strangers and neighbors. When they returned to school each morning they were full of stories, chronicles of new things.

But at 8:20, when the same long lines of boys uncoiled from the chapel at the end of mass, spilling in reverse into the patio and the surrounding courtyards, all order quickly dissolved. The boys had ten minutes until class, ten minutes to organize themselves and their books, ten minutes to visit the bathroom, ten minutes to engage in that all-important gossip about what had happened overnight and who had pulled what stunt. Boys rushed upstairs and back down, and the last stragglers, the three or four cheats every day who had skipped mass and snuck out the back of the school bus, now came darting inside, hoping to dodge in the front door when no priests were looking, and often, thanks to the chaos, succeeding. For ten minutes, everyone tried to move and talk at the same time.

One morning in late 1940, Lundy rang the bell for mass, joined in the assembling of the lines, marched in, listened dutifully for twenty minutes, and then, like all the boys, exploded into the courtyard looking for novelty and *chismes,* gossip and jokes. A crowd of *internos* was in the courtyard, nervously flicking a ball back and forth debating which game they should play—basketball, or HORSE, or stickball, or catch, or any of a hundred contests.

Lundy had no part in this. He was a *zurdo,* a klutz, and rarely participated in the great cleaving contests of *béisbol* and *fútbol* in the courtyard. And the *reguladores* were never exactly popular. Lundy was the uptight kid with the prize wristwatch and the job of keeping them all on schedule. So he went to the second floor, to the office. On his way upstairs that day, eyes always roaming, he glanced at a bulletin board full of notices. There was a letter tacked up there. Written across the top of the paper it said:

THE WHITE HOUSE, WASHINGTON, DC.

You didn't need to understand English to know those words. The letter was addressed to someone Lundy didn't know.

"Who," he asked a passing boy, "is Fidel Castro?"

The session bell rang before he could get an answer. It was a charmless electronic buzzer that had none of the antique pride of Lundy's hand-wrung school bell. It was 8:30. Time for history, geography, Spanish literature, grammar, Greek or Latin, mathematics or biology, depending on the boy or the day. Time to work.

The White House had written in reply to a letter from Fidel which is still in the National Archives in Washington. He wrote it on official school stationery filched from the office after hours. COLEGIO DE DOLORES, it says, over the number of a post office box in Santiago de Cuba.

Fidel wrote in English, but not very good English. The twelve-year-old used brackets to indicate where he was substituting a Spanish word for an English word he didn't know. His handwriting, however, was excellent. The school taught the Palmer Method of penmanship, a regimented system that produced floral cursive lettering and highly ornamented words on tightly ruled lines. Fidel's cursive was flawless, but he made one major mistake right at the start. He misspelled the name of the recipient:

Santiago de Cuba
Nov. 6 1940
Mr. Franklin Roosvelt
President of the United States

My good friend Roosvelt
    I don't know very English, but I know as much as write to you.
    I like to hear the radio, and I am very happy, because I heard in it that you will be President for a new [periodo].
    I am twelve years old. I am a boy but I think very much but I do not think that I am writing to the President of the United States.

Turning the page, Fidel had continued on the back, his English degenerating quickly:

    [I]f you like, give me a ten dollars bill green american, in the letter, because never, I have not seen a ten dollars bill green american and I would like to have one of them. My address is:
    Sr. Fidel Castro
    Colegio Dolores
    Santiago de Cuba
    Oriente, Cuba
    I don't know very English but I know very much Spanish and I suppose you don't know very Spanish but you know very English because you are American but I am not American.
    (Thank you very much)
    Good by. Your friend

Then the signature, worthy of a nobleman. Fidel produced a swirling, picturesque rendition of his name that was a work of art, or at least nerve. The abbreviated first name—just "F."—was overlaid by a vast "C," and at the end of *Castro* the final "o" came back to cross the "t" and link the letters. The signature was so ornate that he wrote his name one more time, in plain print, to make sure they got it:

Fidel Castro

It looked wonderful. But perfection is beyond even the most determined boy, and Fidel undercut his own effort by adding a sloppy, and apparently hurried, postscript:

> *If you want to make your sheaps, I will show to you the biggest (minas) of iron of the land. They are in Mayarí, Oriente Cuba.*

That was it, a page and a quarter.

It is worth noting that Castro's writing wasn't the only writing on the paper. If you turned the letter on its side, there was a second hand, in pencil. There, along the margin, were just two words, in the large and firm writing of an adult. An adult at the U.S. State Department. All it said there was "Castro, Fidel."

Here was the first entry in what would become a very long file.

During the minutes before lunch, Lundy returned to the letter from the White House. "Who," he asked again, "is Fidel Castro?" He'd met the three Castro brothers, certainly, but which was which? They were *internos*, and Lundy didn't know them. Ramón was older, Fidel and Raúl younger.

"That one," someone said, and another: "That's him. There." Different boys all pointed to the courtyard, to a tall boy in a crowd.

Fidel, the tall one. A round face. Arched eyebrows. A Roman nose, and the pale skin of a *gallego*. Lundy wasn't timid. He was a year ahead of Fidel, and also a *regulador*, a statesman in the world of youth. He went straight up to Fidel and blurted out, "I didn't know you had written to Roosevelt."

"Yeah, well," Castro said. "He won the election. But the Americans are assholes. I asked for ten dollars and they didn't send me a cent."

They shook hands and stared at each other. "This is phenomenal," Lundy said.

Castro chatted greedily. He had a high, soft voice, almost feminine. But he was a comfortable speaker, his natural disposition polished in the declamation contests at Dolores, where boys were judged on rhetoric, pacing, and the stentorian tone favored by great Cubans. They learned practical things for the contests: how to speak without notes, use a microphone, stand in the light. Fidel enjoyed an audience, even in the patio.

He disclaimed any great achievement, and then began referring to it as if he'd heard personally from the president of the United States, rather than a correspondence office. In fact, he explained to Lundy, he was quite upset with Roosevelt. The American had also ignored Fidel's offer of good Cuban iron. Everybody knew that Oriente had not just lots of iron, but the best quality, too. How could you build a fleet of battleships without iron from Mayarí?

They would come to know each other, too well. They overlapped for five years at Dolores, both of them star pupils. Then they overlapped again at the University of Havana for four years while earning law degrees. So a connection that endured for twenty years began there, with the letter. The two boys quickly discovered some mutual enthusiasms. They both loved stories about the conquistadors, they discovered. Geography class was a favorite for both, and they shared their detailed plans for traveling the world. They even agreed on some career goals: the best life was to be a famous explorer, and an adventurer, and also a great man of history.

Dolores had film nights, parties that drew in families and day students like Lundy to join the *internos* in watching films that were projected from an RCA Victor machine onto a sheet draped on a wall. Lundy and Fidel sat through several films together. The selection was usually whatever was cheapest to rent, like dreadful Mexican cowboy movies, full of singing heroes, dumb villains, and bad lighting. Lundy ranked films in a way that was common among Dolores boys. Mexican cowboy films were the worst, worse even than films with kissing. There was a middle ground—thrillers, war movies—and then at the top there was one kind of film above all others, the Hollywood Western. The outfits, horses, and guns were the same as in the Mexican films, but these were bigger, more glamorous movies, expansive, with clean sunshine, dirty heroes, and thrilling escapes. John Wayne and Gary Cooper were real men. If film night had included one of these great works of art, then the boys would be ecstatic afterward, lingering in big knots, talking wildly. They would rechoreo-graph the gunfights, reenact the ambushes, and stage the sudden over-turning of villains and heroes all over again, laughing all the while.

But Lundy noticed that Fidel never joined in. When Lundy asked why, Fidel told him, "The wrong side won." He didn't like the American cav-alry. It was the Indians who were brave, who were underdogs, who'd been beaten down by power.

The United States had invaded Cuba in 1898 with the usual mixture of noble sentiment and grasping self-interest. The struggle had already been under way, intermittently, for decades, and was portrayed in American newspapers—then in the heyday of their yellow journalism—as a heroic battle between the native freedom fighters of an island paradise and the corrupt overlords imposed by a cruel European tyranny. Newspaper car-toons depicted Spanish soldiers as bloodthirsty rapists who crushed Cuban liberty—usually a dusky maiden in Greek robes—under their boot heels. American gunrunners and mercenaries—the "freebooters"—who served the Cuban rebels were treated as heroes in the United States. The *New York Tribune* sent a writer, Stephen Crane, on one of these gunrunning mis-sions. The small ship, laden with ammunition, was escorted out of Florida with honors from the U.S. Coast Guard, but soon caught fire in the Straits of Florida and sank. Crane and the crew fled in a dinghy, and his thinly fictionalized account, "The Open Boat," became the most influential short story in American literature.

Presidents as far back as Thomas Jefferson had dreamed of annexing Cuba. With its combination of rich agricultural lands, marketing opportu-nities, and slave society, Cuba was a coveted target of annexation for American planters. In the mid-1800s Spain rejected U.S. offers to buy the island, and by the 1890s, Cuba was routinely portrayed as a natural dependency of the United States. When the war broke out, Mark Twain called it a "pathetic comedy" in the service of building an empire.

By 1898, the Spanish were on the defensive, secure in the cities but unable to dislodge the wild Cuban cavalry, the mambises, who raided the countryside, burning crops and bringing the island to a halt. America then intervened suddenly, and with overwhelming force, annihilating the Spanish navy off the coast of Oriente. This cut off the beleaguered Spanish infantry (including Angel Castro, a quartermaster) from reinforcement, resupply, or withdrawal. Seventeen thousand American troops, including the horseless troop of Wyoming ranchers, Manhattan aristocrats, and Plains Indians known as the Rough Riders, landed in Oriente. Aided by Cuban rebels, they fought several small battles (only 268 Americans were killed or wounded in action; fourteen times that many fell to disease) and had Santiago surrounded. The war lasted 113 days and, as Twain predicted, brought not just Cuba but Puerto Rico, the Philippines, and Guam under U.S. control, creating an instant American empire.

At the Spanish surrender, the American commander refused to allow Cuban rebels to march in his victory parade. The rebels were not even allowed to enter the city and were excluded from the peace negotiations, held in Europe between Spain and the United States.

American businesses invested $30 million in just two years. United Fruit bought two million acres of farmland, at 20 cents per acre. A Wall Street syndicate bought out the Havana street car company. American tobacco and timber companies moved in. By 1901, American business controlled 80 percent of Cuba's mineral exports.

Land reforms introduced by the American government had the effect of turning Cuba into a giant cane field, supplying America under a new system of annual sugar quotas. Throughout the economy, American interests dominated: Americans won the contract to pave Cuban streets with Boston's discarded stones, rather than new ones from a Cuban quarry.

In 1903, the United States simply forced the new Cuban government to sign the Platt Amendment, which guaranteed America's "right to intervene for the preservation of Cuban independence." This was already policy. As early as 1822, U.S. troops made repeated landings in Cuba to hunt pirates, and in 1825, British and American troops staged a joint landing to chase more pirates. The U.S. Marines returned later that year. The policy of intervention was on display in the 113-day war of 1898, and when U.S. forces returned in 1917. Through the 1920s, a series of pro-American presidents were selected from the ranks of the elite. America was behind the dictatorship of General Gerardo Machado between 1925 and 1933, a time of brutal assassinations and open warfare among political gangs. Machado was ousted in August of 1933, and President Roosevelt broke form by refusing to send American troops to intervene directly. The U.S. Navy merely "demonstrated" off Cuban shores. But Roosevelt encouraged

Cuban militarists to undermine the new populist government. After just seventeen days, this liberal administration was overthrown by military coup. Although the Cubans now rescinded the Platt Amendment, Roosevelt had shown that direct intervention was no longer needed. Ambitious Cubans could be found to enforce American interests.

Machado's sudden and violent downfall in 1933 brought down many, including one at distant Dolores. Desiderio Alberto Arnaz y de Acha was the scion of a family that had once owned much of California, and which had ruled over Santiago de Cuba for at least a generation. Desiderio's father was the youngest mayor in Santiago's history, and in 1933 had just taken up a seat in the Cuban Senate, as a supporter of Machado. Desiderio's uncle was head of the Santiago police.

At Dolores, all this meant less than playing guitar. Desiderio sang with a high, clear voice and strummed guitar beautifully during religious pageants and festivals in the patio. The Arnaz family had houses all over Santiago, an old family home just six blocks from the Parque Céspedes, and a brand-new house in Vista Alegre. They had three farms in the countryside, and (best of all, from a boy's perspective) a summer home on exclusive Cayo Smith, the resort island sitting in the throat of Santiago Bay. Desiderio, a member of the Dolores swim team, brought his teammates to the island before a meet. They would swim halfway around the island in the morning, watched by family retainers in a speedboat. In the afternoon they would swim the second half. Desiderio lost his virginity in the boathouse.

This life of privilege came to an abrupt end with the revolution in August 1933. Those who hated Machado hated his cronies. A mob tore through Santiago, lynching Machado supporters in front of their homes. The Arnaz clan—source of mayors, senators, and police chiefs—was next. As the mob came up the hill toward their house, a family servant bundled Desiderio into a car and fled. The frustrated mob looted the home, smashed the piano, tipped over another family car, and eventually set the building on fire, before moving on to sack the Moncada army garrison, setting it, too, on fire. Attacking Moncada, the symbol of military authority in Santiago, was a practiced gesture in any rebellion.

Within days, Desiderio was living in Miami with his father. Unlike Machado's more quick-fingered associates, the Arnaz clan did not manage to leave Cuba with any money, and at seventeen, Desiderio of Dolores took up manual labor, shoveling and sorting cracked tiles, and washing dishes in restaurants. Singing was less onerous, and he soon earned $5 a night for playing his guitar. Even in Florida, Cuban music was then a novelty, an ethnic curiosity. On New Year's Eve, desperate to entertain a bored crowd, Desiderio grabbed a conga drum and began parading through the tables, imitating the rhythmic marching at Santiago's Carnaval. Urging people to follow him around the room, Desiderio invented the conga line, which became a national dance craze. Within months he was a bandleader. Shortening his name from Desiderio Alberto Arnaz y de Acha to Desi Arnaz, he conquered New York. On a film set in Hollywood, he met a redheaded comedienne, Lucille Ball.

The marriage of this popular American actress to an exotic foreigner was a tabloid sensation. Lucille realized that the new medium of television was the perfect way to convert this public fascination into a "reality show" about her life. Ball designed a comedy sketch about a famous actress who marries a zany Cuban. During rehearsals, she discovered it was much funnier if she was portrayed as just an ordinary, talentless American housewife, always trying to crash the showbiz career of her glamorous Cuban husband.

I Love Lucy became the show that made television, number one in the ratings for four of its six years, and still at number one when it shut down in 1957, the year another Cuban was launching his bid for the top. In his despicable autobiography, *A Book,* Arnaz catalogued the whores and starlets he bedded, took credit for inventing Cuban music, and said his only regret was never graduating from Dolores.

The Platt Amendment was gone, but America remained, a set of people, rules, incentives, finances, and values. Before 1898, the Cuban elite had prided themselves on their conservative values and Catholic traditionalism, and they had remained loyal to Spain later than any other country in the Americas. The arrival and departure of American soldiers was only a beginning.

The American military government portrayed Cuba as an unhealthy, festering, backward swamp ruined by disease, and set about ditching, draining, and spewing new regulations about sewers and trash removal. (The Platt Amendment demanded a list of strict hygiene standards for Cuba; failure in any category could lead to American invasion.) They acted as though Cubans were dirty. Open windows were a part of Cuban social custom, a form of transparency that encouraged long chats at the *reja*. But the Americans built their houses back from the roads, and slapped mosquito netting over every window. You couldn't see them or speak to them.

The other American obsession was educational reform. The age of compulsory schooling was raised from nine to fourteen, and the island divided into school districts, with school boards and parent-teacher committees. Reforms benefited many students, but alienated the conservative elite. The American system took away the role of the Catholic Church and substituted a secularized model. The education reforms were administered by a Cuban, but a Cuban chosen by the Americans. (Almost a hundred years after it happened, José Antonio Cubeñas could still identify why this man alienated the traditional families in Santiago. "He was a Cuban," he said, "but a Jew. The people did not want that." When I pressed him on this point, Cubeñas pressed back. "An *atheist* Jew," he said. A practicing Jew might have been acceptable; a secular one was not.)

After American education reforms, Cuba's elite and the increasingly large middle class withdrew steadily into religious schools, away from (Protestant) American values, Jews, and other threats. Dolores, established in 1913 to meet this need, grew quickly, growth that brought funds and connections. But the rise of elite schools came with an attendant failure of public ones: in the 1930s, the private system enrolled three times as many pupils in all grades as the public system. The gap was even more severe in high school, where there were 1,181 private schools to only 21 public. Society had decided that an education beyond reading, writing, and arithmetic was wasted on *macheteros*. About 30 percent of Cubans were illiterate. This wasn't as bad as the figures of 50, 60, or even 90 percent illiteracy invented by Cuban officials after the Revolution, but 30 percent was terrible enough. It did call for a revolution.

That was always a popular idea in Cuba. There were revolutions (failed, attempted, sometimes successful, always loudly declared) in the 1860s, 1870s, and in 1895. There were attempted revolutions in the 1920s, and then in 1933 there was the street revolution that overthrew Machado. Like the 1959 revolution, the one in 1933 had been driven from below by a broad, populist uprising against corruption and dictatorship, before being diverted into the hands of a military man.

Sergeant Fulgencio Batista was that careful man. Batista was part of the military clique that displaced the original civilian government just seventeen days after Machado's overthrow. Batista originally had no gripe other than getting a pay raise, and no constituency other than the military, but as he elbowed his way to the top of the new government, he found it convenient to have allies. He grabbed at the rhetoric of the social movements at hand, declaring himself a revolutionary and a progressive, a nationalist and a patriot. Staying behind the scenes at first, he picked a reformist politician, Ramón Grau, to be the new president, invited students and leftists into the government, and made fine speeches. Batista soon figured out what he really wanted—another pay raise—and within a year he forced Grau out, assuming the presidency himself so that he could extract giant bribes. He kept the Cuban legislature intact, however, which was dominated by a reform movement, and introduced a series of social programs designed to undercut the claim that he was just a power-mad soldier. He infuriated America by instituting a fifty-fifty employment law that reserved half of the jobs in any U.S.-run enterprise for Cubans. He placed the first *Cuban* price quotas on the sugar crop, forcing the Americans to pay a stable rate. And he launched the first national campaign against illiteracy, a "civic-military" campaign that used teachers from the army and was funded by the military budget. Between 1936 and 1940, the Batista government constructed 1,100 new schools. Although the program was not sustained for long and did not reach every part of Cuba, illiteracy dropped by about 10 percent.

Bohemia, Cuba's leading magazine, called the literacy campaign progressive and commendable, but Batista's revolution was a screen for his brutal and corrupt rule. He used martial law to crush pro-democracy strikes in 1935, and despite his avowed nationalism, the 1930s are known to Cuban historians as the "era of puppets" because of the way Batista sent a rotating cast of political hacks to receive instructions from the American ambassador, Jefferson Caffery, and Sumner Welles, FDR's troubleshooter on Cuba.

Resentment of American meddling, and of lingering Spanish influence, fed another round of education reforms. In 1939 the Batista government imposed a unified, nationalist curriculum on all schools, public or private, religious or secular, in Cuba. The rules mandated 228 school days a year, with classes beginning on the first Monday in October and running through the middle of May, and a full month after for intensive examinations. Grades were issued on a 100-point scale. Scores under 59 received a "Disapproval," a category that meant suspension was imminent. A score from 60 to 69 earned "Approval," while 70 to 79 meant "Good" and 80 to 89 was rated "Very Good." Anything 90 or over meant *sobresaliente,* "Superb" or "Excellent." Regulations detailed the total number of hours of chemistry, mathematics, natural history, Cuban history, civics, and psychology necessary to graduate.

The nationalist urge peaked the next year, when Cuba's "New Constitution" came into effect. Promulgated in 1940, it gave Cuba one of the most liberal and idealistic political systems in the world. Cuba was declared to be a broadly enfranchised democracy, with civil, religious, and economic freedoms enshrined in law, and an explicit government mandate to create social justice. Schools were a particular target of the New Constitution:

> All education, public and private, shall be inspired by a spirit of Cubanism and national unity, tending to form in the hearts of students a love for the country, its democratic institutions, and all those who fought for both.

That meant specific lessons blaming the United States for many of Cuba's problems, and, more awkwardly for Dolores, lessons that blamed the Catholic Church for supporting the Spanish side in the War of Independence. The New Constitution also altered not just what was taught, but who could teach it:

> In all teaching centers, public or private, the teaching of the literature, history, and geography of Cuba, as well as of civics and the Constitution must be done by teachers who are Cubans by birth and with textbooks by authors that have that same character.

Since almost all the teachers at Dolores were Spaniards, that meant new Cuban instructors, and new Cuban textbooks, to go along with the new lessons. A Spaniard couldn't even teach geography now.

There was a far graver problem: the New Constitution mandated that high school include a fifth year. Dolores, straining at the seams with over two hundred students, and scrambling to accommodate new staff and lessons, was unable to absorb an entire new grade. For Lundy, Fidel, and a part of each class, that meant transferring to Belén in Havana, which had a large new campus. The Dolores students were submerged in a far bigger student body, amid a city and people they didn't know. Even their diplomas came from Belén, as if Dolores had disappeared. It soon would.

Batista finally stepped down in 1944, and Ramón Grau won the cleanest election in Cuban history. The elections, and the marvelous 1940 constitution, were the high-water mark for democracy in Cuba. The boys at Dolores came of age in this era of hope. When they recalled Cuba, this was what they meant. The early 1940s. The old republic. The time before time.

Cuba was still deeply broken. The wartime prosperity, the rebirth of democracy, seemed wonderful. But in crucial ways the new democracy of 1942 was weightless, a shell. Society was divided, the reality of Cuban politics too hypocritical. The lofty goals were in the hands of democratic institutions—political parties, legislature, press, judiciary, and the police—rotten with corruption. With Batista in retirement, little changed. Cuba was hemmed in by its homegrown culture of *amiguismo,* or economic and political "friendships." Connections opened all doors. Patronage and favoritism determined success. *Amiguismo* drove the cynicism of Cuban society. Squeezing power and decisions through the hands of a few, *amiguismo* choked the economic and political air out of Cuba.

American companies in Cuba supposedly offered a change from that, opportunity built on equality, open dealing, and fairness. One hundred and fifty thousand Cubans worked directly for American companies around the island. These people often adopted American educational practices, cultural values, styles of dress, and even names (in the sugar region where the Castro family lived, common names for Cuban children included Tony, Betty, Nelly, Mike, and Walter). Cubans were becoming more and more American on the outside, but the aspiring middle class discovered that acting American did not translate into equality. Americans kept the best jobs for themselves. Even when Cubans rose up to equal footing with

Americans, they often found the foreigners were getting paid more for doing the same job. Cuban professionals rarely rose above the status of clerks, even when they were more qualified than their U.S. superiors. And Americans, along with other foreigners and the richest Cubans, lived literally and metaphorically apart from the mass of islanders, screened behind walls, air-conditioned, and shielded from accountability.

Americans didn't come to Cuba for equality. For tourist or expatriate, Cuba was an escape from whatever social strictures and mores governed back home. Decade after decade, in tourism advertising, Hollywood films, and Irving Berlin songs, the island was painted as a land of sensual adventure, a place to indulge forbidden urges without limit or care. The reality for visitors and expats—endless rounds of boozing, some mob-run gambling, and discount sex—was hidden behind 1940s silence and euphemism, but everyone knew what was really happening. Hemingway was rude enough to write it down. What foreigners wanted from Cuba, one of his characters confessed, was "cheap whores who can fuck."

Cynicism and hypocrisy were the adders in this garden. Bribery and violence controlled politics. Although it was popular to blame Americans for the failure of democracy in the 1940s, Cuba's Weimar, the rot was Cuban. In 1952, the old tyrant, Batista, staged a new coup. Cubans would not fight for a democracy that was fraudulent and weightless, not even President Prío, who departed the country quietly.

The Society of Jesus opened its first school in 1549, in Messina, Italy, at a time when the Holy Roman Catholic faith had lost much of its dominion to the Protestant Reformation. The Jesuits vowed to "go without questioning wherever the pope might direct," and to take up educational work. Jesuit missionaries went to every corner of the globe, building utopian communities in the jungles of Paraná and even reaching the Tibetan capital by 1661. But it was in education that the order would flourish and find its reputation.

It is often said that the Jesuit order was created to staff the Counter-Reformation, and bring about a restoration of the Catholic world. But the efficient, educated monks of the Society of Jesus were more a reflection of the Renaissance than a rejection of it. Their emphasis on rigorous academics and liberal humanism was mixed with a curriculum of Classical teaching, to create an unprecedented system of education. Within fifty years of their founding they had more than two hundred schools and universities across southern Europe. In 1599, the Society imposed a unified curriculum on them, the *Ratio Studiorum,* or plan of study. It specified classes, books, tests, objectives, schedules, oral exercises, and formulas for answers, and for three centuries, the curriculum gave overwhelming emphasis to Latin, still the lingua franca of Europe's scholar class and the language of daily administration within the Roman Church. Latin at Dolores lit the lamps of ancient knowledge, opening up the rediscovered Classics; the translated Greek works of philosophy, history, and geography; the Roman guides to argument, composition, and oration; the Byzantine volumes of theology and religious statecraft; Cicero, Ovid, Virgil, and Horace.

It wasn't until 1924 that the *Ratio Studiorum* finally received its first major makeover. By the time Fidel Castro was born (perhaps August 13, 1926, although even this mundane detail is treated as a state secret) this new curriculum had been promulgated to Jesuit colleges worldwide, including Dolores. The new *Ratio* preserved the essential appreciation for critical thinking that had motivated the Jesuits from the beginning, but made radical changes, like having students read even Classical authors in translation.

In his *Constitutions,* Loyola wrote that students should be contemplative, even in the midst of activity, and focused at all times. Loyola made the radical suggestion that any activity at all that was not specifically evil could be done for the glory of God if it was done with intention, with that larger purpose of improvement and uplift. He required students to organize their senses, their skills at observation. The *Constitutions* spoke of cultivating your interior so that you really looked at something, heard it, and were present to its reality. The well-rounded student was supposed to be quick at systematically apprehending problems, judging options, reasoning solutions, and imagining results. The skills taught in class were close attention, careful selection, dispassionate appraisal, arrangement of argument, and effective expression. Again and again Loyola mentions the senses: noticing, listening, actively using the eye and ear and other faculties, including imagination and feeling. Although the Jesuits themselves were taught to have no will—they were servants of the pope, dead "as a corpse" to their own desires—they taught the students to feel strongly, to strengthen their own willpower, and to value both cooperation and also the natural competitiveness, the forceful confrontation, that would encourage them to excel.

In math, history, or Spanish class, the Jesuits taught students to examine, question, and wonder. Not in religion: total obedience to the Pope was the only model. Loyola himself cited the example of a wall that is painted white: if the Church tells you the wall is black, you see it as black, say it is black, and *believe* it is black.

The students and teachers of Dolores took long retreats at a mansion outside Santiago, living monastically and reading books like *Rules for Thinking with the Church*. The need for obedience was driven home at one of the last Dolores retreats, a culminating session of three days at the mansion. Here, at a session called "The Meditation on the Two Standards," the boys were given a stark choice. The "two standards" in the title were the battle standards of Christ, on the one hand, and the legions of Hell on the other.

Which would they choose? Enrolling under the flag of Christ, in His army? Or, by refusing, enrolling under the flag of Hell? Which of these alternatives, these Manichaean absolutes? The Padre Rector, Teodoro Berceo, was a short, fat, red-faced priest, but he was a compelling speaker. He would walk among the rapt boys, asking in bleak tones, "What would you do, if death came for you right now?" What would you choose? Which standard?

The students at Dolores were given a maxim, "Ask everybody everything every day," which taught them to seek knowledge actively, to be the initiators of their own education. And the instructors were guided away from chalkboard schooling by another aphorism: "A minimum of precept, a maximum of practice." The emphasis for teaching was on variety and liveliness, in the classroom and out of it. Biology was to be taught not just by textbooks, but by handling animals, by working in a lab, and by hiking expeditions in the Sierra Maestra. Even a math class should be engaging—for the youngest kids at Dolores, there were simple number games posted on the walls, and cubes and triangles to handle on their desks.

According to a Dolores yearbook, the "complete intellectual formation" of the students depended not just on the "splendid laboratories" for chemistry and biology classes, but also the many activities that Loyola believed could be used to glorify God. These included sports, gymnastics classes, arts, music programs, and "excursions to the mountains."

There were plenty of mountains to choose. There were regular trips from Dolores to zones all through the Sierra Maestra. Hikes were intended to train more than the body; they were an extension of botany and biology, opportunities to collect butterflies and birds for the school's small museum. It wasn't enough to say that a fern by the path was a fern. How were ferns similar? Different? Why? Color? Structure? What about soil type, and the advantages of rainfall?

For history, the students were taken hiking along the old fortifications outside Santiago, where the Americans had fought the Spaniards in 1898. The Rough Riders had taken one hill, but the Americans had been repulsed in other places along the ridge line. Pointing to one such spot, the young Fidel told Lundy Aguilar, "This is where we defeated the Americans."

"What do you mean, we?" Lundy replied. "The *gallegos* did it."

The *gallegos* were the Spanish, the imperial power occupying the island. To Lundy and other Cubans, "we" would normally refer to the Cuban side, the Cuban rebels and American troops fighting together. But Fidel saw it the other way around. The Americans coming up the hill were the villains, not the Spaniards defending it.

Either he was being true to his father's service in the Spanish army, or he was already focused on the future, on a larger conflict. It was the Americans who dominated Banes, Oriente, Cuba. It was Americans who dominated Latin America. It was no different than at movie night. Instinctively, Fidel had sided with the Indians. Anyone who confronted that enemy, anyone who opposed the American colonizers, whether in the past, present, or future, was heroic. Even the Spanish imperialists were preferable to the Americans.

On hikes, Fidel liked to be first up the trail. Second tallest in his class, barrel-chested, he had discovered the joy of baseball and basketball, of physical power and skill, of victory. Fidel had arrived at Dolores already tough, with the body of a farm boy, and day hikes and longer camping excursions became part of his training regimen. He volunteered for every hike and became an organizer of them, carrying the Dolores pennant up the slopes of Mount Turquino, at 6,500 feet the highest peak in Cuba, with a long line of students and brothers stretched out behind him.

("They goaded us into sports, excursions to the mountains," Castro recalled of the Jesuits in his interview with Frei Betto, the Brazilian. "All of that exerted a great attraction over me.") Year after year, the Jesuits taught Fidel the peaks that ran along the east coast of Cuba, and the main towns and smallest villages through the mountains. They hiked trails to remote sections of the range, and saw, hidden throughout the most obscure corners, the mountain people, the poor and the crushed, the black, brown, and white peasants who scratched yucca from tiny plots, or tended some-one else's pigs. These people lived almost within sight of Santiago, but it was another Cuba, where illiterate and impoverished people lived in fear of the local landlords, the rent collectors, and the corrupt police and army who backed them up.

Ignatius Loyola believed that a student's task was to stand before another reality, something completely new, alien, or unrecognizable, and, centering his attention, begin to study, comprehend, judge, and come to conclusions. The worst mistake was to refuse to look carefully, to deny yourself that comprehension. A Dolores student couldn't help but study these two utterly different Cubas, each destined to torture the other. When the hikes ended at a trailhead, the boys would ride back into San-tiago in a car, up through the Parque Céspedes, toward school again. Was it possible to ignore the differences? Wasn't it necessary to see the two Cubas reconciled?

Lundy and Fidel began to spend less time together. Lundy found Fidel hard to like: he was showy, a big talker, always promising stunts. Their closest intimacy had lasted months, just film nights and walks in the hills. They would orbit the same institutions for years to come. As students at the same university, they would come to opposite conclusions on the role of violence in politics. They could not agree on the lessons of Cuban his-tory. Or which side in the Cold War was defending the future. Eventually, a piece of newsprint—mere words—would separate them for good.

At the relatively early hour of 11:15 A.M. the boys laid down their pencils for the midday break, a full two hours off. It was traditional in Cuba, and particularly in hot Santiago, to take these long lunches. The city boys—all those who had walked to school—were allowed to set out again, head-ing home for their meal. The *internos,* who were on full board, remained behind, with a group of half-board students, making a colony of more than forty boys at lunch. They put away their books and reported to the long, high-ceilinged dining room before noon. They gathered at tables, this time sorted not by class and division, but by age and affinity, choosing their own seats and alliances at the individual tables. Jose Antonio Cubeñas, Cefarino Catá, and Joaquin Herrera usually sat together.

The lunch menu was a numbing routine: fried eggs, rice, and plantains, sometimes with potatoes or beans, and always with strong coffee laced with milk and sugar, even for the youngest boys. (Sick boys were sometimes given a popular commercial tonic that basically consisted of vitamins in red wine.) There was no meat on Friday, but there also was no meat on most other days. The cooking was the main reason that almost two hundred of the boys at Dolores went home for lunch every day.

After the meal, there came the long recess that was often the high point of the day for the *internos,* who now had the extra companions they would miss so badly every night. They had one hour or ninety minutes. Recess could mean almost anything: games, naps, study, long chats with the brothers, reading comic books, even brief walks outside the building. The Jesuits tried not to structure the break, but they were mostly Spaniards and had a European obsession with soccer. They often tossed out a soccer ball at recess, with subtle or not so subtle encouragement to organize games. But left to their own devices, the boys preferred scratch games of basketball or baseball. The latter was really stickball, a game built for small dimensions and obstacles, easy to play in the street, a patio, or even inside a room.

One day when the main courtyard was occupied, Fidel organized a recess game of stickball in the rear patio, a space atop the *aljibe,* the cistern, in the back of the school. The boys assigned home plate to a spiral staircase leading up to the second floor, with first, second, and third bases distributed around the corners. They had a real baseball bat, but used a *fufa,* a "ball" made of bottle caps taped together. A *fufa* "didn't go anywhere when you hit it," José Antonio Cubeñas recalled, but flew crazily, ricocheting off the walls and ceiling, and taking unexpected bounces. Cubeñas was one of about thirty-five boys watching from the railing over the cistern when Castro came to bat. He swung three times, and he missed three times.

Struck out! On a *fufa!* The jeering was instant. Laughter all around.

Castro looked up, and in the same gesture hurled the bat, hard and high.

It flew up and struck Alcides Núñez in the right arm. Somehow the blow dislocated his shoulder. Castro hadn't been aiming at Núñez specifically— they were friends who had tried to form a volleyball team at Dolores— which only made it worse. As the crying boy was led to the infirmary by a few students, Cubeñas leaned over the railing.

"Animal!" he taunted Castro, below. "Beast!"

"Don't mess in what's none of your business," Castro shot back.

"It is my business," Cubeñas said. "We are all together here."

With everyone watching and waiting, Cubeñas had no idea what to do, so he said, "Either you come up, or I am coming down."

To his horror, Fidel began climbing the circular stairs. Castro looked pale, but he came on, his fists clenched.

As soon as he reached the first floor they attacked each other, wind-milling punches. Cubeñas threw Fidel down, jumped on top of him, and began fending off Castro's punches with his left while delivering several with his right. When he raised his right arm for another blow the arm would not come down: Father Sánchez, a Basque, was holding it.

"WHAT ARE YOU DOING!" he bellowed, and dragged Cubeñas back, separating the boys. Fidel stood up. They faced each other, their chests heaving, red-faced with effort, as Sánchez yelled at them. Cubeñas didn't hear the words.

The crowd of boys fled, dispersed by the priest. Fidel and José Antonio were led off. They were ordered to spend a few hours in the *sala de disciplina,* but that afternoon Castro managed to bolt the school and run around the corner to a city bus stop where no one could see him leave.

The volatile and violent man within the boy Castro had been emerging slowly, always with consequences. As a child at his first small rural school, he'd argued with teachers and fled the building when criticized, by his own account. When he was still not yet a teenager, Fidel had threatened to burn down his father's house if he wasn't sent to a better school. An initial stint with a private tutor—really a foster home—in Santiago had been a disaster, with Fidel, Ramón, and Raúl running wild in the big city, dirty, unruly, rough, and full of coarse country manners and speech. By all accounts, the more toughness and confrontation Fidel showed, the more his father respected and favored him, and Angel Castro set a pattern of promoting Fidel out of trouble. After the tutor, Fidel demanded a proper boarding school, and the boys were sent to LaSalle, run by the Christian

Brothers in Santiago, and then Angel sent them up the hill to Dolores. Fidel had flourished at the school, finally getting the recognition his bright mind deserved, but his rebellious, even domineering, personality, and the fight with Cubeñas, which lasted only seconds, marked a turning point. Soon Fidel would be gone.

At first there was no change. A few days after the fight, Fidel boldly walked up and sat down at the lunch table where Cubeñas and his friends were eating. Castro sat catty-corner from José Antonio, ignoring him, and began eating. Lunch was the usual fried eggs. The salt was sitting in front of José Antonio. Fidel hadn't asked for it, and wouldn't. Herrera made an exaggerated signal with his eyes, looking from José Antonio to the salt, and then at Fidel.

"Salt," José Antonio said, reaching across the table with a long, bony arm.

"Thanks," Fidel said.

That was as much reconciliation as they would ever have. José Antonio believed there was a change after that, not just in his relations with the young Fidel, but in a general queering of the school's atmosphere. It wasn't unknown for boys to fight, but this had been a sharp, fast combat between two of the bigger, more athletic boys at the school. Although inconclusive, the fight had shown one thing nobody at Dolores had ever seen before: Fidel vulnerable. Fidel not so much beaten as shown to be beatable. Everyone had seen him knocked down.

At the end of the fall semester of 1942, Fidel was gone. After five years at Dolores he had jumped schools once again, this time to Belén, in Havana. Lots of Dolores boys were headed that way eventually. Lundy Aguilar was one of many who took his final year of high school at Belén. For many Santiago families, the social connections at the larger Jesuit school in the capital were too advantageous to miss. It is easy to see this move as another promotion for the Castro family, Fidel climbing up from rural schoolhouse in Birán, to the Christian Brothers, to Dolores, and now to Belén. But José Antonio thought the real reason Fidel had left was obvious. The thrown bat, and subsequent fistfight, had made him look simultaneously threatening and weak to other students. He was "exposed," José Antonio said. Fidel had to see himself, and had to be seen, as the top boy at Dolores. And if he couldn't have that, if the students in the patio had seen him down on the ground, then he would go somewhere else.

After the fight—in the first days at the lunch table, and in the long years after, at the University of Havana, and on through their twenties—Fidel and José Antonio engaged in a wary dance. José Antonio's family had land, money, and connections, and in the 1950s Fidel would approach his old antagonist, feigning affection, asking for things, favors that could not be taken by force. During the war years, it was a steady plea, delivered in letters from the mountains: Help me, José Antonio. Help us with money. Help us with information. Send us support. Let us use your farm and your people. Do us this one favor.

But maybe it was really José Antonio who had changed that day, not the atmosphere at the school, or Fidel. Maybe it was José Antonio who saw something to scare him off, something in the way Fidel had come up the circular stairs at the start of that fight, afraid but determined. Something in the way Fidel had gotten back up from the ground as Cubeñas was hauled away by the Basque father.

Fidel kept coming. With fists, or friendship. Even a onetime enemy was a potential ally, a person to be won over again, reconverted. Always, year after year, right through the 1940s and 1950s, Fidel kept pressing José Antonio, gently, for support, friendship, and the necessities of wartime. And always José Antonio withdrew. He smiled, he spoke nicely, and then he withdrew. To the extent possible, he avoided Castro, especially later. He put off answering Castro's letters, or sent back messengers with warm but vague, and even evasive, replies. *Ni sí ni no*, neither yes nor no. He did the minimum, strategically avoiding any outright ruptures with Fidel, but always avoiding cooperation as well. Fidel was a dangerous combination, a bit of a bully, a bit of a dominator, weak enough to pick on the weak, strong enough to fight when cornered. To be his friend would be even more dangerous than to be his enemy.

What Fidel had learned, on the other hand, was that he could take a beating. His reputation during his final semester at Dolores had grown to mythical proportions. After the long double break of lunch and then recess, classes restarted at 1:30. There were just two sessions in the afternoon, often geography and history. Late one afternoon in the fall term, the boys in the front of geography class were listening, still working, but some in the back were forgetting themselves, drifting off or goofing off—whispering, passing notes, wasting their lives.

The geography teacher got angry. This in itself was memorable. The Jesuits could be cold and arbitrary, but they rarely showed a temper. This one pinched a few ears and let fly with an angry lecture. You boys are just drifting through life, he said. You will amount to nothing. There wasn't one among them, not even the best, who lived up to his potential. They didn't even know how to employ the most powerful of all their senses, he said. Did they even know which sense that was?

The boys waited. José Antonio Cubeñas raised a hand. "Sight?" he asked.

No.

Other boys volunteered. Touch?

No.

Taste?

No.

Was it smell? Boys were curling out their fingers now, counting the senses, but the geography instructor only shook his head.

"There is a sixth sense," the padre said. "The sixth sense is common sense."

Duh. The boys groaned with disappointment.

Enrique Hechevarría piped up from the back. He stood right next to Fidel in the school photo. Fidel wasn't even in the room, but at this point, after his letter from the White House, and his fights and stunts, he was the best known student at Dolores. "Padre," Hechevarría offered, "you know Fidel has seven senses."

"Well then, he's not using at least two of them," the priest said.

Bzaam, the bell rang for the end of the day. Cars had been lining up in Clock Street since before 4:00 P.M., and the Dolores bus had ground up the hill, muttering black smoke from a stovepipe exhaust. At 4:15 the doors flew open and more than two hundred boys—the day students, of course—poured out into the narrow street. Those who lived close had the ultimate freedom, the right to walk off into the city, choosing their own route home, or wherever they wanted, diverting through parks, the houses of friends, the department stores on Enramada. Other students rushed off to nearby fields to train for Dolores baseball and soccer teams, while a few unlucky souls would spend more hours in the *sala de disciplina* on the second floor. Being held until six was torture, but the worst offenders could be held as late as 7:30.

Out in the street there was a hot and chaotic unwinding of the day, a mix of fathers, sons, priests, professional drivers, mothers, brothers, and layabouts. Dozens of boys herded onto the Dolores bus, a blue and white embarrassment with the words COLEGIO DOLORES painted over the windows and across the engine cowling, in case anyone doubted who was inside. The bus ran two miles uphill to Vista Alegre, the new suburb where more and more elite families lived.

Only a few boys traveled by car. Some were scooped up by a dad returning from work, but the wealthiest families dispatched a uniformed driver in a gleaming American vehicle. The most spectacular car usually belonged to the Bacardi family, who seemed to always have at least one boy in Dolores. The very youngest of all the Bacardi boys, Facundo, climbed into the family car in Clock Street one afternoon, but never reached home. Later, the family received a ransom note: Facundo had been kidnapped. The police quickly identified the kidnapper, who turned out to be the most obvious suspect, the chauffeur himself. After a few days, officers hunted down the chauffeur's hiding place, where they freed Facundo and shot the driver dead.

The killing was not atypical of police methods in Santiago at that time. The kidnapping of a child was a heinous crime; the Bacardi clan was powerful and wealthy. Perhaps officers thought they could please and cultivate the Bacardis by killing the chauffeur, but the act backfired. The driver had not resisted arrest; he had simply been shot down in cold blood. Rumors spread that the powerful family had ordered the murder. To clear their name, the Bacardis insisted that the officers be put on trial, but the policemen were acquitted and the incident left a bitter taste in Santiago, leaving the impression that police—and perhaps the wealthy— could get away with killing the lowly. After that, the threat of kidnapping convinced more parents to pick up their own children at school, and the number of cars in Clock Street grew, more people waiting outside the building, jockeying for space, parking and double-parking, tooting horns.

The *internos* stayed right there. There were few escapes for them. Lundy did remember seeing Angel Castro out front a few times, picking up his three boys at the start or end of a semester, or liberating them for an after-noon during a rare business trip to Santiago.

But Angel was a true hick, always uncomfortable in Santiago, around the educated. Birán was tiny; the glories of Santiago, the cosmopolitan world of Lundy's parents, the world of a professional class in a busy port city, the life of Enramada and clanging tram cars, of the law courts and social clubs and Cathedral socializing, were infinitely far away from the cane fields where Angel felt at home.

By this time an eighth of Cuba's entire landmass was planted in cane, with more than 400,000 people directly dependent on it for employ-ment. Sugar accounted for about a quarter of the nation's income, and 80 percent of exports, and it was making Angel richer every year.

United Fruit controlled huge sections of the countryside all through Oriente, either directly, through its ownership of hundreds of thousands of acres, or indirectly, through its control of men like Angel Castro. Angel didn't start out wealthy. He was not just a *gallego,* in the Cuban sense meaning anyone from Spain, but an actual *gallego,* a person born in Galicia, the northwest corner of Spain. Wet and achingly poor, green and stony, Galicia produced hard men, like the new Spanish führer, Francisco Franco.

Angel had the hardness of his flinty land. He had come to Cuba as an illiterate mercenary, paid by a wealthy Spaniard to fill his place in the army. A quartermaster in the cavalry, he'd handled supplies, not a weapon. Despite being on the losing, European side in the Cuban War of Indepen-dence, he liked what he saw of the island. This was a big country of rich soil and cheap labor. A man could establish himself. Angel went back to Spain only long enough to collect a bride. Once married, he had immi-grated to Cuba, and settled in Oriente, in the fields around Birán. Angel started with a small farm he worked himself, but his land was surrounded by the fields of United Fruit. He ingratiated himself to the Americans, and became a labor boss, a supplier of *macheteros* to neighboring ranches. The *macheteros* followed the harvest from farm to farm under Angel's direction, as he reaped the benefit of supplying their labor to the truly wealthy. A man like Angel Castro had to be an enforcer, able to mobilize impover-ished men to work in brutal conditions for long hours and criminally low pay. It took a heart of stone, a corrupt soul, and a long whip. The many members of the Castro clan who now live in exile have fought in court about just how bad Angel really was. Fidel's daughter in Spain has said Angel was a rapist and murderer, while Fidel's sister in Miami defended Angel (with a libel suit) as an honest man. But certainly he was a rough man, a provincial, and typical of what was wrong with Cuba. Fidel Castro has described his own father as an "exploiter."

Was Fidel himself innocent? When some imported Haitian laborers at the Castro farm went on strike, refusing to cut cane at the pay rate offered, Angel—and, according to some accounts, the teenage Fidel—rode in among the Haitians on horseback, beating them with the flat of a machete. Angel Castro supplied more than ten thousand blades to United Fruit and other big landowners. The *zafra,* and therefore the economy of Oriente, would come to a halt without him.

By the 1940s Angel had a big ranch—26,000 acres, the second biggest in Oriente—and he liked to claim that he had expanded it by going out at night and moving the fence posts of his neighbor, United Fruit. He also claimed to have taken tractors from the company simply by slapping a different color of paint on them and driving them away. Underneath this amiable front, the jolly forwardness, was a man used to giving orders, tough enough to dominate even those who carried sharp blades every day. He beat his employees, and paid them in coupons redeemable only at his own store. He grew rich in a dirty business.

He'd be waiting by his car in Clock Street on those rare afternoons, ignoring the fathers and chauffeurs. Although barely educated, he was a Spaniard and believed in the inherent superiority of Spaniards, of European culture and people. He approved of the Jesuits on this basis alone, their wool robes and Hapsburg lisps a reminder of home. On the few days that Angel was there on Clock Street, waiting, Fidel and his brothers were able to have a bit of escape, an exception to the routine.

But that was a rare day for any *interno.* Far more often, the twenty-two boarders, including Fidel, Ramón, and Raúl, watched from inside as their classmates dispersed on foot, by car, by bus, in chaos and good cheer, amid clouds of exhaust. By 4:30 almost everyone would be gone. The front doors of the school would swing shut.

José Antonio Cubeñas would climb up to his room. The Castro brothers would split up for different sports, meeting later for dinner. Except for these trips to a nearby baseball diamond, where he was the Dolores pitcher, Fidel rarely left the building.

Around dinnertime, the unlucky students in detention would be let out of the *sala de disciplina* and skip off. Most *internos* did their homework in the late afternoon, before another dull meal in the now quiet dining room. The tropical night stole in suddenly while they ate. In the dark twenty-two boys would climb up to their third-floor rooms, the younger students on the left, the older on the right, two to four boys to a room. By 9:00 P.M. everything was quiet, but for the hushed sound of the Jesuits, who moved about the building at will, crossing the dark courtyard or climbing up to the fourth floor. There was a final round of business when, under stern adult eyes, the *internos* had to kneel and pray before getting into bed.

Sometimes the night inside Dolores was livelier, with a movie, or perhaps a birthday party for one of the boys. The Jesuits would produce a cake, and gather all twenty-two boys to watch the blowing out of the candles. Then the cake would be divided up into thin slices.

The used candles were always gathered up and set aside, ready for the next birthday.

DAYS OF FIRE

The parade was two hours late, but nobody in Santiago cared. Maybe I was the only person in Santiago to even *notice* that the parade was two hours late. For Cubans, inured to long lines, never-ending delays, and decades without difference, the longer this night took to get started, the better. In ancient Santiago, this night was different from all other nights. The first night of Carnaval. The first party of Cuba's week of parties.

In the twenty-first century, an era often called "post-communist," Castro's Cuba was still, among other things, a life sentence to boredom. Numbing routines, endless anomie, empty conformism. The exceptions to this flat lifescape were rare, treasured even more in anticipation than in the event. The later they started Carnaval the better. The more disorganized the better. It only meant that the evening would run later. Communist Party logistics were a tribute to the Lords of Misrule.

There was always time, in Cuba. Time for thousands of ordinary people, black, white, brown, to gather along two designated blocks of a broad avenue, time to have some beer, minutes to flirt, and still more time to wander. Occasionally there was a half-hour set of music, somewhere on a back street. Sometimes even by a live band. So people would wait, then dance like crazy for a few songs, and then, when it was over, they would stand patiently, without worry, ready for whatever happened next, whenever it happened. Equanimity is, in Cuba, a survival adaptation.

July in Santiago de Cuba. The hottest time of the year. In the hottest place. Santiago drops down over rolling hills, toward the long, twisted bay where Spanish sailors had found shelter from the winds. Ringed by volcanoes, the bay was a heat sink, immune to even the faintest Haitian breezes.

Life adapted. Santiago people are famous for walking slowly, which is saying something for Cubans. It was so brutally infernal during the long July afternoons that no one moved in the city during midday, or worked much at all, or even talked. Walking was swimming, the moist air parting around you. When I stepped into one of the mercilessly air-conditioned hotels, my sunglasses would frost over. Only at night did the drama of mere existence ease.

Two hours so far, waiting for the parade, and only now, just after 10:00 P.M., was the temperature down to merely hot, not hell itself. It was merely humid, not the ocean of daytime. You sweated only when you moved. The wind, or lack of wind, was maddening. A breeze fluttered for a few minutes, tantalizing, and then shut off. In the stillness hundreds of Cubans began fanning themselves. Then the breeze erupted again, hot and hard, hurling up the dust generated by the growing crowds, rattling plastic bags in the gutters, pushing scraps of paper in circles. Then nothing.

Although I'd been to Cuba seven times in the last eight years, this was my first night in Santiago. I'd always lingered in the west, in Havana and the tobacco fields of Pinar del Río, or come no further than the central plains, Santa Clara, Trinidad, the Guamuhaya mountains. There had always been nooks to distract me—Sancti Spíritus and Matanzas, Varadero and Cienfuegos—before I could reach Santiago on the miserable buses or the immobilized train system. But somewhere in Santiago there were a few lingering examples of that small minority, the Dolores boys who had never left. And that was enough to put me that very morning on a rusting Ilyushin-18, a Warsaw-pact plane that first saw service in 1965. The four turboprops had stained the tarmac with oil at Havana; as we flew, bumping and bouncing eastward toward Santiago, they trailed smoke. I'd taken a room at the only hotel available, and bought a $5 ticket to Carnaval.

Anyone who showed up at Carnaval with a *ten dollars bill green american* was assured of two seats in a bleacher reserved for hard currency customers. The result was that the white bleacher, elevated on a platform and looking right into the maw of the arc-lit asphalt that would be parade central, was filled with foreigners only (the exception was a pleased Cuban TV crew, allotted free seats and drink tickets). A very excited French couple sat on my left, and two German photography enthusiasts beyond them. On my right I had Socrates, a retired diplomat from Mexico, with a friend from home, José. Both of the Mexicans were in their sixties, but they were feeble old men, liver-spotted, wrinkled, almost trembling. Like most people, they were drunk. Socrates sat in his chair, twisted around backward, his face searching vainly for the waiter.

"Five dollars is a good price," Socrates said in English. He'd been stationed at the embassy in Washington for some very good years and talked like an honorary American. For $5 we each got a lawn chair, packed immovably tight against those to the right and left in a row of forty. Because the waiter was often missing in action, Socrates recommended that, like him, I should order two daiquiris at once, enough to tide us over until the eventual return of the harassed staff.

Right across the avenue was another bleacher, entirely for Cubans. But that bleacher—the only other set of seats for the whole of Santiago on the first night of Carnaval—had been filling up, over the last two hours, with very important comrades. It was the bleacher for Carnaval judges, but also Carnaval officials, and non-Carnaval officials, and families and friends, *maimbe,* the high-ranking civilians in an invisible system of patronage. Except for the two hundred there, all Cubans—thousands already, the crowd growing steadily—were standing, a long and deep line of the public at large, running up both sides of the next long block, and contained behind tall hurricane fencing.

I knew that the parade would run behind schedule. Arriving half an hour after the announced start, I had been among the first to claim a seat, right in the front row. I'd been staring up four broad lanes of the Avenida Victoriano Garzón for two hours now, expecting a parade the whole time. The bleacher filled in, parade marshals stood around frowning, the strong TV lights, hung from cranes overhead, came on, and the crowd grew, thousands and then thousands more.

The overwhelmed waiter finally pushed down our row. Socrates, José, and I ordered a pair of daiquiris each. The breeze blew steadily for a few happy minutes, and if I remained perfectly still, I could feel my face drying, and even my shirt. But the wind died. Seconds later beads of sweat were sliding down my neck.

Two and a half hours. If I was going to sweat without moving, then why not move? "I'm going to find the parade," I told Socrates. I gave him money. "Keep my drinks for me."

"A very good idea to go for a walk," he said, making no effort to rise. He mimed stashing two daiquiris under my chair.

I slid under the railing and dropped five feet down to the asphalt of the *avenida.* A parade marshal glared but did nothing, so watched by thousands of pairs of eyes I marched up the middle of the avenue, alone, toward the city center.

Pressed up against the hurricane fencing were children, a first short row of expectant faces, and behind them, in second and third rows, were their parents, their relatives and neighbors, faces blank. The only excitement was further back, where hundreds of teenagers milled about on the dirt yards of gray prefab apartment blocks. The kids in their faded American T-shirts of hip-hop stars and basketball heroes were shuffling and dodging around in flip-flops, an ambling juvenile version of the old Spanish *paseo,* hundreds of kids circling back and forth, talking, looking, posing, circling again. People dressed for the heat, in either mini skirts or shorts, and the girls in the briefest of shirts, with many boys in none at all.

During Carnaval the state opened its taps, and beer flowed out. Most adults were carrying the evening's chief accessory, a plastic kitchen jug. Translucent, worn from everyday use, in faded yellow, translucent green, and dull blue, they had two uses. When full, they held enough beer to last an hour. When empty, they could be turned over and beaten for applause, or rhythm. A profane plastic batá drum.

A short tanker truck, which would normally carry pesticide or soup, came grinding up the avenue past me and stopped at a row of palm-thatched stalls, where it decanted hundreds of gallons of beer through a fat green hose.

According to a map in the paper, the parade would start in the city center, and the dancers, floats, and musicians would climb up the old Enramada Street, juke their way through the Plaza of Martyrs, and then come marching up the wide Victoriano Garzón toward us. Three intersections along the route, each about a kilometer apart, had been closed off with steel railings and converted into plazas where people could gather to watch. After ten minutes of walking through empty blocks, I reached the first of these cutouts, which had a stage and a tower of speakers. A band had just finished playing. The whole space was ringed with little wooden carts selling food I had never seen in Cuba before: cookies, roast corn, fried and sugared *churos,* popcorn, and roast pork sandwiches.

The beer was bad, and warm. But it cost 12 cents a liter. And they charged by the liter: everyone in line had a plastic jug. One-man kiosks were selling *aguardiente,* clear, cheap, dangerous, sold by the shot in paper cones. Many people had been drinking since morning, and some were already sitting on the curb, feeling no pain.

The shortest line, with only five people in it, was at the booth selling genuine rum, poured into genuine plastic cups. The rum kiosk was three feet wide and two deep. Three men were fitted into this space, nervously measuring out exact shots into the cups.

It was awkward, in another language: *How much does it go?*

He held up four fingers.

I counted out $4 and handed it over. He stood still for a moment, eyeing me, holding the money. Then he conferred with the other two, an encrypted exchange of whispers. They all nodded, and he handed me the bottle.

Four dollars *a bottle.* They laughed when they saw my surprise, but they took the bottle back and returned my four bills, and then accepted an American quarter, the price of one shot. They gave me an unmeasured pour, oily with potential.

Carnaval is a time of reversals, of masques and deceptions, of master and servant trading places. Even the Cuban government threw off restraints here. Beer was gushing; there was all the clear liquor you could drink, and it was cheap; and salted in among the alcohol vendors were a dozen one-man kiosks selling pork sandwiches. The sandwiches were tiny, but at less than 50 cents apiece the hardworking vendors couldn't make them fast enough, their hands glistening with fat as they sliced at a golden pig, layering slivers of gray meat, quivering white fat, and crisp brown skin onto buns. It was terrible, unless you'd just had a big shot of rum.

Here were two things completely uncharacteristic of Cuba: calories and enterprise. Only 2 or 3 percent of Cubans are self-employed, or "self-accounting," in Marxist parlance. In the lean times of the early 1990s the government had allowed a few people to open tiny, one-person businesses like these sandwich carts. As long as you hired no one else, it became legal to be a language tutor, a dog trainer, a flat-tire repairman, or a carpenter. But these people, paid at market rates, were soon making more per month than the 97 percent of Cubans who remained state-employed. Even though the system was restricted to 118 jobs, most of them menial, and tightly licensed, the self-accounting were a threat to a system built on mass control. The state newspaper denounced the self-employed as "piranhas," and Fidel Castro was particularly irritated by the few private restaurants that operated in people's homes, vowing to shut them down several times. When he grumbled during a six-hour speech that there was too much "wimpiness" in Cuba, his aides knew just what to do: tax inspections and harassment shut more restaurants, and the Labor Ministry banned magicians, masseurs, and jewelry makers. The sandwich men had their assistants—usually a wife—hidden behind a wall, for fear of being seen to have an employee.

Santiago has been destroyed by earthquakes many times, so it doesn't look as old as it should. The low houses along the parade route were unlit, struggling to stay upright, full of makeshift rooms and improvised electrical systems, the walls daubed with faded and irrelevant slogans celebrating forgotten heroes. The small 1930s office buildings were what passed for modern in Santiago, except for the rare and titanic state buildings, like a hulking sports complex visible off in the western darkness, an immense box, lifeless, imposing, the front lawn spiked with a piece of Socialist Realist art like a tank trap. Here on the avenue the only sign of life was a single shop, still lit up hours after closing. It was a dollar store, and despite the protests of a security guard, a crowd of women pressed against the glass, pining for the frozen meat, cold beer, baby clothes, kitchen appliances, and shampoo inside.

The avenue topped out at the Plaza of Martyrs, which was dark and quiet, but ringed with people, sitting patiently, fanning themselves. There was no music. Some told me they hadn't seen or heard the parade. They weren't concerned either way.

I could see down the steep hill into the city center. Enramada, the city's original artery, ran down past El Ten Cent, past the Parque Dolores and the radio station where Fidel made his first address to the nation, down past the old, dark movie theater, and the new Communist Party headquarters. Eventually the same street dropped past the Bacardi factory, its red-brick arches still bearing the bat figures seen on rum bottles around the world. Here Enramada expired on the waterfront flats, a wasteland of rail tracks and crumbling customshouses, where wet rats scurried through the miasma.

I didn't go down. The one business operating on the Plaza of Martyrs was selling *guarapo*, sugarcane juice. It was a filthy storefront with a staff of twelve young men in white paper caps. One fed cane into a hand mill;

one turned the mill; a third caught the juice; a fourth poured it into cups; a fifth carved ice, which a sixth put into the cups, while a seventh rang it up, and an eighth served it. The other four watched.

America! they shouted, when they found out where I was from. America! The magic land.

Whenever I walked through the crowd, girls approached with the usual frankness offered to foreign males. *Don't you want a friend, handsome?*

Or, *Are you lonely?*

Or just, *I want to make love to you tonight.*

Where are you from, they called out. *Take me with you, my love.*

As I finished the last of my cane juice I heard a distant crash of drums, followed by the blaring of horns. It was coming from back up at the top of the Victoriano Garzón. Somehow the parade had gotten around behind me.

For a dollar, a pedicab driver huffed, puffed, and sweated his way up the hill, and he dropped me off just in time for Socrates to hand me two cold daiquiris. The first drummers, formed into a rectangle, came banging their way into the light.

Elegguá was in the house. The Santería god of destiny, wearing red and black stripes, inaugurated the evening by marching down the avenue, waving a scepter and greeting the crowd, before passing beneath our raised bleacher, the swaying fringes of his jester's cap almost brushing my big toe.

The parade erupted out of a side street. Apparently there hadn't been enough fuel to drive the floats up through the city, neighborhood by neighborhood, as was traditional. They had assembled near the finish and were only going to cover the last two blocks of the route. Hundreds of marchers mobbed out of a staging area, formed into ranks, and then, with a blast of a whistle, the first "school" suddenly picked up its feet and began marching. Their only instrument was the drum, a plain walking rhythm pounded on dozens of snare, bass, and conga drums. A score of young men, all shirtless, banged in perfect time on brake cylinders from old Fords and Buicks. Struck with a metal rod, the rusty cylinders gave a high pinging backbeat to the looming madness.

A dozen schools representing neighborhoods or *organismos,* meaning a workplace, school, or association, had a hundred marchers each. On reaching the arc-lit section of the roadway, the drum corps and marchers of the first school took up a new step, the distinctive three-forward-and-one-to-the-side maneuver that Desi Arnaz, with a conga tucked under his arm, had converted into a nightclub phenomenon. As the school passed down the first block, people on the hurricane fences took up the beat on their plastic jugs, but this was all anticipation: at the entrance to our block the school came to a new halt, gathered its momentum, and then, with a burst from a whistle, exploded at a run. Socrates shouted his approval, and the French couple took a picture.

There must have been some pattern or purpose to what followed. A dozen men, women, boys, and girls—divided into those groups—broke in every direction at once, making spiraling lines and curving patterns, screaming, leaping, spinning, and dodging, turning back on themselves, and in the middle of this chaos came a pair of abominable snowmen, in outfits made entirely of white chicken feathers, skipping. Then a team of giant sea horses. A group of ancient women, with canes and thick glasses, and dressed entirely in white but for their richly colored necklaces, ambled through the careening formations as though heading to the corner store, not even looking up. Groups of girls in track suits rushed through doing karate. A man—apparently it was a man—in a suit of old paint cans, waddled along, clanging and banging. Elegguá, wandering freely, waved his scepter, always the first presence, always unimportant in himself. Elegguá initiates any ceremony involving rituals of Santería, not because he is great—he is a little god—but because he is an intermediary, a cross between Mercury the Messenger and an Apache trickster, stirring up trouble as he meddles in human affairs. As the "opener of doors," his interventions determine your destiny in life, but he is unreliable. He has been known to forget his missions, to get drunk and fall asleep, or to spend the evening flitting about in the form of an owl, looking for innocent girls to impregnate.

With his blessings in place, the pace increased. The stylized chaos of the first school gave way to a new rival, another hundred people dancing in ecstatic energy down the full width of the avenue. In front of the judges they expanded into the patterns of an American marching band, but with better dancing. The costumes were better, too: men in broad buccaneer hats and shimmering shirts, Carnaval queens in long yellow gowns trailed by attendants, a king waving kindly from beneath the plastic beach umbrella that was his signal of office, and attended by a whole royal family of ecstatic boys and girls. More boys banging more drumsticks on the brake cylinders of more old Chevys. At another point a school of "Jamaicans" came through, who were Cubans from the waterfront, where Jamaican immigrants had settled generations ago. The female Jamaicans flipped their skirt hems; the men wore straw planter hats and had billowing, ruffled sleeves, and they all came down the avenue doing the limbo, and singing as best they could, *leembo leembo la, leembo leembo la, da musi gaw may yew leembo, leembo leembo la.*

The main difference among the schools seemed to be their color schemes, the next one favoring solar yellows and the one after dotted mostly with hot pink, and the following one white. Everyone was slathered in sequins, dancing wildly, and some women had their hats piled high with Carmen Miranda–sized towers of plastic fruit. A glowing girl came forward to be presented to the judges, four attendants helping spread out her velvet cape, decorated with sequins that showed Uncle Sam, running for his life as a locomotive labeled THE REVOLUTION RETURNS bore down on him.

Men in tinfoil helmets. Cowboys. Break dancers. African tribesmen. On and on, one school after another, for three hours, the women gyrating their hips, the men leaping and banging. Capes, banners, more dancers. There were big papier-mâché heads, called *mamaroches*. The *mamaroches* were traditionally caricatures of Santiago's leading citizens, and inside the giant heads the anonymous marchers would belt out ribald songs about the powerful. Tonight there was nothing more risqué than animals and space aliens, painted emerald and turquoise, and seven poorly made dwarves who looked familiar.

Passion makes the powerful nervous. Carnaval was banned by the government of Cuba in 1669, but it proved irrepressible and was relegalized in 1743. The authorities put the insulting *mamaroche* singers on a government payroll in order to control them, but it didn't work, and in 1815 a decree banned Carnaval once more, citing the "moral and physical damage caused by the mixing of classes," and parade-goers who "take the liberty of insulting anybody with indecent songs and offensive sayings." Carnaval was revived again decades later, but was still feared because slaves, using the chaos and costumes of the festival, could escape. Later, anti-Spanish rebels, hidden behind Carnaval masks, moved freely, passing messages and even launching attacks. Fidel Castro timed his first attack on Batista for the dawn following this, Carnaval's first night.

Well after midnight, in a kind of finale, the floats appeared. These were huge contraptions of lights, glitter, and dancing girls, pulled along by old Soviet tractors. The tractors were themselves disguised, under wide skirts of fabric, so that the driver's head and the exhaust pipe were the only things visible above a slowly moving box. Each float vied to be more outlandish than the last, and the biggest was the green and silver one from Crystal, Cuba's favorite beer, which was covered with dancing girls dressed in no more than a dozen rhinestones each. They gyrated on platforms, furiously jiggling their butt cheeks at the judges, their green, blue, and silver feather headdresses swaying wildly.

Social control was still on the agenda. In the usual management-by-shortage, it was the government that doled out cloth, sequins, tinfoil, tractors, generators, fuel, and permits. Where once private beer companies had sponsored floats, now government beer companies sponsored the floats. Where Spanish officials once tried to control the lyrics, now the block committees vetted all routines, ruling out caricatures, silencing songs of protest.

Same dog, the Cubans say, new collar.

When I headed home at 3:00 A.M., the crowds were thronging in the avenues, people drunk enough to need no music for dancing. Children wove wildly through the night, the beer wagons and pork carts still doing a brisk business. Two men staggered into each other accidentally, and fell into a hopeless, inept fistfight, unable to even see what they were swinging at. A man lay on top of a woman in the bushes, groping her, as she pleaded. I overtook a slow-moving Cuban couple just as the woman, in high heels, hunched down in the gutter, pulled up her tube dress, and let loose a heavy stream of urine. "Don't look!" she shouted.

At my hotel, a tall red and gray monstrosity that was about five minutes old, a Toyota taxi was just pulling away. It stopped suddenly, backed up, and the window on my side came down.

"Patricio!" Socrates shouted. He was sitting in the back seat, with a girl on either side of him. José was up front. Socrates leaned out the window. "Where are you going, my friend? The party is just getting started!"

I demurred, but he wouldn't hear of it. "Come with us," he insisted. "Alina here will move over."

"A-*lyyyyy*-sa," she said, and slapped him on the back of the head.

That wasn't my last obstacle. The doorman, wearing the long wool coat and top hat of an English footman, was astonished to see me alone.

"Sir," he said, in a confidential tone. "Don't you need a *chica*?"

The attack came two hours later, long before the blue-black dawn, as I lay asleep, twisting and trembling against the arctic chill of the hotel's centralized air-conditioning. The assault had been carefully timed for 5:00 A.M., the hangover moment.

As I lay unconscious in the icy airlock of my fifteenth-floor room, tossing in the shallow sleep of alcohol and pork fat, the insurgents broke from cover and rushed at the Moncada garrison en masse, shouting *Long live the Revolution!,* or so the newspaper said. The news media, the only defenders of the barracks this time, were a little sleepy, and fired back only with their camera flashes before gently surrendering.

Fifty years to the day after the original July 26, 1953, assault, the attackers were dewy Cuban boy scouts, Young Pioneers in their short pants and red kerchiefs. The Moncada was exactly the same—the battle damage from 1953 had been repaired by Batista, and then painstaking re-created by Castro, down to redrilling each bullet hole—but the targets this time were the attackers themselves. Although membership in the Young Pioneers was mandatory, it was a special honor to be picked for this event. The kids had stayed up all night, meeting in the actual farmhouse that Fidel had used, where Party officials spoke with them about making a deep personal commitment to the Revolution.

Which side were you on? Were you with the people? Or with the enemies of Cuba? Were you really, truly, committed? Were you bound and determined to put your life in the service of the country? The best Young Pioneers could, in their teenage years, join the powerful UJC, the Union of Young Communists. The UJC was a finishing school for cadres that fed its most committed members into the Communist Party of Cuba, at about

7 percent of Cuba's population, the actual vanguard itself. So this reenact-
ment was an opportunity, a path toward that future. Would they take it?
There was only one answer, of course, and the boys and girls had been
bused down to the city, dropped in a parking lot at 4:00 A.M., and then
given their cue.

The real 1953 attack wasn't so organized. About eighty men had left
the farmhouse in a grab bag of vehicles, using four different routes into
Santiago that had not been rehearsed. Many of the young men were from
small towns in western Cuba, and about half got lost in Santiago's twisting streets. With just three dozen men in place, and more courage than
wisdom, Castro launched the attack anyway, riding on the sideboard of a
car as it rushed the Moncada before dawn. The guards fired, surprise was
lost, and the thousand army troops sleeping in the barracks had time to
wake up, routing the assault. Many of the wounded or captured rebels
were tortured, and then summarily executed.

There was one *Dolorino* killed. Renato Guitart, a graduate from 1948.
Although he had arrived at Dolores after Fidel left, Castro was already at
that point recognized for political activism, and by 1952 a famous con-
gressional candidate known for his radio speeches against Batista. Just
twenty-two, Guitart joined the rebels out of idealism, and died that morning in the first volley. Raúl and Fidel Castro both came through without a
scratch.

For the few survivors, there was a mad dash to escape. The Moncada
fortress was located just 850 meters from the Colegio de Dolores, and for
Fidel and Raúl, fleeing was no problem, for they knew every alley. Fidel
ducked into one safe house, later transferred to another, and by that afternoon was in the countryside. Raúl stayed hidden in the city.

Back in Miami, Pepín Bou had dimly recalled the name of a Dolores
alumnus who'd cropped up in some home video. Yivena, or Yivera, or
Llivina, he'd said. Something like that. "Even if I did know someone who
was still there," he'd said, "I wouldn't know him. You know what I
mean?"

For the alumni outside Cuba, those still on the island were an unwelcome reminder that not everyone had made the same choices. But it was
simple enough to find such a person. A telephone shop just off Parque

Céspedes had a phone book that was several decades out of date (not a reproduction, this time, but an actual 1980s phone book). In the timeless stasis of Cuba, these never became obsolete. I flipped through the Ys without luck, but quickly spotted a likely candidate under the LLs: LLIVINA, MIGUEL.

He answered the phone himself. "Oh, Lundy," he said when I mentioned that name. "Okay. He was a good friend of my sister." When I identified myself as an American writer, he switched into English and invited me over. He gave me his unromantic address, which was Calle 15 No. 3, in Vista Alegre.

He didn't ask why I was calling. There was only one reason a foreign journalist would come looking for him. He was Dolores class of 1953, and that was as close as he had brushed up against history.

The remote location of my hotel, a brutalist tower on the northern outskirts, was now an advantage. The Vista Alegre neighborhood was a short walk uphill. I started over in the late afternoon when the sun had dropped toward Havana and the old trees cast shadows to shelter me.

Fifteenth Street was just beyond a traffic circle where six different streets and avenues collided, dividing the lower, older, narrower portions of Santiago from the ring of more spacious suburbs. On the higher side of that split were the stately mansions and elite neighborhoods of the old days, still valued residential properties. A few of the old mansions had been converted into businesses. The first I passed was the Maison de Moda, a fashion center. It had a catwalk equipped with lights in the yard, and two bars and a restaurant. At night the *jineteras* were lined up three deep at the entrance, waiting for the chance to escort a foreign man into the restaurant. Off to the east was the San Juan Motel, an American motor lodge predating the '59 Revolution. On a subsequent visit to Santiago, I caught the maid there stealing my toothpaste.

Many of the boys from Dolores had lived in Vista Alegre, which was a brand-new suburb in the 1930s, hardly developed, high above the city on a breezy hilltop. Although little had been built in the last half century, the neighborhood still had a modern feeling compared to the rest of Santiago. Down below, the houses were Spanish in style, with interior courtyards, separated from the narrow lanes by only two or three feet of sidewalk, all you needed in the era of horse carts. In Vista Alegre, the streets were widened for automobiles, with grassy medians and wide side-walks. The houses, often made of cement, were set behind lawns, many of them now overgrown with thorns and waist-high weeds. The gardeners and servants, declared masters in 1959, had lain down their tools and left. So had many owners, although the houses were usually passed on to relatives.

A few abandoned homes had been converted into *cuarterías,* small apartments made with plywood dividers. Two dozen unrelated people could end up living in one house, the old living room split in half, the bedroom partitioned, even the hallways or a porch split up to make tiny bedrooms. But most houses in Vista Alegre still seemed to be in private hands, often occupied by a solitary old person who had been there for half a century. And sprinkled around the neighborhood were discreet government businesses offering services most Cubans never used: travel agencies, special commissaries, foreign exchange offices, and joint venture bureaucracies in great mansions. I stopped in a small dollar store, unmarked and almost hidden, in what had once been an art nouveau home. In a powerfully air-conditioned room, accompanied by the beeps and dings of a state-of-the-art cash register, a Cuban family with fat children ransacked the coolers for ice cream and sodas. I had never seen obese children in Cuba.

Next door, a Lada pull into the breezeway of a house, disgorging a young white man in a short-sleeve madras shirt and khakis, the uniform of the YUMMIE, or Young Upwardly Mobile Marxist. Clutching a leather folder, he went inside and locked the door. Despite housing shortages he'd somehow ended up with a 1940s style bungalow in good repair. Next door was an older Spanish house with Corinthian columns, a cracked facade, and a crumbling roof. The lawn was split between waist-high weeds and a failed crop of corn.

Miguel Llivina was waiting on his porch. The house, shaded by a large tree, was the same one he had grown up in, the same one he had left every morning in the 1940s to catch the blue bus to Dolores. He pounded the walls with his flat palm, to show me how thick they were. Santiago was known as the Land of Fire, he explained, which referred to more than the heat, or the ardent character of its people. The city was surrounded by extinct volcanoes, which still let loose with tremblers. There had been a

serious earthquake in 1932, so Llivina's father had built this house to survive even a solid shake, with only one story and chicken wire laid inside
the walls as a reinforcement against cracking.

We sat in the sweltering living room. The heights of Vista Alegre were
normally breezy—that is why the wealthy settled here—but the July heat
was still, wet, and merciless. The Land of Fire also had, every July, the
Days of Fire, a nocturnal celebration of the heat itself, marked by building bonfires in the poorer neighborhoods. Heat appealed to the people of
Santiago. It defined them. It justified their self-image as *ardiente,* fiery
souls with uncontrollable passions, both personal and political.

I had arrived at Miguel's house sweaty, and we both remained confined
to our seats (an armchair for me, the sofa for Miguel). It was an Eisenhower living room, with louvered windows and lounge furniture that had
been lovingly tended for decades. We stayed motionless during the hour
of conversation. He was wearing slacks, loafers, and, despite the temperature, a blue dress shirt with the sleeves buttoned at the cuffs. His hair was
almost all white, with just a dusting of the black of his youth.

When I asked about Dolores, Miguel turned in his chair, reaching
unsuccessfully for something on a bookshelf. He called for his son, who
took a thick pile of documents from the shelf, passed them to his father,
and then sat in an armchair matching my own, by my side. He was middle-
aged, fat around the middle, and wore shorts and a velour sport shirt. His
name was also Miguel—"Doctor Miguel Jorge Llivina Lavine," his card
said, "Subdirector of the Center for Educational Studies." He was coughing when he sat down, and the coughing occasionally burst into harsh
fits. Rocking back and forth on his cushion, he cradled an ashtray in his
lap, listening to his father and smoking between rounds of phlegm.

The first thing in the pile of documents was the Dolores yearbook for
1953. He scanned the faces of the very youngest boys in my school photo,
trying to pick himself out, but could not settle on one face, first seeing
himself to the left, then the right. He flipped through his own yearbook
and pointed out his photo, standing among the oldest boys. He wore a
double-breasted navy blue blazer, white pants, and the tightly knotted tie
that Fidel had disdained for his own posing. Miguel's hair was slicked
back, even and shiny, and his face was smooth and round; he'd been
chubbier as a teenager than he was today.

"And here is Uncle Paco," he said, when I showed him Castro's face in my 1941 picture.

Uncle Paco? Was that one of Castro's nicknames? "No," Llivina said. He'd made it up on the spot. Uncle Paco was just a jumble of syllables to substitute for a more dangerous name. Llivina looked at the image of Castro, the small round face under the railing. "He's dressed a little *deshabille*," he said. "Not like the others. A bit messy."

Despite keeping his Dolores yearbook close at hand for fifty years, Miguel said he was not romantic about the old Cuba. Outside the walls of the school there had been a harsh reality. He volunteered that there were a million illiterates in the countryside, and recalled the desperately poor *campesinos* of Oriente surviving on sugarcane and bits of *tasajo*, the scraps of dried, salted beef of the worst quality, imported from Uruguay. "There was equality, and no equality," Miguel said. "The poor in Cuba were a huge class. Public health was in bad shape. Only a minority had access to it. In the *campo*, there were no hospitals. The state hospitals didn't have enough budget. People had to travel to the city for help."

The middle class was in a better situation. "In the 1940s and 1950s the middle class in Cuba was bigger than in many countries in Latin America," Miguel said. Two thirds of Cubans could claim to be middle-class, by some estimates, a figure unparalleled in the region. They had access to good schools like Dolores, private health insurance companies, and the *sociedades mutuales,* cooperatives that offered inexpensive doctor visits. As bad as rural poverty could be in Cuba, Miguel recalled with a shudder his visit to Mexico during a summer break at Dolores. "In Mexico, there was a rich class, and then a huge poor class. The middle class was much smaller than in Cuba."

The priests at Dolores had taught them to look at these problems, not away from them, Miguel said. The education had been excellent and rigorous, focused on preparing them for their special obligations as future leaders of Cuba. His only complaint was that the school, with its strong religious teachings, was lacking in "rationalism." (Fidel Castro agreed, telling Frei Betto that the school had "negative influences . . . such as the non-utilization of rationality, that is to say, the non-development of reasoning and feeling.")

The pages of the yearbook were soft, and Miguel pointed out the entries on the Radio Club and on the basketball team, both of which he had joined. He particularly remembered the outings to the surrounding hills—the famed nature walks where Fidel had absorbed the topography he would use in 1957. Miguel lingered over a picture of Facundo Bacardi, the six-year-old heir to the rum and political dynasty, whose kidnapping had been the most exciting thing that had ever happened at Dolores, Miguel thought. A close second was the military coup on March 10, 1952. All classes were abruptly stopped that day, and the students ordered to assemble in the courtyard. Far away in Havana, Fulgencio Batista had just shoved his way back into power, ending Cuba's experiment in liberal democracy and throwing the beloved 1940 constitution in the trash. Most of the Jesuits, Miguel said, were sympathetic to General Franco, the strutting little strongman who had fought to victory in the Spanish Civil War, imposing a system of proto-fascism on Spain, crushing leftists, and restoring the Church to power. But Batista was no Franco, and this was not Spain. The Padre Prefect assembled the students in their usual formations in the courtyard and spoke quickly, condemning the coup, denouncing Batista, and warning the boys to go home immediately, in case political trouble spread to Santiago. When Miguel finished telling this story, his son snorted.

"Father, no," he said. "Objective conditions did not permit this." Miguel the Younger was an expert on the history of education in Cuba, he explained. He worked at the Ministry of Education in Havana, where he designed the curriculum for teachers colleges—training the trainers, as it were. He was a Communist Party member, one of the 7 percent of Cubans formally enrolled in the machine, and well versed in the Party's practice of constructing secure walls out of language. No teacher at Dolores, he explained, could have condemned Batista. The old system of education in Cuba had been "crude, irrational," he said, using the same language as Fidel and his own father, a system designed to preserve the interests of the elite. The Jesuits had to serve that monolithic interest, which meant they had to support Batista.

By contrast the Revolution had "massified" a "conductive model of pedagogy. Of what does this consist?" Rhetorical questions were safe questions. Words were to be handled at a distance: he spoke of planification and massified pedagogy. A fit of severe coughing then tore into him, cutting off words and even breath. He wheezed, choked, and, forcibly silenced, rocked back and forth in the chair, smoking a cigarette.

Miguel the Elder disagreed now, quietly. Dolores had progressive aspects. The school even "had Negroes, up to a certain point," he said.

"Three!" his son shouted.

They were both right. During the 1940s Dolores had edged away from segregation, allowing a few exemplary black students, though only in auxiliary classes, and then in regular enrollment. By 1955 it was more integrated than American public schools.

Blacks "didn't have the social position" to attend the school, the father said, a little defensively. "Or the money."

Miguel himself had enough of both to go straight on to the United States after graduation. He enrolled as a freshman at another great Jesuit institution, Georgetown University in Washington, D.C. He'd entered the School of Foreign Service there, hoping to become a diplomat or an international businessman, but in the end he'd gone home and become a certified accountant in Santiago.

During four years in Washington he'd became fluent in English, which he tried to demonstrate. But it had been half a century. His pronunciation had decayed and only produced mutual confusion. But in Spanish his native ease helped old memories to the surface. He recalled the names of bars and streets around the Georgetown campus. He remembered climbing earth embankments near the Potomac that had been part of a Nike, an early anti-ballistic missile battery. I had clambered over the same embankments as a teenager, just a few miles from my home.

In the same, easily accessible stack of documents he had a photo of himself lounging in his Georgetown dorm, and another of a snowball fight with some other Cuban students, all of them dressed in natty jackets and ties for this novel experience. Miguel sorted through his sheaf of documents and pulled out the *Directorio de Antiguos Alumnos del Colegio de Dolores.*

The *Directory of Old Alumni* was the last of its kind, published in 1956, with listings and addresses for 3,300 graduates of Dolores reaching back to the founding in 1913. According to its prologue, the booklet had been compiled to satisfy a natural curiosity about Dolores, and "the situation and influence on national life of the alumni who passed through its doors . . . to view, as in a panoramic vista, the works and influence of the college in the national life."

This was of course my own purpose. Here was the control group for Dr. Castro's experiment, brother divided from brother, roommate from roommate, neighbor from neighbor. What was continuous, from that past to this future? And what had ruptured? Everything? Or nothing? Was even this shattering event, the Revolution, incapable of breaking completely from what had come before? Which vanguard was stronger?

Everything had been so neat, before it unraveled. Here was Pepín, his early life summarized in the directory under his proper name:

> *Bou, Leonard José Roberto 1940–47*
> *New Orleans*
> *Chemical Engineer*

Then under *C* were the Castros, their maternal name misspelled, the Ruz turned to Ruiz:

> *Castro Ruiz, Ramón 1939–41*
> *Colono*

That was the eldest, Ramón. *Colono* was an antique term for someone with a large plantation, which is what he would have inherited without his brothers' interference, a position of power. In Cuba, where words had two sides, *colono* was also street slang for a bootlicker, or a flatterer.

Miguel wouldn't even read the next entry under *C.* He looked at it and then handed the booklet back to me. "Here is Uncle Paco," he said. It read:

> *Castro Ruiz, Fidel 1937–42*
> *Abogado*
> *Calle 23 No. 1552 Vedado Habana*

After that was:

> *Castro Ruiz, Raúl 1939–45*
> *Calle 23 No. 1552 Vedado Habana*

The two brothers were living at the same address, in Havana. Fidel, a lawyer, was a candidate for the Cuban Congress in '52, at least until Batista staged his coup. Raúl had no occupation other than shadowing his brother.

There were four Bacardi boys at the school at one time or another, among them:

> *Bacardi, González José Rafael 1945–51*
> *Vista Alegre*

And, of course, my host was listed:

> *Parajon, Miguel M. Llivina*
> *Calle 15 No. 3 Vista Alegre 41216*

That was the same address we were sitting in now. He hadn't moved from his chair.

I asked Miguel what had happened to the boys in the alumni guide, the boys in my photograph. "The first ones to leave, the vanguard, were high-class people," he said. "They were afraid of the confiscations, of the nationalizations of businesses, and industry, and of their land." They often assumed that any privileges and property they lost by departing could be restored by the next government. But there had never been a next government.

"Those who leave the country today come from a different class," Miguel continued, "and are leaving for different reasons. Over forty years, the exodus has continued and even increased sometimes. But those early people had other ambitions."

Not everyone had gone, even if most had. He dug around in his papers and gave me an address in what he called the "Jamaican" neighborhood, down on the flatlands adjacent to the harbor. There was a man there who organized help for the few Dolores alumni who remained in Santiago, making sure they had food and clothing in their old age.

"His name is Segura," Miguel said. "He is older than I am. Jorge Segura. Same years as the Commander."

———

The big house was the main hotel of Santiago, at least symbolically. It was located right on the central plaza, the Parque Céspedes. Built in 1914, its real name was the Casa Granda, and it had a baroque facade that was whitewashed to a blinding purity in the Santiago noon. Babe Ruth and Joe Louis had stayed here, when men wore neckties to breakfast, but now European and Canadian mopes in flip-flops and wife-beaters were packed into the terrace bar, overlooking the square, all day from mid-morning until it closed near midnight. The cans of beer were warm, expensive, and slow to arrive, but there was nowhere else in the city to sit, drink, look at the view, and talk with girls. Or more accurately, to sit, drink, and ignore the girls. The men were Italians, Germans, Dutchmen, Brits and Quebecois, Jamaicans and Bahamians, Americans and Mexicans, but aside from a token effort at saying hello, even those who spoke Spanish didn't bother to talk with their Cuban women. It wasn't about talking. Anyway the women's stories were always too sad or transparently false to earn compassion from the defeated little men who came on vacation here. The men were usually working-class, the kind who took orders at home, and came to Cuba to give them. They counted every dollar and paid for volume, not quality.

Santiago was still the second city of Cuba. The population had more than doubled since 1940, to around 500,000 people, but the city had not expanded, the people being crammed into the same infrastructure or stacked in the efficient apartment towers that were dropped into vacant lots. It was a compact jurisdiction, the Mudejar houses in the center and virtually no suburban sprawl beyond the art nouveau of Vista Alegre. Drive out of Santiago and in just ten minutes you would be looking at it, whole, in the rearview mirror. The laid-back, Caribbean feeling of the city was also intact, but a lot of the isolation had faded. The main highway down the middle of the island was eight lanes wide now, though unpainted, and it was quicker than ever to reach Santiago.

The Big House was at the center of everything, next to the finest old social club, across from the most ancient sites, and overlooking the park, where *jineteras* circulated. The Cubans say, *if you want to eat fish you have to get wet,* and these girls didn't conceal their intentions. Their revealing outfits typically began with absurdly high platform sandals, rose up with a pair of black lycra pants that had windows laddered along the outside of the leg and then summited with an enormous backside, the butt cleavage enhanced and enforced by thong underwear. Spandex tops and huge quantities of crude makeup completed the package. I couldn't stand it. The girls flitted about in the park, intercepting any likely lads headed for the Big House, and the more ambitious ones strolled back and forth in front of the stairs to the hotel, eyed mercilessly by a security guard charged specifically with keeping them out. Any Cuban woman was welcome in the hotel as long as she had a specific foreign man inviting her inside. In a gesture at fairness, Cuban men were actually allowed to enter the terrace with their girlfriends, too, although they were humiliated by having to show the guard that they carried enough U.S. dollars.

There was nothing to do during the afternoon, so I sat in the shade of the balcony like the other men, killing time, drinking bad daiquiris, fending off advances, and watching the *jineteras,* the lucky ones, sit in silence with those they had just met. Descending to the Parque Céspedes, the ancient plaza where the conquistadors had paraded, I sat on a bench and befriended a young braggart who advised me on the superiority of Santiago, although he immediately conceded that he'd never seen anything else. He'd never even been to Havana, he admitted. But there was no reason to go to Havana, for Santiago was better. He explained that Cuba itself was the "greatest country in the world for culture, for education, for advancement, in science and sports. There is no music in the world that is not based on Cuban music. This is the most beautiful country."

He'd been to other countries?

"It doesn't matter," he said. "Everyone knows it is the most beautiful. Christopher Columbus said so."

The plaza was bustling, a crossroads of tourists snapping photographs and young Santiagueros in search of excitement. The benches were nearly full, and couples strolled around the outer edge of the square, knots of girls walked with linked arms, and grinning boys pursued them. Children swerved past the fountain in miniature automobiles, pulled along by parents hauling on a rope. A steady stream of ambitious women—teenage girls, usually in pairs—approached me and made excuses for conversation ("Do you know what time it is?" "What's your name?" "Where are you from?"). Some, assuming I spoke no Spanish, turned to my new friend and asked who I was, and why I was alone. He defended me, which left me time to study the tattoo of a marijuana leaf on his left shoulder, so crude it must have been done with a sewing needle. This was as far as rebellion went in Cuba: smoking dope was one of the only escapes, a way of dropping out mentally, of becoming a passive nonparticipant in the heroics of Cuban history. Unlike imported cocaine, which was vigorously suppressed by the Cuban police, marijuana was grown in Cuba, right in the same mountains where Castro and the guerrillas had fought, and couldn't be eliminated. Weed wasn't exactly tolerated—this fellow had been harassed by the police, he said, just for sporting the tattoo—but you could get away with it. For young people, those who were struggling *en fuego,* living the street life of girls, pimps, and cash, trading sex or whatever they had for a few dollars, marijuana was the least of their problems.

As if on cue, there was a shout, screams, and then a roar of people running. A fight had broken out on the far side of the plaza, and people were rushing toward it, not away. We stood on the benches and watched as a couple of young toughs went at it, throwing punches with their right hands as they used their lefts to grasp and spin each other around. Everyone in the plaza gathered in quickly, and faces lined the balcony of the Big House, but in less than a minute a flying squad of police officers burst through the crowd, ripped the boys apart, and threw them into the back of a van in handcuffs. People applauded the arrest, and then went back to parading through the Parque Céspedes.

"It's not possible to live here," the boy on the bench told me. "We can't survive like this." He detailed the common problems of life—not enough to eat, not enough to drink, not enough real jobs or useful education, too many *comemierdas,* literally shit-eaters, interfering in what was none of their business, and so on. "Even if you work you don't have enough to survive," he explained. "I get paid seven *fulas* a month at my job," he said, using the slang for a U.S. dollar. "I give one to somebody who I owe money. Then I spend one on something to eat. The girls won't pay any attention to you if you don't have money, so you have to invite them for a beer, which costs a dollar up there," he said, pointing to the Big House. "One for you, one for her. Plus something to eat for her. So that's all the money. By the time I get home in the morning, what do I have left for my wife and my baby? Nothing."

He raised his hands, palms out, in disbelief. What could be less fair?

More girls came by. What's your name? *Pepa,* I said. That was what the *jineteras* called all their clients. Where was I from? *Yuma,* the slang for America.

During the next pause the fellow asked me a question I hadn't expected. He wanted to know about the September 11 attacks in America. "We couldn't believe it when we saw it," he said. The TV news in Cuba wasn't always "complete," he explained carefully. Was it all true? Had it really happened like that?

Even Castro had been struck mute, briefly. He'd led tens of thousands of Cubans to the American mission in Havana to present a wreath. Finally, something that could transcend enmity, uniting Cubans with their official enemy.

I told the young man on the bench everything I had seen that day. But such talk was pointless in the Parque Céspedes. The night had come on. The miniature cars went around. The girls continued to stroll past, looking for a way out. *Where are you from? What's your name?*

Pepa Fula de Yuma, I insisted, but the idea was lost in translation. They just couldn't understand me. A foreigner was a rich man. Why come all the way to Cuba if you didn't want to drink beer, make love, and then get something to eat?

Foto Mexicana had taken out advertising in the same Dolores yearbooks that were filled with its own work. The ads listed their address, which I'd found quickly on Enramada, about ten minutes from the school. El Ten Cent was still across the street, with the original Woolworth's sign, but it was empty.

Enramada, one of the oldest streets in Cuba, was still lined on both sides and overhung with commercial signs that predated the Revolution, a thicket of rusty, burned-out 1940s neon and peeling placards with '50s typefaces. In the 1600s the signs had replaced the bower of tree branches that had given the street its original name (literally, "en-branched"). The streets were the oldest things in Santiago, still known by their folk names—Clock Street, Branch Street, Barricade Street. The old Cuban republic and then the Revolution had often slapped new names on them. But people still spoke the original names, the memory of centuries.

Like every business in Cuba, Foto Mexicana was long gone. The address was a hotel school now, where a few rooms were rented to Cubans and the staff were in training to work in tourist hotels, the island's only real industry. The dull yellow building was clean and bustling. Hotel school was a coveted career slot in Cuba, leading to fringe benefits like better food, tips, free shampoo and soap. I knew a man who paid $300 to bribe his son into a hotel school.

From Enramada, it was a couple of blocks to the Colegio de Dolores itself, right on the Plaza Dolores. Its facade was already familiar to me from photographs. As usual in Cuba, the decades had made little impression. It was after 5:00 P.M. when I traipsed up through the plaza and stood in front of the big front door on Clock Street. I rapped twice and felt the door move; it wasn't locked. All was silent. As I was about to peer inside, it opened a crack, and a man, leaning backward in his chair, said, "Can I help you?"

I'd forgotten to prepare a cover story, and so blurted it out: I was interested in the history of the school. Could I see it?

He was a genial man, the kind who rescues Cuba from disaster. He shook his head no, but then he opened the door wider, and I caught a glimpse of the interior, the high ceiling of the entryway, the arched galleries, and the courtyard beyond. Just as it was before? Perhaps. But he wouldn't let me in. I pleaded in a slow, good-natured way, asking just for a peek, making small talk about how far I had come, but it was to no avail.

After he was done rejecting me, I waited. Cubans always have time. He finally said, "Where is your home?"

America, I said, and left the word dangling. He explained that the school, which is what it still was, would be closed during Carnaval. The students would return on Monday, five days from now. Surely I could talk to someone then. Why didn't I try coming back on Monday?

The Plaza Dolores was already quiet, the day winding down. I popped into a bar across Clock Street and brooded over a $1 Cuba Libre, alone with the bartender.

Time cost more money, in a country where credit card transactions were impossible for an American. Downhill on Enramada there was a cash machine, tucked into the entryway of shiny new Communist Party headquarters for Santiago.

A Canadian tourist walked up to the machine, withdrew some American dollars (the only currency available), and then watched in amusement as I tried the same. FUNDS NOT AVAILABLE, the machine said. This electronic enforcement was one of the only effective measures in the fantasy of the U.S. trade embargo, and it wasn't very effective (via the Internet, I soon had a debit card that worked fine in Cuba).

But for today, I was broke. An hour later, I ran into the Canadian at a restaurant. He offered to lend me $400. We walked back up to the Party ATM, and a moment later he handed me the green bills, taking only my promise to repay.

"You need a library card," the guard at the Biblioteca Provincial explained. Santiago's main library was spread through the upper floors of an old commercial building a couple of blocks above the Parque Céspedes, between Saint Faith and Slaughterhouse Streets. I marched up the hill on a hot afternoon to see if the library had, among its vast archives, the old newspaper of Santiago, the *Diario de Cuba*. It was this paper, the voice of Cuba's richest province, that had faithfully recorded the events of life at Dolores in the 1930s and '40s, running photos of school pageants and detailing graduations and victories by the school's baseball team. And it was the *Diario* that had allegedly carried an approving item about the young Fidel's strikebreaking escapades back on the family farm. Several Dolores boys had mentioned the article, but in America, no one carried back copies of this provincial newspaper, not the Library of Congress, the New York Public Library, or the great archival collections of Miami and Tampa universities. I thought I could spend a few days in the Biblioteca Provincial, reading back copies from 1940 and '41. But the guard didn't care what I wanted. "You need a library card or you can't come in," he said. After a few minutes of loitering by the door, I waylaid a library staffer returning from lunch, and she went off with a message. She never returned. Eventually, bored of my pleading, the guard assigned someone to escort me upstairs.

There was a high-ceilinged reading room on the second floor, with yellow light and the sweetly acid smell of fermenting paper. A team of students were assembling huge piles of manila folders, part of a study project on Cuba's economic reforms in the 1970s. A librarian finally appeared to tell me that they would love to help me. My project on reading old newspapers sounded very interesting indeed. Certainly it would be possible to do something, but first I needed a library card. And for that I needed a *responsable.*

Responsable, the Responsible One. A dreaded word in Cuba. Under socialism, everyone had to belong, had to be incorporated within some piece of the system and placed within its chain of responsibilities. You couldn't just get a library card; you had to apply through your *responsable.* This was doubly true for foreigners, who had to "pertain" to some "organism" before they could undertake any kind of official contact in Cuba.

For a decade I had scrupulously avoided having a *responsable.* I had avoided contact with Cuban authorities in all their guises, arriving on tourist visas, and avoiding examination. I flew beneath the radar, switching passports and mumbling my way through immigration as a common tourist. When I overstayed my visa, I played dumb (what visa?). Year after year, I relied on street reporting when possible, and on the rare occasions that official interviews were necessary for some piece of work, I tried to bluff my way in the door, often successfully. Government functionaries in Havana were often less guarded than those in Washington.

I must have been an entry somewhere, in some government file, but shady imprecision, wheedling, and switched-up paperwork had been enough to keep me more or less untraced. I wanted to remain that way, *irresponsable.* But at the library I was up against the need to organize, regulate, categorize, control, channel, and document. There could be no exceptions, not even to read a newspaper.

The librarian suggested that I try making Santiago's official historian of the city into my *responsable.* I walked down past the Parque Céspedes to the address she gave me, where I was refused entry to the building. The guard agreed to send my passport in, and after half an hour in the doorway I was let inside, stepping through a Spanish door into a cool, cobblestone corridor. It was a lovely old building with a small courtyard, built around a fountain. Nothing had been modernized. The doors were old, dark wood, elaborately worked. The courtyard was open to the sky, not roofed with dirty glass and aluminum like so many badly updated buildings in colonial Lima or Bogotá. The ocher walls were interrupted by arches, much like Dolores, that formed shaded galleries. There was a red-tiled roof overhead, higher on the uphill side by an extra floor. Following instructions I went up the open stairway, and as I climbed, a view over the bay opened up, with El Cobre, the Catholic shrine, visible on a hillock more than ten miles away, and then beyond that, the peaks of the Sierra Maestra, pointed and heavily forested. The mountains were either gray-black or flat green, depending on whether they lay beneath cumulus or sunlight.

The historian of the city was out, but her deputy, a jovial, round-bellied intellectual named Omar, had been curious to talk with me. Omar had a secretary, two computers, and a copy machine, in a country where a photo-copier was treated like a loaded gun. He kept an air conditioner blasting to protect the valuable machines, and his secretary was the first woman I had seen in Santiago wearing a sweater.

"Marvelous," Omar said when I explained my interest in 1940s news-papers. "We will help you, of course." The library card could be arranged. And why not interview some of the local historians? He rattled off some names, full of enthusiasm. We agreed, heartily, that the history of Santi-ago—the Jerusalem of the Americas!—had never been properly told. The conquistadors had come here, the great War of Independence had been fought here, and, obviously, Santiago was the *capital moral* of the Revolu-tion. Why, this very building we were sitting in had been the Colegio La Salle, the rival school to Dolores. The Castro brothers had attended La Salle briefly, under the tutelage of the Christian Brothers monks, before trans-ferring up the hill to Dolores and the Jesuits. Doubtless the Commander had been in this very room while a boy!

Of course, Omar said after the requisite pause, this would all have to be coordinated through Havana.

And I would have to find the right *responsable* there, not here. Probably the Casa de Amistad con los Pueblos, the House of Friendship with the Peoples. They ran all bilateral cultural projects of this type. It would only take a few months, he said, until I raised an eyebrow. Then he conceded that getting set up with the House of Friendship could take six months, or more.

And once I had my American university all lined up to sponsor me—what? No university? Then find one!—then the Americans could negoti-ate on my behalf with the House of Friendship, and produce the exchange of letters, in mutually approved language, in triplicate, in English and Spanish, outlining the precise scope of my reading project, the questions I would be researching, and the resources I would be entitled to use while in Cuba. That's all he would need to get started organizing the project here in Santiago.

I knew writers and filmmakers who had charged eagerly into death by enthusiasm, visiting Cuba for years, convinced they were about to get the cooperation they needed and were promised. Most had gotten no further than meetings like this.

On the way out, Omar said he was sure that it would all work out, but I was already regretting showing my face here, or at the library, and soon enough my fears were realized. I'd left him my phone number, and the same afternoon there was a message from him, urging me to CONTACT ANA MARÍA HOUSE OF FRIENDSHIP. The word *URGENTE* was written on the message, underlined twice. I threw the paper away.

For the next three days there were a string of increasingly desperate phone messages. PATRICIO, CALL HOUSE OF FRIENDSHIP OF THE PEOPLES, with a phone number in Havana.

And then, finally, a hand-delivered note, which caught me in the hotel lobby: URGENT MEETING TO DISCUSS YOUR PROJECT WITH ANA MARÍA OF HOUSE OF FRIENDSHIP FRIDAY MY OFFICE 10 A.M. OMAR.

I don't know why, but I actually went to that one. On Friday I climbed back up the stairs at Omar's, the stairs that Fidel, Raúl, and Ramón had climbed. The view was just as good as before.

I arrived a few minutes early, and waited for more than an hour with the sweater-wearing secretary. Some impulse of obedience led me there.

But in the event, neither Omar nor the mysterious *Ana María Amistad Responsable* showed up. After a cold, tense wait, I sprang up and fled, tumbling back down the stairs, leaping the doorway in my eagerness to get out, and then running into the street, like Alberto Casas on one of his jail breaks.

The weekend was starting now, and the heat and the night-long revels of Carnaval had combined to drive the normally quiet daytime streets into utter silence. Nothing moved in Santiago, as if the city were caught between breaths. Even before I reached the door at Dolores I could hear the sound of someone screaming inside.

"WHAAAAA-HEEEEEEYAAAAAA!!!"

The same porter was inside the door, watching a kung fu movie. The TV set was propped on a chair in the middle of the foyer, with two antennas poking up. The black power cord ran off across the floor, hooked to a series of extension cords that covered the forty feet to a plug. Two women were with him. They were so caught up in the movie that they didn't notice me standing in the doorway for more than a minute.

"Hello, friend," the guard said, and went back to watching the movie. Progress.

After a while there was a break, and one of those commercials for cell phones that had begun appearing on Cuban television. Gorgeous young people strolled in the streets of Havana, pausing to make phone calls to other stunning kids. The advertising could be aimed only at the new class of foreign businessmen who oversaw the tourism economy.

The porter didn't object when I stepped inside and watched the next segment of kung fu with him. I introduced myself to his lady friends— neighbors who had just stopped by, in the way that Cubans could spend hours of every day just stopping by. He nodded when I asked if I could see the small room off the entrance—a narrow, cool space with a high ceiling, which had been converted into a minuscule museum dedicated to his time at the school. The room held a dozen black and white photos from the early 1940s, enlarged almost to incoherence, and showing the cracks and rips of the badly treated originals. Mounted around the room were shots of boys in their uniforms or casual clothes.

They showed the boys moving freely through the dining hall, assembling for band practice, and studying. It was possible to pick out him himself in one, only because the caption pointed the way:

Fidel Castro, 5th grade. 2nd of Bachillerato 1937–1942

"Second of Bachillerato" referred to the highest class offered, the baccalaureate course needed to move on to the university. Younger brother Raúl was also pointed out ("1939–45"), but as usual the oldest brother, Ramón, didn't exist. During the first year of the Revolution, Ramón had criticized Fidel in a newspaper article, and since then has lived in comfortable isolation on a tobacco farm in western Cuba. He is occasionally made available to sympathetic biographers of Fidel, but otherwise lives under the cloak that Fidel has thrown over his entire family life.

The photo captions mentioned only one other boy from Dolores: Renato Guitart ("b. 1931–d. 1953"), who died during the Moncada assault on July 26, 1953, which according to the official chronometer of the Cuban Revolution, was Day One. The whole government and party apparatus took its name ("The Revolutionary 26th of July Movement") from that day.

There were different Castro quotes on the walls, enlarged placards that spoke of the importance of schooling, but only in the vaguest terms. ("It is education that converts a living being into a human being. It is education that can empty the jails. I'm an optimist, I believe that ideals prevail over force.") Fidel virtually never talked about Dolores; in his millions of recorded words, there were no genuinely insightful remarks about himself, his origins, his background, or his influences. He acknowledged no influences. He was apart from history, unique in Cuba, self-created, without origins. In his interview decades ago with the Brazilian theologian Frei Betto, Castro had barely conceded that Christian education had affected him at all, and then changed the subject.

It took only a minute to survey this room in detail. Then the guard said, again, that I could not enter the rest of the school, but when he stepped off for something I began touring it anyway. The walls were cracked and the paint dingy, which was normal for Cuba, even before the Revolution. But I could see slogans that had not graced Dolores in the old days: IT IS ALWAYS THE 26TH, one said. And, somewhat defensively, I'M STAYING HERE. Another was rubbed to incoherence: A RE OLU ION WITHOU DANG R IS N T A EVO UTION.

Earlier in the year, Fidel had returned to his hometown, Bíran, to attend the opening of a photo exhibit in a local sugar mill. As usual, Fidel missed the opportunity to reflect on his upbringing. Speaking to an assembly of the students, he said only that "If there's one thing I could reproach myself for, like a pang of regret, it's not having studied much more than I did throughout my life."

This was comedy. Even Castro's worst enemies conceded that he had never, in his whole life, given up his drive to learn, work, and achieve. It was literally impossible to study more than he did. The young Castro had been a tireless polymath, who exceeded in virtually every class and activity. He embodied the Jesuit ideal of relentless effort. He had a phenomenal memory, which was often described as photographic, but which was really the fruit of disciplined application. As a student, Fidel wasted no time: he rose early, worked hard all day, converted even baseball and basketball games into mental training regimens, and stayed up late reading. His curiosity was all-encompassing; he absorbed arcane material quickly, hungry for all forms of mastery and knowledge. Once in power, his own work habits—staying up all night reading reports and then quoting them verbatim at meetings the next day—stood in sharp contrast to the paper shuffling and inertia of the socialist state. Decades of economic disasters have led to many rueful jokes in Cuba (the national motto is said to be "They pretend to pay us, we pretend to work"). The saddest of these comments was the commonplace observation that there was only one man left in Cuba who actually did any work at all. Into his late seventies, Castro was still giving five-hour speeches that regurgitated columns of figures, and even on his hospital bed in 2007 he was photographed reading reports.

By now I had been in the school for half an hour. The kung fu movie was still going, and I asked if I could use the bathroom before leaving. The guard wasn't allowed to let anyone in, he explained.

"I will be quick," I said.

The bathroom was broken anyway, he said. The toilets didn't work.

"I just need a urinal."

He couldn't take me to it.

"I can find it," I said.

He gave in. It was up one flight of stairs, in the back. Use the stairs on the left, he said. And forgive him for the condition of the toilets.

I took the stairs up the right, two at a time before he could stop me. Up on the second floor I began to walk as slowly as possible. All the doors were locked, but I pressed my eye to the cracks between two doors; the room inside was stripped of the old dark wood cabinets that had held the little Birds of Cuba museum. The walls were devoid even of posters, and cheap iron chairs with built-in writing surfaces were packed one against the next, more than forty per room. A chaos of bookcases was pressed against the wall in the back.

The toilets were indescribable. They didn't seem to have worked in years and were jammed with trash and, improbably, several tall boards. I clambered over junk and used a trench urinal in the back.

I came down again, slowly, on the opposite staircase, walking around the patio, counting off the arches. The basketball hoop was still in the same place as some sixty years before. The guard was nowhere in sight, and the two women didn't even look up. I snapped five frames with a camera, putting myself in the same spot as the Foto Mexicana technician in 1941. I just had time to hide the camera.

"There was another fellow here," the guard said, coming back. "About six months ago. A man came, asking the same questions as you do."

He held out a business card, which he had kept in his desk drawer. It read:

Bernardo Souto
Formica Española

with an address in Spain. The porter said he was someone from "before," who had returned to see the school. He'd wandered around, looking, and had left the card. I started to copy down the information, but he gave me the card itself, and then urged me to come visit him again, soon.

Across the street, the same bar was open. It was only five o'clock, and two young couples sat at opposite ends of the room, each pair absorbed in courtship. The bartender shook his head at me, smiling. He couldn't serve me. "It is workers' night." Once a month the bar was required to open itself only to Cuban workers. The prices were changed, and instead of dollars they accepted only coupons, earned at their jobs.

The closer couple broke off lovemaking. "I have a ticket," the young man said. He held it up. Here was another new experience: no Cuban had ever bought me a drink. But I declined. I could drink at the Big House, or a dozen other dollar bars. But he would not see that ticket again for a month.

He apologized, and the bartender apologized, and then the woman apologized, but I found it all delightful. *"Es justo,"* I kept replying to their apologies. *"Es justo."*

Jorge Segura, same years as the Commander, was nervous when I telephoned. He stalled for a while, but I stalled more, and he finally agreed to meet me the next morning, at ten, before it grew too hot. His house was in the low western part of the city, a district of ancient streets and two-story Mudejar houses. By Santiago standards, the architecture was interesting, with a touch of the colonial flavor of Old Havana. But Old Havana had been squared up and repainted with UNESCO money, reborn as Old Havanaland. Segura's neighborhood hadn't received even a whitewash. On the far side of a gritty avenue from the Parque Céspedes, it was a dusty, neglected monotone of cracked plaster and paint that had regressed to some painterly mean, off-white diluted with ocher.

Segura's neighborhood was wrapped around a tiny plaza where a truly ancient tree shaded a swing set and the entrance to Trinity Church. The streets were empty at mid-morning, except for a group of grimly competitive boys playing stickball in the street, using a broomstick, cut short, and a ball made of three plastic bottle caps wrapped in tape. They were quiet, determined, as if some feud were being settled. Every batter nailed almost every pitch of the *fufa,* but the art was in advancing through the bases (a light post, a building corner, and a storm sewer) with complete insouciance. They walked, never ran, moving as slowly as possible, teasing their way to each base, holding up their foot until a fraction of a second before the throw came in. Although they were playing at the intersection of two streets, they were not interrupted by a car more than once an inning.

Up a block, I found one side of the road filled with blackened pieces of a truck engine, all laid out in two parallel lines. Behind them was a soot-blackened Soviet truck, on blocks, with no wheels. The hood was thrown open, a dark mouth without teeth. Lying on the dusty street were both halves of the engine block, six pistons, the manifold and exhaust, the radiator, the starter coil, and the ignition module. It looked like a warning to other cars: turn back! A lean mulatto man, stained darker by grease, was patiently wiping the cylinders with a rag.

It will run again?

Of course, he said.

As I circled blocks, looking for the address, a clutch of women on a stoop called out various proposals. "Come here, handsome!" the oldest one said. And then a younger one: "Don't you need a wife back home?" They giggled into their hands.

There was a plaque on one house, marking the spot where a revolutionary had been killed while fleeing the Moncada attack in 1953. The survivors of the rout that morning had fled into the back streets around lower Santiago, going in all directions, to all fates. Fidel and Raúl had threaded their way to safety on foot. Three of the fugitives had taken shelter in Dolores itself, which was as empty during Carnaval then as it was now. A Jesuit had negotiated their surrender. Others had run to the houses of friends, like this fellow, who had been betrayed in his hideout and murdered during a sudden police raid. Like all frightened bullies, the Batista police were ruthless in revenge.

The army, the police, and the notorious SIM (a hybrid of military men, criminals, and secret police) were all hunting for Castro. If he were captured, he could be tortured or simply gunned down. The Castro family was eager to prevent this, of course, and Fidel's older brother, Ramón, was sent to see various connections around town. Here Fidel's time among the elite served him well: Dolores was thick with families connected to the Church, the political power structure, the Masonic Lodges of Santiago, even the police. Ramón enlisted the Padre Rector of Dolores, who hustled through Santiago, urging the authorities to issue explicit instructions to take Castro alive.

There is some evidence this strategy actually worked. Castro was eventually surprised and captured by an army patrol in the hills. The soldiers were typical of the Cuban army Fidel would face years later: mostly black, overwhelmingly poor, illiterate, and distrustful of Cuba's white ruling class. Fidel was not their liberator, but part of this enemy class. When Castro and the other Moncada survivors surrendered, the government soldiers weren't inclined to accept it. "They are whites!" someone shouted. "Kill them!"

But their officer, Yañes Pelletier—himself black—ordered his men not to fire. He had heard from someone, who had heard from someone, who had heard from someone in Santiago. Fidel Castro Ruz was wanted alive. There would be no memorial plaques for the Castro brothers.

Segura's house turned out to be a modest little Spanish colonial thing on the street beside Trinity Church. It was a single story, attached on both sides to similar houses. Painted a dull ocher, it had wooden louvers on the tall widows, with an iron security grate welded on. A man in his forties answered the door, waved me inside, and said, "My father will be right with you." As soon as I was inside Segura himself appeared, in pajamas. He was seventy-four years old, small, wizened, and slow-moving, but with a lively face, his mind and voice both clear. He pointed me to an iron patio chair in the tiny living room. He had glasses, and hair that was a thorny mixture of gray, white, and black. He made cautious small talk, smiling insincerely. I mentioned Lundy Aguilar and a few other names from Dolores.

"Lundy," Jorge Segura said. "Let's see." Just like Miguel Llirina, he twisted back into his armchair, and reaching behind with a slightly trembling hand, plucked a sheaf of loose documents off a bookshelf. He put the yellow papers and soft manila folders on his lap, sifted through them, and plucked out his Dolores yearbook. It was brown with age. He hadn't even needed to stand to reach it.

He couldn't find Lundy's picture, though. Lundy (and Fidel) were finishing up at the University of Havana by the time Segura graduated from Dolores. Still, they had overlapped for some years, and Segura had always been a tracker of Dolores graduates, then and now. He knew Lundy's later career as an academic, his work writing for newspapers, and that he was living in Miami. Segura was up-to-date on all the old days, slipping me the phone number of Father Dorta-Duque, the Jesuit I'd already sat with during the reunion in Miami. Pepín Bou, looking away from Cuba, had not mentioned Jorge Segura. But Jorge knew all about Pepín Bou. He'd even worked with Pepín at the Moa Bay Mining Company for two years. He was in the headquarters building, doing accounting, while Pepín, a chemical engineer, was out on the refinery site. The two years at Moa Bay were the ones leading up to the nationalization of the plant, Segura explained. They had been through so much together, they were friends. He couldn't find Pepín's picture.

He was only too happy to look back. The student body at Dolores, he recalled, was very intimate, a small and closed society that did not particularly form into groups, bands, or cliques. The students imbibed the sober and timeless culture of the church, and the general rule was one of eager conformism. Not all the families were rich, Segura noted; there were "normal" people as well. He counted his own family as one of the normals: they owned a small store with "only a few things for sale." The "highest" families in the school were the Bacardis and the Macaderos. "There were 238 students during the 1940s. All were white. I remember one Negro, only. Everyone was Spanish. We went to the beach, to dances sometimes.

"I never liked geography. I studied the history of Cuba. Literature. Social studies. We had a lot of masses. A religious life, with moral and civic instruction. How to act as a citizen in Cuba. We never had contact with the other Jesuit schools. My favorite activity was basketball. You know José Antonio Roca? We played on the same team, he was the forward, our star."

He free-associated for a while, an old man's memories of Cuba. "After the harvest, there was three months of poverty, there was no work. I made few visits to the countryside during the 1940s. We went to Bañes," the town near where Fidel Castro grew up. "There were two sides to that place, one for Americans, one for Cubans. There was a central, shared part also, but the Americans had their own colony. There were differences. That sat badly with people. But before the Revolution, that area was very tranquil. In the 1940s the pressure for revolution was very low. Agriculture was the main business of Oriente. Since the price of sugar was guaranteed in that era, everything was stable. I saw a lot of Americans in the streets, on the weekends. Many came. Sometimes they passed me in the street, but they never said anything."

As he talked his eyes ran over papers and then a photograph. "That's Piñon, who fell recently," he said, pointing at one in a group of faces.

After the Revolution, Segura the accountant had became Segura the professor of accounting. Although he was mostly retired, he still held a professorship at the University of Oriente. These days he was usually at home, and rarely out of his bathrobe or pajamas. He was typically found right here in this pale green room, with its neatly kept glass tabletops. The walls were decorated with an accumulation of middle-class signifiers: a map of Spain, landscape paintings. The small space was filled with a matching set of Danish Modern lounge chairs and love seat. All the pieces were carefully covered in white cloth, to extend their years. On the table, there was an old photograph of a woman, her hair bobbed in a 1950s style. It was a black and white picture, but hand-tinted in the weak pastels that signified dress (green) and flesh (pink). It was in a nice frame. Segura called out for tea, and five minutes later the woman in the picture walked into the room with a tray.

Segura had been at Dolores from 1936 to 1946. He'd spent five years in Fidel's company, but they hadn't been close. Even then, he had had an accountant's temperament. Small, slight, modest, he didn't mix well with the overweening force of Fidel's personality. He remembered sitting near Raúl in classes.

"The only thing I can tell you," Segura said, "is the story of how he jumped from the third floor with an umbrella." It began when Fidel had idly suggested that an umbrella could serve as an emergency parachute. Other boys jeered at the notion. Fidel had insisted. Soon there was a dare, and by the end of the school day everyone knew that Fidel was going to jump off the third-floor gallery with only an umbrella.

He had to prove he was right. With everyone watching, he climbed over the third-floor railing and jumped. What happened?

"Nothing," Segura said. "He landed fine." He lowered his voice another notch, to a whisper. "What a shame he didn't crack his head."

A lot of people remembered this same story. Sometimes it was a bedsheet, not an umbrella. From hearing it repeatedly, I'd collated a few mitigating details. Fidel had planned his stunt. He scouted the best spot on the uphill side of the building, where the ground floor rose up, ten feet closer to his launch point. And he had lowered himself over the railing first, dangling down into the courtyard from the bottom rung—cutting another five feet off the drop. Then he had jumped with the open umbrella (or was it the sheet?), which could indeed slow the fall of a twelve-year-old boy, slightly.

That was how you did the impossible. You dogged the problem, worried it, wore it down at the edges, improvised your tools, cut it into smaller, achievable tasks, and then, having made the odds ten feet shorter on one end and five feet shorter on the other, you took a giant leap. If you landed right—more important, if you *acted like you landed right*—then no matter how much it hurt at the time, forever after people would believe that you did it, that you could do the impossible. That you could fly with your umbrella down from the third floor and *no that wasn't a crash that was victory*. That you could run your invasion fleet aground in a swamp, lose all but twelve of your men in ambushes, and then announce *having invaded successfully we are now marching on the capital*.

Segura also overlapped with him at the University of Havana for a few years, but they weren't friends there either. Fidel's life was changing quickly as he stepped onto a larger stage. While Segura was quietly studying accounting, Fidel was cutting a big figure on the campus. Partly it was a change in family fortunes. Angel Castro was getting more and more land of his own, and rented out a larger and larger army of *macheteros*. He made sure that while his oldest son learned the business, his boldest son had everything a young tyro could want in Havana. That meant new American cars and an allowance of thousands of dollars in cash.

Fidel cared so little about money that he often blew through even this fortune, using it to fund his allies in campus politics. The University of Havana was seething with ideological conflict in the late 1940s. Campus factions were allied with the country's political parties, and Fidel tried to push his way to the top of this system, joining an offshoot of the Ortodoxo party during a particularly violent period on campus. The Ortodoxo students were little more than a gang: one prominent student leader who opposed them was assassinated at this time, and in retrospect many discontented Cubans have tried to blame Fidel for the murder. There is no evidence, except the certainty that Fidel did carry a pistol during this period, tucked inside the jacket of his fancy suits. José Antonio Roca had recalled running into Fidel then, on the long steps that cascade down from the university onto the streets of Vedado. Standing together, Roca and Fidel had fallen into an old-friends chat. But Castro insisted on moving to put his back against a wall during the conversation, maneuvering Roca like a shield. As explanation, Castro simply flashed the pistol in his belt. He certainly had to protect himself from armed enemies at the school; whether he participated in shootings himself is speculation. Roca had thought only that Fidel was out of his head. He left quickly and avoided Castro for a while.

As the Jesuits intended, a couple of their students would grow up to lead Cuba, just not in the direction anyone predicted. Aside from Fidel and Raúl, virtually no *Dolorinos* still held positions of significance in Cuba. One exception—the only exception I could find—was Fernando Vecino Alegret, from the class of 1954. He'd been much too young to know Fidel personally, but had served in the Sierra Maestra as a guerrilla fighter and, uniquely, still served at Fidel's side. Alegret had become head of secondary education in Cuba, a post he used to ensure that there were never again schools like Dolores. He was recently promoted to education minister.

"He forgot everything he learned at Dolores," Segura said.

With the louvers closed against the rising heat of the sun, Segura sat in the dark talking of all this in alternating bursts of enthusiasm and hesitance. Although he lowered his voice when talking about him, this was done out of habit. He was old enough, he said, not to worry about any consequences. He hesitated only because he found it depressing to think about how different the world had been back then, how much Cuba and Cubans had changed.

When Segura spoke of change, he made references to "them," and pointed outside, at the people in the neighborhood. Black people. After the Revolution people like him began to leave Cuba and people like "them" had moved in. He rubbed two fingers over his wrist, to make sure I understood. He referred to them as "people down from the hills."

The novelist Pedro Juan Gutiérrez had one of his white narrators relate this urban alienation among commingled races and generations. "The neighborhood was no longer what it used to be," the novel's despicable protagonist complained:

> It filled up with common people from the provinces, uncouth blacks, ragged, dirty, rude people. The buildings crumbled since no one took care of them, and little by little, they became dormitories, thousands of people crowded into them like roaches, skinny, underfed, dirty, unemployed people, drinking rum at all hours, smoking marijuana, beating on drums, and multiplying like rabbits, people without perspective, with limited horizons. Everything made them laugh. What were they laughing at—everything. Nobody was sad or wanted to kill themselves or was terrified for fear the ruins would collapse and bury them alive. Not at all. In the middle of the debacle, they laughed, lived their lives, tried to enjoy themselves as best they could. . . . Born in the ruins, they just kept trying not to give up or let themselves be beaten so severely that at last they were forced to surrender. Anything was possible, everything allowed, except defeat.

Segura wasn't a loathsome racist out of *Dirty Havana Trilogy*, but a decent man carrying obsolete resentments. The world had changed too fast for people like him.

He put the book away, depressed. He leaned forward and lowered his voice. "It's all a disaster," he said. "Look at this place."

"They have announced fish for Monday," Segura added. He pulled out his *libreta*. Like most Cubans, he carried it on his person at all times, even when he was wearing pajamas. The *libreta* was the ration book. He showed me the ration for one person for one month: six pounds of rice, one pound of salt, twenty ounces of "grains," four pounds of raw sugar, one pound of refined sugar, and two liters of oil.

All this added up to 65 percent of a Cuban's nutritional needs. (Even this low figure, produced by the Cubans themselves, was called "very optimistic" by a specialist based in Cuba, Miriam Uriarte of the University of Massachusetts.) There was always something missing, usually several things a month that weren't delivered, just as there were unexpected supplements from time to time, especially for the elderly and children. Macaroni, beans, and "soy protein substitute" might appear, written into the bottom of the *libreta*. But for every extra there were two shortages. Few quotas were met, except sugar. Five pounds a month per person. A pair of plastic tubs, a little tubing, some yeast, and a couple of weeks of patience converted the sugar into *aguardiente*. There was a monthly ration of genuine rum, only enough to fill a single beer bottle. (You had to supply the beer bottle yourself.) The country was brimming with heroic bootleggers, who kept people laughing, who filled the void of ideas and hope, who let Cuba not give up.

Meanwhile there was dried mullet, or would be. Small and oily, salted and reeking, it was a rare source of protein and the only bounty of the sea that came through government hands. Cuba caught loads of other fish, which were frozen and shipped abroad for cash; the lobster harvest was particularly lucrative, but those also went abroad or into tourist hotels. The lobsters were so valuable as hard currency that mere possession of shellfish was a serious crime, yet there was a discreet black market in crustaceans, and old men whispered *lobster lobster* like pimps. You paid them up front. The crustacean would be delivered separately, like a drug deal.

They didn't announce a thing until they were sure it was coming, so the little blue mullets on the ration would likely arrive, eventually. "In August," Segura said by way of example, "we should get the May soap." Like everyone, he kept an eye on what was available outside the system. He found the food at the few, small farmer's markets to be always too expensive for him, except for the mangoes, which cost a peso apiece, and the occasional egg, at two pesos. There were government stores that sold pants for $11 a pair, but he couldn't afford that, and had to wait for his annual ration of clothing—pants, shirt, shoes—even though it really only came every eighteen months or so.

Better to shop at the *candongas*, he said. Cuban soldiers who served in

Angola in the 1980s had brought the word and the concept home with them. Based on the traditional practice of African market women, who laid out their goods anew each morning, *candongas* were tiny venues for selling your own possessions. They were usually just a row of heavily used personal goods—combs, broken watches, shoes, a radio, maybe a shirt or a pair of pants—and they had to be laid out on a cot to bypass the rules against having a business. This is why Cuban men and women could be found walking into the center of town in the early mornings, carrying old army cots, or even folding lawn chairs. They would set up in shaded doorways and then lay out candy, clothing, the carefully cleaned parts of disassembled tools of unknown vintage, and wait all day for a sale. It was government policy to have everyone shop in government stores; the *candongas* only existed because of their association with the Angola veterans, who were given a wide berth by the authorities.

"Fish for Monday," Segura repeated. "It's a disaster. If you don't have dollars, you can't have soap, toothpaste, pork." He continued, muttering a list of ordinary desirables. "The whole world needs everything here. Laundry soap, bath soap, toothpaste, shoes."

He got help from the men he called "the Miami brothers"—exiled alumni from Dolores who remembered their old comrades in Cuba. They sent small shipments of goods a couple of times a year, through the Catholic Church. As an accountant, Jorge was selected to administer a little system for distributing these goods among the remaining alumni. It was a private ration system with its own version of the *libreta*. Segura had taken a blank, hard-backed notebook and divided the pages into precisely ruled columns and rows. Names ran down the left side, a dozen men from the scattered decades of the school's existence. The goods were listed across the top: *Bath soap,* it read in Jorge's rotund, Palmer Method cursive, then *laundry soap toothpaste cooking oil pants shoes socks jackets.*

Jorge whipped out a couple of photos of some Dolores alumni from Miami who had made a visit to Santiago a few years ago. In Miami you could curse and condemn Castro and all his works, and you could listen all day to voices on the radio demanding tougher restrictions on Cuba, less travel and trade. But if you went to the airport in Miami, or Cancún, or Nassau, and boarded a flight to Havana, you would find yourself in the abashed company of Cuban exiles. More than a hundred thousand Cuban-Americans returned to the island every year, and they knew enough to keep quiet on both sides of the Straits. In Cuba, they kept quiet about their politics. And once back in Miami, they kept quiet about having been on the island. Over the years, some of the loudest advocates of cutting off all travel to Cuba had themselves been caught at Miami International returning from visits with their families.

There was always one explanation for why this was not the hypocrisy it seemed: it was an emergency. Cubans from the United States were allowed to return to the island only for "humanitarian emergencies" involving their families. But in Cuba, where temporary was permanent, life was one long emergency.

I told Segura that I would be coming back someday, and drew up my notebooks and the photocopies. Jorge was agitated. He mentioned the surgery he'd had recently, for a urinary problem. Antibiotics were so rare in Cuba that they were often stolen. Poorly equipped hospitals would issue only a single pill at a time—one per patient per day. A man like Jorge, who could have taken his two-week course of antibiotics at home, was instead forced to stay in the hospital for fourteen extra days, waiting for the daily pill.

His recovery was difficult. He spoke haltingly. It was hard, he said, to get . . . the things people needed in such situations . . . virtually impossible . . . to get . . . well . . . "things like _____," he finally said.

Like what?

"_____," he said again, embarrassed. I wrote the word down. I understand, I told him. I will remember.

"*Y una copia de* Baseball Weekly," he added before I could put my pen away. This was his favorite American magazine. He was a Giants fan, and always had been. He'd been following their ups and downs in *Baseball Weekly* since he was a kid. He rattled off the names of a few players. The great _____. The name meant nothing to me. What about _____? I had never heard of him either. How could I not know _____? And _____? They were the greatest Giants players ever!

"And razors," he said, when I tried to cap my pen.

Later, when I'd left the house, and then Santiago, and Cuba, I looked the mystery word up. *Pañales. Diapers.* So, he needed adult diapers to deal with the incontinence that follows urinary tract surgery. No wonder he was reluctant to discuss it.

I did come back to see Segura, after six months. I stopped by the house again, chatted some more, and presented him with a bag of disposable razors, which thrilled him, and an economy-sized bale of forty-eight "super-absorbent" adult incontinence diapers, size medium, which I had bought at a Kmart in New York. I'd carried them through Manhattan, Miami, Nassau, Havana, and then the streets of Santiago. I'd double-bagged them to save myself explanations.

Segura looked confused when I handed them over. I struggled to translate the phrase on the package, *Pañales de . . . de . . . de adultos.*

Diapers? He'd never asked for them. He had no idea what I was talking about. What would he want diapers for? We stared at each other, slack-jawed in mutual incomprehension.

Had I misunderstood him, or heard the wrong word? Or not caught the point of a story? Or was it about someone else? Had it been an earlier problem that had passed? Had he changed his story? Was he too embarrassed to admit he'd needed a diaper? A few strokes of a pen could produce more confusion than comfort.

I left the bale of super-absorbency on the floor of his house, one of those things that fell into the cracks between here and there. Since nothing was wasted in Cuba, the diapers would move, through the ration system in his ledger, or the black market, or to friends of friends, to someone somewhere who needed them.

The magazine was also a flop. *Baseball Weekly* had ceased publication. I had brought Segura a couple of similar magazines, but they were flimsy fanzines, full of steroid-enhanced players whose names he didn't recognize, and cluttered with marketing ploys. Even some of the team names were different.

"Who are the Devil Rays?" he asked me.

Because it is so hilly, Santiago lacks the long, double-humped buses known as *camelos* that are a signature of Cuban life elsewhere. They had been introduced in Santiago in the 1990s, but always burned out their transmissions on the steep hills. In Santiago the best transport was the back of a truck, or a three-wheeled delivery van spitting smoke, or even horse carts, which could carry a dozen people along in the flatter sections of the city. Those with money could catch a yellow plastic *trimoto,* a motorcycle rickshaw. Only tourists could afford the official taxis stashed around the city, but anyone could negotiate a black market cab. Men were usually standing around in the Plaza Dolores and other parks, offering rides.

Looking to kill my Sunday, I hired a fellow to take me to a beach resort down the coast that had scuba diving. He had a filthy Lada, parked discreetly around the corner from Dolores. He told me to lie down in the back seat as we drove out of the city ("Police," he explained). In fifteen minutes we were in farm fields. There was a checkpoint ahead, and the driver veered off the asphalt road, cut down a farm track, made a left at a hut, and drove for half an hour down an increasingly sandy wagon track, until he realized he was lost. A cowboy gave directions, and we cut through a field, around trees, into a riverbed, and came back out on the asphalt road. A mile later the engine died. Using a nail file from my hotel toiletries, the driver filed some grime off the points in the distributor, and the Lada started right up. We drove on, past twenty miles of black sand beaches, to the resort. Like all such hotels, it was a joint venture between the Cubans and foreigners. It had hundreds of rooms, mostly empty, and sweeping views of the coast and the mist-fringed mountains of the Sierra Maestra.

The driver was not allowed to turn into the hotel entrance. I arranged for him to come back after nightfall and then ate a dismal buffet lunch beside the pool with about eighty French people. In the afternoon I joined a dive on a nearby reef, the boat full of agreeable young Europeans on package tours. They had seen little or nothing beyond the resort. One couple had visited Cuba seven times without setting foot in a major city. At the resorts drinks and food were included in the modest weekly price; going anywhere else was losing money.

By 9:00 P.M. I was back in Santiago. There were no black market cabs at the Hotel Santiago, because it stood alone in a sea of crabgrass, too far from busy streets. Instead, the hotel offered a bank of shiny government Mitsubishis. I climbed into the first and mentioned a *paladar* that I had heard about—The Hen, or something like that—and the driver told me he knew it. It wasn't far from the Cathedral. He hit a button on the taxi meter, turned up the air-conditioning, adjusted the radio, rolled up the windows, inquired after my comfort, and we set off.

In Havana, there were dozens of *paladares* sprinkled through the various neighborhoods, but you would rarely find the same place twice, because any given restaurant tended to last only a year or eighteen months before

being shut down. They might be closed for violating the onerous tax regulations, or for seating too many people, or because the owners had used
their profits to flee the country, or because they were ratted out by jealous
neighbors, infuriated at the sight of someone else getting ahead, buying
TVs and clothes, raising fat children, while they themselves lived on the
libreta. But in the end, no matter how many were shut down, there were
always more *paladares* in the capital. Santiago was different: there were only
two legal private restaurants in the city. Havana people always cautioned
that Santiago was *muy revolucionario*, meaning that the second city took its
communism seriously. Central planning was rigidly enforced, capitalism
ruthlessly suppressed, pleasure outlawed. There was no resident population of foreigners to justify the many restaurants of the capital: aside from
the spectacle of prosti-tourism at the Big House, *orientales* were rarely
confronted by the sight of others eating well. *Muy revolucionario* turned
out to mean nothing to eat.

To make time, I asked the cabdriver a simple question: How are things?

"Well, that depends on where you ask the question from," he said. "It's
difficult." He complained about food prices, so I pointed out that there
was more meat for sale than a few years ago.

"Yes," he said, cautiously. "There is a little more. But it's expensive. The
salary for a Cuban . . . well, let's say it's 140 or 150 pesos. You have to buy
food at the farmer's markets, because there is not enough on the ration. If
you want *macho*," he said, using Oriente slang for pork, "you have to buy
it at the markets. And a family needs protein. A family can eat a kilo of
macho in no time. That's not much. But a kilo costs . . . well, it's sold by
the pound, but, two pounds to the kilo . . . well, it's 2.2 pounds to the kilo,
but two pounds costs 40 pesos."

I did the math as best I could. That meant spending about ten days of
your total income for 2.2 pounds of pork?

"Yes."

In the old center of town, where the streets narrowed, we came up
behind a dump truck. It was a big, rotten old beast of a truck, bent, battered, and painted red in the places that showed beneath soot or oil. It sat
there on bald tires, impassive, comfortably squatting across the entire lane
from curb to curb. A dozen men were milling around it, their hands and
arms black with grease, their clothes oily. The taxi driver blew his horn, as

did the driver behind us. There was a lot of shouting, orders were issued, boys stopped to watch, some of the men got on the truck, and then after several minutes a man came out, carrying in one palm a piece of a machine, no bigger than a box of matches. He put it on the truck, climbed up himself, the remaining men all climbed into the bed with him, the engine fired up, the stovepipe behind the cab emitted a great dragon puff of black smoke, and with a grinding of gears it, and then we, began to move.

"I was working for a couple from Curaçao yesterday," the driver said. "You know Curaçao?"

All I knew about Curaçao was that three de Jongh boys at Dolores were descended from a Curaçao family. No, I told him, I didn't know Curaçao personally.

"It's an island," he said. "Anyway, the man told me how his grandparents used to dream about Cuba. They thought Cuba was rich. And it's true, before 1959 Cuba had the highest per capita income in the Caribbean, if not in Latin America. Well, the guy told me that when he was a kid, Curaçao was so poor that people used to dream about coming to Cuba to cut sugarcane for 50 cents a day. Now, he said, it's the Cubans who dream about going to Curaçao to cut sugarcane for 50 cents a day." He looked at me in the mirror. "He was joking, you know. They don't have any sugarcane in Curaçao. But it's true." He drove on for a block. "But Fidel Castro"—the driver actually used the name—"doesn't care about that. Everything has gone wrong. Nothing ever changes. It's like the devil came to this island."

The fare was $2.25, all of which went to the government, because it was an official taxi. I gave him $3, and he thanked me, profusely. He was well dressed, in his early thirties, and had one of the best jobs around. All he had to do was tell a sob story to a foreigner and he could make 75 cents without cutting any sugarcane at all.

The *paladar* had no sign. There were thirty-two people packed around five tables. This was a violation of the law against serving more than twelve customers, but at $7 a plate, the margin was irresistible. And if you gave enough meals to the right people, you wouldn't get in trouble. I'd shared a table at a *paladar* once with the local beat cops, who were eating themselves silly.

It took an hour to get seated. This time I shared my table with a Danish woman and her Mexican boyfriend. The Mexican was depressed. In

Mexico City, he said, when you mentioned Cuba, people began talking about the enormous dignity of the Revolution, about justice, equality, and progress. It was the same in Copenhagen, where he owned a Mexican restaurant. But now he'd seen Cuba. "There is nothing here," he said, speaking quietly, in a kind of shock. Nothing at all. *No hay nada,* he said over and over, almost whispering. "I always thought it was the land of progress," he added. "But this makes Mexico look like a rich country."

We were given menus, but then the owner came out of the kitchen and explained that she had neither pork nor fish nor beef. Just chicken. With rice. We ordered chicken with rice, and beer, and waited.

When it came, the Mexican couldn't believe the food. The Dane barely touched hers. But I have a stomach like a Bedouin dog and gnawed it down to the bone.

"Most of those people went to the States," Miguel Llivina told me, during a second visit to his wire-reinforced house in Vista Alegre. He was going through the pages of his old yearbook. Photographs kept prompting memories, and he spoke like a medium at a séance, reciting slowly as the visions came. "Fernando Alvarez," he said at one point. "He lives in Virginia. He inspects chickens. To see if they are healthy. His oldest brother worked in the oil refinery. I worked there, too. With the Americans. For the Texas Oil Company. They are called Exxon now."

I reminded him that he had already told me this. By the time you reached your seventies you accumulated too many stories, and only those that were taken out and tended, aired and brushed up from time to time, would survive the erosion of age.

Nothing in recent decades had made the same impression on Miguel as high school, and that is true for most people: adolescence is our life. Miguel had done things since Dolores, of course. He showed me some pictures of trips he'd made, before the Revolution. He'd been to Spain in 1949, had gone to summer school in Mexico, and had made a tour of Washington, D.C., that same year. But since 1959 the only place he had visited was Mexico, a single time. He'd gone to visit a Mexican he'd known, who had made a successful career in the Oaxaca tourism office. A very successful career: somehow the man had a private jet, which he'd used to visit Cuba once (Miguel had pictures of himself with the plane on the Santiago tarmac), and a large and elaborate house in Monterrey. He flicked slowly through pictures of a swimming pool, a dining room with a huge banquet table, white sofas and white rugs, a stained glass window, and a pottery collection. "Everything is air-conditioned," Miguel explained. "There are a lot of rich people there."

After closing the album he found, under it, an item that struck him from a new angle. He held it and stared, falling a little inside himself: I gently removed it from his hand: it was an airplane ticket, for a flight on Pan American. The date of the flight was August 10, 1961. The route was from Havana to Miami. The price was $12.50, each way. He'd been forced to pay for a round-trip ticket, even though he wasn't planning to come back.

His father got out, his sister got out, his uncle got out. But even though he had paid for this ticket, Miguel had never gotten the permissions and paperwork together, and he didn't make this flight, or any other. He still thought about America. "You could write a book about the problems I had trying to get there," he said.

There was an arching cry in the street, and Miguel sat up. He went to the door just as a soft knock touched its outside. He opened it to a tall, rail-thin man in a straw cowboy hat. His face and hands were dark from constant sun, his beard was grimy, and he held before him two cardboard pallets filled with several dozen eggs each.

"Eggs," the man said.

Miguel fussed for a while, inspected the eggs, took out his money, and shouted to his wife, Lola, in the back of the house, without reply. He looked at the eggs again, but couldn't make up his mind.

"Come tomorrow," he finally said. "I'm busy. I don't need eggs until tomorrow."

I didn't stay long myself. On the way out Miguel gave me a letter, which he wanted me to pass to an old friend. A really old friend, someone "from before" who lived in New York. Or had lived there. They hadn't seen each other in thirty-five years. Miguel had heard that he'd separated from his wife, and that he'd had a heart attack. "I'm thinking that maybe he died," Miguel said. He gave me the letter, and two addresses for the man. Both of the addresses were from the 1970s.

That might have worked in Cuba, but not in America. In New York I would mail off the letter to the first address, get it back, and mail it to the second, to have it returned again.

Miguel offered to drive me to my hotel. He went off to get the car, and I sat on the porch, in the dark, with his wife. Lola said nothing for a while, so I complimented the pretty backyard and the generous house. "It is a pain to us," she replied. They were too old to take care of the house and needed family. But their children were "lost." One son, the Miguel Jr. I had met, had moved to Havana. The other to Spain. The former they saw annually, the latter never.

"He left with a *problemita*," she explained. A little problem. "Just a bit of paperwork he didn't get. It was just lacking one signature, but because of that, things are not right." This was a reference to a Permit for Residence Abroad, the final and crucial document that allowed Cubans to leave. It was very difficult to get one of these permits, unless you were the son or daughter of a prominent official. And if the paperwork was "not right," the son could not return from Spain, ever. He was one of 200,000 Cubans in Spain now. The Cuban government would use euphemisms other than *problemita*: he had fled without permission, defected, become a *gusano*, a worm, a traitor. So their boy, now a man, stayed in Spain. He had been married here in Cuba and had left his wife and a daughter behind when he bolted. This granddaughter, now a teenager, lived in the house with Miguel and Lola.

"He's waiting until the right moment when things are easier and he can come back," Lola said. "But of course, it has been thirteen years, his wife divorced him, and the girl has no father. It's lamentable."

The girl would be entitled to a Spanish passport when she turned eighteen. "She will leave, because she will have to, because everyone will have to, *lamentablamente*," Lola concluded. "It's the only way to survive."

The car squealed up. It was a 1988 Lada, the final vintage. Somehow these ugly, squared-off Commiecars never made it into the wall calendars about Cuba, where the roads were inhabited only by lacquered Buick 8s and salt-rusted Chevys with Jane Russell curves. Ladas were more common, and were more desirable, since they didn't guzzle fuel and burn through cases of oil like the old American cars. As we started out, Miguel told me that Ladas were becoming popular even in America now. He'd seen it on Cuban television: they were setting up Lada dealerships in New

York and "many other places," because the cars were so fuel-efficient, and inexpensive enough for young people.

We reached the big roundabout where Vista Alegre gave way to the lower city. Down to the left was the old center, Dolores, Enramada, the parade route, and up to the right my hotel, the anonymous, air-conditioned, pimp-riddled Hotel Santiago. I could see my room on the fifteenth floor, but Miguel was seventy and couldn't see across the traffic circle. He took off his glasses, squinted, then put them back on, and squinted again, and then finally took them off. If he had the glasses on, he couldn't see cars approaching from across the circle. And if he took them off, he couldn't read the dials or see the stick shift.

A car shot by. Someone behind us honked. Llivina put the glasses on again, put the car in gear, then took the glasses off. He squinted, looking for anything moving, and then in a swift motion stabbed the glasses onto his face and floored it.

Jorge Segura sent me to see a man named Balbino Rodríguez Romero, another accountant, and another *Dolorino* who remained in Santiago. From the class of 1958, he was one of the last to graduate from the school. Balbino had attended Dolores for nine years. Segura had described him as "a good Catholic," a solid member of the accountants association, and an active participant in events related to the old Dolores. Balbino's address proved to be a small but beautiful 1950s house near the very top of Vista Alegre. Balbino answered the door and it was obvious he was made of different brushstrokes, a spry sixty-one, robust and middle-aged compared to Llivina or Segura. He was fit, with plenty of black in his hair, keen of hearing and quick with a response. Even his clothes were more up-to-date: a polo shirt and nice sneakers. Unlike the older men, he was part of the hard generation that had risen since the Revolution. Physically harder. Even sitting in the chair he had a wiry attentiveness, his focus snapped in, his hands held in front of him, the fingers splayed against each other in an unwavering steeple.

But I didn't have to scrape deep to find the old bourgeois. We settled into the living room, which sat directly over the submerged garage. The duplex house, made of cement, had the usual wide louvers to admit the breezes of Vista Alegre, and Balbino served tiny cups of coffee, which we downed in a gulp. I asked him to tell me about Santiago in the 1950s, and his complaints were not of injustice. "It was a city without much social life," Balbino said. "It had some, but not much. It needed changes. There was no nightlife. There was the Rancho Club, and the what-was-it-called, the one by the airport, the . . . the . . . the Club San Pedro. The city was very *costumbrista*," he said, meaning set in its ways. "But there was a rebirth going on in the 1950s. There was a big plant by the Texas Oil Company, I think it was called, and a cement factory, and a new wheat mill, and the port was rebuilt. The new airport was opened. There were new urban developments, like this one."

He still had one of his history textbooks from Dolores, which had been issued in 1944, just after Fidel left the school. Opening it at random I fell on a lesson about the Platt Amendment, the dagger at the heart of the troubled Cuban-American relationship. In 1903, Cuba was bluntly forced to grant America the right to control the island's foreign policy, and also to intervene in case of domestic instability, or even sanitary catastrophe. The Jesuit textbook reproduced an exchange of letters between the U.S. governor general of Cuba and various Cuban independence leaders over the merits or injustices of the Platt Amendment. Both views were spelled out at the same length, with each side speaking for itself. The American general insisted on the idealistic nature of his country's role in Cuba. The Cuban writers pointed out the hypocrisy of invading the country in the name of freedom and Cuban independence, only to deny them fully to the island. "Which view is correct?" the textbook asked.

The answer was not in doubt: the Dolores textbook stated flatly that the Cuban view of the Platt Amendment was correct, the American view wrong. The Platt Amendment reduced the Cuban state to "a fictional government."

But that was an answer, not a lesson. The students were now required to write an essay analyzing *both* arguments for their strengths and weaknesses. Outside the field of theology, a student of the Jesuits had to find the strong points even in ideas that were naturally repellent.

I asked Balbino what he remembered of Dolores and he laughed. "Seven-thirty A.M. arrival, study hall until 8:00, 8:00 to 8:20 mass, Monday through Friday. Then ten minutes to organize ourselves. Class from 8:30 to 11:15. Then home to eat with your family. About 1:30 classes would start again, and at 4:15 you would finish."

Dolores itself had been founded in 1913. It was "U.S. influence after the war," Balbino said, that drove people to Dolores. Protestant Americans were increasingly visible at all levels of Cuban society. The American-introduced school reforms were strange and unwelcome. The traditional authority of the Catholic Church in teaching, even in public schools, was suddenly supplanted by local parent associations, for example. The elite—what Balbino evasively called "the religious community"—wanted to preserve their way of life, their traditions, their values. An exclusive Catholic school administered by Jesuits looked like just the thing.

"In Dolores there was a strong education," he said. "The Jesuits had teachers who weren't priests. It was strong, very rigorous. The discipline was severe. They'd hit us with whatever they could find at hand—a ruler, an eraser. They'd grab us by the ear," he said, pinching his left lobe, "or by the hair. But they weren't sadists. There was a lot of order. The Jesuits were specialists in forming disciplined minds." He remembered the morning drill, as three hundred boys separated themselves into neat lines, the younger students on the left, the older on the right, and then marched into the chapel in two files, everyone sitting in their seats "in five minutes flat."

The Jesuits, I said, were almost like an army—

"It *is* an army," he countered. "The Company of Jesus is an army."

Discipline, planning, organization, ceaseless effort. "I think Fidel got so far in this life because of the discipline he learned from the Jesuits," Balbino said. "In my opinion the Jesuits trained him to think with discipline. To think and work. That's what they taught. Some learned it, others didn't. The pre-revolutionary society owed a lot to the Jesuits."

While he was in school, the Batista regime was growing increasingly corrupt and ruthless, especially in restive Santiago. "In 1956 the police were killing revolutionary youth and nonrevolutionary youth equally. The police were very violent. The army even more so. The marines less so, they were the only ones who weren't that way. But the others assassinated people before asking a question. And not just killing. They were tortured and mutilated. Castrated. Their eyes were cut out. Batista can never be forgiven. Never."

Balbino became so emotional reciting these crimes that he had to pause for a moment. "I don't know what to say about him," he concluded. "He took power by force, so force was the only way to get rid of him."

Oriente was filled with angry, rebellious young people—what Balbino called "effervescent youth"—in search of a leader. That the rebellion occurred in Oriente was partly circumstance, he said: with the worst inequalities and the most suffering, eastern Cuba was most ready to explode. And it was partly character. Santiago people often described themselves as "hot" or "fiery," slow to move but quick to feel. There was no doubt this was a rebellious region: all the big trouble started in Oriente, from the early slave revolts, to the first aborted War of Independence. Antonio Maceo and Che Guevara would each come charging out of the proud, wild, mountainous east.

"The *oriental* is effervescent," Balbino conceded.

Most effervescent of all was the young Dolores alumnus Fidel Castro. Maybe Fidel was only the second most famous student of the *colegio*. Desi Arnaz was more popular—*I Love Lucy* had been number one in the United States for much of the 1950s—but for serious students, and even the professors, there was only one graduate they really wanted to hear about.

"I was in seventh grade when the *Granma* landed," Balbino said, "and it was much discussed at the school. They talked about the peculiarities of his years at Dolores. There were many anecdotes. How Fidel always liked mountain climbing and hiking. There was a story about Raúl, who brought a parrot to school, and taught it to shout *Salgero veinte cuentas!*," the disciplinary mantra of the most severe Jesuit at the school.

Since we were discussing the revolutionaries, I told him that I had written a book about Che Guevara. I explained that it was a revisionist history that tried to—

"The Che was a great man," Balbino said. His frame had tensed up. The phrase *historia revisionista* had set off something in him. He leaned forward.

"Do you want to know what a hero is?" he said, staring at me intensely. "That is a hero, right there." He was pointing at the black and white picture on a small table. It showed a handsome, fair-haired man in bright sunshine. It was his cousin, Jorge Sotus. This was the brother of the Juan Sotus whom I had met in Puerto Rico—the "James Dean" Sotus, who had been a captain in the anti-Batista underground. To cover for Fidel's invasion down the coast, Jorge had led a diversionary attack in Santiago itself. The timing was all wrong—Fidel and his men were still lost at sea—and most of the Santiago insurgents were gunned down in the streets. Like the Moncada attack, it was a costly failure that nonetheless delivered a psychic shock to the country.

Dolores in 1958 was abuzz with this conflict. There were arguments for and against Castro, there was a strong undercurrent of sympathy. "Fidel was an old student," Balbino said. "They didn't say much, but I think to a certain extent the Jesuits were proud of him."

One of the youngest teachers went further than pride. Father Guzmán, known as "Seven Foot" for his immense height, was one of the few Cuban Jesuits at Dolores and a favorite among the students.

Guzmán, young, passionate, a towering physical presence, secretly enlisted in the July 26th Movement, and in the last months of the war, began wearing their black and red armband under his Jesuit robe. In November or December of 1958 he traveled into the Sierra Maestra to meet with his heroes. He returned a few weeks later, disillusioned.

But many more were swept up in hero worship. Of Fidel, Balbino said, "The youth followed him blindly. Men, women, the old and the young."

A horse went by slowly outside, pulling a wagon full of onions. *Onions onions onions sweet sweet onions,* a man in a straw hat cried, and touched his whip to the horse's back.

Near his old textbook was an unframed photo. Balbino's Dolores class at their First Communion. There were a dozen boys in white tuxedos, sitting stiffly in front of a dark cloth backdrop. Balbino ran his right index finger over the hard paper. "All the rest left. Practically all."

When I left, I walked down through Vista Alegre, passing the neighborhood's Catholic church. I poked my head in there just to confirm what everyone had told me: there, under an archway, was the statue of Ignatius Loyola.

Perform the acts of faith, Loyola said, and faith itself will come. Perform the acts of wisdom, and wisdom will come.

Act, he said. Act and it will.

"Pioneers of communism!" shouted the voice that answered my knock at Dolores, the last time. Of course, the school wasn't called by that name now. Cuban schools today are named by men like Miguel Llivina Jr., given handy sobriquets like the Nguyen Van Troi School, or the Solidarity with Chile School, or School #108. Dolores was called the Manuel María de Mendive School, after a famous teacher no one had heard of. The students just called it the Central School. "Pioneers of communism!" the voice belted again. Carnaval was over. It was Monday afternoon, the end of the school day. The streets of Santiago were so safe, so quiet, that no parents came to pick up their children here. Fuel was so tight that no buses waited. I was alone on Clock Street.

The school doors were closed, but I could hear hundreds and hundreds of children being called to attention, a hubbub that quickly died down into the squeaky shuffling of rubber sneakers on the patio. The squeaks grew tiny, precise. They were lining up

"To arms, valiant ones," the voice shouted. A boy's voice, harsh and instructive, and then some shuffling sound, hundreds of children standing to attention, facing the flag.

"Pioneers of communism," the boy shouted, and as one, the students roared it out, as they did every day: "WE WILL BE LIKE CHE!"

All at once, life. A bell, a great crush of body sounds, voices growing into shrieks, within seconds, laughter and singing. The doors were flung open and a sea of adolescents, boys in red pants and girls in red skirts, came flushing out the door, sweeping all Cuba before them. All the students wore white shirts, with red kerchiefs knotted loosely around the collar.

I turned sideways and pressed in, through the front door, swimming against the stream of children flowing out. The old courtyard was packed with kids in uniform, hordes of them coursing around in circles and clusters, playing hopscotch and patty-cake, skipping rope, shouting and screaming, laughter echoing up the high walls and doubling back down on us, all accompanied by the slap and squeak of rubber sneakers.

There was a chalkboard propped in the courtyard, full of tiny, precise handwriting. It was a list of academic titles, each matched with a figure in a column of numbers down the right.

I approached a cluster of three adults and announced that I would speak to the person in charge. They pointed to a man under the gallery, whose very nondescriptness—khaki trousers and a short-sleeve permanent press shirt with pen in pocket—was the uniform of power in Cuba. He was the principal, or director. I introduced myself as "the visitor who contacted you earlier," mentioned the names of all the historians and institutes and libraries that I had recently walked through, explained that I was making my third "study" here at the school, and asked him to explain the long columns of numbers.

He hesitated, but then began talking, and was soon running on automatic, pointing at the chalk board and giving his briefing. There were seven hundred students. The school held only three grades: tenth through twelfth.

Had I misheard him? Seven hundred students?

"Yes," he said. "Seven hundred. This is a temporary measure."

In 1941 there had been 238 students in the building. The conditions today were overwhelming, but there was little they could do. In fact, even this building would be closed in a year or two, for renovations. In Cuba, it was routine for renovations to take five or even ten years. Often enough, once a useful building did reopen, it was found to be more useful for bureaucrats. A closure could well be permanent.

The curriculum, the director explained, was the same as in every school in Cuba. Not just a set of national requirements, as in the old school system, but a completely centralized lesson plan, detailed down to the wording to be written on a blackboard. Everything was designed for maximum efficiency by pedagogical experts like Miguel the Younger.

Listed on the blackboard were medical school, nuclear technology, accounting, journalism, engineering, and a dozen other career paths in a country dependent on tourism and envelopes from Miami.

The chalkboard was a rationing system for the university. Students picked three careers they wanted to pursue, ordering them in priority. There was no doubt what was most popular: more than two thousand students around the province had applied for medical school. But next to "MEDICINE" the number read "400," the quantity of open places. Bus-boys in restaurants earned more cash than doctors, but obviously some kind of idealism was still strong within these walls.

Each senior was rated on a scale of 100 points. The highest scorers were given first choice; when medicine filled up, the lower scoring students would be given their second picks; the lowest scoring were sent to their third picks. A lot of people ended up becoming agronomists.

I asked where the 100 points came from. "Fifty points are awarded for their grade average, and fifty more come from their exam scores, and so on."

And so on?

"There are other points," he said. "For extracurricular activities, and so on."

And so on. Those who scored less well on the meritocratic measures—grades and exams—could still benefit from other influences. Politics. *Amiguismo*. The Pioneers. The Young Communists. Volunteer labor. All could change scores, and all involved subjective avenues of preference and influence, family and patronage. There was a system, and then there was the improvised Cuban genius for nonsystem, for exceptions and loopholes.

With the school quiet, emptying out, I climbed upstairs. From a third-floor classroom, looking out a tall, thin window, you could see all of Santiago, falling down toward the harbor. The twin bell towers of the Cathedral stood out against the lines of the bay and mountains.

Two men climbed up those bell towers, silhouettes moving against the late afternoon. After a moment they pulled on the ropes, slowly, and the great bells began to sing, and a clapper struck the hour, twenty times or so, at an unhurried pace. Everything by hand.

In a quiet city like this, with so little traffic, so few distractions and distortions, everyone within range of that tolling knew where they lived, which hand-shaped place this was. The bells embraced all within reach.

Down in the Plaza Dolores, a pushcart vendor struggled up the far side of the square, heading up Enramada. *Peanuts,* he cried out, *peanuts.* And then, in song:

> Coco water to clean out your insides,
> Milk fresh from the cow,
> Pineapples and garlic too.

LA CAPITAL

War and mayhem were on the agenda, although we didn't know it. In the last hours of the old year, the gods gathering for their revelations, the rest of us were blissfully ignorant. Up on a rooftop in Havana, the air was cool, the drinks were cool, the party cool, still in its relaxed, early hours. Guests had been arriving since 7:00 P.M., climbing up the four flights of crumbling stairs and huffing onto the cement patio, where our host, Enrique, lived in an improvised cubicle. Pedro Juan Gutiérrez called rooftop living the epitome of Havana life, and Enrique, the brother of a friend, was a prototype of the city: *puro Habanero* back many generations, a sometime roller of cigars, renter of love nests to enamored foreigners, and professional DJ known around the town for his mix tapes, cobbled artfully from the latest global playlists.

The Cuban guests arrived in their best party clothes, oversized blazers or too-tight frocks. The foreigners stumbled onto the roof in sweaty T-shirts and guilty expressions. By 8:00 P.M. some more Cubans arrived in a frenzied state of excitement, throwing air kisses in every direction. But these were Cubans from abroad, prodigal daughters bearing gifts (cash, usually, but clothes and appliances were appreciated). These were the happy middle few, living in America or Europe, able to return annually to families as long as they took no obvious political stance against Cuba. *Gusañeros,* people called them, with a wink: a mash of *gusano,* or worm, and *compañero,* comrade. Half worm because they had fled; half comrade because they came back.

Most Cubans dreamed of leaving, and most never would. But among the trapped on this island were a few volunteers, foreign militants who had chosen to take exile in a country that produced exiles. One of them arrived: a tall, gorgeous woman, her light brown skin dappled with freckles. Many of her colleagues in radical black movements had commandeered American airplanes during the late 1960s and early 1970s. So many planes were turned toward Cuba that *all* U.S. airliners were issued with approach maps for the Havana airport in 1972. These American revolutionaries expected to be greeted as heroes, but Cuba distrusted them, fearing spies and provocateurs, and they were sent to hard labor, to prove themselves through suffering. Outlaw Americans were still sprinkled around the city. The radical journalist who lingered in Havana under a pseudonym. A Black Panther, a cop killer who, broken by years of cutting cane in the fields, had turned introspective and now retailed his story and dime bags of marijuana to the curious foreign leftists who looked him up. There was the CIA turncoat, Philip Agee, the fugitive financier Robert Vesco, last seen under arrest, and the anonymous con man I met, sunning himself on a mega-yacht in the harbor after bolting from a minimum security prison.

The black radical on the roof was lithe and ready to dance. She'd been born in the United States as Cheri Laverne Dalton, and joined the Black Liberation Army, a revolutionary movement calling for a separate black nation in the American southeast. Despite this racial agenda, Cheri had helped white militants carry out a bloody 1981 robbery in New York that left one guard and two police officers dead. She'd fled to Cuba (for once, without hijacking a plane), where she had changed her name to Nehanda Obiodun. She was still wanted in the States for armed bank robbery, racketeering, obstruction of justice, and violating the Hobbs Act, but in Cuba she lived in a bubble of security. Paid the standard salary of a Cuban professional, she sometimes briefed foreign delegations on racial progress in Cuba, but was best known for her work cleaning up the Cuban rap scene. My favorite group, the Free Hole Negroes, had been one of her victims. The band, whose name punned the phrase *frijoles negros,* had become popular for raw, a cappella anthems denouncing racism and repression in Cuba, but such problems could not be mentioned into a microphone, and the Free Hole Negroes were banned from the Havana Rap Festival. After an extended outcry, the band was allowed to appear the next year, but just seconds into their set, it became obvious they had not taken Cheri's—or Nehanda's—advice to change their lyrics. They launched into an uncensored song about racism. Within seconds someone pulled the plug, dropping the stage into darkness. Random blackouts do occur in Cuba, but once the Free Hole Negroes were gone, the electricity came back on.

It wasn't easy being one of these fugitive exiles, betwixt and between,

neither American nor Cuban. The novelist Carlos Eire recalled the shock
of leaving Cuba as a white boy of Irish descent, only to discover in
Florida that he was really a dirty little spick. Cheri had undergone the
reverse, fleeing America as a black nationalist, only to settle in Cuba, the
one place where a *mulata fina* like her would never be called black.

Havana! I loved the capital, bitterly and deeply, an unrequited love
made possible only by distance and loss. The luminous blue-gray hurricane light. The storm spray that left cars, people, and decaying mansions
coated with the white dust of salt. The oily harbor, fuming and ringed
with Spanish forts. The blue streak of the Gulf Stream itself, visible from
the rooftops every day, a world just beyond. Even storm waves broke
against this indestructible city. Havana was battered and defeated on the
outside, ground to the color of dead coral. But the facades, the majestic
banks and great trading companies along the sea-bound avenues, only
looked dead. Inside, the ancient buildings were warrened with unlit, frag-
mentary stairways that led to roach- and rat-infested labyrinths of *cuar-
tería* apartments. Even the sordid smells on the inside of Havana, the
extremes of human defecation, of squalid life, or pigeon coops, were just
as grand in their way as the august Havana that could be photographed.
Life was in ruins in this triumphant city, and always had been.

One fifth of Cubans live in Havana. The people here dropped their *R*'s,
spoke more slowly than in Oriente, and walked faster, though that wasn't
saying much in either case. Habaneros said *frutabomba* where the easterners said *papaya,* and people in Santiago can say what they want, but this
was the cosmopolis, the hard, intransigent, crumbling life of Cuba all in
one package. A global capital of the quixotic, where free market superstars
came to denounce capitalism, apostles of asceticism fell off the wagon,
and most secrets were vulnerable to a $100 bill. The parks were full of
prostitutes, the houses full of liquor, and in this *capital inmoral* of the Revolution, even cocaine. I'd see colonels eating lobster with teenage girls at
3:00 A.M., English rock stars expounding on socialism from the the lawn
of the Nacional, Russian real estate mobsters on three-girls-a-day bend-
ers, Mexican guerrillas turned Marxtrepreneurs, Chilean assassins making
a killing in fruit juice, and the astounding perverts of all nations, wallow-
ing in it.

Despite the 2.2 million who lived here, Havana was notable for its
emptiness, for the quietness of its avenues by day and their inky darkness

at night. The streets were full of spectacular wrecks, black-eyed houses and abandoned hotels, mansions with holed roofs, featureless plains like the Plaza of the Revolution, a gigantic parking lot where legendary rallies had once been held. The novelist Virgilio Piñera described this city—the hungry Havana under the Revolution—as a static place, inherently incomplete, cut off from its own dreams by the sea edge, a theoretical city larded with unerected monuments to unrealized gestures and unpracticed virtues. It was "the city where the whole world went to be lied to." I found Havana dangerous to body and soul, a high-low environment where you could get arrested for nothing but everyone got away with everything.

By 9:00 P.M. on a roof in Chinatown, on New Year's Eve, under the cool canopy of stars, people were starting to sway. Enrique's latest mix tape was pulling them out of their seats: Cuban hip-hop from Paris, Nuyorican soul. A few minutes before ten, a single table of food—paid for by the foreigners—appeared and was wiped clean.

The Chinatown below us was muddy, a crowded but ghostly district of just a few streets, where the ideograms on the walls were unread. There had been Chinese in Cuba since 1847, and the *barrio chino* had ten thousand residents at the start of the twentieth century. Cubans had derided them as drug addicts and homosexuals, and successive governments had restricted their rights, lines of work, and social standing. The Cuban Chinese had taken that message to heart: they deserted Cuba en masse during the spiral of military coups and gangsterism that comprised the 1930s and 1940s. Today there are only about one hundred Chinese left. Their housing had been filled in, and it was an overwhelmingly black neighborhood now.

Before coming up to the party, I had been waiting on the dirty, wet street for Enrique to let me in (a process of bellowing at the roof, waiting, conversing in fourth-floor volumes, and then standing by as he pulled gingerly on a very long piece of string, which curled down through four floors of security grates, broken doorways, concrete obstructions, stairs with and without banisters, and then yanked the bolt). During the wait I asked a very old black man what had happened to the Chinese. He thought a long time. "They go away," he finally said, waving a hand. It was a perfect Cuban answer. Passive. Taking no position on past versus present. Admitting no cause. The Chinese had simply gone away.

Click, the bolt popped. Climbing up, it was a different Cuba even one floor above the street. Homes were the only private space, where people could shut out the block committees, the snoops, the police, and let their guard down. The higher you climbed the more freedom you felt. By the time you reached the roof, the door opened on a little patio, invisible to the world below or even around. Altitude brought out the best in people.

Almost the moment, now. Three men, one tall, one fat, one square, in white set up Batá drums and began, almost casually, beating a tattoo. Fifty guests quieted down, and the drumming rose up, over the taut-faced people, across the brambled skyline of pirated wiring and jury-rigged antennas, sound traveling toward the dome of the old capital, the crumbling towers of the National Theater, toward Old Havana and also out, beyond the ferries in the harbor, beyond the fortresses, to away. The rumba built up, faster, louder, and they started singing.

The trickster, the messenger, the familiar Elegguá was the first to appear, as always. The opener of doorways burst out of the doorway to Enrique's rooftop bedroom, arms akimbo, thrashing. Elegguá looked a lot like a woman this time. One of the women, in fact, from the dance troupe had disappeared into the bedroom twenty minutes before.

Elegguá was wearing the customary red and black stripes, the opposition of life and death. He—she—came out smoking a cigar and howling, greeted by acclamation from the drummers and the crowd, which was now packed tightly around an oval of dance space. Leaping, twisting, and prancing around this circle, Elegguá pounded her feet, spun, and finally, returning to the start of her circle, the keeper of paths sat down on my lap, breathing hard and sweating. She pulled on a bottle of rum and did not even acknowledge me.

The message, and messenger, had worked: other gods paraded onto the roof now, in their order. Powerful Ogún, the thundering war-maker. The pale, blue-clad Yemayá, mistress of the salt seas. The luscious Oshún in yellow, goddess of fresh waters and carnal love. Lastly, Lázaro the cripple, hobbling onto the dance floor with his crutch. He wore a loincloth and was covered with symbolic sores, but Cubans love anyone worse off than they are, and Lázaro was always a favorite, cheered and adored for his ability to take away illness. They all danced in turn, and then together, while the drummers beat wildly and chanted praise. Many in the crowd joined in, singing, shouting, drumming on their own chairs or anything within reach, knocking spoons on tables, firing up their own cigars, calling praise. Now Elegguá noticed she was sitting on me; she forced me to drink and then pass the bottle of rum to others. She exhaled through her cigar, ritually hosing me down with a charge of blue smoke, cleansing me from head to toe. She was so skinny that I could feel the bones inside her legs as she sat on me. When she rose to dance, she stuck the wet stub of the cigar in my mouth, and expected it to be primed and glowing when she returned.

For the rest of the night, strangers approached, smiling, patting me on the back. I didn't know why at first, but they thought it was funny, really nice, that a foreigner had been chosen.

Chosen for what? I asked. People just laughed. *Hijo de Elegguá,* they said, passing another bottle. Everyone had seen it. *Child of Elegguá.*

Whatever door had opened, whatever crossroads loomed, you wouldn't find out until you got there. Off in the dark somewhere, the *babalaos* rattled their turtle bones. Soon the new year came, and in the darkness the old one went.

January 1 again, the keystone date of Cuban history, the axle to the Revolution's endless wheel of time. When I stumbled outside at noon the streets were empty, the winter sun bright and cool. The trees on the Prado twisted in a strong sea wind, their leaves shushing the city. Whitecaps were visible out beyond the end of the Prado walkway, and from a kiosk that sold nothing else I tried to buy a copy of the first newspaper of the year. They were sold out.

The daily newspaper, *Granma,* was named after Castro's boat, the *Granma,* which he'd used to invade Cuba in 1956. The curious name of the boat meant nothing to the revolutionaries, who didn't bother to rechristen it when they bought the yacht in Mexico from an American dentist. He had simply named the boat for his grandmother: *Granma.* Now *Granma* the boat was displayed under glass in a Havana park, and the name had spread. It sounded heroic to Cubans, who didn't realize they were saying *abuelita.* There was a whole province named Granma now, and factories and housing complexes bore the name. But if you said "Granma" everyone knew what you meant: the nation's one daily newspaper. I couldn't help smirking at the title, but there was nothing funny to Cubans about *Granma.* The headlines ("Fidel Castro Celebrates with French

People") were the only headlines they knew. When *Granma* reported in 2006, just a month before he was sidelined by illness, that Castro would probably live to be 120, who was to say different?

This, 2004, wasn't much of a year. Just as Fidel had redrawn the map of Cuba, he had recalculated all calendars. Christmas had been eliminated, July 26 turned into the highlight of the year, and the decades themselves altered with a new chronology. Instead of 1959 there was the "Year of the Liberation." The Cubans had quickly got the hang of this: 1960 was renamed the "The Year of the Agrarian Reform." In 1962, the "Year of Planification," there were planning problems. The next year was "Of Organization," followed by "Of Economy," and then "Of Agriculture." Naming styles changed: the internationalist era of the late 1960s and 1970s had produced the years of Solidarity, Heroic Viet-Nam, Decisive Force, Productivity, and Socialist Emulation.

The 1980s were mostly dedicated to the twenty or twenty-fifth anniversaries of events in Castro's life (these were disguised as Cuban history, but the two were usually presented as one and the same). Nineteen eighty-five was the "Year of the Third Congress of the Communist Party of Cuba," and after that there was a kind of default, perhaps a lack of sufficient ardor, for the exemplary names vanished during the chaotic years of the late 1980s and early 1990s, the clock thrown by the collapse of the Soviet system. By the late 1990s Cuba had switched to a tourism economy, and the slogan-years reappeared as a recitation of long-dead Cubans, José Martí and Antonio Maceo, while the year known as 1997 outside of Cuba had been called "The Year of the 30th Anniversary of the Death in Combat of the Heroic Guerrilla and His Companions." This invented count of years was carried on the front page of every newspaper every day, reprinted in documents, recited ritually by loyal functionaries, and shouted by students.

The years were also counted by the stopwatch system, which dated all events from the Moncada attack of 1953, Day One of Year Zero. So that meant that 1997 was also known officially as "Year 33," a nasty, Khmer Rouge title. Still, for my money the lamest year was 2001, known as the "Year of the Victorious Revolution in the New Millennium," because Cuba alone in the world had refused to celebrate the millennial change in 2000. And according to today's newspaper, I was no longer living in any *Anno Domine* at all, but had embarked on something called the "Year of

Glorious Anniversaries." Nothing epic, or even actionable. Instead of achievements, anniversaries of achievements.

In 1952, the alumni guide for Dolores had listed Fidel Castro Ruiz (*sic*) as "Lawyer, Havana," and that was still true, although he had a bigger house and they spelled his name right in publications. Castro's life had transpired here, in the capital, but he still seemed to dislike the city, pushing resources to any other part of the country at the expense of the metropole. This was justified as support for the overlooked regions, but the city had never been drawn to the puritanical side of the Revolution, had never been as desperate to sacrifice, and Castro knew it.

Everyone in Havana knew him, too. Knew him *personally*. Even me. I'd seen him in the flesh at a small rally, where I crawled in among the cameras to stand close, scrutinizing the lines in his face and the tremble in his hand. Always, Castro was known by his familiar gray beard, which had thinned out, allowing his Celtic skin to gleam through. The beard was surprisingly wide at the bottom, untrimmed bits bristling out past the mortarboards and gold braid of his twill dress uniform. I'd seen him across a huge field another time, a tiny figure in green, giving the same speech as always. I'd also bumped into him in Havana a couple of times, as he marched out of a building to shouts of "Viva!" or swept past the Hotel Inglaterra in the back of a Soviet limousine (just the one car, just the one military attendant in the back with him). I'd learned to watch for him around 11:30 in the morning, when the broad Fifth Avenue was cleared by police for Castro's daily commute. For these regular runs, Castro rode in any of three identical black Mercedes-Benz 560s, in a convoy of jeeps and Ladas, tailed by an ambulance, about a dozen vehicles total. In all, the Castro brothers, their families, and their bodyguards have a fleet of about three hundred cars.

The convoy usually took him to his offices tucked within the large military headquarters on Independence Avenue. There Castro could stand at the center of all flow charts, surrounded by triumphant statistics, pulling levers on imaginary deployments. His personal bureaucracy, the obscure Council of State, then translated these whims for the larger group of about three hundred people who actually ran the country—ministers, deputies, vice-anythings, favorite aides, leading military officers, cabinet secretaries, Party bureaucrats, key players of various kinds. They in turn controlled the larger apparatus of power—the armed forces, the Ministry of the Interior, and revenue-producing business, and the administrative cadre, especially the 780,000-strong Communist Party. The one thing these three hundred people all shared—on an evolutionary model, this was a survival adaptation—was an unwavering and explicit personal loyalty to the one man, to Cyclops himself. This assured that Castro had the final say on any issue he cared to speak about, and allowed him to set the messianic tone of constant crisis, where a standard feature of daily life was the prediction of imminent destruction by powerful enemies within and without Cuba.

By his own count, Castro had stood at the head of the Cuban Revolution for more than half a century. Through his seventies, he was still appearing at rallies, commemorations, and memorials, at openings and closings, at graduations and inductions, welcoming ceremonies and farewell events, banquets and baseball games, TV shows and hurricanes, a well-worn path that eventually put him in the orbit of every person on an island of eleven million. Especially in Havana, it was easy to feel him close, to absorb by osmosis the core value of the system: the Revolution was the man, and vice versa. At night the evening news would recap his movements, and later he would be on one channel, or both, featuring in the documentaries, in special reports, in taped summaries, or in the stupendous speeches that still ran live, sometimes until two or three in the morning. In total, he would command hours of everyone's life on a daily basis. Even on his sickbed, his smallest gestures—sipping orange juice, or reading a letter—were minutely reported. This was taxing for the rest of us, but for Cyclops it was life.

He repeated himself, deliberately. The speeches, the comments, ideas, even gestures, were echoes of previous rallies, events, and speeches. Slogans were made for repetition, for the form they forced onto the mind:

The New Man. The Ten Million Ton Harvest. Fatherland or Death. Socialism or Death. Not One Step Back. Special Period in a Time of Peace. The Heroes of Moncada. The Heroes of Yara. The Martyrs of Imperialism. The Freest People in History. The Sacred Principles of Jose Martí. Be Like Che. I'm Staying Here. It's Always the 26th. Until the Final Victory. Heroes of the Triumph. First Free Territory of the Americas. A Revolution Without Danger Is Not a Revolution. Cuba, Land of Men of Stature.

The public was also enjoined to repeat these phrases, in one voice, day after day, not just the same words but the same accent, the same rhythm. Roberto Robaina, a Castro favorite, had actually been disgraced and sidelined in 1999 for failing to chant "Socialism or Death" with sufficient vigor at a rally.

With the people numbed by slogans, hunger, preoccupation, and prophecies of disaster, the decaying society was ruled from above by that impossible creature, the "revolutionary state." In practice this meant secretive, top-down rule, the masses confined to rubber-stamp rituals. People were told where to stand, and then kept there by the mere possibility of surveillance, by the secret policemen—most of them imaginary—who protected the government from its own people. Occasional show trials, with their cruel theater of power and powerlessness, kept the troublemakers in line. The official doctrine of "Democratic Socialism" was neither: Castroism, the cult of the man himself, was the ideology of Cuba. The Revolution hadn't withered or failed or been abandoned. It had been assassinated by the one who invoked it most.

What next? What world could come after this one? There is no way to have Fidelism without a Fidel. Various pretenders for the throne were mentioned, heirs official (Raúl) and potential (the disgraced Robaina, foreign minister Felipe Pérez Roque, culture minister Armando Hart, and either of the Leál brothers, who ran favored projects for Castro). Fidel himself suggested Elián González. Raúl could run the country as long as Fidel was alive. But whoever came next was to be pitied.

As Cuban dissident Elizardo Sánchez once said to me, "You can't make an elephant out of a hundred rabbits."

The new year, the year of Glorious Anniversaries, started off badly. People woke up hungry that first morning—the ration was down—and found the Revolution stumbling into its second half century. And then at noon, with our headaches finally clearing, the gods delivered their stunner. Even though I'd had Elegguá on my lap, I didn't get the news until I finally found a bookstore selling the newspaper on Obispo Street.

Obispo was the most charming street in Cuba, a narrow path through Old Havana. It began near the royal palms of the Parque Central, ran past the Floridita, where Hemingway quaffed his double daiquiris without sugar, and terminated at the Plaza de Armas and the old forts guarding the harbor. It was a pedestrian street, closed to traffic (although people drive down it anyway). This was the introduction to the old way of life, to narrow sidewalks and stucco houses, crumbling facades propped up with heavy beams that angled into the street. Antennas and brambles of improvised wires were strung overhead; laundry dried on balconies. Tourists plied slowly up and down Obispo, looking for the doorway drunks in Hemingway stories, or for the shadows in Walker Evans photographs. Although *Meester 'Way* made a habit of warming his seat at the Floridita by 10:00 A.M., I thought noon was still too early and stepped right past. Up the block two bookstores faced each other.

On the right was Moderna Poesía, the most important bookstore and publishing house in the old Cuba, in a rounded, art deco building. In Miami the former owners of this store had reopened a clone, also called Moderna Poesía, but the Havana original, with the names still carved in marble, was long shuttered, the windows covered with dusty travel agency posters and the rooms empty. But across the street was a small government bookstore, where I had finally found *Granma.* Half the shelves were covered with murder mysteries, pirated Cuban translations of Agatha Christie and John Grisham. The other half were books about the Revolution. Fidel on Religion. Fidel on Socialism. Fidel on Human Development. Fidel on the Crisis of International Relations. Fidel on the Heroic Events of Moncada.

There were just as many by, or about, Che Guevara.

Explicitly political books, like *Animal Farm* or *The Autumn of the Patriarch,* were effectively banned in Cuba. But literature *without* politics also frightened dictators. In a revolution, the personal was always supposed to be political. The very idea that huge zones of human thought, areas of feeling, and fields of endeavor could lie beyond politics was a threat. Literature could puncture the universe of authority. This is why in Iran, the Islamists criticized Jane Austen. She created a world where men and women chose among dictates of love and conscience, and only love and conscience. One of the few idealists in *Dirty Havana Trilogy* explains why there are no good novels in Cuba: "It terrifies the Old Man to think that any small space set aside for personal freedom might become a space where free ideas were exchanged." Hence a bookstore with no good novels. No good newspapers or magazines. Just police procedurals and propaganda.

A first glance at the newspaper showed there was an item about a new book, "CUBAN BUSINESS IN 1958: A Documented Analysis of the Bourgeoisie," which had just come out. It was "an overall analysis of the Cuban bourgeoisie . . . their habits and way of life, where and how they lived, how they dressed and how they ate." The distinguishing characteristics of this "traitor" class were its "relinquishing its nationality and its principles to embrace extreme right-wing sectors of finance capital."

I held up the newspaper, with its picture of the book party, but the clerk had never heard of the book. There were no copies in this or any other store I visited.

And then, standing out on Obispo, I looked through *Granma* systematically and saw why the newspaper had been sold out. This issue contained the crucial "Letter of the Year," the main Santería prophecy for the year ahead. The Letter was the result of a crucial divination on New Year's Eve. Some eight hundred Santería priests, the leading *babalaos* of Cuba, had gathered in Havana to spend hours in their arcane rituals and devices. After some form of interpretation, and probably a little negotiation and editing, the Letter of the Year was proclaimed to the public. A committee of the highest *babalaos* emerged amid chants and drumming, and their supreme leader, a wrinkled priest named Victor Betancourt, stepped forward to read it.

The most important thing about the Letter is a single phrase that emerges during divination. Cubans, even those who do not follow Santería, pay close attention to this key phrase, knowing that the Letter of the Year will influence the country greatly, one way or another.

"The King will turn in his crown before dying," Betancourt announced. That was the slogan.

A king. A fallen crown. Death. This was dangerous stuff, so before anyone had a chance to even ask, Betancourt volunteered to journalists that the most obvious reading of the divination was wrong. No, he said, it did not refer to Cuba. Nor did it refer to Fidel Castro himself. Nor did it mean that Castro's life or presidency would come to an end in the next 365 days. The phrase had no connection to Castro, at all, Betancourt insisted. The Letter of the Year and the slogan within it both described events far beyond Cuba. It could be any king, anywhere. Any ruler. Any country. "This letter is for all humanity," Betancourt said.

The news was electric, literally. Betancourt released the Letter of the

Year to the press, and within hours the incredible prediction—The King Will Turn in His Crown!—had circulated by e-mail to Miami, and from there worldwide, wherever devout followers of Santería had settled. The Letter of the Year was already being discussed on the AM dial in Miami as I sat reading it in Cuba. In that airy sphere of debate, there was no doubt about the meaning. The king will turn in his crown. Whatever Betancourt said, it meant Castro was finally on the way out.

But Betancourt continued reading, beyond the sensational slogan. The rest of the Letter was full of terrible imagery. The future of "all of humanity," included "war, government collapse, the deaths of prominent personalities and marital infidelity." The Letter went on to describe "the collapse of a government somewhere in the world" and the "enslavement" of a people after a war. The economic news was also bad. The Letter warned of the "rupture" of global commercial relations, an increase in corruption, and trouble in economic markets.

Also, there would be plagues of "grave neurological and psychiatric illnesses, infectious disease and liver aliments, as well as food poisoning and other sicknesses."

And environmental problems, hurricanes, flooding, droughts, and numerous earthquakes.

So that pretty much covered it. The Year of Glorious Anniversaries was going to suck.

The toilet paper at Elizardo Sánchez's house was made from *Granma,* the newspaper, which he cut up into small squares and stacked by the commode. I recalled this while waiting out front, in the shade of an unruly fig tree, for Elizardo to come out.

As usual, I'd had the cabbie leave me at the end of the block, and scuttled up to the gate nervously, looking around to see if anyone was watching. At this house, out of all the houses in Havana, that was a safe bet. A rooster crowed next door, which made me check the time: three in the afternoon. The rooster crowed again, and then Elizardo came out.

He was the most relentless human rights campaigner in Cuba, the most persistent dissident still at large, and the most rebellious pacifist on the island, but he moved like a Cuban, as though he had twenty years to get from the front door to the gate. He came trundling out of the house, nodded, paused, looked around, stepped off the porch heavily, and swung his legs stiffly. He was clean-shaven, tall, big-boned, top-heavy, his skin a kind of translucent parchment. Another pale *gallego,* poured from the same mold as Castro. And Elizardo was *oriental* to boot. I always thought he would be president of Cuba someday, if only because he looked the part.

Elizardo led me inside the chain link fence, padlocked the gate, and then he went to the front door, unlocked that, led us inside, and closed and locked it again. Now I noticed that his hair, an upright shock, had turned completely gray. I'd been to his house in the Miramar suburb two dozen times, and this was the only change I could notice in him.

In 1991, after Sánchez had returned to his home from eleven years in jail, the local block committee had been ordered to screw up a mob and denounce him. This kind of demonstration—called an "act of repudiation"—was a ritual of life in Cuba. His neighbors marched in front of the house, denouncing him as a worm, traitor, enemy of the people, servant of imperialism, and criminal scum. The slogans were pro forma, nothing more inspired than "CASTRO SÍ, YANQUÍS NO." The demonstration was led from in front, and watched from behind, by men in boots with civilian clothes and carrying walkie-talkies. Eventually the mob was encouraged to throw bricks and rocks at the windows, and someone—a someone wearing combat boots—had tried to kick down the front door. The first time I had visited Sánchez I had traced a finger over the black smudge of that boot sole, which had cracked but not broken the door. "They have to do it," Sánchez explained of his neighbors.

Elizardo had repaired the door. Later he added metal *rejas,* or grilles, over the windows. A few years after that he put up a chain link fence, high enough to stop most bricks, with a gate that he kept padlocked. He pointed out the latest addition: broken glass had been cemented into the top of the garden walls and along the roof edge of the house. But this latest measure wasn't to keep mobs, bricks, or the police out. "Crime is up," he explained.

We settled onto opposed sofas in the front room of the house. There was a photo on the wall of Sánchez shaking hands with Ted Kennedy. Another with José Aznar, the former Spanish prime minister.

Sánchez had gone to jail repeatedly on technicalities like buying black market gasoline, which everyone in Cuba does. His real offense was leading the grandly named Human Rights Concordance, which was a loose association of like-minded opposition groups within Cuba. Sánchez and a few hundred people like him around the island were internal dissidents, who refused to go into exile. Cuba had repeatedly allowed Sánchez to leave, in hopes he would not return, but he just went abroad to collect European human rights awards and confer with politicos in America, and always came home. Because of this he was condemned by some exile politicians in Miami as a "collaborator of the Castro regime."

"They found your business card," was the first thing Elizardo told me. I'd left it with him years before, and the police had raided his house, pawed through his files, found the card, and asked him about it. I was one of many journalists who talked to Elizardo, and as a foreigner had de facto immunity. I asked him who "they" were but it was always the same: "MinInt," he said.

The Ministry of the Interior. The bad boys. The domestic security apparatus of Cuba, charged with protecting the country from internal enemies. MinInt was huge. Cuba's 100,000 police officers reported to MinInt, but the organization also controlled a true army of its own, with armored units and infantry, that was designed to discourage any coup attempts by the regular army. MinInt also had elaborate facilities for secret work, for clandestine operations, counterintelligence, and eavesdropping. MinInt was responsible for repression and surveillance. It ran the Special Brigades, the plainclothes thugs who did much of Cuba's dirty work in the middle of the night.

MinInt had spent about five hours copying his hard drive and searching his files, making careful notes, and then leaving everything with him, almost as neat as they'd found it. Sánchez had ties outside, like me, and therefore a level of immunity.

In his living room, Sánchez now detailed for me the latest ways that Cuba was falling apart. The economy was completely dependent on tourism now, which brought in far more money than sugar. But tourism had evaporated after the terrorist attacks on September 11, 2001. Although it had rebounded, it was still vulnerable to hurricanes, politics, and the mood swings of European vacationers. The only bigger money than tourism came from the enemy: Cuban exiles sent about a billion dollars a year back to the island in small remittances to friends and family—far and away the single biggest source of income to Cuba. Although

Washington tried to stifle this transfusion of cash in 2003, the new rules were so easily evaded that the remittances were exactly the same a year later. American restrictions had far less effect than the unemployment rate in Florida.

The regime was getting squeezed from the other side, too, Elizardo said. The costs of running a police state with a centralized, astonishingly inefficient economy were high. Police officers in Cuba were about 1 percent of the population. Like army draftees, these policemen needed to be fed, clothed, trained, and kept somewhat happy, lest they become a threat to, rather than a support for, the government. The number of prisoners was also very high, about another 1 percent of the population. This was a level of per capita incarceration that only a few countries—South Africa, Russia, and the United States—could match. There were about ninety thousand prisoners spread through a chain of remote jails up and down the length of the island, an archipelago of punishment that Cubans called the *cordillera,* or mountain range.

Cuban prisons were filthy and cramped, though not as bad as many others in Latin America. What separated the Cuban justice system from others was its arbitrariness. By law, anyone could be arrested, at any time, and held incommunicado, for any charge or no charge at all. The government was required to charge a suspect within a week, but some people sat in jail for a year before learning what crime they were accused of. Trials were ceremonies, conducted without evidence or the right to choose a lawyer (again, both were guaranteed in law but routinely ignored). The judges, who sat in panels, were a mixture of professionals, who had studied law, and (a Soviet invention) amateurs who were qualified only by their loyalty to the system. These "model workers" and party stalwarts kept the courts subservient. The system was *designed* to be unjust, as Human Rights Watch spelled out:

> Cuba has developed a highly effective machinery of repression. Cuban laws actually guarantee the denial of civil and political rights. Cuba severely restricts free expression, association, and assembly, silencing dissent with heavy prison terms, harassment, or exile. Human rights advocates, journalists, and other independent activists face steady government repression. Cuba refuses to legalize independent labor unions and restricts workers' rights in the international investment sector. The

conditions in Cuba's prisons are inhumane. Cuba's courts fail to ensure fair trials. Nevertheless, Cuba retains the death penalty.

Ordinary criminals were often charged with vague, politically tinged crimes like "dangerousness" or "antisocial activities." Meanwhile, genuine political dissidents were charged with petty criminal acts. In the legal code there was no distinction between political and other crimes. Both populations were mixed together, murderers and pacifists put into one cell. The length of sentences could never be certain: some people were released unexpectedly after serving half their time; others were held in jail without explanation after their designated time was up. Oscar Elías Biscet, a follower of Gandhi and Martin Luther King Jr., had been arrested for advocating civil disobedience in Cuba. Amnesty International started a letter-writing campaign for Biscet, which seemed to work. After serving only a fraction of his sentence, Biscet was released. Cuba took credit for a humanitarian act. Thirty-seven days later he was rearrested.

The dissident groups were routinely penetrated by MinInt officers from Section Four, the bureaucracy that specialized in counterintelligence against internal enemies. Section Four would put sleeper agents into dissident meetings, men and women who hung back for years, quietly listening, until they were trusted, and promoted. After a wave of arrests of real dissidents, several of these supposed dissidents would then appear at a press conference in Havana, announcing that they were loyal revolutionaries and that those arrested had been traitors and mercenaries in the pay of foreign agents.

Trusting people was not wise: the first time I sat down with Sánchez, more than ten years before, he'd announced that everything we said was being recorded. This was no surprise to me: my tape recorder was sitting in the middle of the table. But he pointed overhead, to the light fixture. "Assume they are listening," he said. "Assume that everything you say will be repeated back to you by an official someday. They bug our phones. They can listen whenever they want. I myself have found five microphones in this house. I don't think there are any now. But you never know. They cannot listen to everyone all the time, but if they want, they will find a way. Anyone can be working for them, even you or me." He pointed at the ceiling one more time. "We will never advocate violence," he said, "or anything illegal. We have to comply with the laws. But at the same time the law is an *absurdo*."

The surveillance was often remarkably crude. The phone taps were so bad you could hear the MinInt woman breathing in the background— they just listened to the conversation on an ordinary telephone. Some dissidents would even get in arguments with the clerks eavesdropping on them. The State did not try to hide what it was doing, not from the dissidents: it was better that they knew, that they felt the breath of harassment once in a while. A voice on the phone. A man sitting in the park, taking photographs. Just the possibility of surveillance did most of the government's work.

In the *New York Review of Books* the Romanian writer Norman Manea described the debilitating effect such a system induced:

> The mixture of paranoia and disorientation . . . the ways in which discouragement turns into resignation, then submission. . . . Life as a series of postponements, a tumorlike growth of mistrust and fear, an all-encompassing schizophrenia. A step-by-step reduction of private life, and finally its abolition, as time itself becomes subject to ever increasing taxation and eventually total expropriation by the state: the hours sacrificed to standing in lines, to ritual political meetings and to rallies, on top of the hours of work and the hours of helpless exposure to the inferno of public transportation . . . and when you were finally home in your bird-cage, you found yourself lost, mute, staring into an emptiness that could be defined as infinite despair.

In Cuba the survival adaptation was *doble cara*. You complained on Saturday night about the government; on Sunday morning you went to the plaza and shouted *Viva!* Both statements were sincere, because only the insane remained sane. William Faulkner called it "furious unreality," the hot embrace of the impossible.

Sánchez himself was the subject of a curious attempt at "exposing" him as a MinInt agent. The government had released a dossier on him, with documents claiming that Sánchez had been cooperating secretly for five years, betraying his fellow dissidents. There were even two photographs of Sánchez in compromising situations: in one, he was warmly greeting a three-star official of MinInt; the other showed him sitting on a park bench with a uniformed intelligence agent.

Sánchez laughed when I asked him about the incident: it was a crude attempt at sowing distrust among dissidents, he said. The dossier was fake, but the photographs were genuine. He had met both men after they initiated contact, hinting that they were sympathetic to the dissident cause. As an advocate of a "national dialogue," he had a policy of meeting with anyone in the government who wanted to talk to him, even a MinInt man who smelled like a rat. But Sánchez had insisted on having the meetings in public places. Broad daylight was an unlikely choice for anyone trying to hide; it seemed suited only to the photographer, who had taken a clandestine shot with a long telephoto lens. What secret agent would meet with his uniformed handler, on a busy street, right near his house, at noon?

To me, the release of this MinInt dossier smelled like a ham-handed effort at *Spy vs Spy*. I stayed with the same policy Sánchez had urged on me long ago: I assumed he was telling the truth, without forgetting that it could all be a lie. Cuba in a nutshell.

"Dios mío," Elizardo Sánchez said when I showed him the 1941 photograph, with its 238 faces. "This is the key to Cuba before the Revolution."

As was proving the case across Cuba, I didn't need to introduce the photograph or explain it. He knew what it was, immediately. Sánchez himself was *puro oriental*. He'd grown up in Santiago, and in the 1940s and 1950s had walked by the Colegio Dolores "a million times," he said. But he'd never set foot in the school.

"For me it was impossible to dream of going inside those high walls. My father was a telegrapher. You know," he said, tapping a code onto the tabletop, "he sent letters. So I went to a government school, a public school."

The dominant reality for Dolores students, Sánchez said, was their class. They lived within the bubble of privilege. "They had little contact with the ordinary people," Sánchez said. They were the sons of wealthy landowners, and the scions of successful professionals. They lived in the best neighborhoods, in the biggest houses, surrounded by servants. Their families had cars.

"Half the students were residents, and rarely left the building," Sánchez recalled, not quite accurately. "The other half were day students. They had a special bus, a really nice bus, painted up to read COLEGIO DOLORES, that took them home. I remember seeing that bus going through the streets, heading to their big houses in Vista Alegre. It was a privilege."

Although I had found some in Santiago and would now look for them in Havana, Sánchez assured me that most of the Dolores boys had gone into exile. He was in the unusual position for a Cuban of actually knowing what life was really like for the exiles, since he'd met many while visiting America. He'd even known Lundy Aguilar slightly; although they had grown up on opposite sides of the Dolores walls, they had met in the United States and shared ideas about nonviolence and the importance of dialogue.

Going into exile simply substituted new problems for old ones, Sánchez said. In America, the Cubans were still "strangers," lost to their own roots. Even if they succeeded in re-creating portions of their old Cuban lives in Florida—requalifying in their professions, buying new houses, rebuilding their fortunes—it was never enough, nor entirely genuine. One world had come to an abrupt halt; the other had never quite resumed. They didn't know Cuba, as it was now, and lived without fully participating in the life of America, Spain, Mexico, or wherever they ended up. "There's a double isolation," Sánchez said. "Lundy has said that his clock stopped in 1959. His view of Cuba is of the society before."

But even the boys from Dolores who had never left Cuba were still in isolation, Sánchez suggested. Their privileges, their fortunes, lives, homes, and country had all changed around them, while the culture and values they grew up with were locked in amber.

"Inxilio" was the word Sánchez used. Inxile. Internal exiles. Another coinage to paper over the cracks in reality. *"Inxilio,"* he said, rolling the word slowly.

Pointing to the photo again, Sánchez said, "That saved his life." He told me the story again of the way Castro had been hunted after the Moncada attack, while his brother and the Padre Rector at Dolores had intervened with powerful people to spare Fidel's life. Dolores served "to protect El Jefe when they were looking to catch him," Sánchez said.

From fugitive to hunter of fugitives, from rebel to scourge of rebels.

Castro had spent many of the subsequent decades obsessing over domestic enemies, and Sánchez had quite a list of the opposition groups around Cuba. The best known of these was the Varela Project. Under the guidance of Oswaldo Payá, a long-faced Christian activist whom I'd met in Sánchez's house years before, activists had gathered more than fourteen thousand signatures requesting an open national debate about economic and political changes. Under Cuban law, they were allowed to submit their petition to the National Assembly, but the legislature ignored them, and a year later Castro retaliated by staging a "referendum" in which nine million of Cuba's eleven million citizens signed a statement that the Socialist Revolution was "untouchable." Castro bragged afterward that he'd won 99 percent of the vote.

Payá and Sánchez worked together, but it was risky for dissidents to meet, and they had separate agendas. Payá was convinced that a Christian orientation and legal reforms within Cuba could work; Sánchez thought the regime could be moved by outside forces, like a moderation in U.S. policy and a strengthening of European arm twisting. He was more interested in the construction of civil society, of organizations that could serve as an alternative to the Revolution, a kind of shadow society within the confines of Cuba. He'd introduced me to a team of economists who, working privately in Havana, put out reports on the Cuban economy that used more reliable statistics than those in government reports. There was an association of independent journalists who tapped out dispatches on manual typewriters for internal distribution and publication abroad. There were private librarians, building a network of lending collections where banned, sensitive, or rare volumes were accessible to the public. There were independent lawyers, the *Agramontistas*, who tried to make Cuban courts uphold their own laws.

By cross-indexing their locations throughout Cuba against their leaders' names and their particular focus, Sánchez had made a computer database of the dissident network, a map of the constellation of dissent that he now printed out for me:

> The Escambray Association of Human Rights
> The Humanitarian Association of Followers of Christ the King in
>   Havana
> The National Association of Rafters

The Association for Free Arts
The Association of Political Prisoners and Ex-Prisoners in Güines
The Frank País Independent Library in Santiago

Franz Kafka, Gandhi, Martin Luther King Jr., Jose Martí, Václav Havel, Abraham Lincoln, and dozens of minor Cuban nationalists were commemorated in the names on list. There were Christian groups; women's groups; parallel professional organizations for doctors; youth groups; eco-pacifists; and people in favor of Civil, Human, Political, National, Liberal, and Worker's Rights; alongside the devotees of Peace, Love, Freedom, Democracy, Christianity, and Transition. Far and away the biggest constituency, however, were the private libraries. There were seventy-six of them on Sánchez's list, spread all over the country, in small towns and big cities, and named for a dazzling array of causes, heroes, and dates. Tens of thousands of Cubans had used the private libraries.

A staff member at the New York Public Library, named Robert Kent, had been in touch with a few of the bookish rebels and had come down to Cuba eight more times bringing gifts of books. Fascinated by their movement, he'd returned, and soon came to the notice of MinInt. Bringing books into Cuba was not illegal. Outright banning of books, or shuttering of libraries, was something even the Cuban government couldn't justify. So the American librarian was outed in *Granma*, not as a mild-mannered book-lover from New York City, but as a mysterious CIA agent named "Roberto X." He was not only laboring to split and divide the Cuban people, the newspaper reported, but was plotting to assassinate Carlos Lage, a leading official.

"Roberto X" was arrested in Havana in 1999 and expelled to the stacks of the New York Public Library. Unable to return to Cuba, he had passed me the address of Gisella Delgado, who ran the best-known private library in Havana. With Sánchez's list now in hand, I flagged down a 1954 Pontiac, and the owner, who was running errands, agreed to taxi me to the address for $2. It wasn't far—just on the other side of Vedado, in a crowded, humid apartment in the back of a 1940s building. Delgado was out, but her husband, Hector Palacios, greeted me, unsurprised by the sudden appearance of a journalist: I was the forty-sixth in the last year, he said.

He gave me a glass of tap water and showed me the offending library:

a small room lined with bookshelves, all of them packed with an odd assortment of old and new, moldering copies of *Don Quixote* beside Russian editions of the *Gulag Archipelago,* technical manuals, Cuban histories, textbooks, and reams of uncountable junk. I donated a Spanish copy of *Autumn of the Patriarch* by Gabriel García Márquez, which is about the last days of a green-clad dictator, somnolent inside his palace, who has ruled over a tropical island for a full two hundred years of remorseless decay, until even the harbors have silted up. García Márquez, a frequent visitor to Cuba, declined to say who he had in mind.

No wonder the Cuban government felt threatened. Within months of my visit to the library in Vedado, Cuba suffered its worst round of political arrests in decades. With the attention of Europeans focused on the American invasion of Iraq, Castro ordered an island-wide roundup of seventy-five human rights campaigners, democratic activists, and the leaders of the various independent associations, including ten librarians. Hector Palacios was one of them. After being held incommunicado, and then presented with government lawyers the day before trial, all seventy-five were convicted of being "mercenaries in the pay of the United States," and given sentences ranging from seventeen to twenty-eight years.

The government provided expert advice at the trials, in the form of Eliades Acosta Matos, director of Cuba's National Library. The private libraries were an "aggression" against Cuba, Acosta Matos said. In a subsequent article in *Granma,* he denounced "lies and subversion, such as the 'independent libraries,'" employing the extra quotation marks to imply that they were not private, but foreign-sponsored.

If that wasn't enough expert advice, Castro himself spoke up, complaining that the librarians had circulated several copies of the United Nations Universal Declaration of Human Rights. Castro specifically labeled this document "counterrevolutionary" and demanded an investigation of how it had been smuggled into Cuba. *Animal Farm,* and a biography of Martin Luther King Jr.—presented to the librarians by Jimmy Carter—were also named as counterrevolutionary.

European governments did protest the arrests, and took the symbolic step of freezing diplomatic contacts with Cuba. Castro promptly announced that it was *Cuba* that was breaking off relations, because Europe was meddling in the sovereignty and dignity of Cuba. But the tiff lasted only about eighteen months. At that point Castro transferred a few of the seventy-five out of the remote *cordillera* to the central jail in Havana, Combinado del Este, a model prison where the meals were square and prisoners were allowed to use a pay phone once a month. A dozen of the dissidents were now discovered to have medical problems, and one by one, over the course of months, that dozen were released. Cuba, which had touted the arrests and trials to its people, barely acknowledged the releases at home, but demanded and received credit for this humanitarian gesture in Europe. Diplomatic contacts were restored by eight European nations, including Britain, Germany, and France, all of whom made an explicit pledge to the Cuban government that they would never invite any of the dissidents to embassy cocktail parties in Havana.

The seventy-five were down to about sixty then. Hector Palacios was released after three years, "physically destroyed," he said. Many of those still in jail are senior citizens, with health problems exacerbated by the bad conditions, the poor food, and mistreatment. All face a decade or more behind bars.

The books from Palacios's house were confiscated as evidence, presumably including my *Autumn of the Patriarch*. After the trial, the presiding judge declared that the books were "lacking in usefulness," and ordered them burned.

Cubans have many things to brag about. Once, as I photographed a long line of people waiting for food, a man yelled to me, "Take a picture of our schools." In 1993, perhaps the lowest moment of the disastrous Special Period, when ordinary Cubans were at the point of starvation, I had walked at random into an elementary school and found the children being served heaping portions of ham salad, green peas, and bread, an unimaginable bounty for that time and place. Amid the economic stagnation of the late 1990s, infant mortality in Cuba continued to fall. Thanks to a policy of internal passports and close monitoring of legal residency, Cuba had very little in the way of internal migration and few of the slums typical in the rest of Latin America.

I knew a couple of *jineteros,* Victor and Jorge, who sold fake cigars of the lowest quality in the street. They were always hungry for my sandwiches and old T-shirts, and would watch for me as I left my hotel, sometimes following me around while prattling about how difficult life was in

Cuba. They were particularly outraged by the appearance of slums in Havana, a new phenomenon of the 1990s. These were called the *lleu ipon,* a corruption of the phrase *llego y pongo,* or, roughly, Come and Stay. Victor and Jorge talked so much about the awful shantytowns rising up on the outskirts of the city, hidden away from the sight of tourists, that I impulsively challenged them to show me the worst slum in Havana. They fetched a black market cab, an old black rumbler that reeked of gasoline. Through a cracked windshield, I watched our procession down to and around the harbor, through Regla, and then up the hills on the far side, the breezy heights where Hemingway lived and wrote. We turned left somewhere and rolled slowly past ranks of standardized apartment blocks, the precast concrete that the Revolution had scattered all over the island. The cabdriver wouldn't descend down a muddy track; we got out, crossed a field of soybeans on foot, and came over a ridge to where hundreds of small cement houses were spread out below us. This was it: the worst slum in Havana.

The homes were lined up in perfect rows along wide streets of mud, everything squared away in neat blocks. Each house was painted a different color. Each had a small front yard. We peered inside: two rooms. This wasn't luxury—bare bulbs hung from the ceilings, and only a few of the houses had running water—but they had solid roofing, and sanitary conditions. Blocks without plumbing had their own well with a hand pump. I started giggling.

Victor and Jorge looked confused, and then angry. "Look at how these people have to live," Victor said, trying to fume.

I'd been spending a lot of time recently in Peru, in the *pueblos jovenes* of Lima, where hundreds of thousands of people threw together improvised slums, building their own crude shacks, often of cardboard. Electricity was a dream, and they had to walk a mile to find a water pump, and then wait in a line of two hundred people to get a gallon. Even thatched roofing was considered a luxury there. But Victor and Jorge had never seen Lima, or Bogotá, where the dense slums were filled with desperate war refugees in rags, and gasoline-sniffing children begged through the streets. They'd never seen the steep *favelas* above Rio de Janeiro, crumbling, muddy slums where hovels slid down the hillsides in the rain, and teenage gunmen roamed at will. I'd spent two days amid the million squatters on the flats outside São Paulo going from murder scene to murder. In Cambodia, the young men like Victor and Jorge were living four to a woven mat. This *lleu ipon,* the worst in Havana, would be taken for paradise in such places. Every single resident had a roof, clean water, education, and a doctor.

It is impossible to reconcile the trade-offs Cuba offers. Who would choose one life over another? Thanks to the socialist school system, everyone, even the slum children, could read. Thanks to the socialist political system, they weren't allowed to. Books and magazines were banned, the Internet filtered, and the government monopoly on newspapers was enforced by censors who measured every idea against the words of the Leader.

But even as this machinery of repression ground out a frightened, pacified Cuba, right across the water the Dominican Republic was torn with gang wars, its health, law enforcement, and education systems collapsing, the country bankrupted by a colossal financial fraud engineered by corrupt politicians and wealthy executives. More and more Dominicans took to boats in a desperate bid to reach Puerto Rico and then the U.S. mainland. Which was better? Repression and control, or freedom and chaos? An island with a way out, or one with no exit? A place where no one starved but everyone was hungry, or one where the hungry could hope to become fat?

Cuba, for all its crippling chaos, management whims, bizarre programs, and wasted efforts, had still managed to lift itself into a world player in Olympic sports, and had even put a man in space (albeit on a Soviet mission). The technical university system allowed Cuba to export eighty million doses of hepatitis B vaccine; develop a potent blood pressure medicine, PGP, that was sold worldwide; and even put potential HIV vaccines into trials. Infant mortality had dropped from 100 deaths per 100,000 births before the Revolution to just 5.9 today, a figure that put many American cities to shame.

Castro, always prone to rambling, had sustained his legendary eloquence into old age, and until finally silenced by his 2006 illness, indulged himself in unstoppable diatribes on what he called *el bloqueo,* the blockade, as if the island were ringed by American warships. The American government referred to it as a trade embargo, but in either case it was a net knitted of loopholes, an unenforced fiction of exceptions. The George W. Bush administration simply increased the scale of American hypocrisy: while attacking Cuba verbally, Bush actually expanded trade, under pressure from farm-state congressmen and major American agribusinesses. There had always been a special exemption for disaster aid to Cuba; Archer Daniels Midland, ConAgra, and other companies lobbied for a "reinterpretation" that allowed shipping food year-round, and soon a hundred cargo ships a year were arriving direct from the U.S. with loads of Louisiana rice, Arkansas chicken, and Kansas wheat. During Bush's first three years in office, the U.S. government authorized $780 million in sales to Cuba; another billion soon followed, virtually unnoticed. Year after year it was piling up—apples from Washington State, dairy cows from Vermont—until a Cuban could not sit down to eat without eating American. For once, this meant I could eat well in Cuba, for there were juicy, overbuilt chicken breasts flowing into the Havana harbor, and I knew just the place to get one.

I had taken a room at a private house near the University of Havana. The building was beautiful, with a little patio in back, and you could walk everywhere from this central location. The owner, whom I will call F., spent his earnings on a definitive collection of 1970s rock CDs, almost a thousand records lining the walls of his house. F. was also one of the better (and better supplied) cooks in Havana, turning out huge meals of fried American chicken, yucca, and plantains. F.'s house had the disadvantage of being both legal and illegal, in that he was allowed to rent one room to foreigners—but rented four. Three Air France stewards and an Israeli girl were distributed in the other rooms. The sheets were horrible, and once, when a tax inspector appeared to verify that he was renting only the one room, I'd been thrown onto the street with three minutes' notice. But the food was good, and F. had other talents. In Puerto Rico, the late Alberto Casas had updated the fate of the youngest of three de Jongh brothers, Enrique. Alberto had added, in his shaky Palmer Method handwriting, that rarest of all notations for a Dolores boy, "Cuba." I'd learned that Enrique, who everyone called Kiki, was a prominent architect in Havana, but no one in Miami had spoken to him in decades, or knew his address or phone number, or would search for one, because he was still loyal to the Revolution. I explained all this to F.

I knew enough to time the result. Furrowing the brow of his close-cropped bullet head, F. went to the phone. It wasn't raining, so the connections were good. He called a neighbor. "Who is your friend who is the architect?" Then F. called that man, who referred him to a colleague who was in the architect's association. That man wasn't in, but there was another number for a house next to the one where he might actually be. F. left a message at that house, and then five minutes later, the man called back. He referred F. to yet another number, where someone flipped through an address book while we waited. F. grunted and then wrote a number on a pad.

Fifteen minutes, total. Kiki de Jongh answered on the first ring.

The old Hilton is the tallest structure in central Havana, a modernist slab that leaps twenty-seven stories out of a block-sized plinth in the heart of Vedado. The streets around the Hilton are filled with the iconic leftovers of 1958. On one side is La Rampa, the wide, sloping boulevard down to the sea, where Cuba played out its fantasies. La Rampa was, and is, lined with a couple of movie theaters, Chinese restaurants, several hotels, banks, airline offices, nightclubs, and bars, but most were long closed. One or the other of the movie theaters had a show, but usually not both. The entire front of the Hilton had been commercial space then, but the stores were shuttered. At night, the few tourists and *jineteras* on the surrounding streets didn't linger, preferring darker corners of Havana. The side streets were pricked with smaller towers, like the slender Capri with its pool on top, the ornate palace of the Nacional, and a half-dozen other hotels.

The minimalism of the Hilton was softened by a white and blue color scheme and the swooping lines of the side pavilions, in trapezoids and domes, a curving pool, and around porte cochere full of sputtering taxis. Built at enormous cost in 1957, it had 630 rooms, five restaurants, and was a bad investment. By January of 1959 Castro had moved into the Presidential Suite. His large troop of bodyguards slept in the lobby, draped in ammunition. Instead of paying their bills, they nationalized the hotel, renaming it the Free Havana. In the 1960s and 1970s it had been the only place in Cuba with international phone lines and daily newspapers from abroad. Tourism had now diversified Cuba's points of contact with the world, but the Hilton—the Habana Libre—was still popular with tourists, still a bit glamorous.

In the lobby, nothing had changed since '59. Palm trees reached up into the three-story atrium. The Trader Vic's restaurant in the basement had been kept literally untouched: photos on the walls demonstrated that not even a tiki lamp had been moved. They served the same faux-Polynesian menu, just more slowly.

I sat in the lobby for an hour, waiting for Kiki de Jongh. When I had first called Kiki and mentioned Dolores he had been suspicious, and refused to see me. He was too busy, he said. I would have to arrange an interview through "the government." But I kept him on the telephone and mentioned the names of various of his old schoolmates. I even agreed that he should not meet me at all, that it was inappropriate to speak until I had arranged everything through channels. But in passing I mentioned the book I had written about Che Guevara. He agreed to let me drop a copy at his office; finally, in the midst of confused discussion about the address, he said it would be easier to come get it himself. I couldn't bring him to F.'s house, so I named the Habana Libre and a time. Just before hanging up, his good manners kicked in. He agreed we could talk for "a few minutes."

Kiki had described himself on the phone as "short, though not by the standards of a Cuban, and fat, though not fat like an American." I sat in the lobby looking for someone who would fit that description. It was easy to wait. I had a drink, and a breeze whipped the lush plantings outside the hotel. All foot traffic into the lobby had to flow through one unlocked door. The doormen were like those at all Cuban hotels: uniformed, and more severe than friendly. Their job wasn't to open doors, but to close them—to keep out ordinary Cubans.

Separating foreigners and Cubans was an essential task, complicated and subtle. The Cubans rightly said that their doormen were engaging in security, keeping criminals out. There had been a wave of small bombs planted in Cuban hotels in 1997, by Salvadoran mercenaries, posing as tourists, who took their money and marching orders from a shadowy group of Cuban exiles based in Central America. The bombs were supposed to be tiny, almost symbolic explosions that would knock the legs out from under the tourism economy. But a bomb in the Copacabana Hotel, a few blocks from here, actually killed a thirty-two-year-old Italian tourist. Screening the hotel's guests made sense.

But in Cuba, security always meant more than physical security. In hotels, it meant keeping out all the Cubans who entered hotels for reasons the State did not like. Prostitution was one of those reasons: the State condemned it, but it flourished anyway. Castro was bipolar on the subject, railing against prostitution on television, but then actually bragging that Cuba had "the best educated prostitutes in the world."

I watched the Hilton doormen turn away one Cuban after another. They split apart a couple, turning away the Cuban man while admitting the foreign woman. The pair had been holding hands as they walked through the door, but were physically separated amid objections. She continued in, and the Cuban man waited outside. Then Kiki walked right in, untouched.

What was it? What did the doorman understand about Kiki, immediately? Cubans lived and breathed an idiom of silent signifiers. Kiki walked past the doormen without hesitation, knowing that he would be admitted; the doorman looked but did nothing, also knowing that he would be admitted. It took no conversation to reach this mutual comprehension: in Cuba, the less said the more spoken. Power was inversely proportional to volubility: those who talked most had the least, while the highest-ranking person in any situation was the one who stood silent.

Was it his age? Kiki was seventy-two, his skin touched with liver spots. Maybe the doorman sensed this venerable man was no possible problem. Or maybe it was another quality of Kiki's skin: the pale, even, pink tone. Cubans were infinitely sensitive to skin tone, to the gradations of class expressed in bloodlines.

Maybe it was his clothes? They looked ordinary to me: a wool driving cap, a simple jacket. Perhaps there was something encoded in the crease of his pants, or the cap, beyond my sight.

Or maybe it was simple presumption. A Cuban could bluff his way through doors if he had the right skin, the "foreign" clothes, the well-fed look of money or opportunity, and above all, the *huevos,* the balls, to walk in the door like he owned the place. Whatever Kiki was, it was enough. He shuffled inside without objection, one in a hundred.

He walked steadily but slowly, with the help of an unadorned cane. His hands and wrists showed the bulging veins of the aged, but Kiki had a smooth, untroubled face, and very few wrinkles for a septuagenarian. He wore a yellow short-sleeve shirt, the gray cap, and laid his walking stick across his lap as soon he sat down. He was an architect by profession, precise in his gestures, and almost unique among Dolores boys in his open admiration for the Revolution.

He fell silent when I produced the 1941 photograph. He looked at it for a moment, and then took off, cleaned, and put back on his glasses. With night falling, the ambient light in the huge atrium was barely enough.

"I started in '38," he said without preamble, "and was there ten years." The de Jongh home had been intellectual, cross-cultural, and outward-looking. His ancestors, he explained, were Sephardic Jews, exiled from Spain in the very year that the great Admiral of the Ocean Sea first landed in Cuba. Kiki's people had gone to Holland, acquired a Dutch name, and centuries ago had made the jump to the Caribbean, and eventually Cuba, picking up a Spanish "de" along the way. They were Catholics now, but only by background. Despite going to mass at Dolores every day for ten years, Kiki was not what the Revolution called "a believer." He had the new faith.

His father had been born in Cuba but raised in the United States, and was "one hundred percent American," Kiki said without pride. The most lasting cultural legacy of this "Americanness" was a twenty-nine-volume encyclopedia, in English, that his father had brought back to the island. It was the famous 1911 edition of the *Encyclopaedia Britannica*. Never mind that the book was British, not American: it was his introduction to the English language, to American science, and to global history and culture. Kiki claimed to have read it from A to Z in his youth, all forty thousand entries, absorbing the language that way (he understood English, but declined to speak it).

The 1911 *Britannica* was probably the best encyclopedia ever compiled. The articles were often written by the greatest experts in each field, and ran five or even ten times as long as those in modern encyclopedias, embodying the principle that all knowledge could be made available to all people. Aristocrats practice the art of distinguishing between like things, and Kiki argued that the 1911 edition, the *Britannica's* eleventh, was the "last really good" encyclopedia in the world. Before then, the state of knowledge was not advanced enough for the books to be comprehensive; after that, knowledge became highly specialized, and the age of the generalist declined, as did the *Britannica* series. It was the last moment, he explained, when all the world's learning fit into one set of covers.

The boys at Dolores were "aristocratic," Kiki agreed, when I used that word. They were "an economic, social, and power elite," he said. But they were not particularly right-wing. "Those who left?" he asked himself. "They weren't reactionary." They were just ordinary exemplars of their class. He was making fine distinctions again. The boys from Dolores grew into men who were educated, culturally advanced, and scientifically minded, he said, and accomplished in their fields. They were not the true ruling class of Cuba—not the old-guard plutocrats, or the conservative social elite, or the hard-line reactionaries. Instead, the young men from the photograph were *personally* conservative, but often modern and even progressive in their outlook. They believed in the Jesuit tradition of merit, in a society open to talent, where all were equal before God. They accepted that the Cuba of the 1940s and 1950s was broken and needed fixing. Batista was crushing society. The liberal aspirations of the 1940 constitution had been smashed. Exploitation, corruption, and violence were holding the nation back. "Logically," Kiki said, "the people of Cuba wanted change, including them." Here he tapped the photo.

He was the only *Dolorino* I found who sided plainly with Castro, still. "The problem of Cuba had no solution except the Revolution," Kiki explained with great satisfaction. "It was the only possible solution." At first even these prosperous *Dolorinos* had supported a revolution led by their old schoolmate. They had supported literacy campaigns and land grants and sending doctors into the countryside. But there was, in the end, one aspect of the Revolution that they could not accept. "It affected their economy," Kiki said.

Money. It came down to the laws of economics. His Dolores comrades had been comfortable in pre-revolutionary Cuba. They were "fundamentally accommodated to their position," as Kiki put it. And once Castro's reforms began to hit their pocketbooks—their businesses nationalized, their lands redistributed, their wages put under state control, their country houses turned into dormitories for the masses—they reacted. They became, Kiki now said, "fundamentally reactionary."

"They had to be," he explained. The complacency and sterile thinking of their class left them unable to cope with the changes. They lacked the imagination, the vision, to see the larger necessities of the revolution. "The only thing they were told was to defend the things they had," Kiki said. "If you are taught every day to repeat something, you repeat it."

His reasoning was problematic. The boys from Dolores were mostly from families that were, in the context of 1940s Cuba, liberal and progressive. He was arguing that the Dolores boys weren't inherently reactionary, but then suddenly became reactionary in 1959. That Dolores taught them to think critically, but also to repeat the mindless verities of their class interest.

In the end, it always came down to money, he said. No matter how the boys felt at the start of the Revolution, they had to—*had* to—turn against it in the end. This view of history leapt over the conflicted loyalties of men who supported revolution and then opposed it, and it could not account for the exceptions, men who thought, felt, and acted outside their own class interests, men like Fidel, or Kiki himself. Kiki was bypassing politics entirely, discounting all objections to the new system. The turn from democratic promises to absolute rule. The construction of an all-encompassing surveillance society. The seizures, the shortages, the arrests.

When I cited these objections, Kiki said, "It's true the Revolution was very hard. But no revolution can be weak." Our "few minutes" had now run to an hour, and he had reached his bottom line. "They *have to be* hard," he said with enormous emphasis. "Changing a country is a very difficult task."

He shook his head, the tutor frustrated with a dim student. "What did you expect, Patricio?" he said as he rose to leave. "What did you expect?"

THE HEROIC YEAR

They had to laugh the first time they saw the boat. Nervous, little laughter, the kind that follows a shock to the senses. It was colder out here on the end of the dock than they had expected, with a stiff breeze coming right off the Straits of Florida. January in Key West and you remembered you were on an outlying island, a distant outpost amid deep water.

The wind was bad enough. A huge storm cycle was just starting to lick its way up the Caribbean to Florida, then up the East Coast of the United States, all the way to New England. Twenty-one American air force personnel had just been killed when the wind toppled their radar platform into the sea. Even on the end of a dock, still attached to an island, you could feel it rattle the old navy boards.

And then there was the boat. Somebody made an appreciative whistle. And somebody else, quietly: *Mira; carajo coño!*

And another, saying what all were thinking: *Whose idea was this?*

And, following up: What *did you get us into, Admiral?*

Me? It wasn't me!

So it was nobody's idea. It just happened. Lundy and a dozen men like him had started out with a simple assumption. They would need a boat. And now they remembered that you must be careful what you wish for.

There was nothing unusual about this impulse, the desire for a boat. Nothing unusual in a few Cuban men needing a way to go to sea. Or about Cuban men gathering for a journey, into the Gulf Stream, even in the cold January of 1961. Cubans have always gone back and forth, over treacherous depths, in the most unseaworthy of small craft. Since the 1800s, the Straits had been full of Cubans and Americans in small boats, fleeing one revolution or another, sometimes sneaking a family member out or sending a load of weapons in. There were filibuster gangs of Americans trying to invade Cuba, and exiles and failed coup plotters getting out, decade after decade. The conspirators of 1930s revolutions snuck in and out of Cuba by boat, and in Hemingway's worst book, *To Have and Have Not,* it is revolutionaries who commandeer a small boat for an ultimately fatal trip to Havana. And of course, like his hero, José Martí, Castro himself had done it, crashing ashore (from Mexico) in 1956, aboard the overloaded *Granma.*

On the water all were equal. Exiles, invaders, American adventurers, gunrunners. Whatever the politics or century, they were sooner or later subjects of the sea. And in January, the Straits were in their natural condition: stormy and unpredictable. The Gulf Stream currents were slowed by the contrary winter winds, but also broken up, crosshatched with clashing impulses.

So Lundy and his friends had assumed, from the beginning, before they even knew what they were doing, that the first thing they needed was a boat to do it in. Maybe a fishing boat. Or a yacht. Or a launch. Any old thing. Cubans would go back and forth in whatever floated—inner tubes, surfboards, waterproofed cars, and $25 plastic boats purchased in Florida drugstores. If the weather was right, and if you took the shortest route, the famous ninety miles between Key West and the northern beaches near Havana—and both of those were big ifs—then in perfect conditions you could do it in a bathtub. And of course, people have done it in bathtubs. So Lundy and his friends knew they would need a boat. They were Cubans, there were problems back home, so they were going to need a boat.

But this thing. Lundy scoffed. The Americans had offered them "a boat," but this wasn't a *boat.* It was a goddamn warship! It was a PT, the same kind of ultrafast torpedo boat that the future American president, John F. Kennedy, had commanded during World War II. It wasn't a moldy leftover or outdated relic, either. At eighty feet long and twenty feet wide it was bigger and faster than anything Lundy and the other men had ever ridden. Though made of wood, it still displaced fifty-six tons. They climbed down inside and found that their whole group of volunteers—a dozen like-minded fellows, unsure of what exactly they were volunteering for—could fit inside the bridge. The PT had been stripped of its original equipment—four heavy torpedo launchers and braces of 40mm cannons for fighting aircraft—and the hull emptied out, so that it could carry cargo.

There were three engines, each a powerful twelve-cylinder Packard that guzzled gasoline but could drive the boat into a planing sprint of 41 knots.

So maybe, in a time when no decisions were made, when everything simply occurred, then maybe it was this moment on the dock—out of all the stumbling, sleepwalking steps of a dance—that they themselves first felt what they were in for. Each man had his reasons, his route to the dock, but now they were here. A crew, and now a boat. An eighty-foot-long monstrosity, a brawling, roaring warship, designed for suicide charges against the Japanese fleet.

Up on top of it, on the roof of the bridge, were two long and heavy shapes, concealed beneath canvas. The cloth spray skirts were fixed tight with neat sailor knots, but there was no hiding what was up there, nodding slightly to each wave that penetrated from the choppy Caribbean. Fifty-caliber machine guns. Just enough firepower to prick the crocodile's tail.

In Cuba, 1961 was supposed to be called the Year of Education, but that name didn't stick. In the street and in memory, it was something else. Action engraved itself into consciousness, and what happened in the Year of Education was that everyone learned to read. So people said that if something had happened in 1961, it had happened during the Year of Literacy. If someone had left Cuba during '61, it was during the *Año de Alfabetización*. People in exile didn't think that way, but for Cubans still on the island, that was it, the landmark of temporal navigation. Everything was before, or after, the Year of Literacy.

Cubans breathe hyperbole. A third cousin twice removed is your brother. Your actual brother is your twin. Strangers are esteemed comrades. Anyone who ever got a university degree is addressed as *ingeniero* or *doctor*. Flowers of speech denote the greatness of passion, or event. Cuba is not merely an island but "the pearl of the Antilles." Cuba is not merely beautiful, but, in the quote from Columbus that every schoolchild memorizes and every adult repeats, "the most beautiful land ever seen by human eyes." The government is not merely good, or great, or even perfect, but is *the most perfect form of government ever devised by man in history*.

Even the calendar had to brag. Titles were lathered on like lipstick on an old woman. Because 1958 was a time of war, fear, hope, and rebirth, the novelist Guillermo Cabrera Infante had called it the "Year of Grace." Everyone called 1959 The Triumph. And 1960 was The Reform, for the massive land redistributions. The decades went on, the Cuban government spilling out official names, but only these first, popular names and first, shattering years were engraved with a collective title: everyone called that era the Heroic Years, a name that covered the searing black and white revolution of 1959 through the cascading confrontations that ended at the Cuban Missile Crisis of 1962.

And in that time, there was only one year that was *the* Heroic Year: 1961. The year of education, and of the first reeducation camps. Beginning with a break in Cuban-American relations, and ending with Cuba's tumble into the deep folds of the Soviet cloak. The year of confrontation, open battle, and assassination plots. Sabotage and mass arrest. The Bay of Pigs, cleaving the country into supporters and opponents, unity or exile. The year of stagnation, when the seeds of defeat were planted in the fields of victory. Like all Cubans, the boys from Dolores began 1961 in one country and, whether still at home or suddenly abroad, they ended it in an entirely different place. People had fled the Revolution before, and would do so after, but 1961 was the year that created the Cuban exile as an institution, the year of the first great exodus under Castro, a flood not surpassed until the Mariel Boatlift of 1980, when Castro opened his ports (and jails) to a flotilla of American boats.

Mariel was the bookend, the late flight of those who were desperate. But the earlier, 1961 exodus was a very different wave of emigration, a flight of those who could afford to leave by airplane, or passenger ship, not inner tube. It was an uprooting of those who, even as their world collapsed around them, still had the ability to slip through the narrowing loopholes of the Revolution, to gather money, and manipulate two chaotic governments (their own, and that of their targeted exile) in a rapidly changing situation.

About two thirds of the boys from Dolores cut a path through this wilderness and into foreign exile. The rest found that they, too, had left, even without walking out of their homes.

The Year of Literacy was probably the most selfless and successful act that Fidel Castro ever undertook, with the largest moral component, the

widest support, and most profound impact on Cuba and the world. Starting on the first of January 1961, some 200,000 Cuban volunteers, mostly
very young, were given uniforms, an allowance for food, and an assign-
ment: go into the most backward slums, the most remote corners of the
countryside, climb the steepest mountains, and teach a million peasants to
read in just twelve months.

That January, the first brigades were photographed climbing into cattle
cars for the train ride out of Havana, to the Escambray Mountains in central Cuba and points east. Movie cameras followed them every step of the
way: for those who didn't care to read about it, the literacy campaign was
being memorialized for a film called *El Brigadista*.

These volunteer teachers carried tin hurricane lanterns, donated by
Maoist China. Farmworkers had free time only at night, and most of the
illiterate also lacked electricity. The Chinese lanterns substituted for light-
bulbs and became the symbol of the campaign, the light of knowledge.
East Germany, Czechoslovakia, and the U.S.S.R. also donated tens of
thousand of pairs of eyeglasses, a literal opening of vistas for Cuba's poor.

The students were adults, but began like any child, learning the alphabet, and filling their new notebooks with their first shaping of letters,
trembling curves and hesitant capitals. By instruction, the first words they
would ever write were:

> CUBA
> FIDEL
> RAÚL

Then they would compose their first sentences:

> The Agrarian Reform advances.
> The campaign is strengthening.
> The organizations of the masses are being integrated at the national
>   level.

Classes ran on a continuous basis, more and more of them as the Year
of Literacy went on. As a kind of final exam, every student learning to
read had to compose a letter. Not a regular letter, but a letter to him. The

text was dictated by the teachers, and the newly literate simply copied the sentiments, demonstrating penmanship and conformity together:

> *Fidel,*
>> *I am very proud to know how to read.*
>> *Thanks to you, I can write you this letter to tell you: Fidel, how great you are.*
> *Thank you,*
> *Irma Moquera Barrea*
> *Pinar del Río*

On the 5th of January—just the fifth day of the campaign—a young volunteer teacher named Conrado Benítez reached his post, high in the Escambray Mountains. He wore the uniform of the campaign, a set of military-style green fatigues, with a broad floppy beret, and a black and red armband. Black and red: the revolutionary colors. Conrado Benítez carried a lantern, not a gun, but there were men in the hills who saw him as an invader, a communist, a traitor, and on January 5 they shot him dead.

The government reacted swiftly. Troops pushed through every hamlet of the Escambray, hunting down what they called "bandits." After Benítez was lionized in the newspapers and on radio, there was a flood of new volunteers. The literacy campaign was accelerated, rather than slowed. The very next group of teachers to go into the field was named the Conrado Benítez Brigade.

Just the 5th of January, and the war—anticipated and feared, predicted and denied, talked about and plotted—was under way.

There had been a lot of talk in Miami. It had started with a whisper in 1959, built to a rumbling in 1960, and was now deafening as 1961 started. Every Cuban from Miami to New York seemed to have a gripe about Castro, his draconian revolution, and the need for Cubans to finally do something. People had convened a lot of meetings. There was one going on in Miami in January, with sixty different groups arguing about what to do. The conference was so big that it had to be organized like a trade convention, with booths for each group, and bitter enemies and former betrayals filled the hallways. Some of the talkers were right-wing politicians from the old Cuban parties, and some were Batista cronies, seeking their old fortunes. Others were ex-guerrillas and "true" revolutionaries recently purged by Che Guevara. There was even a contingent from the Cuban-Hebrew Congregation. As would prove usual for *El Exilio,* all that these Cubans could agree upon was what they were against: Fidel Castro. They took a dramatic but empty name—the National Revolutionary Council—and went on protesting, fulminating, releasing declarations, and announcing imminent victories, a cathartic but impotent strategy that would continue for decades without putting a scratch in Castro's Chevrolet.

But as these talkers and shouters, pamphleteers and archivists, demagogues and democrats, demanders and glad-handers all mouthed the great chorus of 1961, there were those whose silence spoke for them. Those who were done talking. The same year would now shed off a splinter group, the doers. There were all kinds of men who vanished into the dark violence of 1961, but perhaps none more surprising than the great democratic activist, Lundy Aguilar. He was one of thousands of Cuban men who evaporated from the streets of South Florida as the winter of discontent gave way to a CIA spring.

In a thicket of rumors was a serpent so large it could not be ignored: in January of 1961 every Cuban already in exile, and many still on the island, knew that some sort of anti-Castro military force was coming together. A big effort. Men kept disappearing with their duffel bags. Everyone knew someone who knew a young man who had gone off to somewhere to do something that couldn't be discussed. War was coming.

January of 1961 brought more than enough young men into Miami to replace, and then follow, those who had already gone off to join the secret military programs. It wasn't hard to see what was happening. Batista himself could be found in the back of a bar in Hialeah, meeting with wealthy men, recruiting, organizing. As far away as New Orleans and Venezuela, plotters, frauds, men of action, mercenaries, smugglers, and agents were weaving their nets.

And now in Miami, lots of new American faces were beginning to turn up. Some of them were just freelance tough guys, or wealthy commie-haters with crazy schemes, the new age filibusters looking for glory. Some crackpots from New Orleans—not a Cuban among them—had already run down to the island in an old boat, shot up some buildings on a beach, and got themselves arrested. But there were other Americans, too, men with suits, sober faces, and U.S. government credentials. They rented offices and settled in to stay. A new administration—the Kennedy kid—would be installed in Washington before the end of the month. New blood. New money. By spring, Miami had the second largest CIA station in the world.

Which is how mission creep took over. Lundy and his friends had begun by talking about innocent things—the fight for democracy, propaganda campaigns about their rights and losses. When the talk turned into action, they discussed getting a boat only to rescue loved ones still in Cuba. They enlisted in a new group set up by Jorge Sotus, the Dolores boy who had been a captain in the Santiago underground. It was called the MRR—the Movimiento Recuperación Revolucionario. But the vague agenda of "recovering" the revolution's ideals was soon being fed with American money, and equipment, and even incitement. The Americans were urging strikes on Cuba's Revolutionary Armed Forces, and sabotage like the burning of crops and the destruction of Cuban industry. With increasing regularity, there were frankly criminal schemes put forward, plans for assassinations, some promoted by the Americans, others generated entirely by groups of Cubans. The American military branches began seconding men and resources to the effort, more and more, faster and faster. So if some Cuban friends got together in the fall of 1960, and started training with a few old rifles and a twenty-two-foot fishing boat, then by January a group of short-haired American men would show up with cash, crates of machine guns, and the keys to *goddamn warships.*

You can't expect young men to turn back from a surprise, from a vision at the end of a dock. You couldn't expect them to stop and think, or to say the weather was too bad, or the implications of the mission too abrupt, or simply, this wasn't what we wanted. Momentum took over, the flow of events.

Whatever they felt, Lundy and his crewmates stowed their gear, started the engines for the first time, unhitched the hawsers, and motored slowly out of the Key West harbor, past low mangrove islands, and almost immediately were into the choppy, miserably cold blue of the Gulf Stream.

The waves were terrible at first, but once the motors were unleashed Lundy couldn't believe what happened. As the boat roared into a deafening, full-throated scream of power, it lifted on plane and the ocean smoothed out. Lundy's position was manning a .50 caliber machine gun, right up on top of the bridge. As he stood with a friend, hair whipping in the wind, they had to hold on tight and take a certain amount of slamming up and down, but their elation was evidence enough. The PT's shape allowed it to plane over the rough parts, and its weight and size allowed it to cut the winter waves right in half with little fuss. It filled them with confidence.

For a few hours, they simply enjoyed it, learning how the boat could twist into the tightest of turns, and even accelerate as it came out of them. How one moment they could flutter along quietly, barely moving, and then burst over the waves like a cavalry charge. There was not a boat in the Caribbean that could outrun, or outmaneuver, theirs.

But it drank a lot of gasoline. An Achilles' heel. The Packard engines were powerful, but thirsty. Almost all travel had to be low and slow, and when the boat did plane up and run fast it had to be on a short leash. After just a few hours of sprinting around, showing off, learning the handling and the feel of their future, shaking the cold sea stomachs out of themselves, getting used to the idea that they were going somewhere on this boat someday, then already they had to turn back for fuel.

So that was the first lesson. Resupply. The Americans had a saying: amateurs talk strategy, professionals talk logistics. January, and everyone was absorbing new lessons.

On just the second day of the year, at the United Nations in New York, Cuba had formally charged that America was preparing to invade the sovereign island, using an army of mercenaries, which was training in Guatemala. This allegation had the benefit of being true: as far back as March of the previous year, President Eisenhower had ordered the CIA to prepare an invasion army of Cuban exiles to overthrow the Revolution, and they really were in Guatemala, training.

So the American *goal* was just what the Cubans alleged. Yet they were wrong about one thing. Instead of a masterful and carefully coordinated plot by the most powerful country in the world, they were facing a chaotic and disorganized array of schemes, often by bumbling amateurs. The professionals weren't so good either: the CIA was working at cross-purposes with itself, in a confusion of overlapping, simultaneous projects to undermine Castro, schemes that involved all sorts of people in and out of American government, the military, the intelligence services, freelance crusaders, NASA, and Mafia hit men. The most extreme CIA measures were eventually lumped together under the title Operation Mongoose, a mishmash of sabotage, raids, assassination attempts, coup plotting, and competing invasion schemes.

The outgoing president, Eisenhower, handed off this jury-rigged and bum-rushed contraption to the incoming John F. Kennedy on inauguration day that January. The young president took up the project without much debate or trepidation: the entire Washington establishment shared the same desire to knock over Castro.

But in Washington and New York the first element of this plan was denial: American diplomacy feigned outrage at Cuba's report of an invasion plan. A day later the American government withdrew its ambassador to Cuba, closed the embassy, and broke off diplomatic contact.

The boats in Key West were the tail of a large dog. The American plan for Cuba was built on the CIA's experience overthrowing the governments of Iran (1953) and Guatemala (1954). In both cases, they had relied on an indigenous elite to do the dirty work, whether army officers staging a coup (Iran) or an invasion by a token force of "patriots" (Guatemala). The CIA believed that Castro could be overthrown in a coup, or killed, with the invasion being merely a backup plan. The idea was to send about three thousand Cuban exiles ashore at Trinidad, in southeastern Cuba. Once in possession of the town and its airstrip, these men would declare themselves the provisional government of a new, free Cuba.

Invading a sovereign country like this raised no eyebrows in Washington. Cuba was fair game. No one blinked at assassination schemes either. In February of '61, the CIA was directly involved in an attempt to poison Castro through a box of cigars. Another plot soon followed, this one to coat his wet suit with a poison. Before the year was out, there would be an attempt to poison Castro's milkshake at a Havana lunch counter. This one failed when the soda jerk lost his nerve.

The core assumption underlying all the American efforts was that by 1961, Cubans were deeply divided. This was partly true. Across the island, in Havana, in Santiago, and even in the Colegio Dolores, there were new and bitter disagreements. The unity and joy of the early, heady days of the Revolution had expired. But these divisions, however real, were not proportioned out the way Americans assumed. The majority of Cubans were still pleased with the direction of their country, and saw Castro as the guarantor of literacy, land for farmers, and the punishing of the guilty. Yet theirs was not the voice that carried furthest. It was the objections and fears of the Cuban elite that reached Washington, echoed in New York, and dominated in Miami. America was listening to the cries of those who had lost land in the redistributions, not those who had gained it.

Castro was slowly spreading his hand over Cuba, touching more and more aspects of life on the island. But at this point, the big corporations and wealthy foreigners had lost out, while Castro had not yet alienated the majority of Cubans by seizing even small Cuban businesses. Life ticked along for most people, more or less the same as before. Castro's own personal popularity was very high. People liked the new order and the urgent summons to rebuild Cuba, to reshape the society, to bring justice to the poor and bread to the hungry. Castro still denied he was a communist, or even a socialist. Those words were not popular with the mass movement of ordinary, middle-class people that had risen up to oppose Batista. So the words were never used.

What wasn't said mattered. Even before taking to the hills of Oriente in 1956, Castro had offered two central ideas: the immediate restoration of Cuba's beloved New Constitution, from 1940, and then free and fair elections within one year. Constitution; elections. This two-part promise was central to Castro's appeal as a student leader at the University of Havana; he spoke of it on Rebel Radio, the guerrillas' clandestine station; it was written into the platform of his July 26th Movement. The 1940 constitution, and then elections.

Because of this moderate agenda, even the head of the Bacardi company, Pepín Bosch, had supported Castro and the guerrillas financially. Other wealthy men helped with money or put their farms at the disposal of the guerrillas. Cuban exiles in New York and Florida had poured money and rifles south to Castro, the great democrat, the principled lawyer who would restore the country to the people. On the island, the middle class responded to these generous ideas in huge numbers, contributing to fund-raising drives for the guerrillas by buying their clandestine "treasury bonds."

Even many Americans in Cuba, including some in the U.S. embassy, expected that Castro—a middle-class *blanco* lawyer talking about democracy and constitutions—would make a ·fine replacement for Batista. A dozen American volunteers found their way into the Sierra Maestra and became guerrilla fighters. The CIA even went as far as sending Castro a token shipment of arms, in an effort to court him. Several American-owned corporations, like the national telephone company, held back taxes due to the Batista government and gave the money to the rebels instead.

But within three months of coming to power Castro began to back-pedal on his claim of free elections within one year. The country had to be put in order first, he said. There was a crisis situation, which demanded delays. Appearing on *Meet the Press* in April 1959, Castro said it would be eighteen months until the elections. By early 1960 the vote was said to be two years away.

In early 1961, the government suggested that it would now need another four years to create the conditions for a national vote. Nobody talked about the 1940 constitution anymore.

It isn't necessary to speculate about what Havana looked like in those January days. Two years into the Revolution, the ordinary street life of the city was recorded on film by a teenager named Orlando Jiménez Leál. Just nineteen, he was a precocious cameraman who had taught himself to master the new generation of small, light cinema cameras that were starting to change documentary filmmaking in America. With integrated sound, fingertip focus, and magazines that held four hundred feet of film, the cameras allowed someone like Leál to turn observation into self-creation. Cuba's most powerful film critic, Guillermo Cabrera Infante, urged his friends in television to lend the nineteen-year-old wunderkind a camera, and to give him the tag ends of film rolls left over from official projects. Leál cobbled together these scraps of film stock and set off into the streets of the city, his finger on the trigger, looking for this transitory Havana, a city pinned between worlds coming and worlds going, the high and low in uncertain relation.

Foreign tourists had deserted Cuba by 1961, scared off by the appearance of barbed wire around government buildings and by new checkpoints on the roads, manned by militiamen exploring their first taste of power. Castro had welcomed the departure of the tourists. He'd closed all the casinos and made a great show of opening the beaches at Varadero and other resorts, which had been restricted to hotel guests under the previous regime. He canceled the 1961 convention of ASTRA, the association of travel agents, announcing that Cuba no longer needed tourism, a parasitical industry that reduced the citizenry to servants and prostitutes. Since the hotels of Havana were empty, the Revolution moved hundreds of poor people down from the mountains and into their empty rooms. The main salon of the Nacional, where Errol Flynn and Winston Churchill had relaxed with drinks and cigars, was converted into a school for tailoring, the high ceiling echoing to the curses of pricked thumbs.

Shooting at night in January, Leál filmed the people of Havana commuting through the darkened port, their faces weary from work. His lens caught the rough water at the Regla ferry docks, the same storm surge that was shaking the old navy dock up in Key West, the same waves that were bobbing Lundy's machine gun up and down. Leál caught the out-of-focus forms of men ashore, and the idlers in bars, drinking and dancing. People still crowded into tiny spaces to celebrate, even if the foreigners were gone. They still played music, and sang, and danced, and got drunk. They still dressed within the social conventions of the pre-revolutionary era, so that even poor men wore skinny neckties and porkpie hats. Black, white, mulatto, they drank from dirty glasses and twirled on the tiny dance floor as musicians scraped at *güiros*. The bars were sweaty, dirty, cheap. Old women lifted their wrinkled arms over their heads to dance the rumba, gallants showed off the funky chicken.

Shot entirely in black and white, under street lamps, the film has no dialogue, only the ambient noise of Havana on an evening in January of 1961. Absolutely nothing happened. But the nineteen-year-old Leál had unwittingly pulled the trigger on the old culture of Cuba, assassinating it with his silver nitrate. His scraps of film, coiled up inside the camera magazine, needed only half a year to force Castro's hand.

It was history that sent Lundy back to the boat in February. At some point, the slow growth of historical truth had bound him to this fate. He had asked to join the MRR group, first of all, because he trusted Jorge Sotus, his friends were in it, and he felt envious that they were doing something. But there was also a "metaphysical" reason. For years, in print and speech, he had warned that Castro could become an absolute tyrant.

He had to live up to his own beliefs. There wasn't any firm decision, or moment of revelation, or sudden insight. He just followed logic to its consequence. "Why not?" he asked himself one day. "I'm a coward, but I have to do something."

Everything was growing: the MRR now had sixty-six men in covert operations, and the CIA had supplied them with a second and now a third PT boat, a little squadron berthed in Key West. They had started out very green in January, but they weren't fools, and learned to run the boat well and to be good soldiers, even if the CIA gave them crappy used boots and only vague information about the future. For Lundy, it was perhaps a Jesuit leftover to believe that everything that could be done, could be done well, even raiding, and he was proud to hold the coveted job of machine gunner on this, their first real mission. They went down to Cuba in February, approaching the northeast coast in the dark, and started probing for the mouth of the Bay of Nipe. The professor, the student of Cervantes and Shakespeare, was on top, clutching the machine gun, and he spent hours peering into the murky night. Even with his crewmates around him, war was a lonely place. Downstairs, amid the regular crew, was one passenger. An MRR operative, to be put ashore inside the bay. His mission was to make contact with internal resistance cells. But they couldn't, for love or money, pierce the darkness and learn exactly where Nipe was. Every shade of blackness in the night was a mystery.

Lundy was by nature dispassionate, an agile dissector of doctrines, seldom angry, proud of his self-control. Standing on the boat in the dark, he didn't *hate* the Revolution, because hate clouded the truth. The literacy campaign and other social programs were fine by him. Class interests meant nothing to him: like Castro, Lundy was only a peripheral member of any elite. His family had lost no broad ranches to the agrarian reforms, nor seen any empires of wealth vanish. It was the love of history, of Greek arguments and valiant citizen-soldiers in Athens and Paris and Philadelphia that had led him, like a catechism, through the same questions, again and again, each one leading to the next.

Does absolute power corrupt, he asked himself as they patrolled in the dense night, *absolutely?*

It must.

Is violence against a tyrant justified?

It was, in the case of Batista, and so it must be once again, in the case of Castro.

And then the old questions, the same ones come around again. *Will you choose? Whose side will you be on? Which standard? If death came for you right now, which side would you be on?*

Last of all, and fraught with the most implications: *Will you act?*

The decision could not be evaded. You had to choose, and act.

But in the night off Nipe, what action was there? There was nothing to see or do. And more nothing. No thing. No form. Shapeless night. An hour went by in silence.

They weren't supposed to talk up on the machine guns, but the waters of Nipe were famous for their quantity of sharks, which led someone to joke that "they" should have eaten "him." This was a reference any Cuban could understand: one of the famous incidents in Castro's life was a long swim through these shark-infested waters.

Everyone knew the story, because the Revolution's propaganda apparatus had already begun mythologizing the events of Castro's life, finding prefiguration in the leader's youth and omen in his feats of superhuman strength. Nipe Bay was one of these moments, and Lundy had heard the story from Castro's own mouth. He had seen Castro twice after the Revolution. The first time was just a brief visit to the Presidential Suite of the Havana Hilton, in the earliest days. Castro had a lot of new friends, but few old ones, and Lundy was gradually able to penetrate the rings of security and hangers-on, the guerrillas with M1 rifles who lounged in armchairs down in the lobby, the crowds of journalists, politicians, beautiful women, and high-ranking *barbudos,* the bearded ones, in the dark hallway of the top floor. Lundy was finally admitted to Castro's suite, which had a sweeping view over Nuevo Vedado and La Rampa, Cuba's national driveway.

They spoke only briefly that first time, enough to exchange best wishes, to laugh at the turns of fate that had brought them to Havana and the presidential suite. As he left, Lundy spied the books on Castro's night table: a volume on Marx that looked, from its smooth spine, like it had never been opened, and a well-thumbed copy of the speeches of Juan Perón. An autocratic populist, Perón had thrilled 1940s Argentina with his rhetoric on behalf of the poor and with his wife, Evita, bedecked in diamonds. Perón talked about progressive themes like universal jobs, health care for all, and pensions for the old, and his supporters had lapped it up, but Perón also gave deranged speeches about Argentina's arsenal of atomic bombs, and even its secret space program. Perón's flights of fancy were a powerful reminder of how far strident nationalism, calls to glory, and the total escape from reality could take a politician.

The story of Nipe Bay had come up about a year later, during their second encounter in the winter of early 1960. Lundy had run into Castro while leaving a Havana TV station. "Hey, Lundy," Castro had called out. They sat down and Fidel quickly turned the conversation to Nipe Bay, his very first attempt at overthrowing a dictator. The dictator that time was Rafael Trujillo, and the country was the Dominican Republic.

Trujillo was a monster who deserved the bullet he eventually got. Another self-styled president-for-life, he spoke of freedom while crushing dissent, gave nationalist speeches while doing whatever the United States wanted, and declared himself the savior of the republic while looting the treasury. Trujillo always wanted to be called by the same intimate street term that Castro liked: *jefe,* or boss. It was a kind of fake intimacy with ordinary people, a suggestion that absolute power did not mean what it seemed.

In the studio Castro told the story of Nipe Bay with relish, even though Lundy knew it already. In 1947, Trujillo had just committed the latest of many outrages, sending his police to massacre a huge number of Haitian immigrants working illegally in his country. It was an act of genocide, immediately infamous worldwide, and in Cuba, Castro joined a badly concealed plot to overthrow Trujillo. About 1,200 men boarded four boats and set sail from Nipe Bay, heading out into the ocean and making a right toward the Dominican Republic. On board the main boat, the *Caridad,* were hundreds of Cuban toughs, many of them from the world of armed political gangs in Havana. Some of Castro's biggest rivals were on the *Caridad* with him, and the disorganized plot lacked clear leadership or even a battle plan.

The one thing they did have on board was ego: everyone had been talking, loudly, about their would-be revolution. The Cuban government knew exactly what they were up to, and an hour or so after the *Caridad* and the other three boats turned out of Nipe Bay, they were intercepted by the coast guard. The *Caridad* was ordered back to port, and the invasion now became a humiliating embarrassment. In a panic, men started throwing their guns overboard. Castro, rather than face arrest, jumped into the shark-infested waters and swam for it.

By his own account, Castro had swum through the night, covering about eight or nine miles, before dragging himself ashore. Most people would drown attempting such a long swim in ocean conditions. Some of Castro's enemies on the *Caridad* later claimed that he had actually left the freighter in a small boat and rowed ashore, but he was a good athlete, fit, and disciplined in a crisis, so he could have swum it.

Lundy himself had already heard a different version—that Castro had indeed swum away from the *Caridad* but had been rescued by fishermen at some point, near death. And Castro hadn't fled the boat to avoid arrest, Lundy thought. He'd fled to avoid being murdered by his rivals, who blamed the talkative Castro for advertising their plot in advance. Castro did have trouble keeping his mouth shut. Just two days after coming ashore, he was back at the University of Havana, giving speeches where he bragged about leading the coup attempt. He even named many of the other participants, who were at that moment under arrest, busily denying their participation.

Whether Castro really swam eight or nine miles, at night, through shark-infested waters, was irrelevant. By 1960 it was already the official mythology that he had. Chairman Mao had to swim the Yangtze; Fidel had to have survived the sharks of Nipe Bay.

The conspiracy of Nipe Bay was a template. It was at once a principled gesture of violence against a corrupt dictator, prefiguring the *Granma* invasion in '56, and also a preview of Castro's appetite for placing himself, sometimes retroactively, at the center of all events. It was a glimpse of megalomania. Fidel described it "like it was the battle of Waterloo," Lundy said. "The appetite was there" in the TV station encounter. In 1960, "he knew he had to control it. But it was there."

All this was a whispered story to fill a dark night watch on the PT boat. But turning back and forth, they simply could not find the mouth of the bay. Nipe had a narrow entrance, hidden by sandbars. All night, darkness and false visions tortured them as the boat growled aimlessly, turning this way and that.

The *zurdo,* the klutz, wasted a lot of effort trying to look martial. He stood at the gun, gripping it, ready to fight. But it felt useless, a toy. The only time they ever fired it was at the start of each mission, as soon as they cleared into international waters. Just one short burst to check that everything worked. When Lundy looked over at Jorge de Moya, who manned the other gun, he saw him equally poised, ready, clutching his .50 caliber, but looking slightly queer.

"How are you doing?" Lundy finally asked.

"I'm fine," de Moya said, "except I can't move my hands." The blood had drained right out of them. "Are you afraid?" de Moya asked.

"I think so," Lundy said.

They probed along the coast like that all night, finding only the wrong places. When the first crack of indigo appeared to the east, they knew how quickly dawn would come. The courier mission was aborted. They turned the boat north and ran for Key West.

Oswald was in Minsk and Kennedy was still in Georgetown when Pepín Bou found himself right back where he had started. In January of 1961, twenty years after bouncing through the hallways of Dolores with a young Fidel and long after leaving the city and the country, he was back in Santiago de Cuba.

After Dolores, Pepín had gone straight to college in America, earning a degree in chemical engineering. In 1955 he and his wife, Celia, moved to New Orleans. Pepín found work with a big American mining firm, the Freeport Sulfur Company. A daughter was born to the couple there, their third, but within two years they returned to Cuba. Freeport wanted a state-of-the-art nickel processing plant in Cuba, employing a new sulfuric acid refinement process, a complicated innovation that extracted much more profit from a given ton of laterite ore, but which required a big investment up front. New machinery required a skilled staff. Cuban engineers were in demand, and Pepín.

In the second half of 1957, Pepín returned to Santiago, but not for long: his family stayed there, while he pushed on to the new site at Moa Bay. It was an area rich in minerals, especially nickel and cobalt, but one of the most isolated places in Cuba. It had a good anchorage, however, which was perfect for shipping in an entire American-built refining plant, assembling it, and then shipping out Cuban nickel, all with hardly any connection to Cuba itself.

Moa Bay was a bad place to work and a worse place to live. The mine sat halfway between Birán, the backwater where the Castros had grown up, and Baracoa, a legendarily remote town that claimed to be the first spot Columbus came ashore in Cuba. That is to say, it was halfway between nowhere and nowhere else. There was no road, just a cart track, which expired in mud during the rainy season. Only the best trucks could get across that way. Most of the mine equipment was brought in by ocean barge, straight from the United States, and the ordinary crews were brought in from Santiago by boat, or via miserable daylong treks in the back of a jolting truck.

The supervising engineers, like Bou, were in a more privileged position. If the weather was good they were flown from Santiago straight into the local airstrip on a DC-3. To make this cost-effective, they had to live at the site for an eleven-day shift. Then they were flown out for four days at home, followed by another eleven days on site. Assembling an industrial site in a wilderness was aggravating, and the long shifts were isolating. The men lived in dormitories, and there was no telephone. The only entertainment was listening to the radio. The nearest people were in a puny village along the coast, with mud streets, one bar that had hitching posts in front, and no whorehouse. Everybody just worked. During 1958 the Freeport equipment was steadily barged in and assembled, and by the fall three out of four refining lines were in operation.

Like the Havana Hilton, the mine was a badly timed investment. By November of '58, more and more towns in Oriente were falling under rebel control, and in early December, a column of guerrillas under Che Guevara broke out of Oriente, storming west into central Cuba and toppling garrisons left and right. At Moa Bay, everyone listened to the radio at night, helpless, disbelieving. The whole east of the country was grinding to a halt, all commercial activity and even daily routines suspended, with strikes breaking out, and underground militias rising up. The replacement crews in Santiago could not be rounded up, and the barges stopped coming. As the guerrilla offensive spread, every American corporation in Cuba suddenly lost its appetite for business. Freeport abruptly ordered the mine shut down and the crews sent home.

Pepín thought it would be a matter of waiting things out. A few months, perhaps.

After January 1, 1959, the chaos began to resolve itself into a semblance of normality. The mine didn't reopen in 1959, but the equipment still needed upkeep, and Freeport kept one engineer on duty at Moa Bay throughout the entire year, serving out the same eleven-day shifts. Pepín had to stand that lonely sentry only a few times, but those days were the worst. History was being made in Havana, the country slowly beginning to wake up to the repercussions of a new era, but Pepín would be sitting in the middle of nowhere, cleaning the equipment and waiting, cleaning and waiting.

In July 1960, still marking time, he served what turned out to be his last shift for Freeport. Without warning, Castro announced in a speech that the government was nationalizing a host of foreign companies. Freeport Sulfur Company was American, of course. Suddenly Moa Bay belonged to the people.

The boys from Dolores were seldom without resources. Pepín found a new job easily enough. His father was head of sales at Bacardi, the most famous distillery in the Caribbean. Pepín landed a desk job in the company's red-brick headquarters edging the Santiago harbor. Pepín's job was connected with a brewery in Santiago that produced Hatuey, the island's favorite beer.

Pepín had always supported the Revolution, but that was no distinction: even top Bacardi executives had supported the guerrillas and had cooperated with the new revolutionary government so eagerly that they welcomed fatigue-wearing revolutionaries into the executive offices to help coordinate production. By some estimates 90 percent of Cubans had sided with the *barbudos* by the time they came to power. Pepín had done nothing to actively support the Revolution—during the fighting, he'd given some money, like many people—but he considered himself a sympathizer.

Sitting on the fence was no longer enough. In early 1961, after he'd been at the brewery just six months, four men in the new uniforms of the Revolutionary Militia appeared at his office door. They were armed but led by a civilian in a tie and jacket, who was carrying a telegram addressed to "Engineer Bou."

"Can you read?" the man asked. He was offering to read the telegram out loud, if Pepín needed that. Bou wanted to snort—could anyone called "engineer" *not* read?—but he restrained himself. It was the Year of Literacy, and the rights of the uneducated were much on everyone's mind.

Engineer Bou took the telegram, and so became the last person to find out the news. The message had come straight from the office of the president of the republic, in Havana. Pepín was to report to the capital in three days. His air ticket and a room at the Hotel Nacional were already reserved.

This was not an invitation to decline. He flew to the capital on the second day, and while checking into the Nacional he ran into another engineer he knew. José Batlle had been a student at Dolores, though not in the same years as Pepín. Still, they knew each other in the way Cubans do: they were *oriental,* they had mutual friends through Dolores, and Batlle had also worked for Freeport Sulfur at Moa Bay. They called to each other by their nicknames, Pepín for the older man and Pepito for the younger.

Soon they realized that the soaring, half-timbered lobby of the Nacional was full of engineers. Mining engineers. *Nickel* mining engineers especially. Most were Moa Bay people. That meant an initiative to restart the plant.

The next morning Pepín and Batlle were picked up in the curving driveway of the Nacional by a government car, with Che Guevara's personal driver, a Cuban navy sailor, at the helm. They were taken to the Banco Nacional, where Che had set up his economic ministry. In the big conference room there, they joined a much larger group of mining engineers, making three dozen people, total. This was a group that Batlle called "the whole world" of Cuban mining. Now they realized that only a small minority of them were from Moa Bay. It had to be a nationwide initiative.

Although they had been told that Fidel Castro himself would attend the meeting, in the end, after a long wait, it was Che who came. He had a big entourage that included some *barbudos,* some bureaucrats, and Pepín's old schoolmate, Raúl Castro. More important, Raúl's wife was there: Vilma Espin, one of the most influential of all revolutionaries. She was an old friend of Pepín's and greeted him warmly, but when Bou nodded at Raúl, smiling, the number two man in Cuba did not acknowledge him. Like Fidel, Raúl was suddenly shedding old versions of himself, along with those who had known him before the fatigues.

Che stood and laid out a new mission in soaring terms. The Revolution was going to restart production of nickel at Moa Bay and increase it at all the older plants, starting immediately. The Revolution needed nickel to barter with the Soviets, who used it to harden the metal in aerospace components, including missiles. In exchange, the Soviets would give their help in other matters.

"Who is disposed to volunteer?" Guevara asked. Only two or three people raised their hands.

Che protested and complained about their lack of patriotism, and then revealed that it didn't really matter whether they wanted to do it. "If you want to work in Cuba," he told the engineers, "then you have to go to the nickel plants."

When Pepín got back to Santiago, he found it was true. A telegram from Havana had beat him to the Bacardi building. Pepín was stopped as he walked in; "Engineer Bou" had been banned from the premises.

So it really was nickel or nothing.

At Dolores the bubble of privilege was trembling without yet bursting. Entering the third full year of the Revolution, the school carried on as much the same as possible, but it was obvious something would soon change. In late January, Belén, the Jesuit sister school in Havana, had been closed by the authorities. Eighty militiamen had taken over the sixty-acre campus, shutting it down and transferring its 1,200 students to public schools. Although the government cited educational reform as the reason for shutting Belén, everyone knew that the school was a nexus of Havana's most recalcitrant families, a rallying point for the Catholic, the wealthy, the stubborn, the obsolete.

Dolores remained open, hopeful that in Santiago, the *ciudad revolucionaria,* there would be less pressure. Each day the students went through the motions as before, the morning mass, the same curriculum, the students cycling in and out of the classrooms as if nothing was going to happen.

The education was as rigorous as ever, but a reactionary atmosphere had crept into the building, an increasing stance of hostility toward the changing world outside. Reflecting the views of their parents, most students had now turned fervently anti-Castro. In mid-January Padre Seven Foot, the teacher who had worn a July 26th armband in 1958 and briefly traveled with the guerrillas, was at the center of a dispute. Even though he had given up on Castro, students taunted him, and parents complained about the presence of a "communist" at the school. Finally the school asked him to take a leave of absence until things had calmed down.

What didn't change was just as important. One of the boys, Bernardo Souto, thought the school was still wonderful, still rigorous, but out of step with the times, unaware of the social changes occurring worldwide as the 1960s swept in. The Revolution outside Dolores merely highlighted what was different within the walls. The school was elite and expensive in a country now ruled by the poor masses. Most noticeably, at a moment when Cuba was abandoning all forms of social and racial discrimination, Dolores was touched with hidebound social views, views that seemed only to deepen as the world outside changed. The school was, Souto recalled, "a little segregationist, a little misogynist."

In late February, in the middle of the morning session, it finally happened. There was a commotion out in the halls. The Jesuits were called together, the teachers brought out of the classes to hear something. Various adults were seen whispering. And then the school bell began to ring out, fast and hard. It wasn't a bell ringing a new hour; it was the last bell, ever. The students were told to assemble in the courtyard. They went through the drill once more, all the boys ranging down the stairs in open order, swirling into the courtyard, forming their neat lines.

Go home, the Padre Prefect said. He stood facing the student body, standing behind the high black railing. The message was simple: go home at once, and for good. The militia was on its way, and the Colegio de Dolores would be closed, permanently.

The boys gathered their things, and went out into the street, standing about as if this was any other day. The militia arrived, searched the building, and posted a guard, who locked the door. The Jesuits who lived in the school were allowed to stay, but even boarding students were forced to leave, with all their things, immediately.

The Jesuit mission in Santiago was over. There was no place for an elite in the new Cuba, even an elite of merit, of talent. There would be only one curriculum, now, nationwide, and only one kind of school, the revolutionary school.

Like other members of the class of 1961, Souto no longer had a school to graduate from, but that spring the Jesuits gave him and the other seniors diplomas, so that they could qualify for higher education. Souto's grand-father had come from Spain penniless, and settled in Santiago impulsively, based on the fine appearance of the city from the deck of a ship. He had built a corner store into a big business with coffee roasters and a ware-house. His grandson took his psuedo-diploma, the last ever granted by Dolores, and reversed the journey, returning to Spain with nothing. He'd been back to Cuba just once, to see Santiago a last time. He'd stopped by Dolores. It was his business card that the guard at the school had kept carefully for so long. Souto settled in Bilbao, the Basque capital, where in 2004, he was a salesman of Formica counters and other kitchen equipment.

When did they know? The very first day, that day of revolution? Or on the tenth? The four hundredth? When did they sense that something had gone wrong?

Or was everything still in play, all results still possible? Do dreams become true, in gradual revelations, or all at once, on a deadline?

Memory was writing Cuban history now, and the curious Cuban art of retrospective prediction ordered all understanding, even as the events occurred—perhaps even before they occurred. The human need for agency, for patterns, gave purpose and shape to the chain of events. People needed a guide, augury in a voice that crystallized the new truths, explaining that things had gone bad, permanently wrong, at just one particular moment. And that moment was usually the one in which each recollecter had made the decision. It was the decision to leave that brought with it the knowl-edge that all was finished, every hope over. Hindsight is twenty Cubans talking about the Revolution.

For Guillermo Cabrera Infante, novelist, film reviewer, and bad-boy intel-lectual of Havana in the Heroic Years, the prophet was a writer he called "the Turk." Cabrera Infante was the editor of *Lunes,* or *Monday,* the Revo-lution's own cultural magazine. *Lunes* had a circulation of 200,000 and a mandate to overturn the culture of pre-revolutionary Cuba. Founded and published by the government itself, *Lunes,* with Cabrera Infante at its head, was supposed to create and chronicle the rise of the new society.

That was also the point of interviewing the Turk (his real name was Nazim Hikmet). He was a celebrated Third World writer, and he came in 1961 to visit Cuba because the island was suddenly at the center of history, a new standard-bearer in an age of decolonization and independence movements. Writers like this were pouring into Havana, global intellectuals rallying to the splendid combination of social justice and tropical intensity. The Colombian Gabriel García Márquez took a job as a staff correspondent for the new revolutionary press agency. Alejo Carpentier quit a comfortable job in Venezuela to move back to Havana. Carlos Fuentes, a Mexican novelist, was waiting in Havana to cheer Castro's arrival. Mario Vargas Llosa, a Peruvian, rushed to Cuba to offer his solidarity to the new government, and returned frequently, as did Julio Cortázar and Jorge Amado. The hemispheric boom in Latin American literature became intimately tied to the setting of Cuba's ambitious revolution, and *Lunes* was constantly taking the measure of these foreign intellectuals, chronicling their enthusiasm for the Revolution and its many projects.

But when the editorial board of *Lunes* invited the Turk to sit down for a formal interview, to chronicle his discoveries about Cuba, they did not get the quotes they were expecting. Although he had come to Cuba in hopes of finding a new thing, a previously unknown iteration of freedom, Hikmet arrived in the spring of 1961 and found something old and familiar: a military regime eerily reminiscent of the "revolutionary" Turkish governments that had repressed freedom in the name of their own power.

"Leave," Hikmet said that day. A poet, he needed only one word.

Cabrera Infante was shocked. So were his colleagues. *Leave Cuba?* Join the crazed exiles, with their war on literacy campaigners and their American paymasters? Why would progressive intellectuals leave Cuba? Of course there were problems. But surely this was no time to run away! The agrarian reforms were long overdue. And why should foreign companies, with corrupt ties to the old dictatorship, get to control the sugar, the telephones, the banking, and every other business of importance in Cuba? Anyone could see that the Revolution's new literacy campaign was a wonder. Only a fascist could be against it.

But this was indeed the very *last* time they would be able to run away, Hikmet warned. He had spent seventeen years in Turkish jails, imprisoned by a military regime that had begun with talk of peace and justice, and then degenerated into a dictatorship. His crime had been to write things that discomfited those in power. He was absolutely sure that Cuba would go down this road as well. It had to.

The Turk spoke in the bleakest, most urgent terms. "Travel," he ordered the assembled writers and editors. He urged them to "invent" trips abroad, immediately, on any excuse, and then stay there. As a last resort, those who couldn't get abroad might be able to protect themselves somewhat by becoming famous, by drawing international attention. "Make yourself seen outside," he counseled them.

But even literary prizes or international friends would not be enough. Sooner or later, they would have to run for it. The time to start planning was *now.* "Above all," he told the disbelieving table, "start to choose your lucky star!"

He meant, your north star. Your escape route. Your destination in exile.

Santiago's Cathedral, a behemoth of ocher plaster with two bell towers, sits right on the Parque Céspedes. In March one weekend, at the end of the main Sunday mass, the families who came out of the church were confronted by an angry crowd. Most of those attending services here—the most important church in eastern Cuba—were white. Most of those in the crowd were black or brown. Most of those leaving church were well-to-do, nicely dressed, keepers of social traditions, the establishment, the included. Most of those in the crowd were humble, the poor, the outsiders and the excluded.

It wasn't anything new to see people gathering outside church. Watching the rich and prominent stroll out of mass on Sunday into the city's main square had been a form of entertainment for centuries. But now the mood was different. The wealthy and the well known were greeted with insults. Arguments started. Threats flew. Then someone slapped an upper-class woman, and the parishioners were suddenly confronted by a rain of blows. As they fled, people were thrown down, the expensive dresses of the women torn by the taunting crowd, the men punched until blood stained their mouths. It was a scuffle, not a massacre, but the dynamic of who was excluded from what had changed. So had the status of the Church.

The rich had never been more than a tiny minority in Cuba, and their traditional power and influence—a system built over centuries—were abruptly gone. The ancient social dynamic of Cuban life—the way people related to one another, the customs, speech, habits, and gestures of daily existence, the divisions among whites and blacks and browns, the role of money, ownership, and labor, the moral force of the Jesuit and the *santero*—all of it was abruptly inverted. Lifetimes of resentment found sudden outlet in symbolic attacks on the aristocracy of Cuba.

Just as Dolores had been closed to silence a center of dissent, in the first days of April it was the turn of Santiago's tennis club and yacht clubs. These symbols of exclusivity were seized and shuttered by the government. The island was now caught in a self-reinforcing, downward spiral: the more the elite attacked Castro, the more tightly he gripped their throats. The more they lost, the more they renewed their attacks. The more they resisted, the more justification Castro and his supporters had for their growing paranoia.

Right from Day One, some people had begun fleeing the new Cuba. At first it was those directly implicated in the previous government. Batista himself flew out of Cuba just four hours into 1959, carrying a million dollars in his suitcase and taking a hundred of his closest friends for company. There was a trickle of departures that first year—the panicked flight of a few millionaires, of some notorious torturers, and of the informers who had blood on their hands. But the air was rendered fresh and pure, and only a few instinctive creatures—the rebellious Alberto Casas, with his hands toughened from milking cows—fled simply because they could. They were considered freaks, at first. Few people sensed anything wrong. On the contrary, Hugh Thomas, the greatest foreign historian of Cuba, said that a "lyric spirit" had descended on Havana in that year, while few people could avoid being "entranced by the nobility, the vigor and the charm of the revolutionaries." Nineteen fifty-nine "was a unique moment of history, golden in promise, the dawn of a new age." But it was also, Thomas noted, the end of one world. And when one world dies, another must be born, a process that cannot be painless.

During 1960 the number of people fleeing increased, with members of the political class and the wealthy beginning to feel some inchoate threat. In that year, those who fled were usually comfortable enough to do so without losing much. But a few ordinary people who were particularly sensitive to their precarious status—a substantial portion of Cuba's Jewish and Chinese communities—headed quietly for the door.

Lundy Aguilar had fled that year, an early departure, the rare philosopher to take his own advice on history. Even as he had supported the anti-Batista struggle in 1958, he had warned in a Havana newspaper that "the vital thing in Cuba is to avoid a situation in which violence triumphs, and where the heroes of today are converted into the oppressors of tomorrow." These sentiments—these premonitions—did not stop Lundy from trying to support the new government. As a noted thinker with personal ties to Castro, he had volunteered in 1959 at the National Institute of Culture, trying to help consolidate the social transformations enacted by the new government, like the lifting of all race-based distinctions and an early program to send "mountain teachers" out to remote villages.

It wasn't hard, as Thomas noted, to see good in what was happening. Castro had started by sharing power, appointing a moderate, traditional politician to serve as president of Cuba. Castro courted public opinion in the United States by appearing in New York and Washington, talking on television, and assuring Cubans and Americans that he would reinstate the New Constitution and set up elections.

But after seven months at his job in the National Institute of Culture, Lundy was convinced that the authoritarian leader he had glimpsed in the TV studio was coming out. Castro dismissed his puppet president and began consolidating his own power. Lundy resigned from the ministry and went back to his books.

In May of 1960 he had been provoked to take up his pen again by the shutting of a right-wing newspaper. This was *Diario de la Marina,* a Havana daily that had grown increasingly strident in criticizing Castro. In May, the government—via an outraged "workers committee"—had stormed the *Diario de la Marina* offices, tossing out the staff and locking the doors. When the revolutionary government refused to allow the paper to reopen, Lundy wrote, for the rival newspaper *Prensa Libre,* his last column:

THE HOUR OF UNANIMITY

Liberty of expression, if it is to be genuine, must be shared by everyone and not the prerogative of any one person. That is the issue here. There is no need to defend the ideas of *Diario de la Marina;* what must be defended is the right of *Diario de la Marina* to express its ideas. And the right of thousands of Cubans to read what they consider worthy of reading. . . . If they begin by persecuting a newspaper for having an idea, they will end persecuting all ideas. . . . The silencing of an organ of public expression, or its unconditional absorption into the government line, means nothing less than the subjection of all real criticism. And since they won't, or can't, refute the argument, they silence the voice. The method is old, the results well known.

And so to Cuba comes the hour of unanimity: the solid and impenetrable totalitarian unanimity. The same fate will now be repeated for all publicity organs. There will be no divergent voices, no possibility of criticism, no public refutations. The control of all methods of expression will speed the labor of persuasion: fear will do the rest. And, beneath the vociferous propaganda, silence will remain. The silence of those who cannot speak. The complicitous silence of those who, being able, do not speak.

Instead of a multiplicity of voices, they prefer the formula of one guide only, one route, and total obedience. So comes the totalitarian unanimity. Because totalitarian unanimity is even worse than censorship. Censorship obliges us to silence our own truth: unanimity forces us to repeat the lies of others.

This was the last defense of free speech ever published in Cuba. The very next day Aguilar was denounced on the radio. Then a group of workers from *Prensa Libre* itself called for the paper to repent and for the author of this offending editorial to be sent "to the wall," meaning, taken out and shot, like one of the Batista assassins. *Prensa Libre* was shut down on the third day. A friend with connections in the government stopped by Lundy's house to suggest that he would be wise to leave Cuba immediately. He departed within days.

All such departures in 1959 and 1960 were incidents, individual acts, when compared with what would come. In January of 1961 the rupture of diplomatic relations with the United States, and the quick tit-for-tat of accusations and confrontations that followed, opened a set of floodgates. By the end of that January flights out of Cuba were packed solid. By March of the Heroic Year, three fourths of the faculty of the University of Havana were living in South Florida.

This diaspora, the Exile, now took shape from a flood of middle-class Cubans. Dolores graduates fled in great numbers that year, but so did ordinary people and even dedicated revolutionaries. Eloy Gutiérrez Menoyo, one of Castro's top commanders during the Revolution, bolted in mid-1961 with a dozen supporters, denouncing Castro for betraying his promises of a "revolution as Cuban as the palm trees" and "bread without terror."

Their way out was smoothed by new American legislation. The U.S. Congress authorized the Cuban Refugee Assistance Program, which allotted $100 a month to each Cuban exile arriving in America, paid for health care, and arranged college loans.

The shuttering of private schools and the creation of a new, revolutionary curriculum during 1961 were guaranteed to alienate the well-to-do families who had been running Cuba up to this point. Opponents of Castro, whether in the State Department, the Catholic Church, or the streets, spread reports that children would be the next victims of Castro's agenda. Godless communists were taking over, according to the gossip of Radio Bemba, the grapevine, and Cuban children would henceforth be subject to brainwashing lessons on the glories of Marxism, turned into robotic cogs for a totalitarian machine. Catholic officials fanned these fears, reminding anyone who would listen that during the Spanish Civil War, churchmen had been shot by the anarchists and the communists, and children had been sent to reeducation camps. Whether it was true, or merely CIA propaganda, the rumors spread like wildfire. As Carlos Eire put it, "Everyone knew someone who had known someone who had known someone whose kid had been sent to Russia." That was enough.

The very first to go were a few students from wealthy and deeply Catholic families in Havana, but as word of this spread it helped fuel a cascading disaster. When the Catholic schools of Havana were closed in January the Church organized an evacuation of about two hundred students, who were flown to Miami and enrolled in similar Catholic boarding schools there. The Church called this Operation Peter Pan, but there was no magic at work. In February, with Dolores shuttered, Santiago families began exporting their children as well. Hundreds, and then thousands, of families signed up to have the Church take away their children. Overwhelmed, the Miami diocese of the Church filled its schools with new children, and then set up five camps across South Florida to accommodate thousands more children who were suddenly appearing. When the camps were full, the Church began to disperse the Cubans to foster homes in Florida, and eventually across the United States.

Here was the Cuban gift for mutually reinforcing self-destruction.

With more children leaving, the Revolution reacted defensively. Castro saw a resource vanishing: boys of military age. First the government banned boys of draft age from leaving. Then it was boys *approaching* military age who were banned. This in turn fed the fears of parents: why did Castro need their sons, if not to reeducate them, to turn them into his rifle-toting New Men? So families began to fake the ages of their male offspring, slipping their sixteen-year-olds out as fifteen-year-olds.

Everyone assumed that this Children's Crusade was temporary. The outgoing boys were told that they would be gone only a matter of months, a semester perhaps. They were simply taking an academic year abroad. Among the families there was a universal expectation that some looming conflict would straighten things out. But they were, as always, underestimating the Revolution.

All year the flights kept going, a thousand children a month in the spring, the number growing fast. One of these Lost Boys—a successful radio executive in Washington, D.C., when he told me this—described his abrupt transplantation from tropical Cuba to a snowbound Kansas, placed with a family who, though kind, spoke no Spanish. He had never seen his parents again. The wry novelist Carlos Eire had himself been a Peter Pan child, exported from a palm frond dream of youth. He had the good fortune to be set down in Miami, amid Spanish speakers, but he and his brothers found themselves crowded into a dingy foster home crawling with cockroaches. They ate gruel and lived under strict regulation, more like inmates in a reform school than children.

By the end of 1961, Peter Pan had swept up 14,048 boys and girls (only a very few of the latter). The Revolution was not "straightened out." Carlos Eire did not see his mother for years. Many Peter Pan children became effective orphans, separated from family permanently. Almost none would set foot in Cuba for the rest of their lives.

Becoming an exile was still possible, legally speaking, and not just for children. For any family seeking to leave the island the first step was to stand in line at the nonexistent American embassy in Havana. With diplomatic relations broken off since January, the U.S. embassy had been formally closed, but you could still pick up paperwork there, which could then be processed through diplomats from Britain (and later Switzerland). Children could get a visa waiver automatically, but adults had to apply, demonstrating that they had financial sponsorship in the United States, meaning family, a friend, an employer, or some connection. Adults could also apply for a special category of visa, a new Cuban refugee quota set up by Congress. Just getting the right paper to apply for the right combination of waivers, applications, visas, and supporting affidavits could take months.

Then came the need for a passport. The Cuban government would not accept the old, pre-revolutionary ones. Everybody had to apply for a new passport, and since this was an obvious prelude to leaving the country, asking for a new passport became the decisive step in the whole process. The American end of the paperwork could be set in motion secretly, but once the government in Cuba received a passport application you had effectively made declaration of your opposition to the Revolution, and there was an immediate response from the government. Inspectors often arrived the same day, unannounced, to confiscate everything in the house. This was done by making a detailed inventory: the number and type of books, the utensils in the kitchen, the nature of each picture or painting on the walls, the types and models of appliances and the size and style of the furniture, the lamps, the clothing in the bureaus, even the toys. All this now belonged to the State. Those leaving Cuba could take nothing with them.

The audit, as this inspection is known, immediately generated its own counter-industry. Cubans learned to sell or give away their possessions before applying for the passport. By the time the inspectors arrived, the house would be empty, cherished books handed out ritualistically to old friends, dresses and their particular memories distributed amid weeping, chairs hauled off by cousins.

The auditors would return on the day before your departure, whether a month or a year later, and verify that every item on the list was still in place. It all belonged to Cuba.

What belonged to Cubans themselves was an increasingly short list, especially for those leaving. The about-to-be-exiles were allowed few items. Two each of shirts and pants. Three each of socks and underwear. One sweater, one hat, one set of pajamas, and one book. Not counting what you were wearing, which led people to put on three shirts. The militia, in turn, began to enforce a new rule against wearing multiples of anything. With each month of 1961 the rules became tighter: the definition of jewelry was extended to include watchbands, the maximum weight of all possessions was detailed, and the dimensions of suitcases specified. The allowances gave rise to a new economy. There was a boom for seamstresses all through 1961, since they could help beat weight restrictions by sewing up special bags, which were sized the absolute maximum permitted but made of the lightest canvas, so that more of the weight allowance went to clothing. It did not matter if this gossamer luggage tore or wore out: it would be used only once.

Those who, after months of such maneuvering, finally made it to the Havana airport found that family separations were made even more wrenching by the long process of examining paperwork, which was conducted after the departing Cubans had been separated into a special lounge. This had been walled off from the rest of the airport with glass and was called *la pecera,* the fishbowl. On the outside, families waited and watched for the four or five hours it took as those departing were searched by Cuban militiamen, who confiscated anything on a checklist of contraband items, weighed the luggage, and counted items of clothing. Guards took children aside and made them drop their pants, peering down into their underwear to make sure that no prohibited items—jewelry, money, and so forth—were being hidden down there. For Carlos Eire, the snap of elastic on his belly that afternoon in the fishbowl, the casual way he had been scrutinized down to his prepubescent *cojones,* was the most embarrassing moment of his life, a stinging symbol of the State's intrusion. Decades later, he admitted that just the sight of a glass coffee table could send him spiraling back to those final hours in Cuba, standing in *la pecera,* looking back through the distorting lens at his father for the last time. Exile started right there.

Miguel Llivina talked of the same thing as everyone else. At least, everyone he knew. His friends and former classmates around Santiago were all suddenly applying for visas to America, or any other country that would have them. They were arranging business abroad, trips to see family, tourism, whatever they could. The world he knew—professional middle-class Santiago—was dissolving. Some were still siding with the Revolution, more were turning against it, but almost regardless of what they believed, people were talking about leaving the country, at least for a little while. After many anxious discussions with his wife, conducted in the hushed tones that suddenly seemed appropriate, Miguel decided that they should follow suit.

Like Pepín Bou and José Batlle, Llivina had gone to work at Moa Bay for a while. The big plant had opened up many jobs for qualified Cubans, and Llivina, an accountant, had done well there. But he had lost his job in late 1958, when the American owners had halted production.

Miguel moved back into his father's house, and during the first year of the Revolution he found work with the Texas Oil Company West Indies Ltd.; as the name indicated, it was the Caribbean subsidiary of the American oil company. The Texas Oil Company owned the only refinery in eastern Cuba, which sat on the far side of Santiago's harbor. Built in the 1950s, the plant was state-of-the-art and had attracted a large number of American and Cuban engineers, technicians, and professionals to Santiago.

The Texas Oil Company plant refined twenty thousand gallons of crude oil daily. As part of its contract with the Cuban government, the company was required to refine "national oil," that is, oil produced in Cuba. But Cuba produced very little of its own oil. In 1960, the Revolution began sending sugar to the Soviet Union, receiving in return regular shipments of Soviet oil (and also of weapons—both heavy and light arms). The Soviet ships, bearing Black Sea crude, began entering Santiago harbor passing Smith Island, where Desi Arnaz had swum. It was now called Granma Island.

The Texas Oil Company was, like other American-owned refineries in Cuba, willing to process this Black Sea oil like any other oil. Despite the tension between Cuba and the United States, this was simply another day at the job for oilmen who were eager to avoid conflicts with their host government. But the U.S. State Department was looking for ways to pressure the Cuban government to return American properties. The State Department urged the American-run refineries to reject the Soviet oil. Reluctantly they agreed. The Cubans promptly countered by declaring that since the Black Sea crude was the property of all Cubans, it was therefore the "national oil" covered by the contracts, just as if it had come out of the Cuban ground. When Texas Oil refused, the Cuban government declared that the company had broken its contract. A barge appeared at the refinery one morning, and a group of Cuban administrators stepped onto the dock. There were no guns present: just clipboards and lawyers. They announced that the plant had been nationalized.

The American manager got in his car and drove home, never to return. But Miguel Llivina, like other Cubans at the plant, and indeed most of the Americans as well, stayed put. He didn't know what else to do, so he kept going to work. History is transcribed from gestures and instants, but the force of events was just as often a liquid accumulation of conflicted and unsteady hearts, millions of nondecisions, passive reactions, and unmade gestures. Survivors are not troublemakers. Invisibility and compliance are the keys to riding out such storms. Most Cubans just waited. They thought they were already masters at that.

Success, when it came, was nearly the end of them. Lundy made his third run with the PT in March. As they prepped the boat at the dock in Key West, looking over the guns and motors, twenty-two Cuban men in uniforms arrived. They climbed aboard and went down into the hold, clattering with a wide array of personal weapons and heavy packs of ammo. There was supposed to be secrecy about the mission, even at this point, but from their fatigues and guns it was obvious they were commandos, and it was inevitable that, in the tight-knit world of Cuban exiles, some on the crew knew some of the men coming on board. So the name of the target came out soon enough: the oil refinery in Santiago. First they would sabotage the big refinery, and then the men would fall back on the Sierra Maestra, where they would link up with local partisans who were fighting Castro.

They left at night, but it wasn't possible to conceal everything—their "secret" base in Key West was right next to a brightly lit marina, so that fishermen and even tourists driving by could see the boat slip out. The trip down was fine, including a refueling stop at a new dock in the Bahamas, and the weather cooperated—bad enough to conceal a small boat on the big sea, but not too nasty. The PT slid in toward the shore of Cuba, northeast of Santiago Bay, in the dark of another night. They dropped off the men, leaving them on a beach in the small hours without incident. The commandos set off to meet a contact and then worked their way around toward the city.

At first light, well off Santiago and running back toward the Bahamas, the squalls on the ocean parted, and Lundy saw a black shape far out ahead of them. In a glance they could all see what ship it was. An American frigate. But it wasn't under American colors. Like the PT boat they were riding, it was a surplus ship from World War II. This one had been sold to the Cuban navy of Batista. Now it was under revolutionary officers and the July 26th flag. It could run at 32 knots, for days. It had four-inch deck guns, which could lob shells about eight miles.

Lundy felt the PT turning under him, and then the deck rising as the boat planed into a sprint at 40 knots. The frigate turned to intercept and also accelerated, throwing up a white bow wave.

Lundy saw a spout of water rising up behind him, an exclamation point lifting out of the PT's wake. And then, as if in reply, the distant crack of the frigate's gun.

The gap between the ships opened. And then again: a splash, followed by the report of the gun trailing over the water. Clutching the machine gun for stability, he knew there was no point firing back. Even at close range the .50 calibers would be useless against a steel frigate.

But the distance kept opening. They didn't dodge, but they didn't run exactly straight either, moving in long and fast lines, just weaving away from the frigate, their thoughts flying out ahead of them toward the Bahamian keys. The frigate kept charging. The CIA had told them they could call for help, but only once they reached international waters. When they thought they were far enough out, they called the assigned frequency, again and again. There was no reply.

Was the frigate getting smaller? It had to be. There were no more shots. In slowed-down time, the frigate shrank, and went hull down over the horizon, until finally Lundy, still holding the .50 caliber atop the bridge, thinking about his children, still believing that he was going down into the sea, saw it vanish.

Eventually, after the long trip home to Key West, they were told the commando mission had been a success. But there were no details. Nor any howls of protest from Cuba.

———

What was true at this point, the last moment of the original Revolution, or the first birth pang of the exile? Who to believe? The gossip on Radio Bemba was whatever truth Cubans themselves broadcast, in fear and expectation, in Santiago or Hialeah. Fantasy. Rumor. Thirdhand facts. In Miami that spring the story spread that a force of exiles was massing in Central America. The MRR couriers that went back to the island, carrying plans and messages, only added to the confusion. Some disappeared or were arrested. Others had been double agents all along. Some succeeded all too well, sending back reports of tremendous successes, new break-throughs, garrisons ready to mutiny, secret armies, the imminent over-throw of Castro and all his works. Within Cuba, the reports were equally wild: mysterious airplanes overhead, secret purges, midnight arrests, para-chutes drifting down over the Escambray, speedboats moving in and off shore as the nights of winter gave way to spring.

A spin of the radio dial was head-spinning. On one frequency, the Revolution had never been stronger. On another, Castro was doomed, in his final hours. Powerful new transmissions started up on the AM dial, declaring in Cuban accents that a new order was coming, that Castro's days were numbered. The only reliable source of news was found amid the denials. No, the president of Guatemala suddenly announced one day, there was no truth to the rumor that groups of armed Cuban exiles were on Guatemalan territory, training. No, American officials said, they didn't have any connection to the new clandestine radio stations. When Castro almost bragged that acts of sabotage had increased, and that millions of dollars' worth of sugarcane had been torched in March and April, the United States said it had not been involved and had no intention of attacking Cuba.

But in the end, there was a set of facts, a bitter truth. Despite all the sabotage and shoot-'em-ups, the couriers and commandos, in the end these exile successes were either imaginary or irrelevant. The resistance groups were either fraudulent or genuine but heavily penetrated by spies who betrayed every plan. The arms shipments, all the tonnage moved by sea, all the parachutes flung down in the night, added up to nothing. Different groups of raiders were led into traps, or arrested as they slept, or wiped out in ambushes, or simply scattered and disbanded in the mountains.

For Lundy, for the men of action, it could not be said to have been a waste. There had been a reason to fight, or to try. But it came to nothing. Out at the refinery in Santiago, Black Sea crude went in, and gasoline, heating oil, and aviation fuel came out.

Miguel Llivina never heard about any acts of sabotage, at least not at the refinery, and there wasn't any spectacular commando attack. Under the new management, things went on, more or less the same. Even in April of 1961.

Just because everyone really is against you doesn't mean you aren't paranoid. In Cuba, there really were strange airplanes overhead, but Castro was never satisfied with reality. Parachutes did indeed drift down over Escambray, but he did not limit himself to that. Arms caches were indeed discovered, but that was no reason not to invent allegations. Anti-Castro guerrillas did try to fight, in the Sierra Maestra and central Cuba, and the CIA really was massing an army to attack. But reality was never enough.

So, with the hour of fate approaching, Castro mobilized his police and army that April to confront the approaching enemy. But he didn't send his troops to the beaches to build defenses, or to the mountains to dig bunkers. In the last days before what would actually turn out to be, for once, the real invasion that Castro was always talking about, Cuba's leader mobilized his resources to defeat the enemy inside Cuba—that is, his own citizens. The police and militia were sent out in April to engage in mass roundups of the usual suspects. Anyone who was associated with disloyal "elements" in Cuban society was under suspicion. They began with the known critics of Castro, especially the hierarchy of the Catholic Church. All the bishops in Cuba were confined to their residences or held by the Department of State Security. Church properties were occupied by the new block committees. But a vast net, thrown in haste, swept up people almost at random. Local authorities, acting on gut instinct, locked up people all over Cuba. The wealthy. The religious. Students and businessmen. Active dissenters and the merely suspicious. The old families and the young toughs. By some accounts, 100,000 Cubans were either arrested, informally detained, or ordered not to leave their houses in the days just before the Bay of Pigs invasion.

But even a broad net, if poorly aimed, will miss some fish. In Santiago,

Dr. David de Jongh, the oldest of the de Jongh brothers, spent the days before the invasion at his medical business, wearing his lab coat, carrying out his duties. But he'd been talking with friends, and was one of those who actually was getting ready. He didn't know what he was getting ready for, but he despised the new government, and remembered Fidel from Dolores all too well.

Radio Bemba, the gossip, said an invasion was coming. David's family was wealthy, with resources, and lands, and hobbies, especially the Cuban love of bird shooting. He gathered together a handful of weapons from their various properties—rifles, shotguns, pistols—and took them to the lab. There, in a kind of secret shelf inside each of the long lab tables, he stored the guns. An amateur searcher would never notice the hidden space, which was surrounded by medical equipment. Whatever happened, whoever came down on which side, he would be ready.

But nobody came to the house to detain him, and nobody came to the lab to search it. He was a respected medical figure. Of the 100,000 names on the list of enemies, he, even with his guns, was missed.

They went out one last time, in April. Instead of the quick overnight dash toward Nipe Bay in the north, it was now a four-, five-, or six-day mission. Refueling in the Bahamas took time, and by April the only infiltration teams that could still be located were operating on Cuba's far southern coast, requiring a longer journey around the crocodile's tail. And the boats themselves were slower, because they weren't carrying just humans anymore.

The American way of war is to do more, to count tons, to total up firepower, to win victory through supply of ammunition. The CIA men in Key West assumed that victory in Cuba depended on equipment, and they put increasing pressure on Lundy and the MRR for more deliveries, faster. The Americans had grown so frustrated with weather cancellations and missed drop-offs by the ghost ships from Key West that they had tried to switch the resupply effort to airplanes. But that was an expensive plan that involved creating an air fleet and rush-training Cuban pilots in the elaborate art of precision airdrops, which required perfect communications, navigation, timing, and flying. The resulting air missions that spring were a disaster: only three out of sixty-eight airdrops actually delivered weapons on time in the right place. So in early April, it was back to the boats.

They went out two boats together this time, both of them wallowing under the weight of their cargoes. Down in the hold of each boat was what the CIA officer accompanying them called a small pack: arms, ammunition, and radios for one hundred men, along with 57mm recoil-less rifles, light machine guns, and medical and food supplies. Two small packs, supplemented with some heavy weapons, would serve two hundred. With a couple more runs they could would equip five hundred men. And the goal was even larger: five of these full packs added up to 2,500 men. You could do this kind of math forever: the more missions the more weapons the more attacks on Castro. The logistical tail was wagging the dog.

They went from Key West to the Bahamas, refueled, and then probed toward the south coast of Cuba. There was no frigate this time, and they managed to get both boats onto the beach in the middle of the night. Lundy waded ashore with the CIA man and waited on the sand for his contact.

And waited. Lundy had driven the boat himself this time, so he was pretty sure this was the right beach. But nobody came. More than an hour went by, but there was no sign of the contact, or his phantom resistance army, eager to take possession of two hundred rifles.

Another screwup. When they had already stayed too long, they heard a speedboat motor running in the distance, and even the CIA man agreed it was time to leave. Getting the boats off the beach took time, and then they motored very quietly to avoid discovery. The PTs were still wallow-ing heavily in the sea and could not move. They would still be in Cuban waters at first light. Having risked so much, so many times, for so little, the crew was in no mood to run more unnecessary risks.

During his own invasion of Cuba, Castro had also been late, lost, and facing daylight in a small boat. He'd thrown his heavy weapons over-board in order to lighten and speed the *Granma* to safety; Lundy's crew decided to do the same, and without further ado began tossing firearms and ammunition for one hundred men into the sea.

The CIA man exploded when he saw what they were doing. "Those weapons belong to the American people," he shouted. When he tried to stop them, another crew member threatened the American, asking Lundy to translate something into English: "Tell him that I will kill him," the crewman said. They went back to throwing things overboard.

Everything they dumped lightened the boat, and now they sprang out of Cuban waters and toward home. In Key West, plans were drawn up for another mission, but time had just run out on their little sideshow.

The first attack occurred on April 15. There had been reports of individual and mysterious airplanes earlier, dropping parachutes or shooting at things, but on the 15th the mystery planes came out of hiding, bursting over the island at dawn and striking a couple of Cuban air force bases, strafing and dropping bombs.

The planes were B-26 bombers, a kind of small, light, fast-strike aircraft developed by the United States for close ground support during World War II. They carried just two men, and were swollen with weapons—eight .50 caliber machine guns, a bed of eight rockets to hit ships and armor, and a belly rack for small bombs, or even napalm. They were designed to fly low, to dodge and shred. On the morning of the 15th they were making "prep" strikes, an attempt to eliminate Cuba's small air force on the ground, before it could join the battle that was about to take place.

At first, there was some confusion. Cuba itself had a squadron of B-26s, which Castro had inherited from the 1950s air force. That was the point: the incoming B-26s that attacked that morning looked like the B-26s already on the ground. Even the paint job was the same. It was supposed to look as if Cuba was being attacked by its own air force, as part of a military mutiny. The pilots were Cuban—but Cuban exiles, of course. And the planes were American, of course, flown out of American-built bases in Central America, where American pilots had trained Cuban exiles to fly them. Americans had paid for, fueled, and armed the planes, and then helped draw up the strike missions. Americans had provided the bombs and bullets. Americans had given the orders. Yet what killed the Bay of Pigs invasion, above all, was the obsession of the Kennedy brothers in Washington to conceal all this, to hide the obvious American role. President Kennedy himself had intervened at the last minute to cut in half the number of air strikes the exile B-26 pilots could make, hoping to reduce the visibility of the American hand. There was no doubt in Washington about the project of overthrowing the government in Cuba; the only question was how to avoid getting caught.

The two preemptive bombing strikes on April 15 were supposed to mangle Cuba's airpower, setting the stage for the invasion. With control of the air, the exile pilots could roam over every land battle, smashing Castro's troops whenever they massed to counterattack. But the raids were flawed in execution (the attacks did little damage) and disastrous in their fundamental misconception. They simply gave Cuba a warning of what was coming. Cuba immediately denounced the air raids at the United Nations. The attacks, a Cuban diplomat told the tense General Assembly in New York that very day, were American aggression. Although the CIA had painted the bombers with Cuban flags, it took the Cuban diplomats only a few hours to produce photographs that showed the attacking airplanes were clearly a different model than the ones in the real Cuban air force. So much for the Kennedy theory of deniability. The air raids, the Cubans announced, were an obvious "prologue to a large-scale invasion."

The U.S. ambassador to the U.N., Adlai Stevenson, vehemently denied any American involvement in the attacks on Cuba. He later said that he had not known the truth, but ignorance of that scale is hard to credit. Miami, Washington, Havana, and New York were all crawling with rumors about U.S. involvement. Newspapers in Central America and Florida had reported on parts of the Bay of Pigs plan. The *New York Times* had published a report about an army of Cuban exiles massing in Central America, and the newspaper pointed out that America was certainly involved, somehow. Half the Cubans in Miami seemed to know someone involved in the invasion or related missions, like Lundy's boat raids.

Castro had been preparing his people for months, warning in speeches that a Yanqui invasion, carried out by a combined force of Cuban exiles and American spies, was imminent. The signs of the coming battle were everywhere. On the 15th of April, everyone who wanted to know already knew.

The April 15 air raids killed only seven people, but they had one huge effect: they led Castro to pronounce out loud a word he had been carefully avoiding for years.

As soon as the bomb debris was cleared away Castro called for a public funeral for the seven dead, to be held the very next day, the 16th. It took place at one of Havana's major intersections, the meeting of two avenues in Vedado, a spot overseen by the Charlie Chaplin Theater on one side and the city's most famous graveyard on the other.

It was not a funeral but a rally. A large crowd of enthusiastic civilians filled the avenues, but a group of armed militiamen was placed between Castro and the television cameras, so that lifted rifles accompanied his cheer lines. Castro spoke for hours, extolling the victims and building up the emotions of the crowd with his rhetorical questions, producing thundering responses.

Here were the choices that created the Cuban tragedy: *Are you with Cuba, or against it? For the fatherland, or the mercenary scum? Our people, or the imperial beast?*

Either or. Zero sum. The denial of any middle ground, or compromise, or choice. *Which standard?*

In the midst of the speech, with everyone caught in the psychic throes of the bond between solitary leader and massed followers, Castro made a comment that went almost unnoticed by the crowd. He said that the Revolution had a "character" and then explained that it was this character that so infuriated the exiles, and the imperialist powers of the world. They

> cannot forgive our being right here under their very noses, or to see how we have made a revolution, a socialist revolution, right here under the very nose of the United States.

He moved on quickly, but that was it. He had blurted it out for the first time: socialist.

While fighting in the Sierra Maestra, Fidel had denied a hundred times that he was Red. The Revolution was democratic, built on a platform of the 1940 constitution and elections. He had mocked the Communist Party of Cuba, calling it a debating club for old men. The communists, Castro said, had spent the war "under the bed." In at least three speeches during his first weeks in power, Castro had denied being a communist or even being influenced by them. Che Guevara called the same allegations "absurd."

The denials had always been countered by rumor and by code words within the new argot of the Revolution. Castro and Guevara both surrounded themselves with aides who were communist. Raúl was a communist, and they all talked in the language of socialism: the rebels were "a vanguard," the new government was engaged in a "struggle" against class and capitalist enemies, and there would be solidarity with "people's regimes" in the Third World and in Eastern Europe. But through 1959, and 1960, and well into 1961, the denials continued, if ever weaker and more evasive. Everyone had strained to hear any direct words of intent from the man known by more and more names.

Finally, here were the words: "a socialist revolution." The spot where Castro spoke is today marked with a bronze plaque marking April 16, 1961, as the birth date of the "socialist character" of Cuba.

People may have been listening for it, but that doesn't mean they heard it. Elizardo Sánchez was a student in Havana in 1961, and a member of a small student group devoted to socialist politics. Since the government had gone to enormous lengths to deny that it was socialist, actual socialists like Sánchez and his friends were a problem. They had to "creep about like four cats," he said. The last thing they expected was an open admission, from Castro himself, that they had been right all along.

At the back of the crowd, blocks from Castro, it wasn't even possible to hear the speech clearly over the excited hum of the assembly. People simply responded to cues. When the militiamen lifted their guns and cheered something Castro had said, the front of the crowd cheered, too, and then the back of the crowd picked it up. The cheering wasn't fake. There was still overwhelming public support in Cuba for the Revolution, but consent wasn't the issue. Even Castro's strongest supporters had to learn their parts by rote. So people went to the rally, and as one participant of that day recalled, unable to conceal his mirth, they shouted:

Long live Cuba!
Long live Fidel!
Long live Socialism!

And then, at the back of the crowd, they all looked around at one another and asked, *What did he just say?*

That was the other thing born in this April of discontent: *doble cara,* two faces, or the flexible loyalty of the moment. Whether you'd heard Castro or not, whether you liked the idea of socialism or not, you still had to applaud the new laws under which you could be arrested.

About the only place they heard him clearly was in Washington. America was already in an advanced state of fear about Castro, and Washington needed no more justifications. As far as the Kennedy brain trust was concerned, Castro was as Red as a baboon's ass. The April 16 speech only confirmed what they wanted to believe.

That very night, President Kennedy signed the final order to launch the invasion. When the ink was dry, a brigade of 1,300 Cuban exiles, already afloat on freighters escorted by U.S. Navy ships, closed on the southern coast of Cuba.

Two Dolores boys, Roberto Mancebo, eighteen, and his younger brother, Jorge, just seventeen, were in the invasion fleet. They were assigned to the exile army's 2nd Battalion, one of the best trained and best equipped in the larger force, which was called the 2506 Brigade. Mancebo, when I found him, was living in South Florida, a social worker for the state. He was reluctant to discuss the invasion and avoided my calls for months. But he finally spent a morning detailing his journey to the Bay of Pigs.

Mancebo had been against Castro from the beginning. In the fall of 1959, the same year he graduated from Dolores, he had enrolled in the Chemistry Department at the University of Oriente. About fifteen boys in the department were alumni of Dolores, all of them passionately anti-communist. There was a lot of rash talking, but during the fall term a dozen of the boys decided to make some simple explosive devices that would scare the authorities. They started with Molotov cocktails, which they set alight and left in trash cans. Then they made a kind of weak plastic explosive, which they used to blow up some mailboxes and park benches in the middle of the night. Betrayed by their own bragging, the boy saboteurs were called in by the police. Nobody had been killed or even injured, and the prankish nature of the small devices was obvious even to the revolutionary militia. They gave Mancebo a lecture on politics and set him free.

Mancebo fled Cuba and turned pro. In January of 1961 he'd gone to Guatemala with La Brigada, as the 2506 called itself, eager to help overthrow the regime. The men had trained hard there, building their own camps. Mancebo recalled that the CIA worked them relentlessly, and in the jungle they were given realistic combat lessons from U.S. Army veterans. As each month of 1961 passed, the equipment improved. M3 rifles from the Korean War. Plenty of machine guns, both light and heavy. Massive 81mm mortars. The best bazookas. Two kinds of recoilless rifles, especially the 75mm version that could slice through any armor. More men began arriving, and they got a second base in Nicaragua to launch the actual operation.

The men were divided up into five battalions, three of infantry, one for heavy weapons, and another for headquarters. But there were still only about 1,500 men in the brigade, about half the number called for in the CIA plan. The manpower was so low that a squad would be labeled a platoon, a platoon a company, and so on up the chart, creating a hollow army. There was plenty of equipment, however. The stuff kept piling in: a whole rented fleet of supply ships, plus fuel, food, and ammo, an entire second fleet of landing craft, scuba gear for commandos, rocket launchers, a squad of heavy American tanks, and plenty of trucks. By March their air force of B-26s arrived, once again the most up-to-date model of American equipment. In almost every case, Mancebo noted, the exiles had smaller numbers, but weapons superior to those of the Cuban troops they would be facing.

The 2nd was charged with holding the left flank of the invasion, and when the fleet moved into the Bay of Pigs at around 11:00 P.M. on the 16th, and most of the ships stopped about a mile offshore of the main invasion site, the 2nd Battalion continued on, almost alone, much further into the bay.

The Bahía de Cochinos—Bay of Pigs—is eight hundred feet deep in some places, which made it impossible for the ships to anchor. And because the beaches were lined with coral reefs, the fleet had to stand far offshore. Mancebo and the other members of the 2nd Battalion therefore had to climb down into small landing boats and make a circuitous approach to their target, the westernmost beach at Playa Larga. But the engines on many landing boats would not run; a CIA officer had insisted on using the wrong fuel. Eventually a few boats sputtered to life and began towing others behind them; but many could not be used at all, others had trouble finding a way through the reefs, and it wasn't until 2:00 A.M. on the 17th that the bulk of the 2nd Battalion finally headed for the beach.

Meanwhile a CIA officer named Grayston L. Lynch decided to go ahead and scout the route. Lynch was one of just two CIA agents who set foot in Cuba during the invasion and will have to stand in for all the other Americans, the hundreds and hundreds of agents and operatives in

Florida and Washington who conceived, planned, and carried out this legendary disaster. Lynch and his frogmen made a quiet approach to the beach at Playa Larga, but here they made a cataclysmic and ludicrous mistake. While still a hundred yards offshore, someone—Lynch declined to say who—accidentally switched on the searchlight they were carrying. A bright beam of light shot up, illuminating the boat and the frogmen in it. Even worse, Lynch couldn't figure out how to turn off the huge light, which was meant to guide in the subsequent landing craft. As desperate seconds went by, and Lynch fumbled, the frogmen tried to smother the light with their bodies. Lynch finally turned it off, but then, miraculously, someone, somehow, knocked it back on again. A second blast of light flooded the boat, the men, and the sky.

Great events have small beginnings. On shore, some Cuban coast guardsmen saw the double flash, assumed a fishing boat was in trouble, and drove a jeep down to the waterline. When they aimed their headlights out to sea, Lynch decided this was the moment to get his war on. He fired the first shots of the invasion, pouring three clips of ammunition into the jeep. Lynch succeeded in knocking out the headlights, and chased off the coast guardsmen, but at the cost of alerting the entire coastline to the invasion.

By the time the 2nd Battalion began trickling in, the coast guard had been able to organize a hasty defense, and Mancebo recalled running across the beach under light fire. Dozens of policemen and some men from a local militia were holed up in a house, fighting back. The defenders were driven out, quickly, and then Mancebo and his unit swept through the small village, facing only the occasional stray shot. The beachhead was secure. They were in Cuba.

Searching the town, the exiles discovered bad news: the village had a microwave transmitter. The CIA's intelligence and planning were off. The invasion had been switched to the Bay of Pigs site because it offered complete isolation. It had neither phone service nor any radio stations, and the agency was expecting to have at least hours, and possibly days, before the Cuban government even knew what was happening. But here was a microwave transmitter, and it was still warm to the touch. Someone had sent word to Havana.

The invasion was now exposed, and behind schedule. By dawn many exile troops were still not ashore. The beachhead all along the bay was secure, but many of the troops were disorganized or poorly led, and hunkered down to wait for supplies. It was common knowledge that American power would decide things, somehow, so there was little initiative on the battlefield. Rather hopefully, the Americans and the Cuban exile leaders believed that the war would be over before it started. Once the landings occurred, Cuban army officers would supposedly defect to the exile cause. Or they would stage a coup, short-circuiting the armed resistance. Castro himself might be chased off by exaggerated reports of an enemy attack, like the president of Guatemala had been in 1954.

But the reverse happened. From the first seconds, ordinary soldiers and militiamen, policemen and civilians, all rallied to Cuba, and therefore to the Revolution, and therefore, ultimately, to Castro. Coast guardsmen and militiamen fought back at once. There was a group of about thirty literacy teachers stationed along the bay who forted up inside their schoolhouse, fighting with rifles until their blackboard was riddled with bullets. Only one teacher, Patria Silva, was taken alive. At the same time, on the far left flank of the invasion, the exile soldiers were surprised to face an aggressive counterattack mounted by about 150 construction workers who had been working on a resort. Equipped with only rifles, the laborers were cut to pieces, but their quick and determined rally signaled that the exile army would face resistance, not welcome.

The worst-case scenario considered by the CIA still assumed that even if something went wrong, and the invaders could not advance, they could always sit tight. With their dominance of the air, superior weapons, and steady resupply from the sea they could hold a defensive line for weeks or even months. A new civilian leadership for Cuba had already been selected (by the CIA), and once put ashore, these men could declare themselves the provisional government of the free territory of Cuba. If necessary, these politicians could even invite U.S. troops ashore to finish the job.

So by dawn on the 17th, Roberto Mancebo and his comrades in the 2nd Battalion had moved out of town and advanced toward Havana about as far as any troops in the invasion would ever reach: less than a mile. They stopped there, holding the left flank, and waited. The 5th Battalion was supposed to have landed behind them, reinforcing and expanding their lines, but there was no sign of those men.

There were some air raids elsewhere that morning by the B-26s of the real Cuban air force, which had survived the prepatory air strikes by the fake Cuban air force. Yet the 2nd Battalion itself wasn't attacked. In relative quiet they worked all morning, digging foxholes and trenches on both sides of a road, setting up overlapping fields of fire for their heavy weapons, and sighting the mortars. They were staring straight out on the only road in their sector, which ran through thick mangrove swamp toward a major Cuban army base. They knew the counterattack would come toward them.

It appeared before noon, in the form of a single truck, packed full of lightly armed militiamen. Troops on foot were scouting the sides of the road, but they were searching quickly, almost jogging, and they didn't spot the camouflaged positions of the 2nd Battalion until they were just seventy-five yards away. Mancebo and other exiles opened up with everything they had, shredding the truck with recoilless rifles. Machine guns cut down the militiamen on foot. The battle lasted twenty-five minutes.

Some survivors crawled into the swamp. Now a pair of exile B-26s appeared overhead to support the 2nd Battalion. These friendly B-26s pounced on another truck that was further down the road and then returned to weave overhead, strafing any Cuban militiamen who were foolish enough to clump together visibly in the muck of the swamp.

The B-26s stayed too long. They used up the last of their ammunition, and Mancebo recalled how they even made a pass over the 2nd Battalion, wiggling their wings in a victory salute. The men on the ground gave a cheer that died in their throats. There was a terrible ripping sound, and then a bright flash of silver over the beachhead. The unknown had arrived.

It was a fighter jet. Cuba did not possess fighter jets. The whole exile invasion plan had been predicated on the sure knowledge, intensely cultivated by the CIA, that Cuba had no fighter jets. Cuba had only a handful of B-26 bombers and a few British Sea Furies, all propeller-driven planes.

But what came overhead was a jet.

The CIA knew that Cuba possessed two American T-33 jets, unarmed training planes that the Agency had therefore written off. But desperation is the mother of invention, and the Cuban air force had bolted machine guns onto the wings of their "unarmed" jets. An improvised ammo feeding system was set up, and the Revolution suddenly had two crude but functional jet fighters.

Now the men in the 2nd Battalion watched in disbelief as the enemy's nonexistent jet, with an almost casual display of speed and power, pawed an exile B-26 out of the sky, sending it spiraling into the swamp right in front of the battalion. Even worse, the jet easily caught up to the second plane as it tried to flee, mauled its propeller engines, and sent it gliding down into the Caribbean.

The jet was disturbing. But quiet quickly returned to Playa Larga. Mancebo spent the rest of the day preparing his .30 caliber machine gun for a fight. They advanced their positions a hundred yards and dug in again. Some Cuban troops appeared at the far end of the road, beyond range, but when they saw the bodies of their comrades they fell back. The 5th Battalion still hadn't appeared, but the exiles were reinforced by men from the main landings further down the beach, who brought some heavy mortars, and even a tank.

That night, in Santiago, David de Jongh listened to his radio in disbelief. An invasion! His guns were hidden at the lab, ready. His friends, his fellow Castro haters, his co-conspirators in a hundred imagined uprisings were ready. But they had been caught completely by surprise. No warning at all. They'd even been in regular contact with an American from the old consulate, hoping for some sort of encouragement.

But nothing. No warning. The people ready to rise up had been given no hint of when the uprising would come. *Why didn't they tell us?* he wailed at the radio.

Tuning through the AM dial, he came across the voice of the invasion, a propaganda station that was already reporting the virtual defeat of Castro. A few hours after hearing the exile radio report that *Santiago de Cuba has been liberated,* David saw Raúl Castro himself driving through the Parque Céspedes in a jeep.

Raúl, recognizing his old schoolmate David, gave a relaxed wave, and went on.

The biggest fight of the invasion started just before midnight. On the road in front of Mancebo, a real Cuban infantry battalion appeared. Not lightly armed militiamen, but a fully equipped force more than twice their size, supported with T-34 tanks and artillery. They came up the road very slowly, probing, covered by a crawling barrage from guns in the rear. But the exiles were in new positions, again carefully camouflaged. The barrage passed over, and the attackers (the 333rd Battalion) came forward. Recoilless rifles stabbed out in the darkness to meet them, piercing a Cuban tank. Mancebo's machine gun cut into the infantry. A second light tank clattered forward and was destroyed.

Ten minutes later they were attacked again. Again, two tanks were destroyed, with heavy losses for the Cuban army. And then fifteen minutes later, a third attack. This time Mancebo was frightened because the sound of the battle had changed. There was something much bigger coming up the road, the evil grinding noise dreaded by infantry everywhere. Heavy armor. Soviet Stalin IIIs, in fact. *Osos,* Mancebo called them. Bears.

The fighting became desperate and almost continuous, with about ten tanks trying to storm forward on top of one another. "Hell," was all Mancebo said, to summarize what that moment had been like. He made a joke about wetting his "soldier pants," and then said, "There was nothing to do but keep shooting. There were tanks in front, and soldiers coming up both sides. We lost many good, young Cuban men. After forty-four years I am almost crying." Then he did start crying.

The swamp favored the defenders. Machine guns swept away the infantry; and first one and then another tank was damaged or destroyed, until the next ones had to turn off the road to get past. But off the road it was swamp. Soft ground or no ground, treacherous, full of trees. The heavy tanks slowed down and became vulnerable as they turned. In the trench next to Mancebo a man popped up, took careful aim with a bazooka, and destroyed one tank as it maneuvered, only to be killed by a shot from the next T-34 in line. But the exiles were dug in and familiar with the terrain. The tank attack faltered, and then the exiles' own M41 tank blasted another T-34, cracking it open.

There was a lull in the fighting around 3:00 A.M., which was broken fifteen minutes later by a large infantry attack. Now machine gunners like Mancebo could fight, and the exiles held their line, calling in mortars. The Cuban infantry attacked for about two hours, but suffered tremendously. The 2nd Battalion had lost only two dead and six injured. After the attackers pulled back, there was another lull, and then a single T-34 tried to push forward at 5:30 A.M., in the last minutes of darkness. Again, it was destroyed by the exiles' M41.

The night battle concluded on a ludicrous note when yet another

Cuban tank raced forward, only to stop short. A hatch opened and the commander climbed out, thinking that he had reached his own infantry. The tank and crew were both taken. And because this was Cuba, the tank commander turned out to be an old army buddy of the 2nd Battalion's own commander.

The quick dawn of April 18 meant they saw everything at once. Smoke poured from sixteen shattered tanks, and hundreds of dead bodies littered the road, with more in the swamp. As many as seven hundred to nine hundred men in a force of two thousand were killed or injured during the night, all by an exile force totaling under two hundred. The 333th became known as "the Lost Battalion." But Mancebo did not gloat over this slaughter. The nighttime attack was a necessity of war, a sacrifice by soldiers pushing for a weakness. The attack failed, but it bought time for the Cuban forces to rally elsewhere and rout the invaders.

In the flush of victory, Mancebo learned that the war had already been lost. During the previous day, the Cuban jets and propeller planes had wrought havoc on the main invasion, shooting down many of the exile aircraft and then strafing the ships. Their reinforcements, the 5th Battalion, had been shot up while trying to land behind schedule in daylight. Many of the landing boats had been destroyed. Now one of their big supply ships was sinking; another, the *Houston,* still carrying their reinforcements, had been hit so hard that it was taking on water, and the captain deliberately ran it aground to save it.

The 5th Battalion reinforcements now had to come ashore, climbing down ropes from the damaged *Houston* to the beach, They had landed in the wrong place, without their heavy weapons. Hours later, when they finally tried to move up the bay to the 2nd Battalion, they met resistance. Six Cuban sailors, acting on their own, had dismounted the machine gun from a patrol boat, dragged it inland, and set it up in a house beside the coastal road. The 5th Battalion—hundreds of men—was stopped and turned back by a scratch force of six.

Now the Cuban air force returned, blasting those few support boats still operating in the Bay of Pigs. More were sunk or damaged; others fled hundreds of miles out to sea, scattering under continuous air assault. After the long night of fighting, the 2nd Battalion learned that most of their ammunition and supplies was either over the horizon or at the bottom of the sea. Counterattacks began again, including strafing by aircraft, but once again Mancebo's experience was atypical. The air attacks were down on the right flank, where there were more roads into the beachhead, and more room for infantry to maneuver.

But soon enough the artillery shells hitting around Mancebo began to increase. Word came down that more tanks and infantry were seen massing ahead of the 2nd Battalion. This flow of Cuban reinforcements was supposed to be delayed by small groups of exile commandos, but the commandos had mostly disappeared. And then as Mancebo waited in the midday heat for what looked to be a huge fight, the trenches were swept with a wild rumor: the beachheads in the south of the bay, the main exile position, were in trouble. This was followed quickly by the even more shocking news that the rumor was true: the infantry in the south were being overrun. Even the headquarters battalion was under attack. FIGHTING ON BEACH was one of the last radio communications that reached the 2nd Battalion.

The 2nd, alone at the top of the bay, was ordered to fall back on these lower units. Mancebo jumped into a truck, and the battalion rolled down the beach road in a convoy of seven vehicles, trying to find the rest of the 2506 Brigade. The *Houston* was visible in the distance, burning and aground, keeled over. Mancebo was witness then to something that has been written out of history: U.S. Navy jets suddenly passed over the beachhead. The Americans were here!

American forces were not supposed to participate, directly, in the battle. At least not at first. The Kennedy brothers were still hoping for some veneer of deniability. The American navy was ordered to stay in international waters, and personal accounts stress that the Cuban exiles did the fighting. It is routinely claimed by brigade veterans that they would have won if they'd had air cover.

But the American jets did appear. The first sweep, which Mancebo saw, was by four U.S. Navy jets that passed over the beach in a combat air patrol, but didn't encounter any Cuban aircraft. The American pilots dipped their wings in salute, and then passed on. Within minutes of their departure, the planes of the Cuban air force had returned to blow up another supply ship. And then, when it was too late in the day to matter, the U.S. jets returned once more, this time making a ground attack on a column of advancing Cuban troops. Huge explosions spiraled up from the site of the attack, and Castro himself later said the American jets had caused many deaths.

As Mancebo, Castro, and the CIA all agree, there *was* American air cover that day.

Castro had raced down from Havana, but he had spent the first full day of battle commanding his forces by radio, from the rear, like a sensible general. Now, on the second full day, he put some theater into the theater of operations. With the enemy lines collapsing, Castro jumped into a car and moved forward, a photographer in tow. Here was the confrontation he had been waiting for, the spectacular assault by his hated Yankee enemy. Yet by the time he arrived at the beach, the third Dolores boy to touch those sands, the fighting was effectively over. He perched on a tank for the photographer, and then climbed inside it. From there he took some potshots at the motionless *Houston,* already bombed to pieces, deliberately grounded, abandoned, on fire, and listed over. That particular tank now sits in Havana, with a plaque explaining that Castro himself used it to sink the *Houston.*

Slowly, all day on the 18th, the wheels fell off the invasion. The exile forces were broken up, isolated, and pushed into the sea. Their few surviving planes made a last effort (flown by CIA officers this time) but were swatted out of the sky by the Cuban jets.

As the fighting sputtered to a confused end, various evacuation plans were proposed, and two American destroyers surged into the bay that afternoon, successfully bluffing the Cuban army into stalling its advance for a few hours. Some exile infantry jumped onto the last landing boats as they fled the beach; others just swam out, toward the horizon, hoping to be picked up. Those who could, made for the sea in rubber life rafts, leaky dinghies, and stolen fishing boats. Some were picked up by the U.S. Navy within a day, others in five days, but one group wandered the ocean in a sailboat for two weeks, starving, without water.

All told, 1,114 members of the brigade were captured. Mancebo was one of them. Late in the afternoon of the 19th, the 2nd Battalion trucks had stopped on the coast road. Some men waited for the end, the obvious surrender that was occurring all around them, but Mancebo was one of dozens who jumped down and ran into the swamp. With no particular plan, he thrashed his way westward, away from the battlefield, with a diminishing band, eaten by mosquitoes, rubbing his legs raw while clambering over mangrove roots. Occasionally they flushed crocodiles from the murky water. After three days only six men remained, and they had covered some thirty miles. They worked their way to the coast again and waded out to a tiny island, hoping to spot a passing ship. But that night, as they slept, they were surprised by Cuban troops and arrested.

The officer leading the revolutionary soldiers asked one question. It was the same one they had been asking themselves. When, their captor wanted to know, were the Americans going to attack?

The survivors of the assault were shoved into makeshift prisons and interrogated individually by the G2, Cuba's military intelligence unit. Although about six hundred "counterrevolutionaries" were executed, these were mostly civilians caught in the pre-invasion roundups, people with records of violence. Only a few of the worst members of the brigade were sent to the wall, for previous crimes under Batista. Instead, Mancebo and the *Brigadistas* were subjected to a television trial that summer, a long ritual of humiliation in which they were lectured on their crimes as mercenaries and terrorists. Cuban prosecutors showed (more or less accurately) that the men had been creatures of a foreign power. Each man was interrogated on television, scrutinized for his ties to the Batista army, and his family tree dissected to reveal ties to the old elite, its institutions, even its schools. Cuban photographers emphasized the presence of blond men among the prisoners, as if to say, these aren't really Cubans. The class status of the "mercenary brigade" was detailed, precisely:

> 100 big landowners
> 24 important property owners
> 67 apartment house owners
> 112 big businessmen
> 194 ex-military men and associates of the Batista tyranny
> 179 economically well off
> 135 industrial magnates
> 112 lumpen and others

(When I asked Mancebo which of these categories described his own family, he circled the first four.)

At trial, Mancebo's history of making explosives in Santiago was cited against him. But it didn't matter: everyone was guilty, and they got the same sentence. The prisoners were sent to the Isle of Pines, the most infamous of Cuban jails, and later distributed to various stops along the *cordillera* of prisons. After almost two years they were traded back to America for a humiliatingly large shipment of tractors and medicines.

After the fiasco, President Kennedy said, "Victory has a hundred fathers, but defeat is an orphan." But wasn't Kennedy himself disinheriting the child? Surely this disaster had a hundred fathers, too: both Kennedy brothers, and the CIA, for its deranged and amateurish plan to attack a swamp, and also Eisenhower, who assumed that the way to deal with Cuba was to invade it. And then, also, all the Wise Men of Washington, the Best and Brightest, who drew their conclusions about the Cuban Revolution by meeting with the heads of American corporations.

A folly, a delusion of the exile mind married to American groupthink, the trick fell apart when exposed to daylight, and Fidel Castro was the only winner.

Victory is a poor teacher. Speaking to *New York Times* journalist Herbert Matthews later that year, Kennedy admitted that a victory at the Bay of Pigs might have had disastrous consequences, encouraging America to engage in more violent gambles, like making war in Laos or the Taiwan Strait.

Such sober lessons were in short supply in Havana. The initial weeks after the April invasion were busy ones, consolidating the victory and disposing of the 2506 Brigade survivors, and it wasn't until May Day that Castro began to publicly revel in his triumph. At a speech that day he announced that "The revolution has no time for elections. There is no more democratic government in Latin America than the revolutionary government." He announced another fait accompli: although Dolores and Belén were both already shuttered, Castro declared that all remaining Catholic and private schools in the country would be closed, and all foreign-born Roman Catholic priests would be expelled.

For the first time since 1952, Castro knew he was secure in his position. Thanks to the victory of David over Goliath, he no longer needed puppet presidents or coalition partners, no more diverse voices or divergent sectors.

Cabrera Infante noted the first hints of a new order in the appearance of new words. Castro had always been prone to long speeches, especially ones about his own victimhood. His most famous oration, "History Will Absolve Me," from his trial in 1952, is striking for its repeated assertions that no one in the entire history of the world has ever faced as much repression or difficulty as Fidel Castro. But soon after the Bay of Pigs, the speeches Castro gave began to sink to a new low of pettiness-per-hour. On July 5, 1961, Castro—introduced as "Prime Minister, Doctor Fidel Castro, the highest leader of the Revolution"—gave a speech on the shortages the island was facing. These were occurring everywhere: food of every kind; equipment like cars, tractors, and buses; necessities like medicine and clothing; everyday items like appliances and toys; more and more things disappearing with each month. Some of these things had been imported from the United States, and the trade embargo was slowly claiming them, a piecemeal process of cutting off one commodity at a time in an effort to punish Cuba. Earlier in the year it had been the turn of the molasses industry to be added to the embargo. Then in summertime it was lard.

Castro entitled his speech on July 5 "The Lard Problem and Imperialism." There was a real lard problem: with Cuba's own food production in free fall, the supply of lard—rendered pig fat—had tumbled. This had triggered rising imports from the United States, which in turn led someone in Washington to seize on blocking lard as the next step in fighting communism in the Americas.

Cubans will fry anything. Lard was the poor person's oil, a gooey necessity for making *tostones* and enriching beans, and when it ran short the grumbling could be heard even by Castro. Castro's TV appearance was billed as addressing the crucial "question of supply" for lard.

But Castro barely mentioned lard, or even food. Instead he digressed into an hours-long description of international relations, detailing the solidarity of the Soviets and the perfidy of the Americans. Shortages, he explained, were not really what they seemed. There were two kinds of shortages in Cuba. The first category were those imposed on Cuba by the imperialists. This was where lard came in for its mention: the American embargo was to blame if Cuba had no pig fat. And then there was a second type of shortage, which wasn't really a shortage at all. These items— Castro refrained from specifying just which ones—were actually missing from Cuba as part of a deliberate choice by the Revolution, their absence the fruition of a careful and long-sighted policy of self-restraint. Cuba was freely choosing not to import "luxuries," Castro said. The so-called shortages were in fact evidence that Cuba's economic power was focused on new priorities, and that the economy was actually stronger, and headed for greater production, than ever before.

"The Lard Problem and Imperialism" wasn't bad as Castro's speeches go. It wasn't one of the six- or seven-hour events that tortured people, and it was full of the typical fireworks of the "highest leader's" thinking, the elaborate reversals of logic that Castro deployed so skillfully, making problems vanish, proportioning out blame and identifying villains, all the small thrills of nationalism and victimhood.

But it didn't put any lard on the table. And it didn't answer burning questions. Where were the fruit vendors? Had the coal carts been silenced by imperialism? Who had taken away all the avocados?

What about all the things that had never come from America in the first place? Who took the plantain?

Acting on Che Guevara's orders, Pepín Bou, and some colleagues including José Batlle from Dolores, returned to the mine at Moa Bay. There was no airplane at first, just a two-day grind in a heavy truck, stopping once in a while to pull the truck out of the mud with a winch.

Batlle had been watching over the decommissioned plant, and it didn't take too long to get the nickel moving again. They cleaned and checked the reactor chambers, refilled them with sulfuric acid, regreased the conveyor belts, and fired it up.

Soon they were back on the eleven-day shifts. The isolation was unnerving. They had an AM radio but no way to talk back to the world. In April the Bay of Pigs invasion was over before they even found out about it. Momentous swings in national life were taking place, all at the indifferent remove of a crackling radio set. On their short stays in Santiago the men struggled to learn and judge what was going on, all while wrestling with a heightened craziness in day-to-day life.

Soon the flights were restored, and the DC-3 pilots would often be their only source of news from the outside world, carrying messages from family members in Santiago and delivering care packages.

In isolation at the remote mine, Bou fretted over leaving the country. Armed militiamen had been stationed at the mine to keep the engineers working, but they had little idea what the engineers really thought. For

Pepín, it was Castro himself who was the prophet. When Bou had heard Fidel listing American companies to be seized on the radio, and had heard that old familiar voice pass through the Fs and come to *Freeport Sulfur Company,* he had blanched. But it wasn't until later, when Castro announced that *Cuban* companies were also being nationalized, that Pepín voiced what he had not yet admitted. When he heard Castro list Bacardi, a symbol of Cuban talent and initiative, as one of the exploiters, a company that had to be "intervened," then Pepín had said it, for the first time, to himself: *We have to get out of here.* On his next break in Santiago, he repeated this, in serious and hushed tones, to Celia: "We have to get out of here."

They quickly made reservations on an obscure flight, a KLM route from Camagüey to Kingston, Jamaica. No one in Camagüey knew who they were; they could slip out unnoticed. But the Bay of Pigs put an end to that, as to so many things. Following the attack, airlines were overwhelmed. The government in Havana announced a temporary cancellation of outbound flights, and then a new system for regulating departures. It was still legal to leave, but the paperwork was suddenly more complicated.

Pepín was in no position to organize a departure. Planning an escape from Moa Bay was impossible. Celia would have to do it.

They had one hope left: their daughter born during the two years in New Orleans. A U.S. citizen, she could get out. And as she was a small child, the Cuban-born parents would be able to accompany her.

They arranged to signal each other in code; when Celia had something ready, she would summon him to a cousin's wedding. There would be a lot of paperwork to arrange, so Celia packed up her Santiago household and moved it to Havana, near the bureacrats. In a sign of how little the expectations of the old Cuba had faded, she traveled to Havana with eighteen suitcases, her maid, and her sister-in-law.

All June, Pepín listened for the sound of the DC-4s. Whenever he heard the daily plane arriving from Santiago, he jumped into a company pickup truck and raced to the airfield. He lingered around nervously at first, trying to find the pilots and engage them in casual talk. He was waiting for them to say, *Pepín, your wife says there is some good news.*

Nothing. Day by day he checked. Gradually the pilots got to know him. He flew his regular journey with them a few times. By late July, whenever they landed they would look for him.

"Pepín," they called out. "Don't worry. There's no news about the wedding yet."

A week later a DC-3 came in. This time the pilot finally smiled when he saw Pepín. He gave a thumbs-up. The cousin was getting married, and soon. Pepín's heart was in his throat, but the pilot explained that he didn't have news of an exact date. Just that it was going to be soon. What Celia was trying to say was that she had arranged to get tourist visas to America.

And then a sharp turn. "There's no wedding," the very next pilot told Pepín. It felt like an *engaño,* a cheap trick. This message from Celia meant that the "engagement" had fallen through. The American government had canceled all tourist visas for Cubans.

There was a DC-3 every day or three, and Pepín always went to the field to meet it. This was the only interruption in his routine of steadily ramping up production. The pilots all knew what he wanted to hear. "There's no date yet," they would call out when they saw him.

In Havana, Celia got rid of most of the suitcases. She practiced loading the remaining four, one for each adult and child in their nuclear family. She made piles, counting out the permitted number of socks, of underwear, filling each bag to the exact capacity. To make sure, she carried the suitcases, one by one, to a scale down the block. Nothing would be left to chance.

The beret was invented for shepherds in the cold hills of the Pyrenees, and the heavy wool and lack of any brim make it uniquely unsuited for the tropics. But when Che Guevara arrived in Moa Bay for an inspection tour of his international nickel trading scheme, he wore his signature black beret. So did the men around him: in the crowd that followed Guevara, there were a half dozen functionaries in uniforms and the useless berets. After two years in power, living in cities, more and more of the *barbudos* were clean-shaven, and the black beret seemed to replace the beard, a sartorial shift, perhaps, from allegiance to the wildly hirsute Castro toward the harder but more dapper man, the impatient Che.

Guevara was also followed that day by his wife and by the photographer Alberto Korda. Korda would later become famous for his iconic image of the Argentine guerrilla commander, the famous shot of Che peering out from under his beret, his eyes full of fire, his rebellious locks flaring. But today Korda was shooting something prosaic. A muddy inspection tour of the Moa Bay plant. No glory, just confirmation of the futility of all inspection tours. The photographs Korda took show Che surrounded by flunkies in berets, men who knew nothing of nickel mining. You could see a few men in tin construction hats in the far background—the engineers and actual workers at the plant.

Bou was desperate to avoid Guevara. He was afraid of somehow betraying himself, even if only by a guilty look. But he couldn't avoid his duties and was tasked with giving Guevara a brief display of the leaching process at work. He took Guevara and the crowd of followers to one of the four "trains," or production lines. He showed off the seventy-foot-high reaction chambers, each twelve feet across, four tanks per train. He showed them the water reservoir, a muddy pond beyond the parking lot. They peered at the conveyor belts, which carried the raw laterite ore. It looked like plain red earth as it marched down the belt, and in a sense it was. Cuban nickel deposits were unusually pure, but that meant just 1.5 percent of the ore was nickel; 98.5 percent was wasted soil. It went into the so-and-so, was transported here-and-there, and this-and-that. Pepín went through the motions for Che, frozen.

Guevara was an amateur scientist, but even he found this too much. "Are you on schedule?" he asked Pepín.

"Everything is fine," Pepín said, nodding. That was it.

A DC-3 came in the very next day. "The wedding is set," the pilot told him, grinning. "Two days."

Now, or never. Without cleaning his hands or changing out of his coveralls, Bou climbed up into the airplane.

He left behind all his clothes and possessions at the mine, a snake starting to shed an old skin. Even the pickup: he just left it sitting by the runway. A few minutes later they were airborne, and as they flew to Santiago, Pepín sat on the floor of the cockpit, smiling and chatting about the wedding, spinning lies. Everything was great. He was giving away his cousin at the ceremony. The party would have plenty of rum. What good times they would all have.

In Santiago he changed his clothes and then went to see his grandmother. "I'm leaving," was all he could say, and that was enough. They both began to cry. Pepín never saw her again.

Celia had all their American paperwork ready. He had to race to Havana. Before boarding, Cuban officials confiscated all Pepín's cash, and the gold band from his wristwatch. Just as the plane was starting to taxi, a jeep carrying four militiamen stopped it. They boarded. They came down the aisle, walked right past Pepín, and removed another passenger. He took the first tranquilizer of his life.

In the air, calmed by the drug and the noisy, drafty reality of movement, he dared to look ahead. He needed to reach Alberto Casas, who had already moved to Miami with his wife, Pepín's sister, Hortensia. How could he reach them?

The passenger at his side, an Englishman, handed Pepín a 1960 American dime. The price of that first call.

But in Miami, Bou saw pay phones, banks of them, set up specially for the emigrants. As many calls as you needed, free. He reached his sister, and by nightfall they had Alberto's roof over their heads, in the neighborhood that wasn't yet known as Little Havana.

In the next few weeks, even when he had money in his pocket, Pepín had trouble paying for anything. He had to stop his hand, and search it; was he paying with that dime? He removed it, time and again, from his hand.

Through July and August, living with Alberto, Pepín couldn't spend any dime. In the fall he finally covered it in tape, to give it a different feeling, and tried going back to spending other dimes, but it was nerve-racking to have to sort through your change, looking to be sure you weren't spending the one. And he liked carrying it: sometimes he took it out and showed it to people, and told his story. By 1962, when the United States was getting Cuba kicked out of the Organization of American States, the tape on the dime was dark with fingering, but he was used to the feel of it now. He kept it in his wallet, through the brinkmanship of the Missile Crisis that October, the end of the Heroic Years. The dime was now a fixture, as familiar to him as Cuba had once been. Into the mid-1960s he carried it, replacing the tape sometimes, noticing the tarnished, filthy metal underneath. After six years Celia finally insisted.

She set the dime aside in a safe place. She eventually had it encased in

Lucite. A big block of plastic, too—several pounds. Too heavy to throw out by accident.

Too big to jump into somebody's pocket and wander off, in search of a pay phone.

It sounded like magnanimity when Castro's speeches first began to change in the summer of '61. He began to talk about the importance of improving Cuban culture, suggesting that, among its victories, the Revolution could also create cultural triumphs. Dance troupes, not just militias. Great architectural commissions, not just shortages. There should be a deepening of culture, and also a broadening of it, and more people making it, and more people having access to it. Everyone was for culture. The only thing Castro didn't say, at first, was what exactly he meant by culture.

In the government paper *Juventud Rebelde,* aimed at Cuba's youth, Cabrera Infante noticed a word he had not seen before: *tramps.* This was a reference to some new kind of enemy to be found in Cuba, part of a warning about unspecified Cubans, traitors who were trying to bring down the Revolution. A polemic was normal, but the word *tramps* bothered him. There was a kind of puritanism at work now.

Into this sudden fever for cleaning up culture dropped the little experimental film that Cabrera Infante had sponsored. Orlando Leál had assembled his shaky footage of the bars and street scenes of Havana on that January night into a short, which he called *PM,* or *Pasado Meridiano.* There was no voice-over, no obvious plot, no agenda, nor any real point other than to embody the style made possible by the light cameras, which had let Leál wind himself intimately inside his subject. In the United States and Europe this kind of cinema verité was all the rage, but in Cuba there was already one avant-garde, the vanguard, and it wasn't interested in a filmmaker's existential self-creation. *PM*—a twenty-minute student film with no dialogue—became what Cabrera Infante called "the beginning of the end . . . the lever of a whole upheaval in the annals of culture under Castro."

PM was scheduled to show at a small Havana theater in June. But the theater owner had to receive permission from Cuba's board of censorship before he could run the film. Film censorship was nothing new, but in the past it had been overheated kissing, or un-Catholic dialogue, that faced scrutiny.

In the summer of 1961 the censors of the Cuban Film Institute were following new criteria, invisible even to them. All they did know was that the enemies were now within and were probably revealed in a failure to conform to the norms of the Revolution. One look at *PM* and the censors panicked: they denied permission, ordered the theater to cancel the screening, prevented the film from being shown anywhere, and confiscated the review copy.

Leál thought the film had been banned because of how it had been been made: entirely outside of government control. "It was a crack in the wall," he told me, in a New York City coffee shop, forty-three years after the events. Film production had to be controlled.

The government was calling for a new filmmaking ethic based on revolutionary consciousness, heroic achievements, and New Men. *PM* showed no such New Men: it was a glimpse of ordinary life, squalid and unchanged, full of Vat 69 bottles, people in fancy clothes, drunks, all of it in the seedy neighborhood of Regla. And despite the presence of some whites, the film showed a largely Afro-Cuban ambiance in Regla, with scenes of noisy rumbas and dancing. This discomfited the nomenclature of the new cultural bureaucracy, who were themselves white, and dedicated to promoting a triumphant vision of a progressive, post-racial society, a scientific paradise that was light-years away from the earthy culture of black Cuba. "We are not like that," one (white) official complained to Leál at the time. "Not just that."

But it is more likely that the ban, and everything that sprang from it, had to do with who had sponsored it. The Revolution was seeking enemies, and found them in *Lunes*, the cultural magazine. *Lunes* was publishing radical thinkers—authors like Trotsky and Jefferson, Sartre and Neruda—and had criticized, harshly, the cultural old guard in Havana. By championing Trotsky, the standard-bearer for disobedient communists, the magazine had offended some of the hard-line Stalinists. That wouldn't have mattered in 1959, or 1960, but after the Bay of Pigs these men—the ones Castro had once mocked for spending the war under their beds—were suddenly wielding power. *PM* became the stalking horse for larger issues.

Sitting in the Manhattan restaurant, discussing all this with Leál, it was remarkable how little he had changed in forty-three years. Though he had filled out somewhat, he was still boyish-looking, still the wunder-kind, with smooth skin, a wide but cautious smile, and a bristling head of hair barely touched with silver. He grew sad as he remembered what had happened next. He'd been at home in Havana one day in late July of '61, still thinking that the worst had passed, that the banning of his film was all that would happen, when the telephone rang. Leál heard his wife answer, and he remembered how nervous she had sounded as she summoned him to the phone.

"The President of the Republic," a voice said, "wants you at the National Library on Friday."

He thought it was a joke. A crank caller. He expelled a gust of disbelieving air and simply put the phone back on its cradle. That's what Leal remembered, decades later. The way he had just hung up the phone.

But you can't hang up on Zeus. Or his attendants, who called right back, furious. This was no joke. He was told to be at the National Library, the night of July 30.

"Nineteen sixty-one was when they shut down the party," Leál said.

It was really an honor, in one sense, to be summoned to the library. There was to be an assembly of the nation's leading intellectuals. The most prominent writers, academics, film and television directors, painters, sculptors, and journalists in Cuba all received the same call.

This great meeting of great minds would occur in the great hall of the National Library, a much maligned construction that Leál called "a fascist, Mussolini building."

Or maybe it wasn't the architecture. On Friday night, Leál and his champion, Cabrera Infante, met in the lobby of the library, full of fear and uncertainty. The writer Nestor Almendros joined them in a hushed conversation. The lobby filled up with other intellectuals. Alfredo Guevara, then as now the leader of the film industry, collected a small circle of whispering acolytes. Finally Castro swept in, and as he passed, called out to Guevara: "Alfredo, I've come to smite you with the light." By speaking this way to the head of Cuba's film production, the Commander was indicating something of his real target.

"And it was just the opposite, of course," Leál sighed now, recollecting. It was not the light of justice that was to smite them, but the beam of a searchlight.

They knew they were in trouble, it was just a question of how much. There were dark, whispered rumors in the lobby: talk of the first purges, of the arrest of homosexuals and other distrusted elements, reports of the arrest, or exile, of prominent figures who were supposedly involved in conspiracies against Castro. The country had become stifled in the last months. The area, and era, of permitted expression was shrinking. There was a sense, Leál recalled, of the "culture closing in, the pressure building."

At the appointed hour the assembled crowd went into the hall in an atmosphere of uncertainty and fear. They left four hours later with greater certainty, and greater fear.

The government leadership was spread out behind a long table on a stage ("It was like the Last Supper," Leál said). Castro was in the middle; Armando Hart, then the minister of culture, was at stage right. Since the evening was billed as a discussion with "the intellectuals," different writers and artists were invited to give comments on the benefit of culture for the masses, and an hour or so was taken up with praise for the new *cinevans,* which toured remote hamlets showing films. There was also a lot of talk about *Lunes,* but not about shutting it down: instead, government officials promised to increase the number of such magazines, to break the "monopoly on ideas" held by *Lunes.* There would be many new magazines, and a broader, diversified, more democratic culture of criticism.

The words were fine, but the speakers were not. Whatever they said, one after another, they sounded nervous. They larded their statements with claims of ardent admiration for the Revolution. After proposing something, they apologized for not serving society more perfectly. As more writers rose, they began to confess to vague errors of judgment. They could not be specific, because they didn't themselves know what they had done wrong. They sensed only a general accusation.

A bootlicker suggested kicking out filmmakers who were ungrateful for the Revolution. At this, someone in the back rows shouted out a protest: "That's what they did to Eisenstein in Russia!" There was laughter and applause, but the heckler had scored a useless point.

Finally one of the poets rose and, almost stuttering, said something so obvious that no one had dared to say it: *I am afraid.* That was his only point. He didn't know why, he confessed. He couldn't think of what he had done wrong. But there was something menacing in the National Library. He named the fear, but again, it did no good. Poets could tremble, but they were faced by men who no longer had any fears.

When Castro finally rose to speak, there wasn't a word out of his mouth before he made a gesture that has become legendary in Cuba: he took off his pistol. Orlando Leál remembered the moment one way, describing how Castro removed his entire gun belt and then coiled it up on the desk. It was, Leál thought, a gesture of disarming, of "deference to intellectuals." But Cabrera Infante described it as just the opposite: he recalled Castro pulling a Browning pistol out of his holster, and then laying it on the table with a heavy thud. The gun was a reminder, Cabrera Infante said, of where real power lay.

Having set the stage, the old debater gave a long talk that has been kept in print and is sold in Cuban bookstores to this day, and that is still issued as required reading to the cadres of the Revolution. Known as "Words to the Intellectuals," the speech went into some detail, but in the end it was only a single phrase that mattered. After the Bay of Pigs, Castro was both confident and aggrieved, and in the mood to separate his enemies from his friends. He spelled out a new guideline for artistic expression which has since become the ideological knife cutting through every day of Cuban life. The phrase has spread to govern all forms of thought, from painting and filmmaking to political ideas and even military obedience. What Castro said that night was simple: *Within the Revolution, everything is permitted,* he told the upturned faces in the National Library. *Outside the Revolution, nothing is permitted.*

The phrase neatly divided the world into two camps. Those "within" the Revolution would have the right to express themselves in art, writing, and film, even to criticize, and to participate in the political system. But those "outside" the system would have no rights.

Loyalty was the declared standard of the land. Loyalty to the Revolution, but ultimately, loyalty to one man, personally. There could only be two groups: those for him, and those against him.

That night at the National Library was the end, for Leál. Castro, of all people, had been his prophet, the one to tip his own hand. "People saw, for the first time, the face of absolute power," Leál said. "It was the first time we understood the repercussions. To be outside the Revolution was to be outside of the Church. There was no space for thinking, no space for reason. There was only one truth, a revolutionary truth. It was religious. If you are not for me, you are against me."

Castro did not invent this idea, or formula, or even phrase. Mussolini had used the same language in the 1930s, while Castro was at Dolores, reading Il Duce's speeches, marinating in an atmosphere of Jesuit sympathy for Catholic strongmen. In Spain, Franco had demanded similar loyalties. The idea has a long pedigree, and a universal appeal to men of authority.

For all its absoluteness, the inside/outside standard was maddeningly vague. The same poem or film or book could be deemed acceptable or unacceptable, loyal or disloyal, depending on the political alignment of its author, the mood of the authorities, the atmosphere in the country, the degree of international scrutiny, and the personal connections between the artist and Cuban leaders. The difference between constructive criticism and serving the enemies of the Revolution lay not in specific words, thoughts, or actions, but in how these words, thoughts, or actions were perceived by the system, by Fidel Castro or his stand-ins. The idea has endured, and the same phrasing appears in Cuban newspapers today, four decades later.

The distinction between inside and outside, between loyalists and traitors, would be drawn at the very top. As Raúl Castro once put it, while silencing a heckler, "There is freedom of speech in Cuba, and I'm talking here."

The meeting at the National Library concluded in the only way it could. *PM* was banned permanently, and *Lunes* was closed within a few issues, buried with a raft of promises that many new magazines would soon replace it. In August the government announced that a new organization, UNEAC, or the National Union of Writers and Artists, would hold exclusive control over "literary production" in Cuba. Control of all printing presses, publishing budgets, even the supply of paper, would be centralized by UNEAC. Only registered members of the union, who submitted their manuscripts for review, would be considered legitimate authors.

Within the Revolution, everything. Outside the Revolution, nothing. By the end of 1961, out of Cuba's roughly two hundred private newspapers, magazines, and newsletters, every single one was placed under state control, along with the country's seven television stations. The costs for violating these rules could be staggering. Cabrera Infante eventually took the advice of his prophet, the Turk, defecting from Cuba and publishing his masterwork, *Three Trapped Tigers,* abroad. A single positive review of this book by the Cuban poet Heberto Padilla led to Padilla's immediate arrest. Padilla vanished, for years. Finally, in 1970, he reappeared as the star of a humiliating show trial, where the poet—beaten and cowed— was forced to confess to a laundry list of imaginary crimes against the Revolution. The only thing not included in his confession was his real crime: a positive book review for an author who lay on the wrong side of Castro's loyalty line.

In the early 1990s, the poet María Elena Cruz Varela was attacked and beaten by her neighborhood block committee, simply because she wrote a poem which declared

> No
> I don't believe in slogans like "fatherland or death."

Her own neighbors tore up the poem and, with security men watching, stuffed the offending lines down her throat, forcing her to eat her own words.

That too was the legacy of 1961, the Year of Literacy. More than 700,000 hungry minds were added to the ranks of readers, but there was less and less to feed them.

Miguel Llivina hadn't believed it back in January of 1961 when he heard that the United States was breaking off diplomatic relations with Cuba. "Everyone thought this was unthinkable," Miguel said, and so he had allowed himself not to think it. But his sister was more skeptical. She had wisely gotten herself a visa to the United States back in 1960, when only the paranoid were doing so. She had wanted to be ready, just in case. She urged Miguel to do the same, but he was busy, doubtful, and patient, so he put it off. Eventually he did walk the four or five blocks to the Ameri- can consulate in Santiago, which was located then in Vista Alegre, and he did apply for his whole family: himself, his wife, and his two boys, the elder almost two, the younger just six months. But the visas hadn't been processed by the time diplomatic relations were cut off. The consulate in

Santiago closed, and the application was lost. It was still possible to reapply, via Havana, but the complications and the increasing restrictions dissuaded him from trying, since he had no real plans to leave.

After April, everything that had been difficult became much harder. "After the Bay of Pigs," he said, "I made so many efforts. So many." He managed to buy a ticket out of Cuba on Pan Am, but the earliest available seat was months away, on August 10. August 10 came and went, and he was told it would be September. Then October.

Meanwhile, paperwork. Getting a visa waiver required sponsors. Miguel's uncle was already in America and agreed to handle their paperwork. But the first application was denied. Miguel couldn't recall why, but later assumed that, because he had dabbled in opposition to Batista, the Americans had his name on "some list from the Revolution."

Miguel's father had known a British man in Cuba, a Mr. McCormick, who "owned a factory." McCormick was in Miami, working with the Americans who were resettling Cuban exiles. McCormick advised Miguel to apply for another visa waiver, and be patient. But again, nothing happened.

In those days telegrams were delivered by messenger boys who blew a whistle as they approached a house. You could hear them going through Vista Alegre, tooting their whistles. Miguel spent the summer waiting for his whistle, the announcement of the imagined telegram bearing news that everything had been set up. They were so eager to go that the family packed its bags and kept them in the front room. At one point, encouraged by his uncle to believe that the waivers were imminent, Miguel actually loaded the suitcases into the car and drove everyone to Havana. Once there, a friend serving in the intelligence apparatus of the new government told him the permission to leave was imminent, but to go back to Santiago and wait there.

"We had everything ready," Miguel recalled. "At night, everybody waited, listening for the telegram whistle. You knew it was the last sound you would hear in Cuba."

They did hear the whistle, occasionally, but it was always far away, a signal for someone else. Another block. Another street. Days went by, then months. They grew tired of looking up when they heard the *wheeeet wheeet* fading away. No one came up the walkway to the house.

Slowly, reluctantly, Miguel came to realize that there was no waiver. His uncle had filed for the application in Miami, while himself residing in St. Louis. It was a jurisdictional mistake, a slipup. "They gave thousands and thousands of visa waivers," Miguel said. "But we didn't get one."

All around Santiago, Miguel's friends and colleagues were hearing that whistle and disappearing into exile. August, September, October all came and went. In St. Louis, his uncle now applied to a Missouri senator's office for help, and this time it worked: a visa waiver quickly appeared. But it was for Miguel alone, without his family. He wouldn't abandon his wife and children in Cuba.

The waivers for the rest of the family didn't arrive until 1962. McCormick, the British man, had finally arranged them. "PERMISSION TO TRAVEL WITHOUT PASSPORT," they read, "MARCH 30 1962."

But 1962 was much too late. The refugee flights had already been halted by then. Pan American wasn't flying to Miami anymore. The tickets were useless. Desperate plans were proposed during 1962 for transporting people out of the country, like putting them in the holds of cargo ships. John Kennedy had put this idea in motion by arranging to buy out the Mancebo brothers and the other prisoners captured at the Bay of Pigs the previous year. In exchange for shipments of tractors and Gerber baby food, Cuba would release the prisoners. These "baby food ships" began arriving in late 1962, and the Cubans of the 2506 Brigade were sent back to Miami.

"I tried to get on the baby food ships," Miguel had told me. He applied for a spot and was given a berth—a bit of cargo hold—for the last of the ships. He resigned from his job at the refinery. A government inspector visited the house and made an inventory of everything in it—how many chairs, how many tables. But in October of 1962 the last ship was "suspended" for "temporary" reasons. In Cuba everything was temporary, forever. The ship never sailed.

When Miguel, years later, applied for exit permits from Cuba, "They kicked me out of my job, just for asking," he said.

In the heat of the late summer of the Heroic Year, Santiago was set afire with a new rumor, which started among the mariners in the harbor and within hours had spread to the stevedores, and then to the warehousemen, and by night to their families. The rumor climbed the hills of Santiago with these people, and in a day or two it had reached the middle class in the city center, and even the rarefied heights of Vista Alegre. The whisper was that a ship full of money had arrived.

The ship was anchored in the long, thin bay, and heavily guarded. It was said to have a cargo of seven tons of money. Not Cuban pesos, or U.S. dollars, or even Soviet rubles, but something new. Although it had been printed in Czechoslovakia, the currency said CUBA on it, and it bore the signature of Che Guevara. A new money for a new country. The old republican peso, the rock-solid peso that had been pegged to the U.S. dollar and was good worldwide, was about to be phased out.

When the rumor first reached him, Dr. David de Jongh, the eldest of the three de Jonghs, had gone to his father's *Encyclopaedia Britannica*. The 1911 edition, the world's knowledge pressed onto translucent Bible paper. A leather so soft that each volume could be rolled up, and so flexible that the collected encyclopedia had to be stacked on their sides because they would not stand on their own. In the de Jongh household the alphabet flowed upward.

David looked under *G*, for gold. He read about 20 karat and 18 karat gold, about how to verify the purity, about touchstones, and aqua regia, and the various methods for dissolving gold in solution. Then he went quickly to see one of Santiago's best known jewelers, a man who normally trafficked in baubles and stones.

"I want gold," David said.

"Oh, yes," the jeweler replied. He understood, with the situation the way it was. "I can maybe find an ounce for you," he offered.

"I'm not buying ounces," David replied. "I want pounds."

He passed on the rumor about the seven tons of new money floating in the harbor. The jeweler was skeptical: Cuba had always had a strong peso, linked closely to the dollar, stable for decades. Nobody would dare touch the peso, a symbol of Cuba's wealth and solvency. Nobody needed pounds of gold.

David did. He insisted. The jeweler smiled at this crazy man, nodded, and was noncommittal.

But a week later, he called back. "Doctor," he said, addressing de Jongh with a new tone of respect.

He had found some gold, he said. A good amount. And more important, he had found that David might be right. The rumor about the currency in the harbor was true. The jeweler had himself already switched some of his money into gold. David wanted pounds, and the jeweler had found seven of them.

It didn't look like much when David came to see it: just a quarter of a gold bar. But seven pounds, at the market price of about U.S. $35 an ounce came to around $4,000. That wasn't a lot of money, but it is equivalent to almost $30,000 in 2006 values. A lot more than other, slower-acting people were about to have.

Once he had the lump, David didn't know what to do with it. How to get it out? Those allowed to leave the country were being searched. You couldn't just walk out with gold: even gold watchbands were being taken at the airports. David thought of burying it under the back lawn somewhere, but that was exactly what everyone would expect: rich people buried their valuables in the backyard. Anyone could examine the ground, looking for signs of disturbance.

David was standing in the backyard with seven pounds of gold in his hand, asking himself, What do I do? He put it in the trash.

At the de Jongh house, family servants burned the household trash every other day in a bin. The bin was always full of ashes and half-burned trash, and David just dropped the gold in, letting it sink to the bottom. He stirred some ashes over it, and burned papers.

Weeks later, in Havana, David de Jongh—*médico* de Jongh—was in Havana on business when he was woken up in his room at the Havana Hilton by a friend. It was 7:00 A.M. on the 4th of August.

"Are you standing up?" his friend asked.

"Yes."

"Well, sit down."

The news was simple: law number 963 had been announced publicly just minutes before. It invalidated all money in circulation. With the stroke of diktat, 462.1 million pesos were rendered valueless, effective immediately. There would be a new, revolutionary money, just as the rumor in Santiago had predicted. All bank accounts (with the exception of those belonging to foreign embassies and the Catholic Church, thanks to its diplomatic status) had already been sealed, and automatically exchanged for new currency. All of the old cash of the Cuban republic was to be turned in by Monday, exchanged at a rate set by the government. All the money in every wallet in Cuba would be toilet paper by Tuesday.

It wasn't the replacement of one money with another that was happening. It was the abolition of money itself. The *uno-por-uno* peso of the old republic was taken out and shot at dawn. Another Cuban cycle of spite-filled self-destruction was occurring. The economy had been shrinking for two years. The rich were fleeing, and the middle class was beginning to unravel. More and more people were leaving and taking their money with them. The confiscation of businesses produced shortages, which produced rationing, which inevitably produced black markets. The nationalization of banks left all financial controls in the hands of the government, and the population began to withdraw even more money from their banks, hoarding it for the black market or changing it into dollars. Government reserves plummeted. The economy was spiraling downward, clipped from both sides by the chaos of nationalization and the shortages of cash in circulation. And now the government feared that private stockpiles of money were being used to finance counterrevolutionary activities. People with cash, bank accounts, piles of silver and gold, were independent, beyond control.

The solution was the same as always: the Revolution would take, without apology, what it needed.

Law 963 paralyzed Cuba, at least for the weekend. Individuals were allowed to keep $500 worth of the old cash, to tide them over. But money was useless: the entire country was shutting down. In Havana that morning, the stores simply closed, unwilling to take the old currency, which was about to become valueless, while the new currency had not been introduced yet. The restaurants around the Hilton didn't bother to open. Out in Santiago the port, and even the lighthouse to guide ships to safety, was shut down.

David stood in front of the hotel's window. You could watch girls swimming in the pool on the roof of the Capri, and see the brand-new Riviera, all aerospace curves in poured concrete, and the spires of the Nacional, and off toward the harbor, the sinuous stretch of the Malecón, hugging the azure waves all the way to Regla and the Moro Castle beyond. David saw, somewhere out the window, the sign he had been waiting for.

Make a permanent memory of this, he said to himself. *Don't forget this.* He photographed the scene into his mind.

I want to see this because I am leaving Cuba.
Because I am leaving.
I am leaving, he said to himself, for the first time.

Not so fast. He raced the Buick to the airport, on the outskirts of the city, but all flights to Santiago were canceled, and then the airport itself shut down. On the way back into town he stopped at the bus station. Not a bus moving. They had no idea when service would resume. It all depended on the new currency.

So the Buick it was. At the Hilton again, he raced upstairs and threw his things into bags.

The phone rang: it was a friend from Santiago, the governor of the Lions Club, who knew he was about to be stuck in Havana. "I want to go with you," he said.

David agreed to take him, with one caveat. "I'm not getting out of the car," he said. "I will drive by your house," he told the man. "You be there in the street with your things. You jump in. If you don't jump, fast, you stay in Havana."

When David pulled up minutes later, the Lions Club governor was there, ready, and he jumped in.

"David," the man's brother called out to de Jongh, "come have some coffee." They were waving him in. The world was ending, and they wanted to sit down and drink coffee. He gunned it.

They left Havana and drove east for two or three hours, fast, before encountering any trouble. There was suddenly a lot of traffic, and then all the cars ahead were moving into the right lane. David could see a line of cars a kilometer long, all in the right lane. The cars were crawling toward a checkpoint. Militiamen were there, looking over the passengers for anti-revolutionary "elements," and apparently searching the cars for stashes of currency.

The left lane, however, was wide open. Without thinking what he was doing, David swerved left and accelerated. The waiting cars ticked by. He rolled steadily down the line, closing on the militiamen. He didn't have an idea in his head.

"If I don't stop," he told the governor, "they will shoot us."

Or would they? As they approached the militia, David kept accelerating compulsively, and the governor simply rolled down his window, leaned out, and, as they passed, he stuck his fist into the air and screamed, with the full authority of the Lions Club, *"PATRIA O MUERTE!"*

Fidel's own slogan. The militiamen threw their fists in the air and answered, as one: *"VENCEREMOS!"* We will win!

David's foot felt locked in place. He drove through, and on, and nothing happened, until eventually they had to stop for gas. They found one of the last stations still open, far enough out from Havana that they either didn't know about the new currency or didn't know what else to do, because they accepted the old money, and the men filled the tank. David and the governor spent everything they could on sandwiches and drinks, before racing onward, eating from their laps as they took turns driving.

They arrived in Santiago at 1:00 A.M., rolling down out of the cool hills into the swampy night of the bay city. Two hours after they arrived, militias closed the roads into Santiago.

Getting home was only a way of leaving. David had scientific habits: you examined evidence, you measured, you laid out a course of deductions, you made a thesis, and then you followed the trail of logical steps, one by one. Denial has no place in the lab.

His deduction had been correct: the new money heralded a complete takeover of the economy, of the mechanisms of trade. The process that began with land reforms and the breaking up of big estates was not an end, sufficient to itself, but part of a permanent thirst for control that could never be quenched.

At the house David called his youngest brother, Kiki, out to the backyard and, acting casually, stirred a stick in the ashes of the trash burner until he hit something solid. "That is about seven pounds of gold," he said. Kiki did not show any surprise. David told him to keep the servants from any sudden impulse to clean out the bin and told him to be ready to move the gold, soon. They would need it on the outside.

Kiki listened. David got an exit visa later in the year and went out like anybody. Arturo followed. Kiki stayed, following his elder brother's instructions. When it was time, and David had everything arranged, Kiki dug the plug of gold out of the ashes. It looked like a filthy fragment of a clay brick, until you wiped it down. Then it gleamed, untarnished.

Kiki delivered the block of ore to a man at a foreign consulate in Santiago. He was a "friend" of David's, and he carried the gold out of Cuba in a diplomatic pouch. It landed in Florida, where David, and then Arturo, were waiting for it, and for Kiki.

The gold, that little survivor of the family fortunes, made it out. But as the months went by, Kiki reported that he himself was delayed.

On September 10, 1961, a Sunday, Catholics in Havana gathered for a traditional procession of the Virgin of La Caridad, the patroness of Cuba. Thousands of regular Catholics were joined at the march by some anti-Castro activists. The police, present in force, initially denied permission to march, then finally granted it. Hundreds of government loyalists were brought to the scene. The tail of the procession had not even left the church, and the head was only a couple of blocks down the street, when someone began shooting. A young man named Arnaldo Socorro fell dead. The crowd fled; the police arrested several Catholic leaders and eventually convicted and jailed them for homicide.

But the immediate effect of the Caridad shooting was far more important: the next day the Ministry of the Interior loudly denounced the Catholic Church as a whole, labeling it a tool of the counterrevolution. Just a day later, September 12, the police began putting under house arrest all Catholic priests who were deemed unreliable, which was most all of them. The rival orders—Dominicans, Franciscans, Carmelites, Christian Brothers, Ursulines, and the Jesuits—were all treated the same. An order of expulsion came down: all foreign priests must leave, and the great majority of Catholic priests were foreign. From across Cuba, 132 of these men, almost all of them Spaniards, were put onboard a Spanish-registered ship, the *Covadonga,* and on September 17 it sailed from Havana harbor with virtually all the Jesuits from the Colegio de Dolores on board. They had been thrown out of many countries before. This was part of being a Jesuit. History taught they would return to Cuba, someday.

Lundy Aguilar's "The Prophet" featured a man sailing out of Havana harbor in despair, and exile was a tragic motif in Cuban life. The Jesuits had company as they sailed away. Before 1961 was through, 67,000 Cubans had fled to the United States. Many others had gone to Spain, the Dominican Republic, and Mexico, where many of the Jesuits ended up, too.

————

Literacy campaigners had been murdered all year, and the last of some two dozen teachers who died was a sixteen-year-old volunteer, killed on the 26th of November. Another martyr. As the Year of Literacy wound down, the spectacle wound up. December 22 was declared the Day of Education, with a massive victory rally in Havana for the teaching volunteers. Their once improvised and enthusiastic effort had a powerful institutional structure now, with a huge bureaucracy, a special anthem, and a spiral of flow charts communicating in a new language of acronymic alliances—ORI, AJR, STE, MINFAR, ME, CTC(R), ANAP, FMC, CDR—which only initiates could understand.

On December 22, the day of the great rally in Havana, statistics, many of them dubious, poured forth: at the rally they announced that 566,817 persons had been taught to read, although later the number was upgraded to precisely 730,212, and still later, the government said "a million" had become literate.

Cuba had jumped into the ranks of the world's best-educated countries almost overnight. General illiteracy dropped from 23.6 percent to 3.9 percent in the span of twelve months, with the stiffest decline among the rural poor, where 42.7 percent had been illiterate. Whatever the real numbers, it was a colossal achievement. *Fidel, how great you are.*

Tens of thousands of the literacy teachers marched up the Malecón in Havana that day, passing for hours, unit by unit, all in uniform. The Conrado Benítez Brigade had multiplied, becoming many such brigades, with company after company of teachers in green. Some of them held up giant pencils, a prop for the photographers on the rooftops.

The main reviewing stand was set up beside the Riviera Hotel, with its high-dive board and its sloping wall of windows. And as they passed, the battalions of teachers repeated the chant they themselves had been taught, by their own teachers, shouting it to the man himself, as he smiled upon them:

FIDEL!

FIDEL!

TELL US WHAT TO DO!

————

Not everyone made it out, then, or easily, or at all, but it still wasn't too late. With the Heroic Year expiring in a frenzy of chants, José Antonio Roca, the old hoops star, sharpened his elbows and drove the lane.

Roca had applied for permission to leave the country much earlier in 1961, but without any result. He'd spent the whole year jumping the hurdles of the new bureaucracy of departure: the health permits and visas and separate certifications of houses, bank accounts, and cars, an inventory of all personal property, and, because he was a dentist, permission from the new state association for dentists. The web of rules was tightening, but many of the old assumptions about rights and civil procedures still lingered, at least in a shadow form. You could still leave, in theory, by asking, by filling out paperwork, by paying, by registering, by playing by the rules. And the government simply lacked experience, the experience of time, in enforcing its new rules. That meant loopholes.

Since the Bay of Pigs, Roca had assumed that, no matter how it happened, he and his family would be leaving, and he had turned his mind to practical questions. The most obvious of these was how to get out with some money or possessions. Those who left were stripped of virtually everything, but Roca looked for a crack in the system and he found it at Guantánamo, the huge American base near Santiago. It hadn't been fenced off completely, yet: Cubans who worked for the American military were allowed to commute into the U.S. base every morning. One of his employees at the dental clinic had a relative who worked at the base, and so effectively left Cuba every morning. For a price, this man agreed to help.

The Cuban government knew that base employees had always been a conduit for back-and-forth smuggling of various kinds and kept them under close scrutiny. But Roca used his dental drills to hollow out the heels on several pairs of shoes. Each day he would give a pair of shoes to the worker, who strolled into Guantánamo on top of a piece of jewelry, or a tightly wadded bundle of U.S. dollars, or bits of the gold that dentists kept for making fillings. It didn't add up to much, unless you were required to leave with nothing at all, but there was satisfaction in knowing that they had beaten the system, and that an old family ring would be waiting for them on the outside.

Not one to wait passively for the play, Roca took up a position near his goal. Late in the fall he took his family to the capital and checked into the

Hotel Capri. But when the exit permit proved elusive, and weeks dragged by, they switched to living in the houses of various friends to save money. The bureaucracy would not budge, right through December and the end of the Year of Literacy. Since those who left Cuba were by definition tainted, the risk-averse bureaucrats in Havana were stalling. Even completed exit permits would sit unsigned for weeks. Roca struggled with one evasive bureaucrat, who insisted that he simply had no time to handle the family's application. Finally José Antonio went to his house at 5:00 A.M., waiting in the street for the man to emerge for work, and then presented him with the paper needing his signature right there, on the sidewalk. The man rubbed sleep from his eyes and signed.

In late December, José Antonio, Carmelina, and their children were finally given seats on a flight. They would leave on the sixth day of the new year, 1962. When they arrived at the airport, their luggage was searched to the usual stringent standards, and a policeman confiscated a gold chain from around Carmelina's neck. But to their own disbelief, the family walked out of the fishbowl, crossed the tarmac, and climbed the mobile stairs to take their seats.

The flight was brief, less than an hour passing over the hues of the ocean, tropical green, then North Atlantic blue, and then the muddy coastal waters of Florida, and finally the black runway in Miami. Such a short trip, José Antonio recalled, but in that one crowded hour, "winter gave way to spring."

AVENUE OF THE PRESIDENTS

Granma was in favor of Fidel Castro. Since its first issue in 1965, Cuba's national newspaper had been full of enthusiastic praise for the Leader, and despite all the decades and misadventures, the editors had never yet found space for a single word against him. Fidel, known in the streets as the Horse, the Beard, Crazy, This Fellow, The Boss, Him, or just Uncle So-and-So, was identified in the pages of *Grandmother* by a variety of titles:

> Leader
> Maximum Leader
> Major
> Doctor
> First Vice Minister
> President
> Prime Minister
> President and Prime Minister
> First Secretary
> Commander
> Commander in Chief
> Invincible Marshal of the Republic

Granma needed multiple titles. They wrote about Castro not just every day, but on most pages of every issue. He was mentioned in about a third of the articles, including those on the sports page, and even in theater reviews.

Perhaps the most shocking thing about *Granma* was the paper it was printed on, a gray and faintly greasy newsprint with strange bits of fiber and black spots dotting the page. The red ink in the big headlines ("Raúl Meets with Italian Foreign Minister") was prone to bleeding out, and the smaller black-type paeans to the State Visit by the President of Burundi, or the Comments by the Chief of the North Korean Armed Forces smudged on your fingers. The photographs were flat, developed in old chemicals and printed with diluted ink. A smudge on Castro's face could set off an orgy of speculation in Miami (wasn't it deliberate? a signal from Cuban journalists?). Smudges everywhere else drew no such attention.

Granma was utterly reliable. Come hell or high water, *Granma* was on the street. Since 1965, the one thing that had never faltered in Cuba was the message. The headlines in *Granma,* applied daily in small doses, added up to a seamless worldview:

> The Struggle Continues and Will Continue
> The Force of the Revolution Must Be Expressed
> An Atomized Society Can Have No Force for Anything
> We Have Begun to See the First Fruits
> For Development, for Progress, for Justice
> For Caribbean Integration
> Emulation Among Combines Will Increase Efficiency

Poet and novelist Reinaldo Arenas described *Granma* as the "first wonder" of Cuban socialism:

> It's the only newspaper in the world in which the events that the newspaper reports on have nothing whatsoever to do with reality. It is the most optimistic newspaper in the world, and among the most frequent verbs you will find in its headlines are *inspire, conquer, overthrow, achieve, optimize.* . . . It's also the newspaper with the largest potato and sugar harvests in all the world, although we ourselves never see those products anywhere. It has no obituaries, and when somebody is shot by the firing squad the newspaper says that the person died in a state of grace, proclaiming the virtues of the newspaper editor who had the person shot.

The "newspaper editor" was of course the one man, the Horse himself, who appointed the men who chose the men who directed the men who actually wrote, edited, and printed *Granma.*

On the day known as "18 JANUARY YEAR OF THE GLORIOUS

ANNIVERSARIES," or eighteen days after my rooftop party, the news-paper had exciting news: there was an election coming. Cubans would be voting directly for their provincial delegates and national deputies. The emphasis was not on who was elected—a foregone conclusion—but on how. The goal cited in *Granma* was to improve the "organization of elec-toral roundtables" and "the functioning of the system of communica-tions." Form was substance.

But the election itself was actually small news today, at the bottom of the front page. A much larger and lavishly illustrated article with red head-lines and bullet points covered the top front of the paper, and this was, of course, a lovingly detailed account of Castro's latest statements on a variety of topics, taken from a long television appearance the night before. Castro had sat in a TV studio with two men from the electoral commission, dis-cussing the elections, and he had done the talking. The other men were supposed to start things off, and then intervene with gentle questions only when one of Fidel's twenty-five-minute monologues petered into a digres-sion that not even he could fathom.

Castro was old and weak, but not yet silenced by illness, and he had spoken at length last night, extemporaneously, wagging his finger in the air, reciting the astonishing array of statistics he kept memorized for this purpose, using familiar language about the sanctity, sovereignty, inde-pendence, justice, efficiency, and morality of the Cuban system. But then he had explained that the logic of his argument had best been expressed once before, on the occasion of another election. He picked up some pages and began reading aloud. The television program now consisted of Castro sitting in a chair reading a speech from the early 1990s as two men watched. Then, the next morning, here was the nation's leading newspa-per describing the television show, and serving up the old speech anew.

Cuba had to conserve everything in the Special Period, even words. There might be small modifications in the language, and the packaging was changed, but the Cuban system concentrated on delivering the same clear messages again and again, a drumbeat to the Revolution's march.

The very first of these themes was always the same: unity. Today, preparing the public for the upcoming election, *Granma* called for "unity against those who want to divide us, weaken us, demoralize us." Unity was mentioned in the first and second paragraphs of the article, and most of the rest, and also at the bottom of the page, in an entire article devoted to unity. This one exhorted the people to vote with unity, and various key phrases were put in all capital letters (VOTE UNITED!) or in boldface (Make the United Vote a Reality!).

Dissent, to any degree, in any form, in any place, at any time, was not just weakness but a betrayal. This was the purpose of Cuban elections: they served as periodic loyalty oaths, mechanisms to enact fealty. Cuba was always improving on the "quality" of its electoral system, meaning the ability of state organizations to control and mobilize people. Up to a year before the vote, the "organizations of the masses and students" would be charged with "clarifying" the "correct" manner of voting, *Granma* said. The propaganda machine would kick in a few months before the date. Only at the last minute would anyone learn what they were voting for, and how.

In 1997 there had been local elections, and Cubans had been allowed to choose one of several candidates for each municipal post. All the candidates, without exception, were loyal revolutionaries from slates approved by the Party and its many organisms, so the result was merely the ratification of the government's own policies. But seven years later the 1997 elections had been discovered to contain a vital weakness. The candidates were competing against one another. Competition was inefficient, a wasted replication of talent and effort, and had now been improved upon. In this new election, candidates would no longer vie for the attention of the voter. This time it was a matter of simple ratification: the government had one position for every single candidate. All the voter had to do was put a check mark next to the eight or nine names. It was a plebiscite, not an election, with abstention as the only alternative to saying yes.

But the new election had been improved even beyond this. At the bottom of the ballot this time there was a large circle, next to the words "ALL OF THE ABOVE." You could put one check mark there and let the Revolution do all the hard work of picking the right people. Unity in gesture was crucial. Any form of individual choice—anything less than complete conformity in every detail—was, in the words of *Granma,* an opening to "imperialism" and "traitors." Even showing up late at the polling station was a form of weakness. Vote early, *Granma* said, and vote united.

The second theme, here and everywhere, was equally blunt: patriotism. "The fatherland needs you," the newspaper said. Nationalism, hyperbole, and false pride marched in step. Cubans were not merely free, the minister of information and communications said, but "the freest people on earth." The candidates for office were not merely good, *Granma* said, they were the "most modest and humble of candidates." The election was not merely democratic, it was, the paper continued, "the most democratic that has ever been employed in the world," with "new and creative methods" unknown in the darkness beyond Cuba. No other election had ever been so well prepared and organized.

The ceaseless tolling of such superlatives, of achievements, records, and improvements, was a vital part of building an alternative universe, of constructing what Czeslaw Milosz called the "Captive Mind" of those living amid universal deceit and loyalty rituals. Every harvest set some record, if not for size than for being done in the "most heroic" conditions or for the "unprecedented" difficulties. Castro would begin half his speeches by saying "I UNDERSTAND . . . THAT THIS EVENT . . . HAS SET . . . SOME KIND OF RECORD . . . FOR ATTENDANCE." Castro's birthday, once unremarked, was now a nationwide event, with orchestrations of loyalty beneath photo murals of the Leader, all reported breathlessly on Cuban TV, and then distilled the next day in the pages of *Granma*. Among the scintillating international dispatches in *Granma* was this news:

> "On his birthday, the Olympic team sends . . . a message of admiration, respect and support to the main inspiration of Cuban sport, President Fidel Castro," said Humberto Rodríguez, president of the Cuban Sports Institute.

For those who ignored the instructions to live, think, and act united, a cartoon inside the newspaper reinforced the electoral message. There was a four-panel strip that showed friendly Cubans waiting for a *camello* bus and discussing the new election. The punch line was, "The best thing is to vote united to advance and defend the Revolution!"

Posters about the candidates were plastered all over Havana, listing their names and résumés. Even a quick glance revealed that every candidate was either a member of the Communist Party or one of its affiliates, like the Party-controlled Union of Young Communists, or the Party-controlled labor union (actually, most candidates were members of *all* these groups). Among thousand of local candidates in this election, only three were not communists, and these three were all Protestant preachers, who worked with the government and were urging their flocks to cooperate with the socialist system.

Castro, however, insisted on television and then in the newspaper that there was absolutely "no intervention by the Party" in the election. The masses themselves had nominated communists for 98 percent of the openings. This point was so important that he repeated it again later, almost verbatim, and then veered off into dangerous comparisons. By contrast with Cuba, other countries were false democracies, where the candidates were chosen by political parties, he explained.

Money was "the great elector," Castro said. Politicians in the United States were bought and sold "in the same manner used to sell soda, beer, or cars . . . any of the millions of articles that are sold in the market."

True enough, in a way. But maybe it was a bad idea to mention that in other countries there actually were millions of articles for sale in the markets.

The baseball stadium is in an ancient neighborhood of Havana called El Cerro, or the Peak. In the nineteenth century, a series of plagues drove the rich to build airy second homes on the small rise of El Cerro, just a couple of miles from the harbor. A century later the houses were decayed, rotten, and lovely, like so much in Cuba: hundreds of them lined a long avenue, more than a mile of colonnaded porches, rococo pediments, and rusted ironwork.

Half a dozen people had assured me that there was definitely no baseball in Havana this weekend. Both of Havana's teams, the Industriales and the Metropolitanos, were on the road. No baseball. Definitely not. Cabdrivers, neighbors, hotel concierges, old friends, and strangers had all informed me there was definitely no baseball. But come Saturday night, the TV in F.'s kitchen was blaring a pregame show. I could see an Industriales pitcher warming up in the bullpen, and asked F. where they were playing. "Right here," he said. "That is the Estadio Latinoamericano, in El Cerro."

I went out in the street, flagged down a black market cab, and was at the stadium in under fifteen minutes. I paid a dollar for my ticket— Cubans paid 7 cents—and stormed inside, helping myself to one of the many free seats behind home plate. There was a large bus tour of Canadian tourists here, underdressed for the cold but genial and glad for my company. The bleachers were only a quarter full. I managed to catch, live, the last warm-up pitches by the same hurler I had seen on TV.

I was looking forward to a little nostalgic baseball, the old-time game for which Cuba was famous. Players were paid nothing, rode their bikes to work, and batted and fielded with the desperate heart of true talent. Just five years before, I'd had a fantastic evening right here in the same stadium, seeing exactly that. The Cubans had put on a mind-numbing display of talent, especially Omar Linares. At the Atlanta Olympics of 1996, Linares had rained hits on the Americans and finally crushed the Japanese with an impossible batting average of .487, bringing home the gold. He was the Satchel Paige of our day, a legendary talent kept out of the American big leagues by politics. He was famous for refusing all offers to defect to the United States, where he could have earned millions. Instead he had always chosen to return to Cuba, where he served in the National Assembly, preaching the virtues of loyalty to the Revolution and hard work.

Linares had started that long-ago night with a memorable display of his most famous quality—his blinding speed on the basepaths. As the first batter up, he'd been walked by a clumsy starter. Then Linares had somehow disappeared, only to reappear at second base a half second later. After just a few more pitches he rematerialized at third without anyone having seen a thing. Then he'd blown home on a wild pitch, accompanied by the roar of the crowd.

Not tonight. Linares had finally "retired early," to take a lucrative contract with the Chunichi Dragons in Japan. Like all loyal Cuban athletes, artists, and musicians—the ones who went abroad only with permission— the money Linares earned while overseas didn't go to him. It went to the Cuban Sports Federation, which arranged the contracts and received the hard currency. This allowed the government to keep up to 80 percent of the money that a performer, like the late Rubén González of the Buena Vista Social Club, earned. Thus Linares's yen were turned into lead by the alchemy of the Revolution, which paid him a fraction of his earnings in Cuban currency.

When the game started, it was clear that the generation of Linares had passed. The Industriales pitcher threw three stinkers, all three of which were clocked for bases. Two runs got in before some fans had even noticed that the game had started.

A cold front had blown in. Night winds tortured the stadium. The Cuban players weren't used to this kind of weather, the low forties, the very coldest it ever gets in Havana. Their game was stiff, clumsy, almost amateurish. Both teams began smacking singles, doubles, home runs, more singles. It was raining baseballs in the outfield, but stupid errors abounded, and the sides came and went with equal incompetence. Shivering first basemen dropped everything that bounced their way. Both teams burned through their bullpens, changing pitchers after each new disaster, and the game slid toward absurdity. The weather miserable, the crowd became increasingly surly as the score ran up. About four thousand people cheered or booed, depending. Most of them were teenagers, and since cans of beer cost a *fula* each, they couldn't afford to get even a little drunk. A bored teenager is dangerous.

Béisbol goes so deep into Cuba that it can't be dug out. It arrived in the 1860s, brought in by Cuban students returning from the United States, and played by American sailors loading sugar. By the 1890s, *béisbol* had become a Cuban game, a point of nationalist pride in their struggle against Spanish identity and rule. Cuban exiles had carried the game to the Dominican Republic and the rest of the Caribbean. *Béisbol* still entwined Cuba and America like two tongues in one mouth. As I sat on a sticky, cold metal seat, there was *un squeezeplay,* followed by a *flai* to the outfield, which was caught by a *fildeador* for an *aut.* The Industriales could barely *pitchear* at all, so that *jonrón* followed a *tubey* ("two base"), which followed a *tribey.* Inning after inning I waited in vain for that supreme display of competence, *el double play.*

The Canadians went home in the bottom of the fifth, leaving me in the company of two Cuban big shots who somehow had tickets right behind home plate. They spent the entirety of each inning yelling at the players. *Fag fag fag you homo you fucking monkey you fag.* They did this in front of their children, getting more and more furious as the game ground down into farce. They weren't for either side: they were against both. *You fag,* they yelled. *I'm going to fuck your wife just like I fucked your sister you cocksuck-*

ing fag you fag fag fag. They had plenty of money for beer. They were getting red-eyed, sloppy on their feet. When the Industriales came in from the field at the end of the inning, both men leaned out to taunt them. One of the Industriales fielders held out his hand, in a gesture of reconciliation, and when one of drunkards took it, still saying *you are shit you fag,* the ballplayer gave one clean jerk and flipped him headfirst over the wall. The drunkard landed on his head, sprayed with beer, and the ballplayer was gone.

The visiting team, from Santiago de Cuba, had a surprising number of fans behind its dugout—almost a thousand, it seemed. The Industriales still had a strong home advantage, but this was the Yankees–Red Sox rivalry of Cuba and only the *orientales* seemed to be enjoying it. During the sixth inning (a cascade of grounders that amounted to nothing), a small fight broke out in the crowd near the Santiago bench. I could see flailing punches and a half-dozen teenagers battling, and then the police waded into the fight.

The crowd around me, on the Havana side of the stadium, began to hoot, and gradually the people behind me began to raise a steady, orchestrated chant, which spread through our section of the bleachers and built up to a roar. The fight over on the other side had finally given hundreds of people something to get excited about:

PAL-E-STI-NO!

PAL-E-STI-NO!

PAL-E-STI-NO!

"Palestinian" was an insulting nickname for easterners. During the 1990s, Havana's population had been swollen by tens of thousands, possibly hundreds of thousands, of easterners looking for work. Because they were without residency permits, without ration cards, they were said to be stateless, i.e., Palestinians.

And since there was never enough money for new housing, or social services, or even food, *Habaneros* liked to blame the *Palestinos* for crowding, for the shortages, for the lack of jobs, for social problems, for crime, and for starting fights in the Estadio Latinoamericano.

A thousand people now:

PAL-E-STI-NO!
PAL-E-STI-NO!
PAL-E-STI-NO!

The hard drunks in the power seats had recuperated from the earlier upending, and were on their feet again, turned toward the crowd, inciting them. They waved their arms, ordering people to stand up. A minute ago they'd been heaping insults on their own team; now they couldn't assault the visitors fast enough. The usual atavistic accusation: *Them. Outsiders. The Palestinos. They are the source of the problems. Them.*

For the average person, less vicious, maybe it was just the ancient rivalry between Cuba's two cities. But the mass of voices was a force, a message. *This is our town. We decide things here.*

A dozen police officers were needed to break it up. They finally dragged away five or six young men. The chant died out slowly, and the bullies turned their full attention back to insulting the sexuality of the players.

A cold, boring inning later, I got curious about the *Palestinos,* and walked over to the far side of the stadium, shooting pictures, snooping, eavesdropping. I don't worry about safety much in Cuba. Crime is low, weapons rare. Philip Agee, the former CIA spy who had become a turncoat and exposed many of America's worst plots to murder Castro, had recently opened a travel agency in Havana. He'd boasted that the island was a stress-free travel destination. "Take a break from anxiety and tension and come to Cuba," he advised tourists. The island was "well known for having the safest streets in the Western Hemisphere."

But crime was rising, a dangerous situation where precedent and experience were a poor guide. While I was bent over, composing a shot of the deserted bleachers, something tingled quietly in my subconscious, and I whipped around to find two gangly teenage boys sitting right behind me. They were pressed too close together, looking furiously at the field, as if they'd had no thought in the world except to watch the game from ten inches behind my ass. One of the buckles on my camera bag was now open.

Look asshole, I have eyes, I can see, I blurted at the closer one. I jabbed a finger at him, and he fell back in innocence, rolling his eyes, insisting he wasn't doing anything. They both got up and walked away.

Grab them? They were young, strong, and mean. Two of them. There was no need to debate who could get away with what. Call the police? For what? I hadn't seen anything. If I made even an allegation against them they could get caught up in the nightmare of the legal system. Better to leave it alone. I dropped down a level and walked fast across the stadium. I rebuckled the camera bag and settled into my seat.

I spotted the two boys watching me, from new seats, much closer than before. When they saw me spot them, they flicked their heads back to the baseball game.

I don't like being chased out of places. Fear makes me physically ill, so I don't always recognize what is happening. Leave when you are ready to leave. Stay until midnight, just to prove you don't always leave, every time.

Seventh inning, top and then bottom. More hits. Top of the eighth. More hits. The pitchers were throwing wild, the batters laughed, and the crowd was increasingly restive. At the bottom of the eighth, three minutes to midnight, the Industriales were up 14–11, and I went for the exit tunnel.

No taxis, no buses. Just the usual Cuba at midnight. A trickle of baseball fans simply walked off, heading confidently into the dark streets of El Cerro. I asked the staff where to find a cab at midnight, but I already knew their answer: nowhere. There were never any taxis at the stadium, because Cubans couldn't afford them and foreigners like the Canadians arrived and left in special tour buses. And, one elderly attendant confessed, there wasn't a single working phone anywhere in the building to call for a cab.

After the Linares game, I'd stood right here, asking the same questions. Then as now, the only hope for a ride was up on a major avenue, four blocks away. You could just make out the cars up there, passing by in a whiz. The deaf old comrade manning the stadium gate pointed his finger up the street, and I obeyed.

Halfway up, I stopped to tie my shoe, even though it was well tied. Three boys stopped and watched me. *They are definitely not following me.* I ignored them, tightened up my camera bag, and went on, faster. More people ahead of me, also boys. Up at the avenue, everything was fine, *there will be a car soon.*

I stood in plain sight, waiting for cars. In the empty intersection the boys felt too close, so I turned back toward the stadium, but found another six teenagers coming up the alley, animated, spread out. The new group called out to the old group, in gruff bursts of encrypted street Spanish that bounced off my ears.

Nothing is wrong. I went back across the avenue. *There will be a car soon.* I moved down the road a dozen yards. *Soon.*

It was quiet for a long time, four or maybe ten seconds. Perception was beginning to squeeze into a tube. The shortest of all the boys, maybe twelve, walked up. He asked if I needed a cab. "No," I said. *Well yes you do.*

"Actually," I told him, "yes, I do."

He hesitated. "So . . ." he said, and unable to think, he asked again. Did I need a cab?

His clumsy little lie now broke, like a fever. He'd repeated himself because it was a script. A setup. They were—

Three coming fast. I saw it now but restrained myself. Do it one way and play it another. Muttering to the kid, I put my back to a column and looked right *four big muggers.*

They were smiling, walking in quickly. Left, right, and also ahead. All the adrenaline in my body released at once, taking one second to tighten all my muscles and speed my heart, dilate my eyes and lungs, flood my bloodstream with clotting agents and cover my face in sweat. *Two in front.*

That was it then. No need to discuss who could get away with what. Someone on the left jumped a railing, to get behind me and my column, and I rocketed forward, looked at the skinny boy in the eyes and asked loudly, "Can you tell me something?" He froze.

I juked around him, faked a punch at the second kid, and broke into a run, slamming away another hand that grabbed at the camera bag and slipping into the open.

Even as I ran I could not accept what was happening. *They aren't chasing me,* I thought, despite the quick slapping of sneakers that came from behind.

I looked. Halfway down the first block, I looked over my shoulder. It was much worse than I feared. Amazing what your eye can record in a quarter second. The sallow yellow of his palm, reaching out to grab, the hand just a foot away, so close I can still see the dirt under his nails. The Hawaiian shirt, open over a white T-shirt. Shorts. A jaunty fade for a haircut, with a fake part on the right, buzzed into the nappy hair with clippers. Behind him, a half-dozen other forms, running in.

I ran faster. Huge strides with my long legs, arms pumping, straight as an arrow down the middle of the street. The sound of shoes on asphalt diminished. I could see the stadium, which looked to be three kilometers away, not three blocks.

AYÚDAME, I bellowed, running hard and screaming it again, *AYÚDAME AYÚDAME AYÚDAME!!!*

In the middle of the second intersection the slapping of sneakers stopped. I sprinted a half block more, just to be sure, and looked back in time to see the boys disappearing around the far corner, onto the avenue where we had started.

The short, determined kid in the Hawaiian shirt was the last to vanish, and did not look back. If they were caught assaulting a tourist they were likely to get severe jail terms. Six, eight, ten years in crowded, harsh conditions. More if they had a record.

Run, assholes. I was bent over, gasping for breath, almost blacked out. *Fuck you Fuck you Fuck you Fuck you You fucking shit-eaters.* I wanted to hurt them. To see them afraid. I wanted to split their skulls open.

Your turn to run, assholes.

Run.

By the time I woke up the election was over. I had gone to bed at 1:00 A.M. in a state of nervous disbelief, which gradually deteriorated with the passing hours into a fevered paranoia. I tossed on the polyester sheets, bundled up against the unfamiliar cold, agonized by a war between exhaustion and jittery energy in my endocrine system.

Whenever sleep began to close over me, a hand reached out of the darkness, a hand connected to a cruel, delighted face. The face was connected to a yellow Hawaiian shirt. But it was not fear that coursed through me; it was rage.

I wanted to smash them. To crush them. I imagined flying slowly over the city, hunting down the boys as they fled before me, helpless and terrified. I imagined attacking them with knives, with rocks, with sticks, my feet and fists, anything. How quickly I grabbed for that live wire, the mastery over life and death. A few seconds in an alley, and I was full of hatred and the lust for power. My own little dictator.

I kept jolting out of bed. I tried sitting up, or pacing the dark hall of the house. At 4:00 A.M., trembling in my sheets, I heard the roosters of Havana crowing to one another. One was next door, and others responded from many blocks away. The last time I checked my watch it was 4:30 A.M. I drifted in the foggy realm of semiconsciousness for the next few hours.

I rose at ten, only because I had to find aspirin. For some reason I could barely move my neck. I couldn't recall suffering any injury during the attack. Had I forgotten something? Had they yanked the camera bag hard enough to sprain my neck? Had I twisted it while slinking out of someone's reach? Did my fake punch really pack that much theater?

At breakfast, the neck was so painful that I could barely tip my head back to drink the coffee that F. served me. When I told him what had happened, in the alley, he looked at me with wide-eyed fear. Foreigners brought trouble, first on themselves, and then on those around them. The money was always balanced against this.

And now it was election day. F. brought the television into the kitchen, put it on the counter, plugged it in, turned it on, and a figure in green appeared. Him. Here he was, live, voting in a small city in eastern Cuba, trailed by cameras and hordes of election officials.

Fidel was being watched by a group of journalists, who were described as the "international press." There was a long delay, and several staged discussions between the Commander and the election officials about how exactly one filled out the ballot. Then He made His mark, folded over the paper, and inserted it halfway into a ballot box.

He paused there, looking up expectantly. This was stagecraft he knew well: as he waited, dozens of cameras flashed, and soundmen shoved in closer for position. He waited for the media, and when the substance was done—the display of voting—he pushed the paper into the box like an afterthought.

F. was clutching the breakfast table like a drowning man. "What a farce," he muttered. "It's like Galileo Galilei. The Pope made him say one thing, but he knew it was another."

I asked F. if he was going to vote. "I voted hours ago," he said. He'd gone up the street at dawn, like all his neighbors, and had waited at the polling place. Then he put a check mark in the "all of the above" circle, just as the propaganda demanded. He went on with his day.

Although the vote today was nominally secret, done privately on a folded piece of paper, F. was convinced that the government knew exactly how he had voted. He pointed out that the "secret" ballots had individual serial numbers. And as each voter entered the station, his name and the number from his ID card were noted down. Couldn't these factors be cross-indexed somehow? Maybe they had other ways of knowing. For every real secret policeman there were ninety-nine imaginary ones. You had to be safe and do what you were told: vote early, vote united. Support the system or face the consequences.

Half an hour ahead of the midday sun, I walked up the street one block. The polling station for this neighborhood was in a television studio. The résumés of the five candidates were taped to the inside of the glass by the front door. Each sheet read roughly the same: a name in bold letters, a photo, the details of age and residence, and then the official organization that the candidate "pertained" to: PCC, CDR, CTC, MTT, ACRC, and so on. The groups were listed in order of importance. PCC was the Communist Party of Cuba; CDR was the acronym for the Committees for the Defense of the Revolution, the famous block committees. There were more than 130,000 CDRs around the island, one for every large building or residential block in urban Cuba, and they were scattered in most rural areas. Although Castro liked to boast that 91 percent of the population was enrolled in the CDR system, that was actually the number of people who were monitored *by* it. The elderly participants who actually administered the CDRs numbered over 2 million, out of 11 million on the island. Directed by block captains, these people were responsible for watching every person entering and evaluating homes for their revolutionary atmosphere, and tracking their neighbors' participation in revolutionary activities. Nonparticipation was a problem and was enforced by unarmed vigilante groups ("popular revolutionary vigilance detachments") who coordinated with the police to ensure compliance. The most ardent members of these CDR detachments were promoted to the notorious "Rapid Action Brigades," who could be mobilized at a moment's notice to control public events, or stage "acts of repudiation" against dissidents. And the most devoted members of the Rapid Action Brigades were in turn promoted to the Special Brigades, the most elite units within the machinery of repression, who formed a kind of shock troop specializing in beating square pegs into round holes.

By law, the block committee was required to verify that each youngster was being taught proper "Marxist-Leninist values" inside the home; parents who insisted, for religious or political reasons, on teaching their children anti-communist beliefs could, and did, lose custody. The children were sent off to boarding schools. But block committees were as varied as the blocks they represented; some were staffed by hard-core supporters of the system, who, motivated by the basest forms of envy and resentment, snitched on their neighbors, denouncing those who bought black market food or muttered petty criticisms of the regime. Other CDRs were composed of time-serving retirees who looked the other way, tolerated all sorts of dissent, refused to rat out private enterprise, and put up with unrevolutionary citizens. It simply depended on the people within the system. Then there was the CTC, the Confederation of Cuban Workers, which was an overarching, state-run labor organization that claimed to be a union for the workers, but which answered to the government and allowed neither strikes nor independent voices.

Each candidate offered a biography, of which this one from under the glass was typical: he'd been a member of his local block committee for forty-two years; had volunteered on twenty sugar harvests and helped pick eighteen coffee crops; had a long career as a driver for various state enterprises; had participated in "various" May Day events; had served an "international mission" in Angola for three years and been sent to the Soviet Union in 1984; had "participated actively in the battle of ideas which liberates our people" and had signed a declaration that socialism was "untouchable"; as well as organized rallies demanding the return of Elián González. He had earned the "Internationalist Combatant Medal First Class" as well as three other nonmilitary medals, five certificates for attending various anniversaries and congresses, two "distinctions" for meritorious labors, and the Order of Lázaro Peña Heroic Workers of the Republic of Cuba in both second and third classes.

The polling room was still. Four people sat on chairs. The ballot box was on an end table. The ballot forms were stacked next to it. A clipboard to check off the names of the neighborhood voters as they came in. A red, white, and blue flag (for Cuba) and a red and black one (for the Revolutionary July 26th Movement).

No one was voting. By noon, 154 of the 194 registered voters in the ward had already voted. When I came back five hours later the same four people were still sitting there, and the total was still 154 of 194.

The results were a sweep for socialism: all five candidates had been elected. The people of this CDR had, like those in every neighborhood across Cuba, voted early, and together. They had been "united," as requested.

Elizardo Sánchez and a dozen other Cubans had fanned out during election day to observe the vote. Working in pairs, using preprinted tally forms, they had dropped in unannounced at polling places and collected the end-of-day tallies. They weren't well received—within twenty minutes, Sánchez had been joined at his local polling place by more than twenty men with walkie-talkies—but (as Sánchez reminded them) it was legal for Cubans to enter and observe the voting process, *Granma* had said so right on the front page, and Fidel had stood on TV and invited the world to come watch a Cuban election. The dissidents were allowed to collect their data and leave.

Sánchez described the tallies as accurate, at the level of the polling places. But somewhere higher up the chain—at the provincial level—the tallies began to look suspicious.

Most of the neighborhood polling places they checked had the same number of voters as mine—across the city, it was almost always just under 200 per CDR, with only a couple carrying 201 or 189. In the typical district, 180-something voters had shown up, out of 190-something. With 194 registered voters, but only 154 votes, the precinct had an extremely low turnout by Cuban standards. Of those 154 voters, 151 had voted straight down the Party line. The half-dozen abstainers in the typical district were "almost heroic," Sánchez told me. More than thirty locals hadn't shown up to say yes to the system. The difference between CDRs might be political, but it was more likely economic: my voting place was in a once posh neighborhood in the center of Havana. As it had been half a century ago, it was disproportionately white and middle-class. These people could afford the little risks of refusing to say yes to the system. Out in the big Revolution-built housing projects of East Havana the vote was more solidly for the Revolution because the people were more solidly for the Revolution. They were disproportionately black, often from the poor class that had lost the least and gained the most. And it was easier to control people in the uniform blocks, where everyone was equally poor, than in the private courtyards and hidden entrances of the older housing stock.

———

By the time I got to Kiki de Jongh's neighborhood on election night it was dark. A beautiful Caribbean night, cool and windy, the moist ocean air brushing softly over the city. The sky had cleared after weeks of cloud, fog, haze, cold, and rain. Havana throws up less light during the night than other cities; a dense field of stars stood out like pinpricks on black velvet. The moon would be in its last quarter, but hadn't slipped into sight yet.

Standing on the dark street, looking for his address, I was afraid again. Some Cubans came down the sidewalk, making my spine tingle, but it was just a couple of couples, deep in conversation. I held myself steady as their group split around me and passed downhill, still talking.

The cabdriver had dropped me at the wrong intersection, off by four blocks. I headed downhill, glad now that those four Cubans were within earshot. Counting houses, I ticked off the addresses and studied the avenue, a short, steep one I'd never visited before. It was luxurious beyond anything I had encountered in Cuba. The roadway was divided, with a manicured park running down the middle. The trees were in excellent shape, the bushes carved into precise topiary, an unnatural restraint on the riot of tropical greenery. At least the sidewalks were Cuban: they were broken up, with occasional sinkholes and unfinished repair jobs. But there were nice benches, and no disastrous piles of garbage or rusting equipment. Too nice. This was the Avenue of Presidents, classier even than Fifth Avenue in Miramar, the suburban strand that had been the preferred remove of the ruling class in the 1950s.

The houses here were set back from the road, behind chain link fences and high screens of bushes. Pre-revolutionary houses, with Spanish tiles and ornate bric-a-brac. There were a few tall apartment buildings, and I walked down, passing the first tower and coming to the second, which was finally the address Kiki had given me. The building was twenty stories tall, well maintained, each floor cut by a single slab of white cement that reached out of the building to yield balconies. It was dramatic, and self-conscious. The home of an architect. The single elevator refused to appear, and eventually I walked up.

Kiki greeted me in the dark and led me through nine rooms to his study (there were more rooms; I only saw nine). The floors were marble, but the walls were made of little more than air. Some of the outside walls consisted entirely of wood louvers, while the rooms were separated from one another with grilles. It wasn't a rich household, by the standards of somewhere else. But in Cuba it was a palace, not just large but elegant, neat, and glamorous.

"I'm very concerned about your project," Kiki announced, once we had taken seats in the study. Although he had never agreed to give me an interview at all, Kiki had nonetheless asked me to drop by, and began by explaining that there were several things he could not discuss. The first was Fidel Castro himself: Kiki swore up and down that he would not breathe one word about the human being he had known at Dolores. Although they had overlapped for almost the same years, Kiki was six years younger, a lifetime of difference to children. They'd barely noticed each other.

Kiki would talk only about history. It was important, he said, to not misunderstand things. Not to misinterpret them. He explained, again, that the boys from Dolores were nobody, and meant nothing. The Revolution was made by history, by huge currents. It was vast, a product of the impersonal masses, not something that could be traced back to "a group of boys." I nodded my agreement, but this did not allay him.

"You Americans are the best in the world at making a small thing stand for a big thing," Kiki warned. "It's just like *Time* magazine. They always focus on one thing, and make it stand for everything.

"It's not these people," he said. He tapped the 1941 picture for emphasis. The image seemed to exert a magnetic pull on him. He picked it up, turned it to the light, and fondled the page, squinting through his glasses, adjusting them, searching for faces. "It's not these people," he repeated. The Jesuit temperament had produced few of what Kiki called "extremists," or the radicals who appeared in history books.

If the boys in the photo had not become extremists, then what had they become?

Kiki paused, and then said, "The majority of these people are professional." He was guessing. "Serious," he said. "Cultured. Well placed. A fundamentally religious group. Or at least with elements of religion. They educated their children, and are defined by their families. I'll bet they are, as a group, the least divorced, the least damaged, the least involved in drugs or alcohol. They contribute enormously to the economy of the

United States. I'm sure these are the most stable families, the honest types. Working people. Well behaved, with a huge role in the economy, aiding the United States. Most of them went broke, and have done very well with their skills, their work."

It pleased him to predict. To speculate, so that I could go to Miami and see for myself.

"A few have stayed," he said, almost defensively. "Not many."

Did he miss them?

He nodded. "Logically," he said.

His little studio office was covered with lithographs of Viking ships and Spanish caravels, and one wall held a display case showing a model of his latest architectural project. It looked like a *bohío* at first glance, the traditional Cuban hut. But it was in fact a *cabaña* for a tourist hotel in western Cuba. It was meant to be part of a larger renovation of a hotel complex in Pinar del Río, but in the end only the little *cabaña* had been built. He had other designs in his folder, sketches of apartment blocks, high rise hotels, even a modern version of the traditional tobacco drying shed. But none of these had ever been constructed: the tourist *cabaña* was the sum total of his work for the Revolution.

There had been big architectural dreams, at the beginning. Castro had authorized a burst of progressive building designs in the 1960s and 1970s. The Revolution had put up many new school campuses, including a swooping set of domed buildings outside Havana for dance students and other artists. These eccentric buildings and dramatic rehearsal spaces had been a showpiece, springing like mushrooms from a former golf course. But the flat roofs needed a lot of maintenance, and the domed ones leaked. The school had been abandoned by now, and creepers grew down through the shattered skylights. Kiki's own apartment building, on the Avenue of the Presidents, had fared better. People would not be pushed out of apartments in Cuba and did their own maintenance if they had to. Kiki had been here since it was built in 1968, and he or his family would be here until the end. It was full of space, air, and good views, all commodities that were rationed. All housing went to the sympathetic and deserving, but some housing was more sympathetic than others, and some people more deserving.

He felt around in the dark, past his Acer computer, and drew one of his portfolios close, and presented me with a drawing. This is why he had asked me to come over. It was a precise sketch of a modern Cuban house, white, low, and long. The sketch had been given a light color wash of azure windows and green lawn. The lines of the house added up to the horizontal minimalism of the "new" parts of Cuba, that is, the mid-century buildings. It looked like a house you could find just up the Avenue of the Presidents, or the cracked home of Balbino Rodríguez in Vista Alegre above Santiago.

This was Kiki's own work, a concept sketch. For the entrance, he had designed a curtain wall of glass—swirling Fiestaware reds and yellows—so that the house would light up at night like a party beacon. The land-scaping details were thick sketch lines, but it looked like there was a swimming pool in back. The legend read, "PLAN FOR BOU FAMILY HOUSE, 1958." He put it in an envelope and asked me to send it to Pepín Bou. How long had it been, I asked, since they talked? "Oh," he said, and made a gesture as if washing his hands. "I imagine it was '58. But he is a magnificent person, first-quality, just like José Antonio Roca and Lundy Aguilar."

Near the door, I touched the envelope and asked if the house had ever been built. Kiki laughed. "No," he said. "That's when the Commander came along."

I walked home. It was about a mile, in the darkness, and it seemed to take an hour. Climbing the avenue, watching for trouble, crossing the back streets of Vedado, drawing the usual curious stares from the few people about. The University of Havana was lit up in some places, but in the darkness along its forbidding walls, a lean and powerful drunk wheeled toward me, howling and demanding money when he saw I was a foreigner. My heart kept beating. I held the reins of my tyrant; no war tonight.

Eventually I slid past the front steps of the university, down past the silent and shuttered polling place, toward F.'s house. The steps, now vast and empty, had been the stage for much of Castro's life. In the late 1940s José Antonio Roca had seen him here, a pistol tucked into his waistband as insurance in the days of "happy trigger" student gangs. In the 1990s I'd come closer to Cyclops here than anywhere else, standing thirty feet away as he addressed another rally. His voice was surprisingly soft and high, and his way of speaking so clear, so un-Cuban in its precise diction, that even a child could understand him. He'd been led away that day, his trembling gait and palsied hands supported by Foreign Minister Felipe Pérez Roque. Like so many of the boys from Dolores, time would close over him, and all his secrets. This had been my eleventh visit to Cuba. Now that I knew I was leaving, maybe for the last time, it was easy. I slept hard.

WINTER

The last Ice Age pressed down hard on New York City, flattening it for a hundred thousand years, piling up terminal moraines like Long Island. Washington Heights, the northernmost, and tallest, section of the island of Manhattan, is a pile of topsoil and mud slowly crushed into schist, the softest and flakiest of rocks. The neighborhood is narrow, taking the north–south shape that survived the passing ice, and peers down on Harlem and the domes of Columbia University. The taller apartment buildings, propped on the very top of the schist ridges, gaze west toward the Hudson, over a shockingly green vista of forested Manhattan and New Jersey. Peregrine falcons live on the tallest buildings, and mostly Dominican people live inside them. They call the neighborhood *Santo Domingo Norte,* but Puerto Ricans, Hasidic Jews, and African Muslims live on the avenues, along with the occasional Cuban.

When I arrived at 187th Street it was mid-afternoon but already as dark as urban evenings ever get. Snow was falling, thick and fat flakes, as it had been all day. There were seven inches of powder. The black of asphalt was gone. Parked cars and iron railings were cartoon shapes. The sidewalks were white; the yards white; even the few people in the streets had accumulations of snow on their hats and shoulders, and moved slowly, as silent as snowmen. The hush was broken by the shriek of a Dominican boy shooting down 187th on a garbage bag.

José Antonio Cubeñas came slowly to the front door of his nine-story red-brick building. He took a full minute to cover the distance of just twenty feet across the lobby. He wasn't feeble or injured; his progress was slowed because he hesitated, stopping to look behind him, unsure of something, occasionally backtracking a few steps, pausing to listen and look. Finally he reached the glass door, let me into the lobby, shook my hand quickly, and then hurried back toward his apartment, the very first one on the ground floor, just around the corner. "My wife has Alzheimer's," he called over his shoulder, as he turned out of sight.

Inside his apartment, I stomped my boots on a mat, shedding a layer of slush. The apartment, and the building, had a hard-to-define quality, a studied normalcy. The building was red-brick and unadorned, all right angles and straight lines. The apartment was one of many identical units, which themselves sat in a sea of similar blocks, all from the postwar boom, everything made from plain brick, glass, steel, aluminum, and cement, never trying to look like anything fancy. José Antonio's apartment was on the ground floor, the windows covered with heavy curtains against street noise and other intrusions.

Of the many *antiguos alumnos* I had now met, few could claim to know Fidel Castro as Cubeñas did. He had gone beyond Dolores with Castro, one of the few who was in nearly continuous contact with him through the 1940s and 1950s, right through the war against Batista. Everything about Cubeñas looked, as Pedro Haber said, *superinteligente*. He was rail-thin, and his hair had receded back across his forehead, which exaggerated the size of his skull. Cubeñas was a tall, bony man, eighty years old, but it was not hard to see the strength that had been in him. He had thick fingers and large hands covered with bulging blue-green veins that snaked down his wrists. The veins disappeared under the cuffs of his cardigan, which he wore over a tan, long-sleeve guayabera. His fine hair was black on what remained of the top, and white on the sides. And like his comrades in Cuba, he did not have to leave his living room to reach a stash of yearbooks, letters, and photographs from the old days. An end table and a larger coffee table were both covered with letters in Spanish, obscure pamphlets on Cuban projects, and heavy pages curled up at the edges with age.

José Antonio had been more guarded than anyone else when I first called, reluctant and protected. How had I learned his name and number? Where was I calling from? Who had I talked to? Why?

Now, as he settled onto a love seat, facing the armchair carefully prepared for me, he apologized. "Coming from Cuba, you have apprehension when someone comes looking for you," he said. He leaned back, flaring his hands in theatrical skepticism. He called it a "Miami" reaction that was not really appropriate in New York. Indeed, it was Pedro Haber in Miami who had given me the phone digits, warning that Cubeñas would be afraid, and insisting that I speak "in strictest confidence," without disclosing who had given up Cubeña's phone number. Exile was a long catalogue of bitter encounters with journalists, officials, rivals, and accusers, and the distrust of outsiders was fundamental.

Cubeñas kept this jaundiced view of the world at a slow bubble throughout our many interviews. As soon as we sat down he began to describe the old Cuba, and explained that the rise of Batista in the 1930s was a conspiracy by Americans. American companies were behind this, and other things. Nobody knew the real story, because deceptions and lies had supplanted the true history of Cuba. He cited one famous incident in the 1940s, often described in history books, in which the sight of American sailors pissing on a statue of José Martí had sparked a Cuban nationalist outburst in Havana. This incident had never happened, Cubeñas explained. It was staged by a young Castro. Fidel had paid the American sailors to piss on Martí, and provided the photographer, to generate propaganda.

"I know for a fact that the government is listening to all my phone calls," Cubeñas told me. He didn't specify which government. It didn't matter. Larger forces were at work.

It is hard to be Cuban and not believe in conspiracies. Cubeñas had been born into an era when the American role in Cuba was not one of occasional meddling and sabotage, but rather outright control of politics and the economy. American domination was so widespread in his youth that it was "a moral and economic scandal," he said. The symbiotic relationship brought out the worst in both societies: rotten corruption, profiteering, rigged elections, self-dealing, and hypocrisy. From the very beginning in 1898, American officials had pursued self-interest, pushing an agricultural "reform" that did nothing for the poor, but made it easy for American corporations to buy up huge tracts of land. They promptly turned Cuba "into a giant cane field," Cubeñas said, making the island totally dependent on the annual U.S. sugar quota for economic survival. The Americans made unwelcome changes, trying to secularize the school system along American lines. This was when he told me how they had appointed an atheist Jew to run the education system. "A Cuban," he had clarified, but a Jew, and an atheist Jew to boot. "That is not what the people wanted."

Like Lundy Aguilar, Cubeñas was a lawyer who'd dedicated his life to writing, another Cuban pamphleteer who'd spent decades turning out articles, columns, and booklets, his mind filled with plans for new parties and constitutions, reforms to Cuba and the exile movement, revised frameworks for speculative transitions, and manifestos and essays on pre- serving Castilian language, republican values, and Catholic influence. Most were self-published, circulated within the little Philadelphia of Cuban intellectuals.

I'd been told that Cubeñas was a member of the Royal Academy of Spain. He reached behind him and drew from the pile of papers on the end table an impressively thick sheet of actual parchment, which was from the Academy in Madrid. Cubeñas was a corresponding member, a distinction, but one that he made little of.

"Class of '45, same as him," Cubeñas said abruptly. "I'm not going to say his name. I'm talking about the Big Chief down there."

He kept this promise, mostly. He talked instead of "him" or "that fel- low," like when he said that "Once that fellow is gone, Cuba will recover in three years, you'll see."

His wife, Elsie, came into the room now. Her hair was white, and she moved at a slow pace, picking her way through the furniture, distracted, not speaking or looking up.

"She's not that bad," José Antonio said, "but she forgets almost every- thing." She was aware that something was missing, so she looked for it. If the front door was open she would walk out, sure at some level that it could be out there. She knew all the rooms, but did not know them, and tapped the walls as she moved about, surprised to see furniture. She was on her own island, without memory or expectation.

The TV in the apartment was turned to Univision. The screen showed a *telenovela,* a soap opera, but the sound was off. Cubeñas helped Elsie sit on the sofa across from us, turned her to face the screen, and she watched it, fighting off sleep. Her head nodded, bobbed, fell, and lifted up again. When I looked over minutes later she was wide awake and rose to walk around the room. As José Antonio and I spoke, going over documents, she opened the door to the coat closet, then closed it, tried the locked front door, and gradually worked around the four walls of the room, She came back and tried the closet again. Then she sat down and began weeping.

José spoke to her softly, in a quiet Oriente accent. *Cálmate, cálmate mi amor, qué quiéres, estoy aquí mí vida.* He fetched a glass of orange juice from the kitchen and put her hand around the glass until she sensed it and drank. She was a pretty woman, her hair and clothing neat, even her gestures with the glass graceful.

"She is diabetic," he said. The sugar made an instant improvement in her mood, and she sat motionless in her chair now, watching the *telenovela*. José Antonio's patience and gentle manner never varied, but there was a translucent, dried-out pain in him. Even with someone at hand, he was alone.

Cubeñas and Fidel were not merely classmates and *internos* at Dolores. They had graduated from University of Havana law school together, in 1950. They had been student cohorts for a dozen years all together, but only the time at Dolores was indelible. It was the shared experience of being boarders that made for their intense and ultimately explosive relationship.

"We were twenty-two *internos* living in the school," Cubeñas said. Another twenty were on half board. Because these students stayed for lunch every day, during the long two-hour break when most students went home, they were considered part of the *interno* group. They were present for not just the meal, but for recess, when the pecking order at the school was established with contests and games. Cubeñas referred to "all forty of us together" as the core group at the school.

The three Cubeñas brothers shared a small room, catty-corner from the room of the Castros. The relationship between José Antonio and Fidel had started off well, and they often sat on opposite sides of a long table at lunch or dinner so they could talk better. Cubeñas rattled off the names of the other boys who sat with him, typically: José Antonio Roca, David de Jongh, the class clown Enrique Hechevaría, and sometimes the colorless Raúl Castro, too.

According to Cubeñas, the young Raúl was interested in communism, but Fidel preferred fascism. He read the speeches of Mussolini, repeating them (as a joke) from the balcony at Dolores, waving his hands stiffly in imitation of the dictator at a rally. Castro also read *Mein Kampf,* Cubeñas said. He even recalled Castro going to sleep with the book, then waking up and starting right in reading it again. When Poland was invaded, Fidel had marched into the patio holding over his head a newspaper that reported "NOT ONE POLISH AIRPLANE REMAINS." "Our first victory," Fidel said.

But these were thoughtless flirtations, a fascination common enough in 1939, when half the world believed strongmen of one stripe or another—Hitler, Mussolini, Franco, Stalin—were the future. Castro was interested in global events, in the rise of the war, in Europe and Hitler, in the Danzig corridor and the Molotov Ribbentrop pact, but chiefly with how these events affected Cuba. He was never a real fascist, Cubeñas said, and was definitely not an anti-Semite. On the contrary: Fidel explained at the time that he could not be "with" the fascists because they were against the Jews. And he could not be against the Jews because he, Fidel, was one. He volunteered that he was descended, through his grandmother, from Jews.

I asked Cubeñas what was the single most striking characteristic of the young Castro.

"He was very dirty," Cubeñas said. "We called him *bola de churde,* ball of filth."

Raúl's nickname was also bad. "We called him *La Pulga, La Pulgita,*" he said. The Flea, or Little Flea. It came from the way Raúl buzzed around his brothers, sticking his nose in the business of the older boys. Raúl wasn't as dim as Ramón, the eldest Castro, but he wasn't a Fidel, either. "He only used his head to keep his cap warm," Cubeñas said.

Fidel was the academic leader. He wasn't the very best student at Dolores—Lundy got better grades—but Fidel seemed to inhale books on any and all topics, devouring not just what was assigned, but anything else he could get his hands on. With a combination of natural ability and trained discipline, he developed a phenomenal memory, one that gave him a nearly photographic recall of details. When they studied at night, Cubeñas would hold a textbook and ask drill questions. Fidel would answer, easily and quickly, showing his usual mastery of the subject. But what Cubeñas remembered was that Fidel would finish his answers by casually mentioning the page number that Cubeñas was looking at.

"There were many more intelligent than Fidel," Cubeñas said. "What Fidel had was memory."

Fidel seemed to feel some pressure. Something was driving him, something he needed to overcome. And Cubeñas—along with most everyone else—knew what it was. "Fidel had a *gravísimo* problem," he said. "It was that he was a bastard. He was the only *hijo de puta* who came to the school."

Fidel had indeed been a literal bastard. When Ramón, Fidel, and Raúl had been born, their father had not been married to their mother, Lina Ruz, a cook, a servant girl half Angel's age. Angel later married Lina, and at some point in their Dolores years Ramón, Fidel, and Raúl were legally recognized as Angel's heirs, perhaps when Fidel was sixteen.

Out in the countryside of Oriente, even in a busy town like Banes, casual family arrangements could be ignored, but in a big and pretentious city like Santiago, among boys from elite families with ancient Spanish surnames, legitimacy still had its prerogatives. *Hijo de puta* was one of the most routine insults in Cuba, and Cubeñas remembered seeing Fidel hide the sting of that taunt, pretending he felt nothing.

Denied one kind of legitimacy, he sought another, making himself the leader in all things, the organizer, the prima donna, the orchestrator of games, trips, and entertainments. He would announce there was going to be a baseball game; assign the boys to teams himself; then insist on pitching, umpiring, keeping score, and calling the game like a radio announcer. When he came to bat he would make his own decision about whether a pitch had been a strike or a ball. If he got a hit, it was the best hit of the game. If he swung and missed, it was lousy pitching. He acted as if he ran the school, rather than attended it. Cubeñas called Fidel a *gallito,* a little rooster. He puffed himself up and would never back down, at least in public. He was a bully, brave on the outside but "always a coward, inside."

During finals, Fidel and Cubeñas had studied together for the history test, the one that they and most of the boys at Dolores took most seriously. The short questions were easy enough to anticipate, but the exam ended with a surprise topic, requiring a long essay.

Cubeñas was confident. So was Fidel, with his superb memory. Cubeñas raced through the exam and came to the dreaded essay question. Who was more influential, the exam asked: Frederick the Great of Prussia or Peter the Great of Russia?

Cubeñas was the first to drop his pencil and turn in his exam. He waited outside the classroom. Fidel was the next student out.

"Which did you answer?" he asked Cubeñas. "I picked Frederick."

"Well, I answered Peter."

When the exams were scored, both had passed with the remark *sobre-saliente,* or excellent, but Cubeñas had a perfect 100, and Fidel was a cou-

ple of points behind. The Jesuits posted the results: they encouraged this
kind of intellectual rivalry, what Loyola called the natural desire to com-
pete. But Fidel didn't like being second and showed it for a while.

Cubeñas loved retelling the story of their famous fight at the railing
above the cistern. By his account he'd given Fidel a thrashing. He was
probably the only person alive who could say that. Cubeñas called him a
coward, but not every boy would have marched up the circular staircase,
into the face of an enemy.

According to Cubeñas, the next year when Fidel went home for summer
vacation he had a chance to hone his skills at beating on the weak. This
would have been in 1941 or perhaps 1942. In the midst of World War II the
demand for sugar and the shortage of labor had driven Cubans to import
a lot of *macheteros* from Haiti. Back in Banes, Angel Castro was getting
rich on the migrant workers. The black Haitians were generally treated
with racist contempt by white Cubans and were allotted even worse pay
and food than Cuban *macheteros*. The Haitians refused to work in these
conditions, and soon there was an informal strike at the Castro farm.

Angel didn't like rebels. He sent in Fidel to break the strike. "He broke
it on horseback," Cubeñas said, riding in among the Haitians and beating
them with the flat of his machete. The Haitians took up their work again.
Cubeñas hadn't seen any of this, but said he'd read it in the newspaper,
before confirming it with Fidel himself.

The world of Dolores began to break up. After the 1942 school year,
Fidel was transferred to Belén in Havana. Lundy and at least half the boys
in each graduating class went on to Belén. It was the best way to get polish and social contacts in the capital, and Dolores was anyway overloaded
by a requirement for a new fifth year of school.

But Cubeñas preferred to see his own agency at work. It wasn't educational reform that sent Fidel to Belén, it was the fistfight. After that day,
Fidel had felt his ambitions thwarted. He could not dominate. The boys
there had seen him knocked down.

"He tried to impose himself on me," Cubeñas said bitterly. "I fought
him and won in front of forty-five boys. *That* was why he went to
Havana."

Fidel may have left, but he and Cubeñas were far from done. Both boys
arrived at the University of Havana as freshmen together and overlapped

there until winning their law school degrees in 1950. After that, Cubeñas went home, setting up a law practice in Manzanillo and supervising his father's farm.

"Our farm was in the first foothills of the Sierra Maestra," Cubeñas told me. It was a big spread, 150 *caballerías,* or about a thousand acres. It lay on the inland, or north side, of the mountain range and was separated from Santiago de Cuba by a range of steep hills that, for a hundred miles west of the city, were not crossed by a single road.

In December of 1956 Castro brought his fighters here, where they could ambush, flee, regroup, hide, and fight again, using the convoluted terrain to evade their powerful enemies.

But to do that, they needed Cubeñas. "There were only two roads into the Sierra" in this region, Cubeñas explained, "and both of them passed through our land." Immediately upon landing, the guerrillas began to need things—bullets, guns, medicine, food, money, clothing, boots, and information.

"All the supplies had to go up those roads. Everybody knew it. The Batista government knew it, but they didn't do anything about it because the soldiers were afraid they'd get shot if they came up the roads. So they declared them open roads."

Cubeñas had a legal office in Manzanillo, serving as a notary and dealing with people from all walks of life.

Between his practice in the city, where he heard gossip all day, and his house on the farm, where he could see everyone who came and went from the mountains passing along a road just fifty yards away, he knew more than most people.

In 1957, marijuana growers were among the only people who regularly took motor vehicles up the tiny, rutted tracks. They packed their crop into metal cracker tins and drove back to Manzanillo. The smugglers were willing to bring supplies uphill, and Castro allegedly declared, in these first desperate months, that "if the marijuana ends, the revolution ends."

Fidel and Raúl were operating from a series of camps, most of them only an hour from the Cubeñas farm by horse. But in the subsequent two years of fighting Cubeñas never went up to see his schoolmates once. Not that he wasn't invited: in February of '57, just three months into the war, Raúl wrote him a letter asking for money and supplies, and recalling their friendship. He urged Cubeñas to come to the Sierra, and signed off dramatically that "if the bullets respect me" he would give Cubeñas a hug "after the triumph." Raúl's older brother added a postscript, scratching out "a hug for everyone, Fidel."

Caridad Fernández, the army chief in Manzanillo, came to visit his law practice one day. Caridad had a woman's name, but he was a vicious soldier, a trusted crony of Batista sent to Manzanillo to crush the festering insurgency. Caridad accused Cubeñas of being involved with his old friend Castro. Cubeñas, he said, heard everything on his farm. He knew the guerrillas' plans, the location of their camps. As a notary he was in touch with the poor of Manzanillo and could learn which Batista official might be assassinated next. Cubeñas would have to become an informer for the government.

Cubeñas did not deny it. "Yes," he said. "You know that I do speak to everyone. I do know all the conspiracies." But he served neither side. "If I hear that something is going to happen to you, specifically," he promised Caridad, "then I will seek you out right away and tell you. And the same is true for Fidel. If I hear a specific conspiracy against him, I'll warn him."

Caridad measured the utility of this—a lot of Batista officers were being assassinated—and left Cubeñas alone for the rest of the war.

Having connections was more dangerous than useful. Any association with the guerrillas could be fatal. In February of 1958, the American journalist Herbert Matthews, working for the *New York Times,* came to Oriente looking for Castro and his guerrilla army. After an exchange of messages, Matthews was given permission to join the guerrillas, and a guide brought him up to the Sierra. Like everyone else, he had to pass through the Cubeñas farm to reach the rebel camps. Cubeñas played no direct role in the assignation, but one of his employees acted as a guide, showing Matthews the way. The resulting article, appearing on the front page of the *Times,* put the lie to government claims that Fidel Castro had been killed and caused a sensation in both America and Cuba.

The interview's fallout was felt in Havana and foreign capitals, but what José Antonio Roca remembered was the immediate and very local reaction. Matthews had been careful not to reveal how he had reached the guerrillas, but *Bohemia,* Cuba's premier magazine, was less discreet. *Bohemia* ran a follow-up article about the *New York Times* scoop and casually printed the name of the guide.

"It was a death sentence," Cubeñas said. The agents of the SIM secret police would not hesitate to arrest and torture the guide.

But *Bohemia* was printed in Havana and distributed throughout Oriente using the local bus services. The incriminating issue had arrived in Santiago first. A friend there called Cubeñas to warn him. The next bus to Manzanillo would be carrying a load of fresh *Bohemias*, dropping stacks at small towns along the way.

Cubeñas jumped into his car and rushed to the nearest crossroads. He didn't have to wait long before the bus for Manzanillo appeared. He tried to convince the driver to hand over the entire stack of *Bohemias*, but the man wouldn't; the magazines belonged to the vendors. He unloaded some for local use and kept back others for Manzanillo. Cubeñas had to wait in the terminal for the newsboys to show up, and then bought every copy. This gave him a few hours. Cubeñas had time to warn the guide, who went uphill at a fast clip. Having missed their man, the police had missed their chance.

People often say that Castro came to power on January 1, 1959, but that is wrong. He came to Santiago on January 1, 1959. Power was in Havana, eight days away. It was Che Guevara who rushed into the capital, while Fidel stayed in his tent. He had not left Oriente with their advancing columns; only now, with the battle won elsewhere, did he do what armies always did in Cuba, which was march into Santiago. The city surrendered joyfully to the rebels, a day of ecstatic revels that fully confirmed the population's belief that they sat at the center of world history. Castro gave his first address to the nation from the radio station on Enramada, declaring the city the "moral capital" of Cuba.

Arturo de Jongh, the middle of the three brothers, had the pleasure of liberating the city himself. He had joined the guerrillas just two weeks before the end of the war, part of the last-minute flood of support that made Batista fold his hand. Arturo hadn't even received a weapon by the time the war ended, and woke up that last morning among a big group of recruits. They'd bunked in El Cobre, on the far side of Santiago Bay, just outside the city proper. Santiago was surrounded, but the police and the army had held out. Now, with dawn, there was no Batista for them to hold out for.

The defeated and the victorious lost all discipline. The worst of Batista's torturers and cronies scattered into hiding that morning, and the rebels in El Cobre made a sudden rush for the city. Arturo jumped onto an overloaded jeep that had been commandeered by a July 26th officer and was spattered with Cuban flags and rebel banners. They sputtered toward the city with no idea what to expect. When they crested the hilly section of the Carretera Central, they were directly in front of the Rancho Club, one of Arturo's old hangouts. The view is spectacular, right down Santiago Bay and over the entire city. They rolled down, parading into the avenues amid disbelief and cheers, to surging crowds. Cuban flags had sprung out like daisies from every building. There had been days and days to prepare; thousands of civilians appeared in red and black armbands, the colors of the July 26th Movement. The officer drove around, honking the horn, looking at the city, trying to find other officers, and at one point Arturo just stepped off the jeep and went home, getting back into his own bed that night.

The other Dolores boys didn't quit. Fidel went to a radio station and announced that the rebels were in charge of the country. Raúl went out and made sure that was true, rounding up about seventy enemies from Santiago's streets—police spies and army officers, mostly—and machine-gunning them into a ditch.

Cubeñas wasn't one of those who rushed into Santiago. He remained his withdrawn self. It wasn't until six months later that he stirred. He was finally rousted out by a letter from Celia Sánchez, the effective head of Fidel's operations. The rebels needed to staff a government. At Celia Sánchez's instruction, Cubeñas went to see Calixto García, the new governor in Oriente. Cubeñas carried the letter, written in a feminine hand on official Rebel Army stationery from the General Command:

Havana

Dear Calixto,
The carrier of this note is Dr. José Antonio Cubeñas, a great friend and comrade of ours. It serves you two, and Oriente, to know each other. Work together.
Talk to him, he can help you now greatly.
Hugs,
Celia Sánchez
6/18/59

Six months into power, but again, Cubeñas was evasive, and eluded the new government's embrace.

Discerning the future didn't require a seer or a prophet, Cubeñas said. "All who knew Fidel Castro knew what he was going to do. All his intimate friends knew. No one who was close to him stayed with him. He was always amoral. Not immoral, but amoral. He couldn't be loyal to anything."

During the long afternoon we talked, that was one of the few times Cubeñas broke his rule: he actually allowed himself to say the words "Fidel" and "Castro." His wife was agitated again, and we'd already talked for hours. It was night. I left, struggling through the snow and then descending to the subway system, using an elevator because the tunnel entrance was so deeply buried.

I returned to Washington Heights in other seasons. Cubeñas was always ready to talk but kept his arms around his papers, his letters and pamphlets. He was going to publish them himself. He hinted at secrets held back and would wave old letters in front of my face, refusing to let me read them. But he would grow tired and leave them lying on the table as he went for water, and they would turn out to be more old letters, cryptic, secondary, dim photocopies of ordinary communications. One, from the late 1940s, was a note from Fidel encouraging Cubeñas to come back to Havana to study for a law school exam with him. Cubeñas insisted that Castro was proposing that they cheat on the test. The phrasing was ambiguous, but not to Cubeñas. "You see?" he said. "You see?" A cheater.

To me it was more interesting that in 1948 Castro had owned a sheet of stationery from the Cuban Senate. He'd probably stolen it while visiting some politician. The young Fidel was on the move in the capital, spending time in political circles, dropping in on government, helping, arranging, building, pushing, and filching.

In Miami a year later, I ran into Cubeñas while visiting with some Dolores people. He was on his own. His wife had deteriorated to the point where he could no longer care for her, he explained. She was in a home in Miami now, which meant he was spending far more time in Florida. It was an improvement for both of them. He was looking brighter, almost relieved. The friends around him appreciated his talk of the old days. Dressed up in a blue blazer, with a pin in his lapel, he managed to smile.

———

It took me all that same year to find the other José Antonio. That was José Antonio Roca, the dentist. A chain of phone calls led to an apartment complex in Bailey's Crossroads, Virginia. When I tucked my mother's station wagon into a huge black parking lot, on the bright morning before Christmas, I was early, and sat in the car looking up.

I'd grown up seven miles from here. My mother still lived in the same house. For my whole life I'd passed by without even noticing the huge residential towers that dominated the crossroads. These were three nearly identical slabs of brown, and Roca lived on the twentieth floor of one. That is about as high as one can live in the Washington area.

Bailey's Crossroads is less a suburb of Washington than a coordinate. Most people know it by numbers: it is squeezed between 395 and 66, exactly where 7 crosses 244, with 50 close by. Amid the asphalt are retail outlets with deliberately generic names (The Chicken Place, Total Value Shopping, City Diner); it is both everywhere and nowhere. It is a very American place, with few traces of the federal red-brick housing thrown up during World War II. Driving here I'd passed a Central American neighborhood and then the largest mosque in the Washington area, and had come finally to rows of big apartment complexes like this one, which were full of middle-class people. Some were the rising young apparatchiks of the Beltway-Industrial complex, who liked easy parking. Others were elderly people who had downscaled from bigger houses.

The towers didn't block the wind but channeled the air, accelerating it. The station wagon shook in its parking place, and I saw ice in the storm drains. Underdressed, I struggled upwind to the sidewalk, battled around to various wrong entrances, and finally found the building. In the lobby I had to collect a parking pass, go back to the car, leave the pass, and return through the arctic insult.

José Antonio Roca was dead center in the 1941 photo, above the railing, almost shoulder to shoulder with Lundy Aguilar. Alberto Casas had written "VA/Spain" next to Roca in the list. This modest condo was the VA. And in the summer they went to a house they owned in Spain for a few months. They were leaving in a few days for Miami, to be with their children for a month.

As we sat down in the white living room, Roca marveled at the photo. He'd seen it but never owned a copy. Glancing over Alberto Casas's list of names, he noticed how many of the boys in his row were already marked *en paz descansa.*

The survivors mentioned Roca. He was tall, the flag bearer, a good student, a leader, but that wasn't why they remembered him. It was because he was the agile star of the Dolores basketball team. Now here he was, a retired dentist, thick around the middle, with a full head of gray hair. He wore a plaid shirt, with a Montblanc pen tucked in the pocket, black corduroy pants, and slippers.

Roca sat in an armchair, beside a table covered with a crèche, a manger-in-Bethlehem extravaganza of miniature barns, Wise Men, lambs and donkeys, humble shepherds in cloaks and sandals. The crèche was laid across burlap sacking, which Roca said made it look more like the Middle East. Roca talked with the manner of a man recalling a shipwreck from the vantage of a warm hearth. He bubbled over with enthusiasm for little things, showing me pictures of his six children, all but the last born in Cuba, detailing their successful careers (two children, and one grandchild, were dentists). He introduced his wife, Carmelina, when she came in with a tray of sharp Cuban coffee, by saying that she was far more interesting than he was. And he presented me with a copy of his self-published autobiography, bound in a cream cover with a picture of him and Carmelina. He had called it *Recuerdos.*

Pepín Bou had already lent me his copy, saying, "He wrote it for his family. It's not the greatest book ever written, but it tells his story with great feeling." True enough. The short text, loaded with family photos, rushed through his youth, Dolores, and the time of the Revolution. He'd become a dentist and president of Santiago's dental association. But most of his book was about his good times with family and friends, either in Cuba or later in America.

In reality his landing in the United States had been extremely tough. After arrival he was told that, like other Cuban professionals, his accreditation was worthless in America. Only West Virginia, desperate for dentists, would give him a one-year waiver to practice. So they moved to Welch, West Virginia. There were many difficulties that year—a cold winter, a new language, and a small home they struggled to keep heated—but José Antonio drilled a lot of teeth. Looking back, he couldn't contain his gratitude to the people in Welch, who "were magnificent, they couldn't have been better." Carmelina, dressed in a housecoat and slippers, bobbed her curls in agreement.

Looking for a way to requalify as a dentist, José Antonio settled on Washington, D.C. The city had a large Jesuit university, Georgetown, with a dental school. Through a Jesuit in West Virginia, José Antonio arranged introductions, and drove to Washington eight times that year to take necessary exams. The school allowed him to enter directly into the second year of their program. The Rocas moved to Arlington, Virginia, the next fall, and for three years José Antonio studied by day and worked nights as a waiter at Blackie's House of Beef. Carmelina drove a school bus.

José Antonio's memoir was long on the Virginias, but short on Dolores, and I prompted him to tell the story of what Lundy Aguilar had called "The Night," meaning the night Roca had scored more points than anyone. "I scored sixty-two points once, a record," he conceded, throwing up his hands. He didn't have braggadocio. He didn't care about basketball.

Not like some people. "Fidel was a fanatic supporter of the team," Roca recalled, "fanatic." Basketball was Castro's favorite sport, but as the best pitcher at Dolores, he was needed on the diamond. So Fidel invented a fan club for the basketball team, declaring himself president. At the last game of the season, Roca came off the floor, sweaty and exhausted, to find Castro confronting him. "José Antonio," he called out. "Look how many votes I'm getting for you." Fidel flashed a handful of tickets discarded by fans leaving the gym. You were supposed to write your pick for MVP of the season on the back.

"Fidel stood by the door, asking them for their tickets. Some of them didn't have any opinion, and so . . ." He didn't finish the sentence. Castro turned each one over and wrote JOSÉ ANTONIO ROCA.

Roca became MVP, of course, but he could never understand why Fidel did it. Roca probably would have won anyway. And even he didn't care that much about the MVP.

Why try so hard? What did this kid need from José Antonio Roca?

Roca's glory days at Dolores were interrupted when his family ran short of money. Not everyone at the Colegio de Dolores came from wealth, or even the middle class. ("The Jesuits," Roca said, "if someone had qualities, they wanted him. So there were the sons of Bacardis, of industrialists, but also of barbers, and of tailors.")

His father had worked for El Encanto, the best department store in Cuba, which had a branch in Santiago, right on Enramada. But José Antonio's father was using the back door. He was El Encanto's *cobrador,* a collection agent paid a commission to walk around the city all day, gathering small payments against El Encanto's installment plan.

The year after José Antonio posed in the Dolores photograph, El Encanto introduced a pay-by-mail scheme. His father lost the 2 percent commission they depended on. The family could no longer afford private school and was too proud to accept when the Jesuits offered to waive their fees. At the age of seventeen, Cubeñas dropped out of school, moved to Las Tunas, six hours from Santiago, and tried peddling life insurance to strangers. He made almost no money and had an emotional realization while meeting with his boss: the man's shoes were worn out, his jacket ratty. High school looked a lot more promising. Back in Santiago after twelve months, he enrolled in one of the city's public high schools as a fourth year student. But Dolores offered him a job coaching his old basketball team, and the Jesuits allowed him to attend the extra fifth year classes required by Cuban law. By doubling up, he graduated with a Dolores diploma alongside his original classmates.

Rushing toward middle-class stability, José Antonio raced through dental school in a year less than normal and set up a practice in Santiago at the age of twenty-four. Soon he was president of the association for Dolores alumni. His memoir was thick with tales of good times at the Ciudamar Yacht Club in Santiago, where he played dominoes with friends and appeared at formal events, presenting or receiving awards in a white suit, in a room full of white suits.

The Moncada attack of 1953 interrupted the good times. Roca had been woken up at dawn by the sound of gunfire, as surprised as everyone else in Cuba. Even Castro's old friends had no idea of the mission. Fidel had been in touch, writing letters about how they would play basketball together someday, but he didn't want anyone that he already knew involved in the attack, José Antonio suggested. "He didn't want anybody from Dolores. He was afraid we wouldn't follow him. All the boys he looked for when preparing his coup were much younger, of little preparation, of very little culture." By *culture* he meant personal character, or backbone. The only Dolores boy in the attack (aside from Fidel and Raúl) was the almost beardless Renato Guitart Rosell, the twenty-two-year-old commemorated on the walls of the small museum at Dolores today. In Cuban histories, Renato was "Fidel's right arm," a chief planner of the attack. But Renato was Carmelina's distant cousin. "He was very impressionable," she said. A romantic young man carried off by history. He was a "follower," she said, "not a boy who could act as an equal to Fidel."

The 1956 attack was less of a surprise. This time, Castro was in Mexico with a big group of anti-Batista men, preparing to overthrow the government. This was no secret: Fidel had announced to journalists that he was about to invade the island. The government knew he was coming, and so did a wide network of supporters. On November 27, 1956, using a fake name, Castro sent them a telegram from Mexico that read, in its entirety:

OBRA PEDIDA AGOTADA

The three words (meaning, roughly, "WORK SOUGHT EXHAUSTED") were meaningless fakery. Three words meant three days. It was the signal for sympathizers in Santiago to rise up in three days, with another Moncada-style assault in the city center that would serve to divert the army from Fidel's landing.

Castro's invasion was a success, of course, but as successes go, this one was highly Cuban. After sending the telegram, Castro discovered that the *Granma* held only eighty men, so that more than half the rebel army was left behind. A storm put them behind schedule. Taking on water, they threw away much of their heavy weapons and ammunition.

On November 30, Roca was woken up in Santiago before dawn by the sound of gunfire. ("Once again," as he put it.) The Santiago underground made its big effort, and rebels, led by men like Jorge Sotus, shot up several police posts around town and even fired a few mortar rounds into the Moncada. Sotus, wearing a set of homemade fatigues with a July 26 armband, even seized a police station for several hours. But the distraction they created was wasted, and so were the lives of the men who fell. Castro was still roaming the ocean, and the attack was crushed. It served only to alert the army to watch for Castro. Two days behind schedule, the

Granma ground ashore in a swamp, lost. The men marched inland, but were soon spotted by airplanes. Castro lost most of his men in the first two days. Only a mythological dozen guerrillas actually reached their rendezvous point in the Sierra Maestra.

Roca was thirty-four that day, a dentist, fully engaged in civic life, a regular visitor to the American naval base in Caimanera. No rebel, in other words. But he discovered that men he knew, like Sotus, were participants in the day's uprising. And the survivors of the failed Santiago attack were now scattered in the city, hunted. It was like 1953 again, when the police and army had pursued and murdered rebels around the city.

What could a dentist do? The next night he found out. As Roca was smoking his evening cigar, a friend stopped by and mentioned a curious thing. He'd heard that an unknown person was hiding in a garden behind a certain house. Nobody knew who this man was, but then again it was obvious, because the police and the army were looking for him. So somebody had to get him out.

The somebody, Roca learned, was him. Roca's friend revealed that he had been given a signal, a few notes to whistle, so that the fugitive would recognize them. But Roca's friend couldn't whistle. José Antonio would have to come along to provide the music.

They drove over to the address and then stood in the street, feeling obvious and unsure. Still blinded by their own headlights, they peered into the dark area behind the house without seeing anything. Roca tried to whistle the notes with a dry mouth. He tried again. It was pathetic. This wasn't his line of work.

The man came out anyway, businesslike. He got into the car, gave an address, and the three of them drove through a city teeming with nervous police officers and army troops. They did not talk. The address was right in the city center. They climbed up to a second-floor apartment, all together for appearance's sake, and then the man closed the blinds and told them to leave.

The underground recovered from the failed November 30 uprising. Castro and his motley band opened communication with Santiago. By December of 1956 Castro was directing his first attacks, and recruits from Santiago were starting to filter up into the hills near the farm of the other José Antonio, Cubeñas.

Roca tried to stay out of it. He knew people who sympathized, and he remembered his old Dolores classmates. But that first night, driving the car through Santiago, he thought he could still stay out of it. He had just helped one person, that was all.

He went home, sat in his usual chair, and lit a new cigar. The friend recalled seeing that Roca's hand trembled as he held the match.

Unfortunately the People's Revolution needed a friend with a car. Roca had succeeded in staying out of things for a while, but during 1957, as the guerrillas in the mountains spread out, sparring with the Cuban army, the urban underground began to braid itself through Santiago. Roca was one of many people who made small financial donations to the movement, even as his career was blossoming, and he regularly filled his dental chair with some of the top people in Santiago.

By early 1958, the urban underground was both far larger and far riskier than Fidel's guerrilla group in the mountains. Even at its very largest peak, the guerrilla force never held more than eight hundred or nine hundred full-time fighters in the Sierra. But thousands of Cubans were now in clandestine militias in towns and cities across Cuba. In the Sierra, Fidel had a chef, a mistress, and bodyguards, and the incompetent and demoralized government troops never once dislodged him from his principal strongholds. After the first few skirmishes, Castro himself didn't even participate in the fighting, taking only symbolic potshots at retreating soldiers in the distance with a sniper's rifle.

By contrast the covert war in the cities was brutal and its leaders highly vulnerable. Good men began to disappear. Batista became serious about the war, in his fashion. He replaced the honest army chief for Oriente with a corrupt man who required kickbacks from legitimate businesses, and who soon controlled all the illegal ones, from smuggling to whorehouses, and even the numbers game in the poor streets of Santiago. This money was used to buy loyalty and pay thousands of informers to rat out the urban rebels. The official branch of SIM, the military intelligence men, was expanded, and Batista sent in a notorious gangster-politician named Rolando Masferrer—an old rival of Castro's from Havana days— to head a death squad that roamed Oriente at night, murdering those suspected of ties to the rebel movement. Newspapers were afraid to report the assassinations, but so many corpses were turning up on the outskirts of Santiago, often showing signs of torture, with mutilated faces and tied hands, that they described the victims as *Vertillon 166,* an autopsy code understood to mean "assassinated."

In Santiago itself, the *subterráneo* leaned heavily on its wealthy and powerful supporters, both for money and for the crucial safe houses. Roca started with money. Aside from his own contributions, he volunteered in 1958 to be a sort of *cobrador* for the rebels, collecting donations from ten of his own friends and contacts. The dental practice was perfect cover, because anyone could make an appointment, come in, and have privacy to sit in his chair and hand over money. Then Roca would clean their teeth so it looked like something had been done.

But the money grew. At the start of 1958 it was just the donations of his ten friends. But he was soon entrusted with the donations of other circles of friends, regularly carrying thousands of dollars to the rebels. By spring he was handing money directly to Celia Sánchez, Fidel's most trusted assistant, $10,000 at a time. As the amounts of money grew larger, the rebels began to issue their own receipts, in the form of bonds, in denominations of 1, 10, and 100 pesos. At first Roca sold bonds to supporters. But in the summer of '58, the rebel treasurer for Oriente was killed by SIM. Although he wasn't even an official member of the July 26th Movement ("practically speaking, I was"), they gave him the engraved lead stamps, or seals, that the movement used to print its bonds. Essentially, the mint. There was only one set. If he were caught with them it would be impossible to survive.

But he was more than a bagman. People smuggling was a regular business. He moved Lester Rodríguez, the number two leader of the urban underground, to a safe house, and then to a boat. And in July of 1958, he moved Frank País, the number one leader, from house to house in Santiago on several occasions. José Antonio knew places to put people. Someone from the dentists' association had a disused summer house on Cayo Smith. A friend from Dolores had an uncle who was a rabid *Fidelista,* with a small farm he could lend out. If one safe house was "burned," meaning exposed to suspicion in some way, then he would swoop in with the car and evacuate somebody. Usually they sat in the back, with a gun concealed beneath a newspaper, ready in case they were stopped by the police on their increasingly frequent patrols. Carmelina began to accompany him and was particularly cold-blooded. One morning they had two men with submachine guns in the back when José Antonio turned a corner and was stopped by police. Carmelina leaned out, flashed a big smile, and explained they were taking some patients to the dental office for an emergency. The police waved them along.

The greatest risk was always the car. The *subterráneo* had moved more than a hundred men so far, mostly passing them up into the Sierra, but sometimes helping them down out of it, either back to Santiago, or to other parts of Cuba, or even to the United States.

In late July, Roca once again moved Frank País, taking him from a safe house in Vista Alegre to another down in the city center. País had changed identities, taking the code name David, and often had to change locations, too, because the police, backed by the SIM agents, were searching whole neighborhoods house by house.

Roca dropped off País—or David—in Santiago's downtown and went home. With experience he had grown calmer.

A couple of days later Roca was working on a patient when he was interrupted and told there was an urgent call. The receptionist said it was someone named David, so he thought it might be País. But it was another David: David de Jongh, the eldest of the three brothers. They'd known each other at Dolores, and David was a doctor. He knew that Roca was in the underground and had called because he had just heard a burst of gunfire. Something was happening. David de Jongh could see out his window as they talked: police were moving around. Roca realized that the doctor's office was close to the house where he had left País. Although the safe house was well hidden, tucked behind another house, it was stocked with clues, like fifty pairs of boots and a collection of Coleman stoves. The neighbors had seen a man shuttling two dozen rifles to a car, badly concealed under a single sheet of newsprint.

Frank País was doomed to become the hero everyone wanted. Deeply religious, idealistic, and democratic-minded, an anti-Fidel, he had spent his last days in the safe house reorganizing the rebel forces, putting the clandestine urban groups on an equal footing with the guerrilla fighters in the hills. The city had sacrificed as much as the rural guerrillas. But the rise to equality of this *llano* (plains, or lowlands) was an implicit challenge to the *sierra* (mountains). Fidel had staked the Revolution to the idea of a heroic guerrilla force climbing through the forests. A conflict between these two views was inevitable, and in one of his last acts, Frank warned that the rebel movement was in danger of sliding into gangsterism, the war of personalities and rival leaders. Amid all this drafting of memos, dispatching of letters, discussions of plans, and bullets-and-beans logistics, Frank found time to propose marriage to his longtime sweetheart, a member of the movement named América. (For a honeymoon, he proposed hiking into the mountains to see Castro.)

País knew his time was running out. He had already escaped out the back door of a safe house as the police came in the front, and his brother had been killed.

On the 30th of July police and SIM agents began registering houses on a cross street near the hideout. Frank dawdled a few critical minutes, sending others to safety but neglecting to put on the priest's robes that he carried for exactly this purpose. The first two men to leave the house climbed into a car, and then calmly asked permission from the police to drive the wrong way down the street, against traffic, to reach the corner. This theater of misdirection worked and they were sent on their way. But when Frank stepped outside and got in a car, a SIM officer said loudly, "Colonel, do you know who that is? It's Frank País."

They dragged him between two houses, beat him, and then shot him dead with a submachine gun.

Afterward, the officer in charge made all the SIM men fire a shot into the corpse. That way everyone was equally guilty. This was the cascade of shots that David de Jongh had heard. This was the news he had brought to José Antonio by phone.

With País dead, the conflict between the *llano* and the *sierra* was over. Frank's successor, code-named Daniel, tried to preserve the independence of the underground, and told José Antonio (who was his dentist) of a private fear that Castro might actually be a communist. But Roca, like most people, "never suspected" such a thing and dismissed Daniel's worries. And soon Daniel was killed. Castro then reorganized the militias and insisted, stridently, repeatedly, that they surrender their weapons to the *sierra* for distribution among the guerrilla troops.

The urban network was being weakened from both sides. Roca tried to lie low for a while, but too many people knew who his friends were. Early one morning in November an American appeared at the clinic. He was particularly huge, sweaty, and improbable. He arrived at Roca's office claiming, in crude Spanish, that he had a toothache that needed emergency treatment, and he wouldn't take no for an answer. After nearly forcing his way into the dental chair, he looked around conspiratorially and then took off one of his shoes. Inside was a letter. It was an introduction from a mutual acquaintance, asking for help sending the American up to the mountains, to join Fidel.

The shoe trick was strange. That wasn't how the rebels did things. And although Roca knew the "mutual acquaintance," he didn't know him well, and had never seen his handwriting. How could he tell if it was real? And this guy, this huge, sweating, monstrosity from abroad, was going to become a guerrilla, running around in the mountains?

Roca stalled, pretending not to know what it was all about. The mutual friend was mistaken. The American must have been looking for a different dentist. The Sierra Maestra? He didn't know about the rebels or the mountains.

After a few minutes, the American left. Roca went right to a phone and called a neighbor named Basilio, an American who worked at the U.S. consulate. José Antonio suspected that his name wasn't really Basilio, and that the American was actually the CIA man in the city. He asked Basilio if he knew of some big, crazy American who was in Santiago, looking for the guerrillas. Basilio checked, and then called back. Someone at the consulate had in fact heard about the American, talking too loudly about joining the movement.

Basilio suggested that Roca be very careful, but it was November of 1958 now, and the season of amateurs was over. They were still on the phone, discussing what to do, when SIM agents rushed the door of the clinic and arrested José Antonio.

They blindfolded him with a handkerchief when they took him out. That was a very bad sign.

It was only mid-morning, but instead of a short drive to a police station, there was a long drive, up, out of town, many turns, and then a long ride, ending with a very slow drive on dirt. When Roca, blind but attuned to the other senses, felt the asphalt give way to dirt, he grew truly afraid.

The car stopped somewhere. They took him out and put him on his knees in a sugarcane field. He heard voices in the distance and then a couple of shots. The longest minutes of his life passed by. He was going to be a *Vertillon 166* in the papers. The sugarcane smelled incredibly strong.

Then cold metal pressed against the back of his head. They didn't beat him or torture him. They didn't touch him. They just put the gun barrel where he could feel it, and then someone spoke in the quiet and hard tone of a man with nothing to lose. If Roca didn't immediately name all his contacts in the July 26th Movement, they would kill him right now. A bullet through the head.

He wouldn't. They pulled the trigger.

Click. The gun wasn't loaded.

Just the *click* of the hammer falling on an empty chamber.

He was taken back into the city. Still blindfolded, Roca listened to the sounds of the car, felt its turns and speeds, recognized the descent into the center of Santiago. There was a sudden turn off a fast street, and then he was out. The voices were now those of sentries, and of command. This had to be Moncada, the main barracks. They took off the blindfold. Although the facade of the building had been spattered with bullet holes during the 1953 attack, the holes had already been filled in and painted over by 1958. It wasn't very well done: you could still see where some of the shots had struck. A cosmetic gesture for a hollow regime. Soon, Castro would have the bullet holes reinstalled.

Roca was in a different situation now. He was led inside, processed by police officers, and then interrogated by men who seemed to have learned their technique from a Hollywood film. They shined bright lights in his eyes, hiding themselves from view while asking the same questions again and again. He gave no answers, or diverted them with stories of his innocence, his loyalty, and his quiet life as the dentist to various people they might have heard of. He did not know what they were talking about. The Sierra? Fidel Castro? Sure, they'd been at Dolores together, but that was it. He wasn't involved in the underground. The questioners did not touch him, not even once, and gave up after a couple of hours.

They locked José Antonio in a room with another prisoner. A woman. They didn't know each other, but she was some kind of rebel supporter who had been picked up. They were kept under observation and ordered not to move from their chairs, and not to speak to each other or even look at each other. Roca sat, motionless, perfectly silent, recalling the smell of the sugarcane.

Eleven hours went by like that. Just sitting. No questions. No beatings. No food or water. No bathroom trips. No sound. Not even movement. He never spoke to the woman or learned who she was. Power was restraining itself.

Or being restrained. As soon as Carmelina heard the news she called everyone she knew, which was a lot of people. She came from a large and prestigious clan herself, and José Antonio had been president of the dental association, several times. He was a member of the Ciudamar Yacht Club. His photograph had been in all the newspapers, repeatedly. Carmelina told everyone the same thing: her husband was in the hands of SIM.

The revolution against Batista was largely a phenomenon of class. This class: the middle class, the professionals and technocrats, the engineers and lawyers. People like Fidel Castro. It was a revolution of lawyers and of dentists. These were the people in Cuba who could literally afford to rebel, to risk things in pursuit of the better instincts of Cuban nationalism and democracy.

Kiki de Jongh had argued that Frank País and the poor boys around him were more important than any group of Dolores alumni. But the poor were the disposable ones, and did the dying, and the killing. Many of Che Guevara's best soldiers were street urchins, barely into their teens, and the most famous assassin in the July 26th Movement was a fourteen-year-old boy from the slums of Havana. But the Revolution was a cause, an organization, and it was made overwhelmingly by people from the middle of Cuban society, made for the proletariat, not by it. On the radio, Castro called himself "a son of the oppressor class," and his camp followers bragged that socialist revolution had occurred in Cuba, before anywhere else in Latin America, precisely because Cuba was more advanced, with a larger, stronger middle class, better-educated professionals, and a complete bourgeoisie ready to throw off Batista.

Lundy Aguilar had argued in one of his books that people at the bottom of Cuban society—blacks in particular—had been disinclined to support Castro because they feared all revolutions equally, and repressions fell on them first and heaviest. It was the middle, reacting against the cruelty of Batista, the nakedness of his greed, and the lies of his American friends, that made it happen. Decade by decade they had tried politics, new constitutions, civil resistance, and general strikes. When they saw, in 1958, that nothing peaceful could stop Batista, that torture and assassination were going to be the rule, even for them, they threw their support to Castro.

It didn't hurt Roca's case that he also knew the mayor and the archbishop of Santiago. After Carmelina raised an alarm, both men called Moncada to insist that her husband be freed. Within hours the newspapers also heard what was happening and made inquiries.

Roca had been taken in mid-morning. After the trip to the sugarcane field, he'd been questioned for two hours, and then he'd sat in his chair for eleven hours. And then, at what must have been nearly midnight, the army commander at Moncada suddenly appeared. They had met before, in other circumstances (he was "a good man," according to José Antonio).

"Dentist," the officer said, "don't be afraid. The whole city is up, clamoring for your freedom."

After the commander left, another officer, a lieutenant who was a notorious enforcer, came in. He was said to have personally killed a long list of men in the underground.

"Doctor," the lieutenant told him, "you have many friends. But you are lying to us. You have the face of a shit-eater. We know who you know. Someday we will catch you."

Then Roca was set free. He walked out, called Carmelina, and went home.

Which is how it worked in Batista's Cuba. The old Cuba, where flags rippled at sunset against blue seas. A poor boy would be found stiff and cold in the sugarcane fields, the morning after his arrest, and be listed as *Vertillon 166*. A boy from Dolores would go home with a warning, and sit in his usual chair, and smoke a *puro*.

Roca was done. He ended his fund-raising, told Celia Sánchez that he was resigning as treasurer, and surrendered the lead seals for the guerrilla bonds to another supporter. Fidel himself sent word that Roca should flee into the mountains and become the dentist to his troops, but that wasn't the point for Roca. José Antonio wanted to get out, not go deeper in. He had never intended to do anything more than whistle once, in the dark, or maybe give some money. "I had a mortgage, and my family," he said. "I wasn't like Fidel or Che Guevara, who renounced everything. I always loved my family."

He made sure that everyone in Santiago knew that he had quit the movement completely. Before it was too late, he would become a dentist again.

But it was later than that. The Masferrer death squads didn't care that he had resigned. As José Antonio was sitting at home one night with Carmelina, they heard the roar of a car in the street. Just as they looked up, whoever was driving past unleashed a volley of shots from a submachine gun.

Like a lot of Santiago houses, theirs was made of very thin wood, with louvers everywhere. The bullets punched holes through the louvers in front, passed through the interior walls, and then exited out the back of the house. Neither they nor their kids were hurt.

And then a few weeks later it happened again. A slower car. A more carefully aimed, sustained burst of gunfire into the house. They were sleeping this time, and once again the bullets passed over them, through the house, without striking anyone. The bullets just flew off into the night.

When it was time to leave, for my mother's house, I told Roca that I'd been in El Encanto, his father's store. Enramada wasn't much of a place to be seen anymore. The Foto Mexicana studio was gone; El Ten Cent was shabby and shuttered. But El Encanto was still open, sort of. It was now a State store, but there was almost nothing to sell. The marble floor was still lovely, and the old glass showcases were there, empty but for a museum-like display of Warsaw Pact engineering books. The whole sales floor was dark and cool. The only real business in the place came from a few stand-up racks right by the front door, where they sold notepaper and cheap pens.

"I haven't been back since the day I left," Roca said, his big hands—basketball-sized hands, too big for a dentist—resting flat on the armrests of his chair. "I always thought I would go back when Fidel was out, but I don't believe it now. And anyway, his brother Raúl is strong." He meant Raúl was tough, as iron-hard as Fidel. Roca illustrated this by making a muscle with his biceps, pounding on it with the other hand, but the blow wasn't a hard one, as Alberto Casas's would have been. It was just a symbolic tap on the sleeve of his cardigan.

The view out the window behind him was captivating. We towered over the asphalt crossroads of shopping malls and highways. In thirty-five years this was the first time I had seen the geostrategic sprawl of the city from on high. The suburban belt of government began behind us near the CIA building in Langley, and ran in, toward the Pentagon. Straight out ahead was Arlington, the Potomac, and then Washington. The highways all around us fed bridges—Chain, Key, Memorial, 14th Street—that aimed at the federal city. Then there was the great oblong Mall. The State Department. The monuments of this new Rome, all in their rows.

The last thing Roca told me was that he had run into Basilio once. The CIA man from the consulate. He was a legend among people in the Santiago underground, because he'd helped get visas for some of them, saving their lives. Basilio had been seen in Panama and was rumored to have been involved in bringing down Manuel Noriega there. And then about a decade ago, Roca had gone to a party, a random evening in Washington where the accidental round of drinks, dinners, and picnics always meant running into government types. The party was at a private house, and José Antonio immediately recognized Basilio, standing in the kitchen. He hadn't set eyes on the CIA man in decades.

Roca reintroduced himself, reminding Basilio how they had met.

The man looked at him with no expression at all. Standing in the kitchen, he said his name wasn't Basilio. They hadn't met before. It was a mistake.

Then he left the party.

KEY BISCAYNE

When I flew out of Havana the last time I was carrying four envelopes, all addressed to America. Jorge Segura had given me two of them. One was for his brother Carlos, who lived in South Florida. He wanted me to stamp and mail it inside the United States, so that it would arrive quickly and safely, and then call as well.

The second letter was to Pedro Haber, the reunion organizer in Miami, and described an annual meeting for *Dolorinos* in Santiago, an alumni group he called the Family of Dolores:

Santiago de Cuba

Pedro Haber
Florida, U.S.A.
Dear Brother Pedro:

I'm taking advantage of a friend who is traveling to the USA to send you these lines.

I hope you have received my letter of December 20. I inform you of the following activities:

A mass the previous Sunday the 5th, in the church of the Sacred Family of Vista Alegre, officiated by our spiritual leader RP Jorge Contelles SJ; we commemorated the second return of the Company of Jesus to Cuba, 1854, and the Saint Mary Mother of God. A good quantity of Dolorinos *attended (16), the Dead were remembered (7), and then a few words from P. Contelles, with 40 for very modest refreshments and drinks.*

I am putting together a calendar of the activities of the [new] year, I will send you a copy. We will probably celebrate on the first of June an activity to commemorate the fifth anniversary of the creation of the Family of Dolores. In reality it was May 31, but as that fell on a Saturday we opted to celebrate it on Sunday. I will send you the program.

Once again I insist that you send us a copy of the alumni magazine, receiving it would bring us a huge spiritual delight.

If you have a chance to send a ribbon for a typewriter, I would thank you.

My affections to all the brothers from Dolores, I always include them in my prayers.

We are brothers in Christ,

An embrace,

CP Jorge R. Segura

Everybody had a title. Dear Brother. P for Padre, or RP and SJ, the Reverend Padre, Society of Jesus. Even Jorge was "CP Jorge," or a certified public accountant.

The third letter was given to me by a man in a Havana street. Having known me for two minutes, he asked me to wait, went inside and dashed off a paragraph to his uncle in "Oonion City," New Jersey. He left the envelope open, just as Jorge did. It was to show you had nothing to hide.

In theory, there is normal service for letters between Cuba and the United States—one of the only routine daily interactions between the two governments. But letters mailed from the island to America could take six weeks, or six days, or four months, and some just disappeared. Mail heading the other way, into Cuba, was even less likely to arrive. In Virginia, José Antonio Roca had talked of mailing four letters to Jorge Segura in Santiago, but not one had arrived. He blamed Segura's "situation with the government," but it seemed unlikely that the MinInt agents were combing the mail of an elderly accountant. Cuban postal workers sometimes cut open envelopes from abroad, looking for money. But there was also the plain ineptness of Cuban government services. I had once sent a letter, wrapped around a $20 bill, to a friend in Havana. Six months later the envelope was returned, unopened, with a notation in perfect cursive: *Returned due to death of addressee.* Two years later the dead man wrote me from the same address, asking why I never sent him $20 bills anymore.

So hand delivery was best, especially in the case of the large envelope from Kiki de Jongh for Pepín Bou. After mailing the others, including Jorge's letter to his brother, I called the brother's South Florida number.

"He hardly ever gives me any help," Segura had told me. "Just a pair of pants one time, and a hundred dollars many years ago. Call and tell him how difficult things are for me. Make it sound bad, but not too bad."

Carlos answered and spoke fine English, but was gruff. He had graduated from Dolores in "I think it was '42, or '43," but he hadn't seen the photograph of all of them together and didn't care to. Despite overlapping with the Castro brothers, he said he hadn't known them, "and I don't think I missed anything there."

I tried to start the your-brother-is-bad-but-not-too-bad speech, but Carlos cut me off. "Nothing about those people interests me," he said. "I left Cuba thirty-three years ago. I got a hard time leaving the island, whoo. Like the Yews say, never again."

He paused, as if remembering something. "I don't want anything to do with those people," he finally said.

"So thank you," he said. And then hung up.

Pepín Bou laughed and shook his head when I handed him the envelope from Kiki de Jongh and he saw what slid out. A colorful little sketch of a house that never was. The house the Bou family might have lived in now.

"A lot of time gone by," Pepín said, holding the sketch and smiling. "A lot of time gone by."

He didn't need the drawing to remember the plan for the house. He leaned back and described it, waving over his wife. "That was for a beautiful spot outside the city, with a tremendous view over the bay," he said, handing her the sketch. "Oh, that was a beautiful spot. It was going to be the family house. But it was 1958, and it was never built."

Pepín had moved many times in his life. Just now he had moved for what he hoped was the last time. He'd traded the house with the swimming pool for a condo in a tower, near where the crabgrass touched the ocean. It was just a mile away from the old place, still on the familiar Key Biscayne. Instead of no view and some crossed palms, he had a wide sweep of glass looking out to sea in two directions. The lobby of the building was a concoction of white gilding, buffed brass rails, glass, and dappled marble, but their new apartment was soothing, with white sofas, wall-to-wall carpeting, and pictures and photographs in gold frames around the walls. It was more manageable than a house.

A sea breeze rattled the windows. It was a hazy day, and the winds were shifting around. One moment they were battering the windows on the east, the next they were striking the south. Then they fell silent. The barometer was changing, one weather system giving way to another.

Someone leaves Cuba in a boat almost every day of the year, regardless of conditions, and today was no exception. Tonight, near midnight, a group of six people would slip off a beach in Cuba, in a small boat with a worn outboard, trusting themselves to the pilot and the gods. A storm was coming, but they did not wait. The U.S. Coast Guard intercepted about 1,500 Cubans a year at sea, and a bit of foul weather might hide their small boat.

Pepín could see far over the ocean from here, just water for twenty miles. With a telescope at dawn, he might even spot them coming over.

We looked over the house sketch. It was "very modernist, very 1950s Cuban," Bou said. The house looked very American to me, but that was the point. It had been a time of intense connection between the two countries. With his wife standing behind him, pressing down on his shoulders, Pepín recalled all the tourists in Santiago then. The whole world was flooding into Cuba, bringing money and something intangible.

"To think in 1960 they had the ASTA convention, or whatever you call it, the association of all the travel agents, in Havana. Fidel boycotted it. He said he didn't want tourism. He didn't want prostitution, either, but now everyone is a prostitute. He didn't want tourism. Now everyone is a tourist. He didn't want arms. *¿Armas para qué?* That was his favorite speech. Why would we need arms? Everybody was brothers. Now they are armed to the teeth.

"All the world has its history," he said, without further explanation.

He inquired about Kiki. They hadn't seen each other since 1958, but Pepín wasn't expecting that to change. When we had started all this, a couple of years before, he'd told me that no *Dolorinos* remained in Cuba. Then he'd admitted that there had to be some. Finally he'd concluded that "even if I did know someone who was still there, I wouldn't know him." That was how he felt about Kiki.

"I thank him" for the drawing, Pepín said. "But I don't want to talk to him. That's bullshit. I respect him, but I don't agree with him."

I had never seen him at a Dolores reunion. Miami Springs isn't that far away. Why didn't he go?

"I went to a few of those," Pepín said. "You go to those reunions and you don't know who anyone is, and the ones who were there last year are dead. Personally, I find it depressing."

I'd known for a while that Lundy and Vera were going to sell their house. Now Pepín mentioned that they had already bought a condo right here, in the same building. Two floors down.

High school all over. They'd started out in the same building. Now they would end that way. The old life remade in foreign climes.

Kendall is a neighborhood that would be considered a neighborhood only in Miami. It lies south of Little Havana and its Cuban kitsch, west of Coral Gables, with its absurd bridal shops and *quinceañera* extravaganzas, and had none of the exclusion of Key Biscayne out in the ocean. Kendall was the flat, fecund stretch of green and asphalt that you passed as you shot south out of the city, on an elevated expressway, peering down from Route 826 at 90 miles an hour. It was cut into pieces by 826 and the South Dixie Highway, and crosscut by 878, and divided by drainage canals, a railroad, and unexpected wild corners. Cement and stoplights in one direction, verdant saw grass and vines in another. The telephone lines and the stop signs were in the grip of creepers, and all the streets the same, so that reaching David de Jongh meant telling 85th Street from 85th Place, which were both found off 85th Avenue. I drove around a cul-de-sac of modest ranches and stopped the car. There was a spatter of rain, and I was early, so I sat and waited. The house had nice ornamentation— cut glass lanterns in front, a heavy knocker, bits of brass, spur stones, the usual Cuban love of too much.

Up north when you read about Miami it was all about alligators stealing the family dog out of the backyard, or picnics that were interrupted by Indian pythons that had slithered off cargo ships, or five-foot-long monitor lizards that were released into the canals by panicked pet owners. Miami was where old men went out for their daily swim and were yanked under by bull sharks, a tropical freak show of crooked politicians, fraudulent elections, luxury cars, and lowbrow dingbats running pyramid schemes and self-improvement rackets. You could get the antenna and mirrors ripped off your rental car by gangs of macaques. Everyone was here to party except the immigrants, the Haitians and Cubans.

Out on the ocean, a full day into their journey, the six would-be exiles who had left Cuba were in the grip of the Gulf Stream, a dark blue conveyor belt. Even the best boat could be swamped here. The rain was brief and intermittent, but it looked to be coming in, hard.

Of the de Jongh brothers, only Kiki had stayed behind in Cuba. This was the house of David, a paradise that might look like hell to some people: surrounded by roaring freeways and swamps full of invaders, the block was quiet, handsome, and clean. The house was trim, the paint fresh.

David's wife, Elena, let me inside, and had me wait alone at a glass table, on a glassed-in porch. On the way through the house I'd only glimpsed the shelves, the end tables, and the mantelpiece, crowded with art, collectibles, figurines, books, knickknacks, and souvenirs. Everything bright, accumulated, a feast for the eye. After a few minutes David came out to the porch, tall, grave, slow-moving, his hands and scalp dotted with liver spots. Despite recent surgery, he moved with authority. He didn't bother to shake my hand. He just sat down at the table and said, "Yes?"

I showed him the photo. I flipped over the picture, ran through Alberto Casas's list of names, and pointed out himself and his brothers in different rows. He tried to act unimpressed, but after a minute he was fingering it, hungry. He ran his eyes over it. "Hechevarría!" he said, stopping abruptly over a face. He whistled twice. A blast over his teeth. Elena appeared. "Guess who that is," he said, and grew frustrated when she didn't have an answer.

"Hechevarría," he said. "It's Hechevarría!" She wasn't as excited. He looked cross. I noted that whenever he wanted something—a glass of water, a coffee, or help remembering a name—he whistled like that.

Elena sat down at the table. Like all the wives of the boys from Dolores that I had met, she seemed ten or fifteen years younger than her husband, although they were both seventy-nine. Her hair was an airy copper suspension of hair spray and willpower. David, by contrast, had missed a big spot while shaving his throat. A fringe of thin white hair surrounded his head. He was similar to Kiki: the same compact head and thin lips, the same precise manner of speaking.

Elena had visited Dolores and remembered the boys in general, if not their particular boyish faces. She was from one of the oldest families in Santiago, the Portuondos. She led me into the living room, to the Portuondo arms and crest on a wood plaque. Many of the paintings on the walls were her own work, consistently good oil landscapes of Cuba. Not a Cuba that had or did exist, but the elemental one of resonances. She showed me a painting of Santiago Bay, the blue water dotted with sailboats.

"It was wonderful," she said. "A paradise. Every summer day was wonderful. People went for three-month vacations. Almost everybody had a boat, a small boat to go around in the bay at five o'clock in the afternoon, just calling out, *Hi, hello, how are you.*" She stood in the living room, waving graciously at other boaters, floating in the sunshine. Paradise was just childhood, in the end.

Back on the porch I punctured the atmosphere by asking about Kiki's recent visit. After I'd interviewed him in Havana, but before my arrival in Kendall, Kiki had made a surprise visit to Miami, his first ever. It was always a monumental thing for a family to be reunited across the Straits, and the brothers hadn't seen each other in decades. But the visit hadn't been terrific. Kiki hadn't even told his brothers he was coming. They found out from Radio Bemba; a friend of a friend mentioned that Kiki's wife was coming to see family in America. When they found out Kiki was coming, too, they still didn't communicate, and nobody arranged anything. Only at the last minute, when Kiki was about to leave for the airport, did the three brothers come together, at this house. After embraces they sat down and avoided any topic even remotely contentious.

"We didn't talk about Cuba," David said. "Or the house. Nothing."

"Just family," Elena added grimly. "How is your brother-in-law, and so on."

No discussion of "the house," that most symbolic of all exile obsessions, with its promise of restoration and return. No mention of Him, Cyclops, the Horse. Their old friend. No talk of ration books in Cuba, nor of dubious elections in Florida. After an hour Kiki went back to Havana, willingly. To the very thing that David abhorred.

How could David explain that?

"I don't know," he replied. "There is a saying in Spanish, *al vino, vino; al pan, pan.* Wine is wine, bread is bread. I would say to him, To me, you are a mystery." The mystery was how Kiki could still believe. "I understand some people believe in Muhammad. Some people believe in Buddha. But thirty, forty years on? You have seen what it is. There is no way you could be fooled."

David and Kiki now spoke of politics, through me. I read back some of Kiki's comments and explanations. How he had called the Revolution "a necessity," for example. "The Revolution was something necessary, yes," David agreed, nodding. "But communism, no."

Kiki had argued that the rich fled Cuba because the Revolution took away their wealth. Because it was in their economic interest to do so.

"We don't care about money," Elena said curtly. David nodded slowly. "I left nothing behind," he added after a moment.

Nothing of value, he meant. All the things that he and Elena had abandoned in Cuba were just things, not important in the long run. Things could be replaced. What mattered was freedom. Having room to breathe, to make their own lives. "We can't live like that," David said, of Kiki's Cuba.

David told a story about keys. So many Cuban exiles remembered the keys: the keys to homes, to automobiles, to workplaces, the intimate essence of security and control, of one's place in life. Keys were symbols of the Enlightenment, and of Elegguá, the opener of doors and pathways.

"I used to carry all my keys on a ring here on my belt," David said, touching his right side. The de Jongh family was "rich," he explained, with many properties and buildings. As the eldest son and a medical doctor, David had a lot of keys. By 1959 he had built up a successful laboratory and blood bank in Santiago.

"You don't just build a laboratory," David said. Kiki had been the architect on the project. First they studied building plans in the Sears Roebuck catalogue, and then together they drove "all over the republic," looking at laboratories and hospitals, seeing how they were built, the way they were laid out to collect northern light, with a soft floor to protect the feet of the weak and ill. "We visited every place we could find," David said. "Every building, every laboratory. We studied every instrument. We did everything ourselves. We even produced our own reagents for the lab work, too. It was a dedicated effort on my part. It took many months, a year."

The lab and clinic that Kiki designed became David's little domain, and the keys on that key chain—for the company cars, the different doors of the different buildings—were always at his side. He could identify each key, just by fingertip, without thinking or looking. "I was very *dexterous,* very *agile,* in picking out a key," he said, mixing precise English words into his Spanish. He mimed the action of reaching down and whipping a key off the ring without looking, a blur of motion.

Then the Revolution. In 1959 the economy began to fall apart. In 1960 the confiscations began. In 1961, the militias began rounding up people like him, who were known to be against Castro. He was his own prophet, hiding his gold in the ashes, his rifles in the lab, and telling his staff that the end was near. "I remember the staff were all there once, and I said to them, One day you will see me leaving Cuba. They said, No, this is your life, your laboratory, you can't leave them. But I said, Yes, I'll take my keys and when I go out the door for the last time, I'll throw them behind me."

This was exactly what David had done. When he left the laboratory for the last time, he threw the keys over his shoulder. "I told them, wherever I go, I'll build a new blood bank. I'll build a new laboratory. And I'll be a free man." Now he didn't miss the keys or the things they opened. Not the cars. Not the labs. Not the house. Not the stamp collection he had built up carefully, over many years, and then left in a drawer. In America, after much trouble he had forged his life over. A new blood bank. A new laboratory. A new house. A new car. A new set of keys. "We would give it away again ten times over, if we had to," he said as Elena nodded.

What made David angry was something else that was lost: respect. He fell into an unsolicited rant about the decline in American culture. The United States, he said, was now hated all over the world not for our foreign policy or economic power, but because we mocked our own symbols of authority. David blamed it on television. It had all started with *McHale's Navy* and *F Troop*. These were ancient shows in black and white that had been the basest, most obsolete reruns of my youth. They outraged David. They encouraged people to laugh at the flag, the military uniform, all "the emblems of the country. Those things are sacred."

Next thing you knew, Roseanne was mocking the national anthem, spitting on the ground. He was speaking faster and faster. Roseanne *infuriated* him. "If Fidel was out and I was in," he said, jabbing two fingers into the table, "she would be shot by sunset. I would shoot her. When the sun came up in the morning she would *not . . . be . . . alive.*" Jab, jab, jab.

Once he was done shooting comedians David was ready for Fidel. David was "absolutely sure" that Castro had directed the September 11 attacks on New York and Washington. The hijackers had trained in Florida.

Nothing could move in Florida without the knowledge of Castro's spy networks. Therefore it was "not possible" that Castro was *not* involved. I challenged him for evidence, but David had the only evidence he needed: Castro's character. He picked up the photo. "I'm here," he said. "Fidel is here." He dragged a nail across the picture. "For many years we were together. We played baseball many times. I know him from a child—"

He came to an abrupt halt. "My God," he said, staring at the spot where his fingertip had landed. "It's Santangelo!"

Now it began to rain. Not just rain, but the sudden onset of a tropical storm. The wind blew up and a minute later the downpour was so loud on the glass roof that David and I could not speak. It grew dark, and palm fronds showered down everywhere, along with seedpods and sticks. Kendall was getting hit.

Out at sea a squall like this would throw up crisscrossing swells that slammed at little boats, shake loose the screws in their motors, pry at their amateur seams and crudely constructed equipment. The storm would look for a way to break them. Six people, wet and cold in an open boat, would begin to doubt. It was two hundred miles to Miami, and a storm could double or even triple that distance while dragging out the trip for days. Rafters were sometimes pushed by storms as far as the Bahamas or the Carolinas. About 950 Cubans a year landed in South Florida. So the odds weren't bad. All they had to do was survive the hard squalls like this one.

When the rain retreated, I mentioned the *Encyclopaedia Britannica* to David. His face changed. "Kiki has it?" he asked.

No. Kiki had reminisced about the *Britannica,* but he didn't have it anymore.

"Oh, it was magnificent," David said. "And that edition!"

Another de Jongh family lecture on the genius of the 1911 edition. All the knowledge of the world in one package, David said. All about aqua regia and touchstones. About gold. David brushed his hands over the memory of those soft leather covers and mimed rolling a whole volume up into a tube. Then he slashed his hand horizontally through the air, recalling the way his father piled them in upright stacks, rather than linear rows, so that the thin paper and leather wouldn't bend.

Arturo de Jongh now came into the house. The middle brother of the three, he introduced himself, but fled into the kitchen, where he talked quietly with David's wife. He was the least assertive of the brothers. Arturo was the one who had joined the guerrillas for the last two weeks of the war, liberating Santiago without a weapon. He had always been hard for me to interview, because in his late sixties he was usually flying or driving somewhere in Florida to broker a new real estate deal. His corporate masters had big money at stake, so he could never get away to talk with me.

Now that I had seen all three brothers, I asked David to try once more to explain the differences. How did he and Arturo end up here, and Kiki there?

"Explain Kiki," David said. He wasn't repeating my question. He was ordering me to answer it myself. He tapped the photo, lying on the glass table. "Same father. Same mother. Same city. Same school. Same university."

Same but for the result. The conclusions they drew from their own lives were diametrically opposed, a negation of the other's existence. They were like David's reagents, cultured in the same petri dish and then put to utterly different purposes.

That was it. Explain Kiki? There was no explanation. When nations sink, people make life rafts from a flotsam of ideas and stories, old keys and dimes blackened by age. Life was held together with ideology, loyalty, ambition. We are all drowning this way, but the Cubans, like the Jews, understand what it is to stay afloat.

On the way out, David left me in the living room for a while. Going to the bathroom takes a long time when you are old. I studied Elena's paintings. Voluptuous green hills. The elderly city that she called by its full name, Santiago de Cuba. The bay dotted with sails. The water was calm. Everybody had a boat.

David let me out a moment later, just after I'd finished inventorying the walking sticks in his umbrella stand. Here was something he and Kiki had in common. Back in Havana, Kiki had his walking stick. And here in Miami, David had nine.

————

The next night, many of the most important figures in El Exilio were gathering at the Biltmore Hotel in Coral Gables. The event was a cocktail party and fund-raising dinner in honor of Václav Havel, the former dissident and outgoing president of the Czech Republic. Cubans were paying $1,000 a table to sit near Havel's halo and hear his anti-communist philosophy.

The Biltmore is an embarrassing Moorish fantasia from 1926, with a central tower in yellow and long wings on each side containing vaulted banquet and meeting rooms. Havel would appear first at a cocktail party in one wing, where he could embrace former political prisoners in solidarity. But the room could contain only about two hundred people in a city where more than twenty thousand describe themselves as former political prisoners of Castro. The organizers had focused on the usual names. Ileana Ros-Lehtinen, the Republican congresswoman from Miami, was one of the first faces I recognized when I came into the room. There was also a list of players from the Cuban American National Foundation (CANF). In the 1980s the group had held a kind of monopoly in Washington, the go-to group on Cuban issues, but their strident leader, Jorge Más Canosa, had died abruptly in 1997 (though Jorge Más was from Santiago, and one of his brothers had gone to Dolores, he wasn't himself a Jesuit product). CANF had been gravely weakened in recent years, as hard-line supporters defected to Cuban Liberty Council, moderates dropping away to the left.

Among the former were the *plantados,* the hardest of the hard-line men who had come out of Castro's prisons. The *plantados* were honored for the length of their sentences and were rejectionists by nature, proudly to the right of Genghis Khan. In Castro's jails, they had sometimes gone naked rather than wear communist clothing. Here in Miami they were the refuseniks, opposed to any dialogue, contact, or commercial opening to Havana, under any conditions.

The *plantados* wore name tags that listed their sentences. Havel, who endured four years under arrest, waded into the crowd and was embraced by Huber Matos ("20 Years in Jail"). The Velvet Revolution and Operation Mongoose were together at last. Matos had been a soldier his whole life, first as a major for Batista, then as a *comandante* against him, and one of Fidel's most trusted commanders. Then Matos had tried to overthrow

Castro and had served twenty years, mostly in the notorious Isle of Pines prison. Now Matos was one of the most ardent advocates of violence against Cuba. Havel moved on to shake more hands ("Luis Gonzáles Infante, 16 Years in Prison"), but Matos spoke up for more violence. He praised Havel as "one of our own," but then told me that the Czech was just plain wrong about Cuba. Havel was advocating a Velvet Revolution model, or undermining communism from within, peacefully, with civil disobedience. Matos offered a different prescription: *militarismo.* The Cuban army had a long tradition of overthrowing leaders, he said approvingly. Officers within the Revolutionary Armed Forces could be convinced to toss out Castro. The *plantado* answer for the future of Cuba was the same one for many centuries. Force.

I asked Matos why a Velvet Revolution wasn't possible in Cuba. "The difference," Matos said, "is the Czech Republic is in the heart of Europe. They had contact with other countries all around. But Cuba is an island." But it was the *plantados* themselves who demanded isolation. They wanted maximum hostility and minimal contact. Anyone who stayed behind in Cuba was useless. They denigrated the internal dissidents, people like Elizardo Sánchez and Hector Palacios. These inxiles speaking of electoral reform and human rights were naive, hopelessly compromised, even collaborators.

Behind Matos, Mr. 16-Years-in-Prison nodded, and then condemned the internal dissidents. "Václav Havel considers it correct. But we see it as not the correct line to free Cuba." The next government in Havana would have to come from Miami, he said, because there could be absolutely no participation by *corruptos,* which meant anyone involved in the old system at all.

There was an exile left in the room. Most Cuban-Americans were younger than the *plantados,* and more recent in exile. Right behind Matos were two fresh arrivals, dissidents named Maritza Lugo and Marco Torres, who had come to America within the last year. Torres had served five years in Cuban jails, and Lugo had been arrested more than thirty times. Torres, wearing a long-sleeve guayabera and staring intently at his glass of white wine, had left Havana just two months before. "There are a lot of political differences in this room," he said quietly. "We want concessions. The *Exilio* is not putting the interests of Cuba first."

Lugo, who had left the island eight months before, volunteered, "I'm no *plantado*." Wearing a new gold dress and matching shoes, she surveyed the high-ceilinged room, a woman watching a fund-raiser for the first time. "There are a lot of groups within the exile," she said. "There are some discrepancies of opinion, but that's Cuban." She herself supported Havel and the nonviolent approach. The older generation of *plantados* "struggled for so many years, was jailed for so long, saw their families killed, their friends executed. These people don't know another route to power except through force.

"Miami is very different," Lugo mused. "It's a radical change, so different from Cuba." She pointed to a vast centerpiece of grapes, cascading down onto a serving table covered with cheese and crackers. "The food is very different," she said. "But there's a lot of it."

Havel's dinner speech disappointed the *plantados*. At an event that raised about $100,000 for him, they got only two sentences in English and the rest in Czech. At dinner, he returned again and again to the theme of nonviolence, to the moral authority that comes from embracing the enemy.

Cuban exiles should push for maximum opening and contact with Cuba, not because it would help the inxiles, but because it would change the exiles. They were the ones who needed to adjust to the reality of the internal dissidents, Havel said.

What Czechoslovakia and Cuba had shared, Havel said, was the "permanent state of dissimulation" required by living under communism, a "closed system of dogmas" dependent on "hollow and mendacious language." The only thing that could shatter a state built on lies was principle. "The mysterious, radiant energy that comes from free speech and free actions turns out to be more powerful," Havel concluded, "than the strongest army." He called this the power of the powerless.

Changes in Cuba would come sooner than anyone might imagine. The first cracks would be almost imperceptible. It would begin with "inconspicuous and slow events."

I wanted Havel to be right, but my dreams didn't believe him. That night, falling asleep in the Holiday Inn in Little Havana, I had troubling, violent dreams of a dystopian Cuba, richer and freer in all the wrong ways, divided, filled with crime and vainglorious wealth. Where would the infant mortality rate go when businessmen and politicians divided up the spoils? What would happen when the boys outside the Estadio Latinoamericano shoved society downward, into a devil-take-the-hindmost whirl of pistols and drug money? It was enough to make me miss the hand that throttled me. Once Cyclops was gone, everyone would miss that comforting iron fist.

There was no realistic plan in Miami, nor in Havana either. The only plan in Cuba was for a succession, not a transition. The older brother gave way to the younger brother, quietly, in 2006. Fidel's funeral will surely be the largest and most emotional in Latin American history. I fully expect to see even his enemies crying down both sides of their *doble caras.*

Then Raúl. At Dolores he was *La Pulgita,* the Flea, colorless, forgettable. He was either an inflexible, charmless, and violent ideologue, or a warm family man, depending on whom you listened to. The truth is that nobody knows him or what he will do. If he has any instinct for survival, he will announce the day after Fidel's funeral that nothing is going to change, and then start changing everything. This could allow Cuba to pass through a gradual conversion of some sort, on its own terms. In the streets Raúl was known as *el chino,* and maybe he could indeed pursue the Chinese model, opening the economy to profit and property, everything managed by a dictatorship of the Party and the military. If the average person benefited, the Chinese model might be possible.

But what new Cuba could be born from this rotten thing, this pile of crumbling expectations surrounded by vultures? Economic changes would produce wealth, but also disparity; then social tension, increasing crime, factionalism, and the collapse of some parts of Cuban society. The *plantados* and thousands of other exiles vowed to leap into boats heading back to reclaim their houses. This could spark a civil war. Cuba has fought itself before.

Strange and little reported events were occurring in far parts of the country. Spontaneous acts of dissent. Just before Fidel fell ill, a group calling itself the Mothers in White appeared suddenly one morning in Havana, marching to the Malecón to commemorate loved ones who died fleeing the island. They went to the water and threw in wreaths.

Within minutes of their appearance, the Mothers in White were under surveillance. The police arrived. A dial-a-mob was mobilized from local block committees, confronted the Mothers in White, surrounding them, shouting insults, tossing trash, and chanting:

FIDEL, FIDEL,
THIS NEIGHBORHOOD BELONGS TO FIDEL.

About fifty of the women were detained. Castro's reaction came a few days later. During a six-hour speech, he said there would be no more tolerance of "traitors and mercenaries." Opponents would not be allowed to go "one millimeter" beyond what the people would tolerate. Then the Cyclops, the Horse, Him, the *bola de churda,* turned on a Jesuitical dime and denied that there even was such an opposition in Cuba.

"The much publicized dissidence, or alleged opposition in Cuba, exists only in the fevered minds of the Cuban-American mafia and the bureaucrats in the White House," he said to cheering and applause.

"You would think that the Revolution had only a few hours left," he added, to laughter.

The day after Havel's speech I was out on the key again. The Aguilar household was upended. Lundy and Vera had bought the new condo below Pepín Bou's, but weren't moved in yet. There were decades of accumulated material, a household of carefully constructed identity to be packed and reallocated for the last time. Old age was its own exile, a stripping away of the self. The senses, the quickness of the intellect, the granular details—were slipping away. Life became a regression, from the sufficiency at birth to the hollowness of even the fullest old age.

His son Lou met me in the driveway of the house. He was wearing a blue T-shirt and jeans. We chatted and he gave me the same warning.

"He has Alzheimer's," Lou said. "He's lost it. It's over."

How did Lou know it was Alzheimer's?

"He keeps repeating himself," he said.

The Alzheimer's was true. When Lundy had first talked of the raider boat back in 1961, describing what powerful motors it had, what a marvelous boat it was, the superb handling, and the crack of cannon fire from a Cuban frigate, his mind was clear. The old memories were good.

But tangles of proteins were slowly grabbing at his brain cells. When I called him on the phone now, he sometimes stopped abruptly, losing track of the conversation.

"Who is this?" he had said to me, astonished. "What do you want?"

Vera always arranged my visits for late morning, when Lundy was at his best. We would talk, and then finish with lunch. Lundy was worried about the deep divisions within the United States, where politics increasingly consisted of opposed groups who denied the legitimacy and even language of the opposition. The future of Cuba was also hard to see. Civil war was possible, he acknowledged. "It will take generations to restore the society," he said. Lundy had learned from Castro himself to be "a peaceful revolutionary," he said. Violent overthrows could produce only new governments built on force and the strongman. "I never argue with someone who has a gun," he added.

"Maybe the future is here," Lundy suggested. It was a radical idea for a Cuban. It was heresy to acknowledge that there would be no satisfying end to this story. There would be no *reconquista,* no triumphant reentry, no fitting of old keys into the houses of memory. Cuban-Americans could "go back to the island slowly, over time," Lundy suggested. "Over time" meant decades, generations, centuries. Cubans might become like the Jews, defined by their floating state, reciting what was lost in an ancient homeland.

I left the old house for the last time, steering around the lizards and stopping back on the main drag, Crandon Boulevard. Key Biscayne had only one of everything, but that was all you needed. I bought a coffee and a *Miami Herald* at the standup window of La Carreta. The coffee was good Cuban stuff, espresso with the sugar mixed right into the grounds. The steam carmelized the sugar, and the black honey that emerged was smothered in a froth of hot milk.

The *Herald* carried a small item. Yesterday, before dawn, right here on Key Biscayne, six Cubans had come ashore. Their pilot must have been good. He'd sailed through two coast guards and a storm, and brought them right into Biscayne Bay, to a point where they could see the purple neon towers of downtown Miami in the distance. Then the smuggler had turned left and aimed for the first beach he saw. Just outside the surf line, he'd tossed his six passengers overboard and then motored off to fend for himself. The money was so good—tens of thousand of dollars a trip—that many skippers went back to Cuba immediately.

The six had staggered ashore and found themselves in Crandon Park Beach, half a mile from here. Standing in the crabgrass, beneath the baobabs, their feet were wet, but officially dry. In accordance with American law, the six were taken by police to a detention center, processed, and released. They would have legal residency a day later—today sometime— and, if history was any guide, would be connected with family members and working at jobs within the week. I drove by their landing spot on the way out.

I went back to Key Biscayne several times after that. Lundy and Vera finally moved into the new apartment, and it was a good spot. Their other son, George, a film producer, had bought the house from them, keeping it in the family. In the new condo, two floors below Pepín, they had a simpler life. Someone was always vacuuming the hallways, polishing the elevator, or clipping the grass out front. It was smaller than the house, but Lundy found room for his battalions of Saxons, Cuban irregulars, and Waterloo victors, and his swords and muskets were hanging on a wall.

Lundy paid less and less attention to these things. He was now captivated by the view, by the wall of glass in the living room. The vista wasn't as lofty as in Pepín's place, but was more intimate, a tree-level view right into a thick grove of Malay and Panama Tall palm. There were a few baobabs off to the left, imitating the great ceibas of Cuba, the holy trees where Santería spirits gathered. Out ahead were mangroves, some of the last stands in Miami. Aside from the mangroves, all the trees were imports from somewhere else. And aside from the green, all you could see was the washed-out sky.

"I love these trees," Lundy told me over and over. "You can't see any buses or streets."

Just trees, swaying and waving their arms in silence.

"I love those trees."

The last thing I had to see was Belén, which stands to the west of Miami. It had been in Havana until 1961, and then was refounded in Miami in 1963, by and for Cubans fleeing Castro. Several of the Jesuit priests from

Dolores joined the staff, but most were from the other Jesuit schools, in Cienfuegos and Havana. Like their teachers, the students from Dolores were subsumed into this mother school on arrival in Miami. Dolores, in this way, had disappeared.

The new campus was out near the Palmetto Expressway, facing the humid interior of Florida. The new Belén campus that had sprung up was more like a college than a high school, a collection of linked buildings backed with playing fields.

In the lobby right where you walked in, there was a photo of the old Belén in Havana. You had to show what you had lost. And across, smack-dab in the middle of the other wall, was the current school photograph. Not the entire school body—with more than a thousand students, the boys of today's Belén would not fit in any viewfinder. Instead of a group portrait of the senior class, there was a pointillist composition of several hundred individual portraits in tight columns. The boys were wearing neckties. Although there were Colombians, Dominicans, Venezuelans, even Mexicans, it was overwhelmingly a class of second- or even third-generation Cuban-Americans, fluent in Spanish, but at home in America. The Boys from Belén were seventeen and eighteen. The only Cuba they knew was a story. In the whole class of 2004 there was not one black face.

The school had an inner courtyard, a patio in the old vernacular, but this was a mundane oval of poured concrete. Efficient, cost-effective, the Florida way. There were good playing fields out back, a theater, modern science labs, and well-equipped classrooms. They were especially strong at sports.

School was ending. Out front, cars started queuing up at about 2:45 P.M. The first few filled the parking lot, but more and more kept coming. They double-parked in long rows. By 3:10 a traffic jam of sixty cars spilled out the driveway and into the street. One man drove a BMW convertible, another sat reading the paper in a battered Honda Civic. Women were doing their hair or talking on the phone, sometimes both, as they waited for their sons. Many were driving the boat-sized Lincoln Navigators, Chevy Suburbans, and huge SUVs that are the status brands in Miami, America's capital of luxury cars. Two people arrived in Hummer H2s, one swathed in dark windows, one topped with banks of fog lights and chromed from stem to stern.

At 3:15 the students came pouring out. A sea of boys, some in what passed for formal outfits. That meant white, collared shirts and blue trousers. Nobody wore a tie. Many, who were heading for the practice fields or gym, were already in the sweatpants or gym shorts of the Belén teams, the Wolverines. Everything was colored Colegio de Belén blue.

Acknowledgments

I would like to thank Beth Segal for her true and constant support. I am greatly indebted to Dan Frank for his trust, and his sharp editorial scalpel, and must mention the many lessons learned from Elizabeth Hightower, Tom Miller, and Annie Dillard. I owe thanks to the Canadian stranger with his cash, and to the countless Cubans who contributed to the making of this story, over many years, teaching and welcoming me across their island. Some have been given pseudonyms out of necessity.

I was also accompanied on my long journey to Cuba by many friends, who year after year forced me to see everything new again for the first time. Thanks to Clara Jefferey, Tom Watson, and Dan Klaidman, who was the first to say, many years ago, "I saw a photo once. . . ." I'd also like to thank Fran Bigman, and the NYU journalism school for the research support of Jason Boog, Danielle Renwick, Dietrick Knauth, Dorsey Kindler, Ruth Fowler, and Polya Lesova.

Lastly, this book would have been impossible without the kindness and cooperation of the men from Dolores and their families. Pepín Bou; Lundy Aguilar; David, Arturo, and Kiki de Jongh; Pedro Haber; José Antonio Cubeñas; Robert Mancebo; Miguel Llivina; Alberto Casas; Jorge Segura; José Antonio Roca; Bernardo Souto; Balbino Rodríguez Romero; Juan Sotus; Daniel Domenech; and many others opened their memories, homes, archives, and passions to me. Their wives, more often than not Sacred Heart girls, deserve my deepest gratitude for putting up with all these stories one more time. Any errors are the fault of the author, or memory, or the deliberate suppression of documentation within Cuba, or Elegguá.

Index

Patrick Symmes is the author of *Chasing Che* and writes for *Harper's Magazine*, *Outside*, *GQ*, and *Condé Nast Traveler*. He lives in New York City.

A NOTE ON THE TYPE

The text of this book was set in Monotype Columbus, a contemporary face designed specifically for digital typesetting by Patricia Saunders. Released on the quincentenary of Christopher Columbus's 1492 voyage from Spain to the Americas, Monotype Columbus has a distinctly Spanish flavor to its letterforms. Saunders did, in fact, draw inspiration from fonts created by Jorge Coci in sixteenth-century Spain, as well as from italic fonts by the brilliant typographer, Robert Granjon, to create this lively and highly readable face.

Composed by Creative Graphics,
Allentown, Pennsylvania

Printed and bound by Berryville Graphics,
Berryville, Virginia

Designed by M. Kristen Bearse